Republics of Myth

Republics of Myth

National Narratives and the US-Iran Conflict

Hussein Banai, Malcolm Byrne, and John Tirman

Johns Hopkins University Press

Baltimore

© 2022 Hussein Banai, Malcolm Byrne, and John Tirman
All rights reserved. Published 2022
Printed in the United States of America on acid-free paper
9 8 7 6 5 4 3 2 1

Johns Hopkins University Press
2715 North Charles Street
Baltimore, Maryland 21218-4363
www.press.jhu.edu

Library Cataloging-in-Publication Data is available.
ISBN-13: 978-1-4214-4331-7 (hardcover)
ISBN-13: 978-1-4214-4332-4 (electronic)

A catalog record for this book is available from the British Library.

*Special discounts are available for bulk purchases of this book. For more
information, please contact Special Sales at specialsales@jh.edu.*

To James Blight and janet Lang,
with warm admiration and respect

Contents

Acknowledgments   ix
Acronyms   xi

Introduction
Foundations of a Conflict   1

1 The Narrative Trap   18

2 The Fraught US-Iran Relationship, from Mosaddeq to Khomeini   54

3 The Iran-Iraq War   79

4 Rafsanjani and the Post-Khomeini Order   103

5 Khatami and the Possibility of Dialogue   128

6 The Shadow of Khobar in Washington   151

7 Bush in the Khatami Era   *172*

8 The Iraq War and Its Consequences   *197*

9 The Nuclear File under Bush 43   *222*

10 Obama Enters   *251*

11 Rouhani, Zarif, and the Nuclear Deal   *276*

12 Trump and Regeneration through Violence   *305*

Conclusion
Narratives and National Interests   *331*

Notes   *347*

About the Authors   *405*

Index   *407*

Contents

Acknowledgments

The three of us thank Jim Blight and janet Lang, who were integral to the first three critical oral history conferences we convened. They are the originators of this method, which convenes policy makers and scholars, along with voluminous, original documents, to discuss particular periods and episodes of history. Their use of critical oral history has shed new light on the Cuban Missile Crisis, the Vietnam War, and several other important cases of US foreign policy.

Among those who participated in those five meetings, we are particularly grateful to Thomas Pickering and Bruce Riedel, who helped the project in innumerable ways. We thank the dozens of others who participated in the conferences. Those were convened with the gracious assistance of the Rockefeller Foundation's conference center at Bellagio, Italy; the Arca Foundation's center at Musgrove, Georgia; the Massachusetts Institute of Technology; and Goodenough College in London, England. A number of colleagues supported the project in substantial ways, most notably Mahsa Rouhi, David Weinberg, Casey Johnson, and Bridget Peak.

We also thank our donors, the Carnegie Corporation of New York and especially Stephen Del Rosso; the boards, leadership, and staffs of the Arca Foundation and Brenn Foundation; Cynthia and John Reed; and Wade Greene of the Rockefeller Financial Services.

We greatly appreciate the opportunity to collaborate with Laura Davulis and her colleagues at Johns Hopkins University Press.

Huss Banai thanks his coauthors, John and Malcolm, for their friendship, support, and patience (especially in the writing phase of this project). He also thanks friends and colleagues at Brown University, Occidental College, and Indiana University for their support and encouragement at various points in the life cycle of this project. For their unconditional love and support, he thanks Tracey, Elyse, and Eleanor.

Malcolm Byrne thanks friends and colleagues at the National Security Archive and the many longtime supporters of the Archive's Iran-U.S. Relations Project—in Iran, in the United States, and elsewhere. Love and thanks as always to Leila and Kian.

John Tirman thanks MIT professor Richard Samuels, director of the Center for International Studies, for his encouragement and support; Kurt Fendt, director of the MIT Active Archive Initiative and the creator of the website associated with this project, which is https://us-iran.mit.edu; Robin Straus, my literary agent; and Nike and Coco Tirman.

Acronyms

ABM	Anti-Ballistic Missile
AIPAC	American Israel Public Affairs Committee
AWACS	Airborne Warning and Control System
CIA	Central Intelligence Agency
CW	chemical weapons
DOD	Department of Defense
EU	European Union
EU3	France, Germany, and the United Kingdom
FBI	Federal Bureau of Investigation
GCC	Gulf Cooperation Council
IAEA	International Atomic Energy Agency
IED	improvised explosive device
ILSA	Iran and Libya Sanctions Act
INF	Intermediate-Range Nuclear Forces
IRGC	Islamic Revolutionary Guard Corps

IRI	Islamic Republic of Iran
ISIS	Islamic State of Iraq and Syria
JCPOA	Joint Comprehensive Plan of Action
JCS	Joint Chiefs of Staff
JPOA	Joint Plan of Action
MEK	People's Mojahedin of Iran (also referred to as MKO)
NIE	National Intelligence Estimate
NPT	Non-Proliferation Treaty
NRA	National Rifle Association
NSC	National Security Council
NSS	National Security Strategy
OIC	Organization of Islamic Conference/Cooperation
P5+1	Permanent UN Security Council Members + Germany
PGOI	Provisional Government of Iran
SCIRI	Supreme Council for the Islamic Revolution in Iraq
SNSC	Supreme National Security Council (Iran)
SOFA	Status of Forces Agreement
UNSC	United Nations Security Council
WMD	weapons of mass destruction

Republics of Myth

Introduction
Foundations of a Conflict

For more than forty years, the United States and the Islamic Republic of Iran (IRI) have been enmeshed in a cold war, punctuated by small eruptions of violence or covert action, with each relentlessly declaiming the other as aggressive and fanatical. Remarkably, in the midst of this routine outrage and maneuvering, the two came to an agreement on a difficult, complex issue: Iran's nuclear program. Then, abruptly, that sole achievement was unraveled. How and why did this happen?

As to the achievement, the simple answer is that the two men elected as president of their respective countries—Barack Obama in 2008 and 2012, and Hassan Rouhani in 2013—were prepared to negotiate more seriously than the two nations had before. Aided by America's other negotiating partners, which were France, Britain, Russia, China, and Germany; by UN and US sanctions that increasingly squeezed Iran's economy; and by the mounting, violent disorder in the region stemming from the Iraq War and the rebellions of the "Arab Spring," each side had powerful incentives and openings to reach a pact. With skilled negotiators and a favorable climate of world opinion, the breakthroughs came. Iran's nuclear program, the most worrying aspect of which was a large and growing number of centrifuges potentially capable of producing uranium that could be fabricated into weapons, was sharply constrained—indeed, rolled back—by the agreement that was to last for the ensuing ten to fifteen years, with some constraints being permanent.

Then it came apart, and that demise was also attributed to a personality—Donald J. Trump, elected president about sixteen months after the deal was signed. Trump had vowed during his White House campaign to scuttle the Joint Comprehensive Plan of Action (JCPOA), the full name of the Iran deal, which had always been a *bête noire* of the Republican Party and its increasingly extreme leadership.

This common template for explaining the Iran nuclear deal's roller coaster ride is sturdy but incomplete. The JCPOA did not spring from the heads of Obama and Rouhani like Athena from the head of Zeus, nor was it later a victim of Trump's whims alone. The Iran deal was instead the culmination of at least eighteen years of fitful, contentious, and miscalculated attempts to build a relationship between Washington and Tehran. Negotiators, policy makers, opinion leaders, and the publics had to overcome deeply ingrained mistrust of each other. It is a distrust borne of actual events and accusations in the relationship. And because they exert powerful influence on political leaders, the two countries' national narratives constantly clash, an undertow that subverts attempts at a normal relationship.

A national narrative is a story a nation tells about itself. Narratives are typically complex, weaving actual history with myth. They are composed of cultural artifacts and trappings, often borrowing from religious tales and folklore, and exalting the nation in uniquely heroic expressions. As we explain in the next chapter, the American national narrative, rooted in the myth of the frontier and burnished with a certain self-glorifying idealism, tells a story of persistent expansion on the continent and beyond. The Iranian national narrative conveys, among many diverse elements, deep suspicion of foreign involvement in Iran, spurred by centuries of domination by non-Persians.

The two nations came into conflict not only because their respective narratives are conflictual but also because specific events brought them into confrontation—which the narratives enabled and reinforced—as did conventional national interests. This dynamic, moreover, gave rise to another narrative, that of the fraught relationship itself. The slings and arrows of that specific, bilateral narrative—the US-led coup against Mosaddeq, the Iranian takeover of the American embassy in Tehran, with much more in between and afterward—fit the larger national narratives that span centuries before the two countries ever encountered each other.

Precisely how these narratives shaped the US-Iran confrontation, the fitful search for some sort of accommodation, and the missed opportunities to create a functional state-to-state relationship constitute the subject of this book.

■ A Brief History

The relationship between the IRI and the United States was fraught from the beginning. The revolutionaries in Tehran saw Washington as the power looming behind the throne of the deposed shah, Mohammad Reza Pahlavi, whose long reign was enabled by US and British power and intrigue. Most notable was the coup the two powers engineered to remove a popular prime minister, Mohammad Mosaddeq, in 1953, restoring the young shah to a stronger political position and supporting him for more than two decades. The shah fell in 1979, due not only to repression but also to lavishness and corruption enabled by

American petrodollars. American elites failed to see the situation for what it was and dug themselves into a deeper hole by allowing the ailing shah into New York for medical treatment. This, for the Khomeini-led masses, was the final straw; they overran the embassy and held its staff hostage for 444 days.

The animus became even more deadly during the 1980–88 Iran-Iraq War. The Carter and then Reagan administrations supported Saddam Hussein with intelligence, political legitimacy, nonlethal military equipment, and financial credits—probably saving his regime when the tide of war turned against him. Only after Khomeini died in 1988 did the possibility arise for some rapprochement, signaled by President George H. W. Bush, but the chance slipped away in the tumult of Desert Storm in 1991 and the collapse of the Soviet Union several months later.

Beginning with the election of Mohammad Khatami in 1997—an enormously consequential event in the politics of Iran—the two adversaries commenced as never before an improvised series of moves to build a better bilateral relationship. These moves were intended not to "normalize" the relationship, which seemed far-fetched at the time, but to transform it into one with regular, direct communication; some discussion of mutual concerns; and more efficient troubleshooting. These modest but achievable goals seemed feasible with Bill Clinton having begun his second term as president just seven months before Khatami was inaugurated. Clinton had hardly been embracing Tehran with open arms before Khatami's arrival. He issued several executive orders banning investment in Iran's energy sector, for example, and signed the Iran and Libya Sanctions Act in 1996, all of which cheered Iran's opponents. Just as significant as sanctions was Clinton's palpable anger when in June 1996 nineteen US Air Force personnel were killed in a truck-bomb explosion at Khobar Towers near an air base in Saudi Arabia. Iran was fingered as the culprit, and Clinton actively considered a retaliatory attack on Iran.

In light of Clinton's actions and attitudes, it was not a given that he would respond favorably to the surprise election of the reformer Khatami. A cleric with a rank just below ayatollah and a descendent of the Prophet Mohammad, Khatami was something of a mystery to US policy makers, as indeed Iranian politics had always been. Soon into his presidency, however, Khatami was making gestures indicating that he sought a fresh beginning with the United States. The gestures were largely rhetorical; in one important instance in January 1998, he spoke at length with Christiane Amanpour of CNN and said, among much else, "I respect the American nation because of their great civilization." He was also opening up social space in Iran, loosening the restrictive revolutionary practices that, in the West, appeared highly repressive.

As a result, the Clinton foreign policy team began to see Khatami as something new and possibly agreeable. The question for them was how to take advantage of this new attitude in Tehran, assuming that it would last and not be subverted by hard-liners. So began a back-and-forth process of signaling, preparing publics for a new approach, some policy changes, and a considerable amount of confusion about what was unfolding.

Very little seemed to be tangibly achieved by the Clinton administration in advancing relations with Iran by the time of its exit in January 2001. As we argue later, the awkward and at times even hostile exchanges with Iran appeared to be fruitless and very much beholden to past events and long-held prejudices. The beginning of something more favorable was nevertheless developing. This continued, for a short time, during the George W. Bush administration. Relations with Iran were not a major issue in the Bush-Gore election in 2000, although the Israeli-Palestinian issue and threats made by Saddam Hussein were somewhat prominent. The Bush team was visibly more interested in a potential confrontation with China in its early months and had neglected the potential for a terrorist attack arising from the Mideast. With the September 11, 2001, attacks by Al-Qaeda, the US policy focus shifted abruptly. For relations with Iran, which had been in limbo for several months, this had a twofold effect.

First was a promising cooperation on post-9/11 action. Khatami had been reelected just that summer, and while his star had dimmed owing to a student uprising that state security forces harshly subdued in 1999, he remained relatively popular in the eyes of most Americans. Thus, his expressions of empathy with the victims of the Al-Qaeda attack and the Iranian people's outpouring of solidarity in candlelight vigils and the like showed a seemingly authentic sense of caring. This attitude took a more concrete form when Iran played a very positive role at the December 2001 Bonn conference following the collapse of the Taliban's state. Conversations between Iran's envoy, Javad Zarif, and US ambassador James Dobbins were particularly promising. Even after President Bush surprisingly included Iran in his "axis of evil" reference in the February 2002 State of the Union speech, Iranians pursued a better relationship through the diplomatic channel afforded by state building in Afghanistan.

Again, however, it was apparently all for naught. For the second impact of the 9/11 attacks was America's elevated fear of terrorism, and Iran had long been identified as a terror-sponsoring state. The most vivid memory of Iran in America was the US embassy hostage taking of 1979–81, and the Islamic Republic had been charged with terrorist sprees from then on. That the United States went to war in Afghanistan against the Taliban and Al-Qaeda and then eighteen months later in Iraq against Saddam Hussein—two mortal enemies of Iran—did not lessen Americans' wariness of Iran or Iranians' fear of a hostile United States suddenly encircling their homeland. Many in Iran believed, as did many Americans, that the United States would make Iran its next regime-change target after Saddam Hussein was removed from power in March 2003. The public disclosure of a covert nuclear program in Iran in 2002 added to the tension on both sides.

Perhaps as a result of that fear in Tehran, the Khatami government, with the apparent approval of the supreme leader, Ali Khamenei, wrote an unaddressed letter or memo that was faxed by the Swiss ambassador in Tehran to the US State Department seeking a "grand bargain" on all outstanding issues. These included the nuclear file, recently galvanized by accusations about a secret enrichment facility at Natanz; a vow to stop supporting militant Palestinian organizations and to resolve differences with Israel; and a pledge to cease support for political violence more broadly. The letter was ignored by officials in Washington.

Still, the Bush administration did allow for some progress as Iran engaged on its nuclear program with France, Germany, and the United Kingdom (EU3), as well as the International Atomic Energy Agency (IAEA). A 2004 accord in which Iran agreed to suspend enrichment and accept inspections appeared to be an important step forward. In the final months of Khatami's government, new proposals from Iran were put forward by negotiator Hassan Rouhani, including relatively sharp constraints on enrichment and other nuclear activities and an extensive inspections regime. The EU3 countered with a few more conditions, but Iran declined the proposal because it did not recognize Iran's right to enrich uranium, a norm Iran insists was established in the bedrock Non-Proliferation Treaty (NPT) of 1968.

The election of Ahmadinejad in 2005 (and his inauguration just after the EU3 proposal) threw that progress off course for a time; he restarted enrichment and raised the level of bumptious rhetoric, even as the parties continued to discuss comprehensive proposals for stopping Iran's enrichment of uranium. A 2006 proposal from the West, including the United States, demanded an end to enrichment—the major stumbling block throughout negotiations—which Iran promptly rejected. But the rejection was tempered by acknowledging that the proposal contained constructive ideas.

This back-and-forth on the nuclear issue was occurring as the US war in Iraq was intensifying. The anti-occupation insurgencies in Anbar Province, mainly Sunni Arabs, were to clash with Iran-backed Shi'a militias, and both were dangerous to US forces. The 2003 invasion and resulting occupation stirred sectarianism so violent that it became in 2005–7 an outright civil war. Iran was playing a key role in backing the likes of Muqtada al-Sadr, the firebrand Shi'a cleric who commanded a militia and was a major voice lambasting the US presence in Iraq. Virtually all Shi'a politicians, who represented 60 percent of the Iraqi population, were beholden to Iran; many had lived there during Saddam's reign of terror against Shi'as. The war was fractious: US military and political leaders contended that Revolutionary Guard Corps operatives were directly killing American soldiers. All sides pursued their objectives through the multifaceted use of violence.

The mounting mayhem in Iraq coincided with a change in the Iranian government's public face—namely, the feisty Mahmoud Ahmadinejad, elected in June 2005 to the presidency, replacing the placating Khatami. Ahmadinejad's questioning the Nazi Holocaust and his confrontational statement, drawing on Khomeini, that this "occupation regime over Jerusalem [Israel] must vanish from the page of time" rattled regional and bilateral relations, particularly as his hard-line supporters widely used the provocative interpretation to mean that "Israel must be wiped off the face of the Earth." Given the closeness of the United States and Israel, such incendiary statements were bound to singe whatever working relations were enlivened by the nuclear talks. The rhetoric also brought the pro-Israel lobby ever more forcefully into the domestic political whirlwind around nuclear negotiations.

It is remarkable that these disruptions—Iraq violence, Holocaust denial, harsh rhetoric on both sides—did not derail the nuclear talks completely. They resumed in 2008. By then, with Russia and China participating, the group included all five permanent members of the United Nations Security Council (UNSC), plus Germany, hence their designation P5+1. The UNSC was increasingly the generator of sanctions, prompted by the United States, to constrain Iran and exert negotiating pressure. The 2008 offer from the P5+1 was similar to the 2006 offer, with some sweeteners if Iran would quit enrichment, including membership in the World Trade Organization. Again, progress remained elusive. Later that year, Barack Obama was elected president, and he proposed in April 2009 that suspension of enrichment would no longer be a condition for negotiation. A few weeks later, Iran was suddenly beset by a major political crisis following an allegedly fraudulent presidential election in June 2009, with large-scale street protests following. It did persist with nuclear matters, however, among them requesting fuel for a small research reactor that then became a focus of multilateral talks.

This took two tracks. One was the so-called Vienna Group (United States, Russia, France, and the IAEA), which guaranteed fuel if Iran would ship out an equivalent amount of enriched uranium to a third country. Iran stalled on this confidence-building measure, while enrichment centrifuges continued to spin. A second initiative, this by Turkey and Brazil, essentially aimed to achieve a similar fuel swap and resulted in a signed agreement with Iran, known as the Tehran Declaration. The United States, then about to impose strong sanctions on Iran, quashed the agreement within a day of its signing in June 2010.

The P5+1 and Iran convened again in Istanbul in April 2012 for the talks that would lead to the deal. Ahmadinejad was still president, but as became known later, he was (contrary to the typical depiction of him in the United States) negotiating seriously at the formal talks and through back channels. The proposals each side put on the table in 2012–13, before Rouhani's election, were very close to the final JCPOA in 2015. The sticking point then and later was how much enrichment would be allowed—the total material, the level of enrichment, the number of centrifuges, the source of fuel, and the length of an agreement. Issues of cooperation on the research reactor, transparency of Iran's nuclear program, IAEA inspections, and the like proved far less trouble-some. The series of talks that first achieved the interim agreement in November 2013 and the final accord in July 2015 proceeded much as arms control negotiations usually do, with broad political objectives ap-parent, technical specialists ensuring the agreement's integrity, and all hands on deck to find work-arounds to political or technical obstacles. Notably, and again typically for arms control negotiations, the talks and final accord excluded other issues—regional security (the civil war in Syria especially), human rights, support for terrorism, US military in-tervention in the region, and other such hot-button concerns.

Trump campaigned on scuttling the JCPOA, probably his most specific campaign promise regarding foreign policy, and it was clear from the start of his time in office that he wanted the United States out of the deal, with the explicit hope that the deal with the remaining partners would then collapse. He used language as incendiary toward Obama as toward Iran, but he made no secret of his dislike of Iran and the need to reverse its gains in the region. Notably, Iran was again de-picted as cheating (the IAEA confirmed Iran's fealty to the pact), devi-ous, and hell-bent on violence toward neighbors (especially Israel). Many of the people close to Trump were those that for many years urged a US policy of regime change in Tehran, including the possibil-ity of going to war with the Islamic Republic. The brief respite of the Obama years was clearly over, but a restoration of sorts loomed when Joe Biden took the presidency and reengaged with Iran to revive the nuclear agreement.

■ Elements of Constancy and Change

What this brief history does not convey are the personal qualities that ultimately are so important to how events unfold, as well as the broader set of relationships and unofficial actors trying to influence the course of US-Iran relations. The final deal was achieved by Rouhani, Obama, and their principal negotiators, Javad Zarif, Iran's foreign minister, and John Kerry, the US secretary of state. Both Zarif and Kerry began their tenures in 2013, but they knew each other from earlier, when Zarif served first under Khatami as Iran's envoy to the United Nations (2002–7) and Kerry was a prominent member of the Senate Committee on Foreign Relations (later chairman) and Democratic nominee for president (2004). This familiarity, forged in countless informal meetings and exchanges, was aided by Zarif's intimate knowledge of the United States, where for more than a decade he lived and was educated. This familiarity was important not only because Zarif understood American politics better than his predecessors and other Iranian clerics and politicians but also because he had so many opportunities to interact with US elites.

Throughout these years, and indeed preceding Khatami's election in 1997, the trajectory of the bilateral relationship was bent one way or another by several competing forces in each country. Most prominently in America was the pro-Israel lobby, mainly the American Israel Public Affairs Committee (AIPAC), as well as numerous other organizations pleading Israel's case. AIPAC and its offshoot, the Washington Institute for Near East Policy, populated policy circles throughout the period, helped to formulate Clinton's signature initiative for the region—"dual containment" of Iran and Iraq—and strongly influenced the news media coverage of Iran.

Working the other side of the street, pro–arms control and pro-détente, was a less well-organized but sizable cohort of civil society groups, scientists, former diplomats, and intellectuals. This included "Track 2" meetings, for example, those convened by Pugwash, the venerable worldwide organization of scientists; lobbying action based on sophisticated policy analysis by the Arms Control Association and the Union of Concerned Scientists, among others; a steady stream of articles in the *New York Review of Books, Bulletin of the Atomic Scientists,* online venues like the Huffington Post, and the elite dailies; and academic and policy conferences that enabled shared analysis and networks across borders. That is to say, there was for more than two decades a "norm cascade," establishing the value and feasibility of handling the Iran nuclear problem diplomatically, which was started and sustained mainly by civil society organizations, given intellectual muscle by scholars, and supported by private, grant-making foundations.

In Iran, domestic politics played a significant role as well. Khatami's election was a shock to conservative elites, and they worked from the beginning to narrow the new president's room to maneuver. The complex governance structure of Iran allows for restraints on popularly elected legislators and governors, and the president, who enjoys no exception in this respect, is not as powerful as in most political systems. The Guardian Council, for example, vets the candidates running for office and may disqualify any who do not meet its standards for piety. This led in 2004 to the overturning of the reform parliament—the Majles—that had been elected in 2000. Pressure on reformers is relentlessly exerted by the Islamic Revolutionary Guard Corps (IRGC), the dominant security force in Iran that is close to the supreme leader and generally aligns with hard-liners. The IRGC essentially threatened a coup d'état against Khatami if he failed to deal severely with the student demonstrators in 1999, but they habitually exert influence indirectly. Street violence by a paramilitary force, the Basij, is common. The conservative press, such as the newspaper *Kayhan*, signals the thinking of the hard-liner elite and has the informal power of intimidation.

At the same time, the popular pressure for reform (political reforms, loosening of social strictures, and an overhaul of the clumsy and corrupt economic system) was quite apparent in most elections. Khatami won the presidency in 1997 and 2001; no reformist stood in the 2005 election; Mir-Hossein Mousavi identified with reform aspirations in the 2009 election, which many believe he would have won in a clean vote count; and the pragmatist and reform-minded Rouhani won a large-margin victory in 2013 and was reelected in 2017. So popular sentiment for reconnecting with the world through an end to sanctions was apparent. And the end of sanctions would come only with a nuclear settlement.

In both countries, the hostility toward the other is long-standing and difficult to dislodge. Opinion surveys in the United States consistently show suspicion of Iran's motives and opposition to much of its foreign policy among the public and opinion makers. In Iran, while young people embrace American popular culture and technology, the official line is to resist US "imperialism." The US alliance with the "Zionists" is widely derided by Iran's public. So the hurdles for negotiators of the nuclear deal were high—not only the usual problems of negotiating a technically complex agreement (with seven parties, no less), not just two countries with sharply different understandings of geostrategic reality, but two publics reared on narratives that encouraged suspicion of the other and were not eager to take risks for an accord.

The depth and rigidity of these attitudes, which persisted after the nuclear deal was completed, stem from national narratives that have been nurtured and grown steadily over many decades and have intensified since the Iranian Revolution in 1979. As noted earlier, every nation has its myths and legends, as well as a unifying social and political narrative about itself and its challengers. For Iran, the United States looms large, because Iran has long suffered under foreign occupation and influence. A sense of betrayal at the hands of Arabs, Turks, Britons, Russians, and Americans is acute, and it is strongly reinforced by a recurring insistence on victimhood, or martyrdom, in Shi'a Islam. The unifying perspective of these centuries of foreign domination in modern parlance is *imperialism*, which Iranians of all political stripes freely accuse America of imposing.

The American national narrative has also come into play most powerfully via the frontier myth, which regards American expansion from seventeenth-century New England as divinely sanctioned. The wilderness—the frontier—would be tamed, savages would be dispatched, and bounty would be reaped. This vision informed continental expansion, and when that frontier closed in the late nineteenth century, many political leaders thought the new American frontier to lie abroad. In America's encounter with the Middle East particularly, the frontier myth remains rousing and relevant. The wild places would be subdued by imposing Western civilization, the savages would be tamed like so many Apaches or Seminoles, and the bounty of oil would be collected.

The frontier thesis has fit neatly into America's dealings with Iran. The specific instance of disruption that has conformed to that narrative is the hostage taking at the US embassy in November 1979. That and the triumph of the apocalyptic Khomeini lent credence to the widely held depiction of Iran as being run by "mad mullahs." Like Arabs who had challenged US activities in the region—Nasser, Arafat, Assad, Saddam, Qaddafi—the new rulers of Iran looked like "savages," all the more so because of their theocracy.

These two national narratives—which we examine in detail in the next chapter—had no obvious path to resolution or some kind of joint understanding, much less a single narrative. US imperialism and Iranian irrationality became the sturdy pillars of how one viewed the other. Throughout the post-1979 era, these frames of reference often guided policy makers in both countries. In Washington, this penchant for seeing Iranian actions and overtures as duplicitous and conniving, prone to violence and sheer anti-Americanism, may have led decision makers to poor choices when Iran was open to a more constructive relationship. A series of violent incidents attributed to Iran—two bombings in Buenos Aires in the early 1990s, the assassination of Kurdish activists in Berlin in 1992, hostage taking in Lebanon in 1986–92, and the 1982 bombing of US Marine Corps barracks in Beirut, among others—shaped US perceptions of Iranian intrigue such that when the

Khobar Towers bombing took place, a ready-made assumption pointed to Iran. The same dynamic was at work during the Iraq War, when US commanding general David Petraeus exclusively accused Iran of fomenting anti-occupation violence in Iraq.

Similarly, Iran has for years routinely accused the United States of plotting regime change, taking actions to undermine Islam, fomenting ethnic divisions in Iran, encircling Iran militarily, imposing sanctions without justification, conducting cyberwarfare against Iran, sponsoring a "velvet revolution" against the Islamic Republic, et cetera, even accusing the West of altering Iran's climate to produce drought. These many complaints typically take form as Iran's potential victimhood at the hands of the imperialist aggressor, but averted by Iran's capacity to resist. Many observers point out that this conforms to long-standing cultural tropes, such as the martyrdom of Imam Hussein, the grandson of the Prophet who was betrayed and slain by a rival.

In the face of these durable narratives—which contained enough factual bits and pieces to remain robust—the elements of positive change were all the more essential to move the relationship from outright hostility to something like cooperation. These elements derived from state interests, an international system that rewards compliance to widely held norms, the nurturing of newly applicable norms to the Iranian nuclear imbroglio, and communication channels supplementing, or instead of, traditional diplomatic channels that were afforded by new technologies and conveyed through global civil society. Each of these will be explored later, but it is worth noting that each element reflects one or more theories of international relations.

The powerful engine of state interests, reflecting realist theory, has been obviously at work throughout the relationship and in the nuclear negotiations and JCPOA specifically. For the United States, the interest was to keep Iran contained, its revolutionary impulses subdued, the flow of oil from the Persian Gulf unimpeded, and its support for anti-Israel violence neutered. Iran's state interest above all else has been regime survival. As a corollary of that objective, it has sought to break free of constraints that harm its economy and political influence in the region—thus the desire to end US and UN sanctions. The United States and Iran have had some overlapping interests, mainly sustaining the oil and gas trade, and opposition to the Taliban in Afghanistan and Saddam Hussein in Iraq. Cooperation was possible, and sometimes extensive, in pursuing the latter interests. It is worth noting, however, that the articulation of these interests underscores the profound imbalance in the relationship: Iran's interests, particularly regime survival, were existential; the United States, while pestered by Iran, rarely considered it to be a top global concern.

The international norms that most affected Iran's nuclear program were those barring nuclear weapons proliferation and promoting the rules—such as transparency—embodied in international institutions like the NPT and the IAEA. One can say that this is explained by both realist theory (states have interests in maintaining credible international institutions) and liberal internationalism (collective rule making and enforcement are constituents of a liberal global order). Another set of norms, noted earlier, coalesced around the central salience of negotiations as being strongly preferred to war. While this would seem always to be preferred, in the Iran case the deeply rooted bias that regards Iranian leaders as both irrational and cheaters, "rug merchants" who will fool the West's negotiators and are determined to destroy Israel, militated against the norms favoring diplomacy. The latter, derisive set of attitudes is what Trump carried into the White House and implemented as policy by withdrawing from the JCPOA and imposing new sanctions. Even the Biden administration was relatively slow to pursue the campaign promise of rejoining the JCPOA and spoke of new conditions along the way.

That Iran had a perspective on security and its place in the world that should be honored became commonplace even in popular accounts of the nuclear controversy. It reflects, in this way, constructivist theory that emphasizes the role in global politics of ideas, including the narratives or discourses of the subaltern. The Iranians' arduous insistence on equal status and respect in negotiations has an account in critical or postcolonial theory as well, in which those who have been excluded from the dominant political systems (principally colonized peoples in the global south) struggle to gain a voice and the capacity for autonomous action.

The guiding ambition in this book is not to prove one theory or another but to demonstrate how national narratives, as well as national security narratives, have dominated at pivotal junctures of the relationship. The narratives may reinforce a calculation of interest, but they sometimes work against such formulas. Narratives can express aspirations akin to liberal internationalism—support for universal human rights, to cite one American hope—while they can also be parochial and premodern. Ideas matter significantly, but narratives tend to draw on long-standing cultural formations and are relatively maladaptive to new conditions, quite different from what most constructivists consider to be ideational power in international relations.

The broad, nearly chaotic eighteen-year process that led to a historic nuclear agreement, only to have it disrupted precipitously, can insightfully be examined through this lens of understanding national narratives and how they apply to real-world problems. The same can be said for other matters besetting the relationship, notably Iraq, Israel, and US regime-change efforts, among others. That process and those issues—what they were and how they unfolded, and refracted through the lens of national narratives—are the subjects of this book.

The Narrative Trap

1 Every nation or nation-state has a narrative, a story that defines what it is—its origins and history, characteristics, claims to legitimacy, values, mission, and destiny. These defining stories are an essential component of nationalism, sometimes contrived by a state needing to establish its bona fides, sometimes more gradual and organically grown. They typically convey a sense of belonging, pride, and unity. In all cases, narratives are "socially constructed," often filled with fictitious claims, populist in tone, and readily manipulated by elites to gain some political advantage.

Both the United States and Iran have well-formed national narratives, very different from each other and with several internal inconsistencies. Each has a powerful grip on national consciousness, discourse, and political behavior—not a comprehensive grip, and not always a decisive grip, but remarkably strong and durable. Even in this age of a multiplicity of voices via new media, which are global in scope and richly multicultural, the long-standing national narratives continue to define much of our countries' deliberations, policy making, and practice in the domestic and world arena. They are cohering ideologies and moral guides to action, for better or for worse, and serve as a bedrock of identity and self-realization.

National narratives and nationalism itself grew often from the dissolution of kingdoms and other forms of personalized political authority. These "imagined communities," in Benedict Anderson's reckoning, were made possible by vernacular printed communications, the printed language serving both as a common bond and as a revolutionary social and political invention.[1] Nationalism can also rise within empires and monarchy, as Iran itself shows; the conveyed sense of national unity and identity braced the crown and its legitimacy, with the monarch representing nationhood rather than deriving authority from his own divinity or power. In other instances, monarchy was gradually giving way to popular sovereignty, and nationalism was an engine of that change, as was the case in Britain's Glorious Revolution.[2] Anderson's focus on nationalism's appearance in colonies and postcolonial states is notable in the American case because colonies possessed defined territories, a common (imperial) language, and institutions of governance—all essential to state building and to the emergence of liberatory nationalism.

A nation typically has territory and a state; it also has cultural characteristics common to the many who see themselves as belonging to that nation. In addition to language, such characteristics may include religion, traditions of everyday life, ceremonies and rituals, and a shared history. It may contain multiple "ethnicities," although this is frequently contested in everyday politics: in the United States, African Americans and other groups are targets of bigotry that include denying their place in the American nation; in Iran, the Baha'i and some other groups face similar discrimination by the Persian majority. The divisiveness over ethnicity—"purity," in effect—besets any definition of nationhood. National narratives, however, tend to gloss over such difference and speak of the nation as a unified body, no matter how badly ruptured, as was the case of slavery and Jim Crow in the United States. With ethnicity also comes language, and the unifying power of language is at the core of nationhood. The use of Spanish in America is, as a result, one of the most tendentious aspects of public debates over immigration and belonging.

All of these cultural symbols and practices make up the features of particular nations, but nationalism—the adulation of a particular nation—also requires a story. The mundane rituals and social practices must be enlivened and ennobled by a national narrative, customarily a mix of the mythological and an elaborated set of historical assertions. This story serves many purposes. It describes the uniqueness of the nation, its particular characteristics that explain a certain greatness. All members of the nation share in that greatness. "The task of nationalists is to rediscover the unique cultural genius of the nation and restore to a people its authentic cultural identity," observed Anthony D. Smith, a leading scholar of nationalism. "This emphasis upon national individuality helps to explain why nationalisms are so often accompanied and fueled by the labors of intellectuals intent on tracing the 'roots' and 'character' of the nation through such disciplines as history, archeology, anthropology, sociology, linguistics, and folklore." The objective for nationalists, he noted, is "to achieve the fullest expression of all three national ideals," that is, of autonomy, unity, and identity.[3]

Those nationalists, moreover, must be able to exert political as well as cultural power to shape and sustain a national narrative. In complex societies, such as America and Iran, more than one narrative can be detected. The history of black people in America or that of indigenous tribes are very different stories from the dominant, white European settler account. The master narrative, which accumulates mountains of details to nourish its main themes, can encompass some difficult truths and contradictions in the national tale. Racism in America and the Civil War itself are alkalinized by placing art like *Huckleberry Finn* and *Gone with the Wind* in a nationalist canon, or making the lives of Abraham Lincoln and Martin Luther King Jr. indisputably heroic. The normative trauma of slavery becomes, in this telling, a story ultimately about American "values" prevailing and healing. The American narrative palette, you see, is wide and diverse.

So too in Iran. One icon of Iran's national self-regard is the Cyrus Cylinder, an artifact of the reign of Cyrus the Great in the sixth century BCE and held to be among the first declarations of human rights—specifically, a right of return of displaced peoples and the right to worship freely (both claims, however, are disputed by scholars). Undoubtedly a remarkable document, its placement in the Iranian national narrative is unabashed. Yet it was discovered only in 1879 and, more importantly, had no continuous political or cultural resonance in Iran, as did, in contrast, the Magna Carta's influence on English political evolution. The last shah used the cylinder to celebrate the 2500th anniversary of Cyrus's reign, and much was made of its supposed human rights originality. The Islamic Republic also exalted the cylinder and displayed it (on loan from the British Museum) in 2010. The wound of Iran's deplorable human rights record, indefensible under any of its regimes, is somehow partly repaired or obscured by the presence of the cylinder.

Political exigencies and political actors inevitably influence national narratives and the way they are used. Nationalism and, by implication, national narratives include ideological statements, understandings, prescriptions, and warnings—ways to interpret the world as agents of destiny. Ideology in this sense is not merely a particular lens used to grasp the meaning of life and the world around us, but a guide to action, a prompt to fulfill the mission or purpose of one's nation. (It would be the rare national narrative that depicts the nation as passive.) One might say that the narrative is the story, ideology is the exegesis, and nationalism is the sentiment or moral fuel. They are not the same, and they will not always appear in the same way: one can take a narrative, even one with fabulous features, interpret its ideas in different ways, and be moved by different parts of the story at different times. As is discussed later, the high regard given to the pioneer in the American narrative can be taken as idolizing the covered-wagon settlers battling Indians to civilize the frontier; one could also, alternatively, promote as paragon a pioneer in science or exploration or art. Even within the former, the pioneer could evoke feelings of national pride for subduing the savages or for exploiting the land—for adventurousness or husbandry. The political actors seizing the narrative device of the courageous pioneer typically use it to enliven an ideology of rugged individualism in the service of a certain kind of nation building.

While national narratives and nationalism are made up of cultural elements, their purpose is almost always political—defining and legitimating a politically powerful class, using symbols but not being merely symbolic. Defining political power and those who legitimately can exercise it also means creating boundaries and markers for political action. The Greek myths, for example, were in part folklore and religion and in part a legitimation of a certain group of invaders whose system of monarchical or elite rule was integrated through mythology into a universal template of (divine) justice.

The US-Iran confrontation, as argued later, is rooted in conflicting narratives, and it also has a narrative of its own—a national security narrative about the two nations' relationship. Because narratives have historically contingent origins, events such as the overthrow of Mohammad Mosaddeq by the Central Intelligence Agency (CIA) in 1953 and the 1979 US embassy hostage taking resonate prominently. It is not sentimentally charged nationalism that is clashing, although nationalist feelings are roused, but very different interpretations of events—a story that is told and retold and fit into broader, richer tales that pose the other as an existential enemy.

These stories and sentiments nourish national self-consciousness—identity, norms, goals—while also serving to preserve power relations internally. One can see a good amount of subterfuge inherent in national narratives. "Nationalist ideology suffers from pervasive false consciousness," Ernest Gellner asserted in *Nations and Nationalism*. "Its myths invert reality: it claims to defend folk culture while in fact it is forging high culture; it claims to protect an old folk society while in fact helping to build up an anonymous mass society." It holds itself "as a manifest and self-evident principle . . . violated only by some perverse blindness." And, perhaps most importantly, "it preaches and defends cultural diversity, when in fact it imposes homogeneity both inside and, to a lesser degree, between political units."[4] This fundamental deception—mythmaking, corruption of history, and imagined community—is rarely if ever haphazard or randomly contrived. Though it may be woven by many hands and appear in many forms, it is constructed in such a way as to embrace popular sentiments of all social and economic strata in the service of national prominence and, typically, a privileged class.

The popularity and acceptance of the narrative derive from many sources—pride in one's people and place, the sense of specialness it conveys, a defense against obscurity or meaninglessness. As we shall see, the American and Iranian national narratives serve different purposes for each nation. But the myths, legends, historical episodes, cultural artifacts, and blandishments that compose narratives all are fueled by sentiment—an essential glue to bind the nation together. Sentiment at the core of nationalism and as a fruit of the national narrative is not necessarily inspiring or heartwarming. It can be a relentless shadow of pessimism. As the British philosopher Isaiah Berlin explained in his 1972 essay "The Bent Twig,"

Nationalism is an inflamed condition of national consciousness. . . . It usually seems to be caused by wounds, some form of collective humiliation. It may be that this happened in German lands because they had remained on the edges of the great renaissance of Western Europe. . . . To be the object of contempt or patronizing tolerance on the part of proud neighbors is one of the most traumatic experiences that individuals or societies can suffer. The response, as often as not, is pathological exaggeration of one's real or imagined virtues, and resentment and hostility toward the proud, the happy, the successful.[5]

Berlin explored in a number of books and essays the rise of German nationalism, an outgrowth of Romanticism and a reaction to French universalism, beginning in the eighteenth century. That is, the *philosophes'* insistence on reducing all social and political thought and action to a common standard (whether derived by rationalist or empiricist means)[6] deprived specific nations of their unique cultures and character. The first theorist of nationalism, in Berlin's reckoning, was Johann Gottfried Herder, the late eighteenth-century German philosopher who "rejected the absolute criteria of progress then fashionable in Paris: no culture is a mere means towards another; every human achievement, every human society is to be judged by its own internal standards. . . . Cosmopolitanism is the shedding of all that makes one most human, most oneself."[7] This acclaim for the unique value of local or national cultures is the stuff of nationalism and national narratives alike as they became the dominant political thrust in Europe a century later and in Africa and Asia two centuries later. "Germans must be Germans and not third-rate Frenchmen; life lies in remaining steeped in one's own language, tradition, local feeling; uniformity is death. The tree of (science-dominated) knowledge kills the tree of life."[8]

The power of national myths, social and cultural practices, and language in shaping a narrative that is politically animated by patriotic fervor became obvious in the nineteenth and twentieth centuries. But not all aspects of a national narrative are as salient as others at any given time. Why was the US-Iran confrontation so much more belligerent after 1979 than before? Did the national narratives—and the emergent national security narrative—shape political behavior, or did political actors merely use national narratives to justify their actions? "Only some narratives," wrote Ronald Krebs, "become dominant, an accepted 'common sense' about the world, and thus set the boundaries of what actors can legitimately articulate in public, what they can collectively (though not individually) imagine, and what is politically possible." Dominant narratives, he continued, "privilege a range of policies and impede the legitimation of others, and fundamental change in national security policy—in its basic orientation, as opposed to the effort expended or the means employed—hinges on change in the dominant narrative."[9]

The national narratives that animate nationalism are, in sum, socially constructed over time, tend to serve the interests of specific elites, are populist in tone and lit by sentiment, and honor particular cultural myths and social practices. How narratives affect political behavior and international relations, particularly alongside or juxtaposed against state interests or global norms, is our pivotal question. The United States and Iran, especially in their relationship to each other, provide some insights.

▪ Iran's National Narrative

Like a great river that has different springs and occasionally divides in half to circumvent an island, Iranian nationhood and its narrative have two sources and currents—the largely polytheistic Persian history stretching back to Cyrus, and the story of Shi'a Islam that is rooted in the "Karbala Paradigm" of Imam Hussein. They are significantly dissimilar, but in places complementary. Tributaries feed them. Political leaders of all stripes sail with the river's flow. The public sees no reason to divert or dam the waters that seem to replenish Iranian cultural identity and political outlook.

Nationalism was slow to emerge in the Middle East and indeed most of Asia and Africa, and in Iran the social and political conditions of the second half of the nineteenth century provided a fragile stage for its debut. The Qajar dynasty (1785–1925), which was actually Turkmen in origin, was widely regarded as weak, indecisive, and corrupt—ripe for an uprising. It was not merely incompetence that stirred a new nationalism, however, but the perception and reality of the Qajar shah selling Iran's resources to foreigners, Britain and Russia in particular. While some modernizers in the shah's circle saw these concessions as the only feasible way to upgrade railroads, communications, extractive industries, and governance itself, the deals struck were outrageously generous to foreigners. Nothing comparable had occurred in Turkey, Egypt, or Tunisia, which also aspired to Western-style modernity.

In consequence, two things happened. The reigning Qajar monarch, Naser al-Din Shah, violated his subjects' tolerance for the selling of Iran's assets, the breaking point coming in 1890 when a tobacco concession, sold to an Englishman, gave away the rights to grow, sell, or export Iranian tobacco. Stirred by newspaper articles and pamphlets, a nationwide protest rocked the country and the government. The Shi'a clergy, importantly, led the movement, and eventually the shah backed down. Because of the months-long crisis and the organizing of protestors, a significant form of nationalism coalesced, one that was fundamentally anti-foreign and mixed religious and secular leadership.[10] The constitutional movement, culminating in a full-blown revolution in 1906 that established an elected parliament and constrained royal power, typically is traced to the tobacco protest.

The other consequence of the Qajars' ineptitude was the growth of an intellectual space where a new national narrative was forged. This narrative, nurtured by anti-monarchical and anti-cleric intellectuals Mirza Fatali Akhundzadeh and his protégé Mirza Aqa Khan Kermani, harkened back to the age of Cyrus as the foundation of a secular, Aryan nation that had continuous linkages to the present day. The glories of the Persian Empire, which extended from the Mediterranean to present-day India and Central Asia, reflected on the Iran struggling to emerge from the doldrums of the Qajar period. Notably, this conjured depiction also linked Iran to Europe through the racial trope of the Aryan nation—not wholly surprising, since the Aryan myth was a concoction of European Orientalists to begin with. Some common roots of Sanskrit, Persian, Greek, and Latin led European intellectuals obsessed with racial origins to seek an original tribe or nation that would connect these traditions, and these musings in effect invented an Aryan race.

In the 1890s, Kermani was among the first Iranians to adopt this line of thinking, and he elaborated a narrative that encompassed the Achaemenid Empire founded by Cyrus and bypassed several hundred years of occupation by Arabs (considered then and now to be an inferior race) to keep the narration's lineage intact. The story of the Aryans was a gallant one, with whiteness and European brotherhood as its defining characteristics. These stories Kermani and like-minded writers fabricated sought to undermine the legitimacy of the Qajars, who were Turkmen in origin and spoke Turkish at court, as well as the *ulama*, the religious establishment, which of course could lay no claim to Cyrus and the Achaemenids. Both, in Kermani's reckoning, were obstacles to Persian modernization.

Iran's political trajectory in this period reflected the rise of the clergy as the most prominent check against arbitrary rule. In large measure, the Constitutional Revolution occurred because Islamic and secular visions of constitutionalism could not be reconciled. Sheikh Fazlollah Noori, whose execution at the hands of constitutionalists would become a potent symbol of clerical resistance against secular, Westoxified visions of modern statehood, built his opposition on the emergent narrative of Islamic unity that Jamal al-Din al-Afghani and other Muslim leaders had awakened in the public imagination.

The nationalist vision gained traction politically only after the final demise of the Qajars and the rise of Reza Khan, a military officer who led a coup d'état in 1921 to reverse the loss of Iranian territory to the Russians and the British. The "Great Game" between Russia and Britain for control of Western Asia at that point involved the nearly complete loss of Iranian sovereignty outside of Tehran. Reza Khan, who commanded the Persian Cossack Brigade, subdued foreign and domestic challenges to the central state; he was appointed prime minister in 1923 and was made shah by parliament in 1925—partially at the insistence of the clergy—taking the name Reza Shah Pahlavi. As he consolidated power, he modeled himself after the Turkish general who salvaged the Republic of Turkey out of the defeated remnants of the Ottoman Sultanate, Mustapha Kemal, or Atatürk. In this modeling of the Turkish nationalist, Reza Shah was secular, Europe oriented, and a builder of a strong state. As part of that state building, he embraced the Aryan narrative.

It was a narrative that suited the new monarch as a nationalist who was determined to modernize Iran along secular lines. "This pre-Islamic frenzy—very much vivid throughout the Pahlavi period to this day—is one of the founding pillars of ideological Iranian nationalism," observed scholar Reza Zia-Ebrahimi. "Pre-Islamic Iran also conveniently seemed to possess what the Qajar era did not (power and progress) while its temporal remoteness made it a more suitable starting point for a genealogical narrative of the Iranian community."[11] The Aryan myth, then, served as the nationalists' imaginary of noble origins, unsullied by religion or "dirty" foreign contamination, in which Persians thrived in an idyllic and just nation.

This account insists that the lineage of this extraordinary race up to the twentieth century was corrupted by Arabs in particular, who earned harsh disapproval by Kermani and later writers as backward, uncivilized "lizard eaters" that, among other sins, brought Islam to Iran. This divergent path explained the decaying condition of Iran under the Qajars, in the nationalist view, and thus it was all the more urgent to assert the primacy of the Aryan nation as a guiding light toward modernization. Rejection of all things Arab, even Arab loanwords in Persian, was part of the nationalists' project, their route to Persian (and Aryan) purity.[12] The political power of this national narrative grew with the half-century reign of the Pahlavis and was never extinguished from Iran, even in the revolutionary period since 1979.

In this same period, however, from the tobacco protests to the 1921 coup, another strain of nationalism grew and thrived, however tenuously, in the form of liberal constitutionalism. This effort was broadly anti-absolutist and insistent on a written constitution to secure popular sovereignty, rule of law, and individual rights. It drew significantly on Enlightenment values in contrast to the Aryan myth, and indeed the 1906 constitution was based on a European (Belgian) constitution. Many of the nationalists saw constitutional government as a bulwark against undue foreign influence. A parliament, or Majles, was founded. Voting rights and the like were circumscribed and thereby dominated by elites and the wealthy, but the principles of popular sovereignty nonetheless took root. The secular constitutional tradition endured nominally until the 1979 revolution, its democratic principles more often honored in their breach during Reza Shah's increasingly authoritarian reign. Even before then, the country descended into political turmoil, during which one of the key achievements of the constitutional revolution—that the Majles would protect the nation from foreign encroachments—was subverted by continuing British and Russian intrigue. In fact, an Anglo-Russian agreement in 1907 divided Iran into respective spheres of influence and control, which the two empires exploited at will. This foreign intrigue (as well as considerable lawlessness by various tribes in the countryside) prompted Reza Khan's coup.

While suspicion and rejection of foreign influence are a common theme of the Iranian national narrative in all its forms, Reza Shah acted

The Narrative Trap

on other nationalists' aspirations as well, such as unifying the nation within its borders and promoting a broad adoption of the Persian language. His vehicle of unification and order, the military, was a frequent feature of twentieth-century nationalists such as Atatürk (a general and genuine military hero), Mussolini, Horthy, Franco, Peron, Nasser, and so on. The great leaders of ancient Persia—Cyrus, Darius, Xerxes—were military conquerors, a theme not lost on the shah and his circle, who drew on the ancients to propel their version of modernism.

Reza Shah's twenty years in power became increasingly autocratic, dismissing the promise of the constitutional revolution, but he was wholly dedicated to the project of utilizing the distant past—the Aryan myth—to forge a new national consciousness. It was the flowering of Kermani's vision. This project introduced a particular cultural discourse about the Achaemenid Empire while diminishing the importance of the *ulama* and the tribal chieftains.

This politically attuned agenda utilized cultural means to write the new narrative, to make it visible and audible. Architecture, museums, memorials and mausoleums, and other public landmarks were designed to invoke the glories of the pre-Islamic past; ancient cities gone to seed were revitalized to become destinations of pilgrimage; and a discourse of starting anew, occasioned in part by the failures of the constitutional movement, focused on how the collective memory of ancient Persia was a formidable alternative to Arab (Islamic) decay. The men who undertook this sizable task "genuinely believed in the Aryan superiority of the Iranian nation and endeavored to revive its cultural expressions, deciding and defining the parameters of that nation's new 'heritage'" while mindful of Western influences and determined to modernize Iran.[13] "The continual process of depicting the past was not only projected as sets of events and forms that could be renewed, but also as a vivid collective memory that must be reawakened," and so in cultural reconstructions the Pahlavi elite, for example, "consistently privileged the image of Ahura Mazda over Ali, or

Cyrus over Hossein, as the 'true' signifiers of Iranian identity."[14] As the prominent Iranian intellectual Said Nafisi lamented in 1935, "We forget, or we seem to have forgotten, all our past historical brilliance, our struggle against Babylon, Athens, Sparta, Rome, and Byzantium; and we seem not to want the memory of our military deeds and our humanitarian and civilizing principles to remain alive."[15]

The strategy of nation building through this narrative included formal education. In part, that manifested as a determined effort to permeate Iran and its many different ethnic groups with the Persian language, which itself was an attempt to coerce Azeris, Arabs, Kurds, and others to identify with the national, Persian project—*e pluribus unum*, so to speak.[16] The promotion of the Aryan myth in school textbooks persisted into the post-1979 period. By the late Pahlavi period, then, this national narrative was well established in Iran, culminating in the widely ridiculed 1971 commemoration of the Persian Empire by Mohammad Reza Shah, the son of the first Pahlavi, in a lavish event attended by many world leaders. The shah stood at the tomb of Cyrus (which was empty) and intoned, according to a report, "'O Cyrus, great King, King of Kings, Achaemenian King, King of the land of Iran . . . I, the Shahanshah of Iran, offer thee salutations from myself and from my nation.' He promised to safeguard the traditions of humanism and benevolence and noted that 'the Iranian flag is flying today as triumphantly' as it flew in the time of Cyrus. 'Rest in peace,' he said, 'for we are awake, and we will always stay awake.'"[17] (The extravagance of this event is sometimes credited with feeding the discontent that ultimately led to the shah's demise.)

This version of the national narrative held that there was a continuous Persian nation populated by an Aryan race with a specific geography, Iran (and beyond), speaking Persian, and with a distinct character and culture of greatness that transcended various non-Persian rulers or interlopers. This narrative instills a demand for respect for this remarkable civilization. It demands integrity and a certain homogeneity within Iran. And while the Persian nation has at times identified with other Aryan peoples, it resists foreign intrusion.[18]

The other narrative account of the Iranian nation is rooted in its devotion to Islam and has become an official narrative since the 1979 revolution. Islam was introduced in Iran by the conquering armies of Arabs beginning in the seventh century CE, and gradually the various parts of Iran converted to Islam from Zoroastrianism, although pockets of non-Muslim communities, including Jews and Christians, persisted. By the ninth century, Islam was dominant. Moreover, foreign rulers were also dominant, first the Arab Umayyad, ruling mainly from present-day Iraq and their caliphate, and then nearly eight centuries of Turkish rulers until the rise of Reza Shah. Throughout, Persian identity was maintained via language and other cultural traditions, as well as by the development of a separate branch of Islam, Shi'a Islam, which was mainly (though not exclusively) Iranian.

Shi'ism came to Iran following one of the many invasions it endured, this in 1501 CE by the Safavids, a Kurdish tribe that was culturally Turkish. Esmā'il, the Safavid charismatic leader, invaded from Azerbaijan, seized the throne at Tabriz, and declared Twelver Shi'ism (beholden to the "hidden," or twelfth, imam destined to return) the state religion on pain of death. He defeated Uzbek and other occupying tribes and unified the country. The adoption of Shi'ism brought Iran into conflict with its Arab and Ottoman neighbors, who remained Sunni, and this confrontation—involving actual politics and armed violence, as well as the foundation myth of Shi'ism—persists vividly to this day.

The foundation story involves the bloody end of Hussein, grandson of the Prophet Mohammad and son of Ali, a cousin and son-in-law of Mohammad who was among the closest companions of the founder of Islam. A complex succession struggle ensued upon Mohammad's death in 632 CE. One faction regarded Ali as the rightful successor but was outflanked by others of the Umayyad dynasty who were able to control the caliphate for years to come. A treaty had been made that would return the caliphate to the Prophet's family: Ali, who served briefly as caliph, and his older son Hassan were murdered, and Hussein was next in line. But the treaty's terms were revoked, and in 680 Hussein, citing his own legitimate claim to the caliphate, refused to pledge allegiance to Yazid, the Umayyad caliph. Soon after, on a journey across the plain of Karbala (in present-day Iraq, just south of Baghdad), possibly to initiate a revolt against Yazid, Hussein and his entourage were attacked by forces loyal to Yazid, and Hussein was murdered, his body mutilated and beheaded.

This betrayal then became a rallying cry for the faction loyal to Ali, the *Shī'atu 'Alī* (the Party of Ali, from which the name Shi'ite or Shi'a is derived). The split between Sunni and Shi'a was cleaved by many events in this early period, but the assassination of Hussein and his family was the most dramatic violation. Not only was there betrayal, but Ali and Hussein embodied virtuous qualities of piety and humility, in contrast to the tyrannical Umayyad caliphs.

This narrative is central to Shi'ism. Interpretive texts, passion plays, informal folklore, and rituals have placed the martyrdom of Imam Hussein as the fulcrum of the sect. It appears in these forms as a premonition of Adam, Moses, Jesus, Mohammad, and other religious figures. It organizes worship, observance, and coping with everyday life. The entirety of the martyrdom story and its expression is what scholar Michael M. J. Fischer calls the "Karbala Paradigm":

> There are, then, three parts to the notion of paradigm: (a) a story expandable to be all-inclusive of history, cosmology, and life's problems; (b) a background contrast against which the story is given heightened perceptual value: in this case, primarily Sunni conceptions, but other religions at times serve the same function; and (c) ritual or physical drama to embody the story and maintain high levels of emotional investment:

the rituals of daily worship (prayer, purity rules, dietary rules); pilgrimage to the tombs of 'Ali in Najaf, Husayn in Karbala, the other Imams and the hajj; preachments (*rawda*), morning processions (*ta'ziya*), and passion plays of Muharram (*shabih*).[19]

The Karbala Paradigm is a structure of belief and action, organizing more than religious observance alone. The martyrdom of Hussein spoke to a sense of injustice, maltreatment administered by despotic, illegitimate rulers. As Iran careened into the revolutionary period of the late 1970s, the symbolic uses of Karbala multiplied. The shah was Yazid, the tyrant (or, in earlier biblical terms, Pharaoh), and the growing numbers of protestors raised the banner of Ali and Hussein, the martyred ones, as indeed martyrs to the shah's repression multiplied. Martyrdom was a central motif of revolution and, later, of the Iran-Iraq War. The breadth and depth of protest against the shah were astounding; thousands died and thousands more were imprisoned, and they came from all walks of life. In the growing street protests a chant would echo, "Every day is Ashura, and everywhere is Karbala."[20] Ayatollah Khomeini and other Shi'a leaders explicitly made these connections and extolled the blood sacrifice of martyrs.

The ouster of Mosaddeq ushered in a twenty-five-year accommodation with the West, and the United States in particular, as US military and economic aid poured into Iran. While the shah and his cohort welcomed this, for many Iranian nationalists it was evidence of a new form of foreign domination. The intellectual avatar of this critique was Jalal Al-e Ahmad, whose 1962 book *Gharbzadegi*, which translates as "Westoxification," was enormously influential. He described Western influence as a plague that threatened to overwhelm Iranian culture. The book, as well as the argument, added powerfully to the longtime Iranian narrative that included suspicion of foreigners, and in this case it was taken up by the growing Shi'a opposition and the secular opposition to the shah as well.

As many observers have noted, the revolution culminating in the exile of the shah and the establishment of the Islamic Republic in 1979 occurred in the Islamic idiom because leftist political parties, news media, and other organizing had been ruthlessly banned. As a result, the Karbala story was ideal for the revolution: its Manichean structure of good versus evil, the centrality of martyrdom and sacrifice (and action over passivity), the acts of betrayal and deception that Hussein suffered, and the foreignness of the dark forces of the Umayyads all privileged the Karbala myth as an emergent national narrative.

Once the protest movement achieved its goals, it faced a paradox of power: during the period of protest, the opposition posed as the victim of tyranny, but then how did the shift in roles affect that narrative claim? One of the easiest answers to that dilemma was positioning the United States as Pharaoh, or the Great Satan, aligning it with Israel as a mortal enemy of Islam and Iran. In this formulation—based on the irrefutable history of the CIA-backed coup against Mosaddeq and durable support for the shah—several of the tropes of the Iranian narrative come alive, particularly those of foreign intrigue, domination, and betrayal. Transferring Pharaoh from the White Palace to the White House is a key to understanding how the national narrative unfolds in real politics.[21]

The new state in the 1980s also needed to deal with the lingering attraction of the Aryan myth and the attachment to Cyrus, Xerxes, Darius, and the pantheon of ancient Persian heroes. Pre-Islamic culture, as a continuous and sustaining source that nourishes modern Iran, does not coexist easily with the Karbala story as the dominant shape of national identity.

At first disparaging the pre-Islamic past (as have, dramatically and destructively, the Taliban in Afghanistan and the Islamic State in Syria), the Islamic Republic came to embrace the glories of this past as a suitable precursor to the arrival of Islam. This attitude required a refurbished version of events, of course, as the Pahlavi-era school textbooks and other cultural institutions had not merely exalted the Aryan period but denigrated the foreign armies and ideology of Islam, seeking to nationalize, in effect, the early period of Islam. Similarly, the Islamic leadership has allowed the continuation of highly popular non-Islamic traditions such as the celebration of *Nowruz*—Persian New Year. The troublesome facts of foreign dominance could be dismissed as small annoyances in the boundless magnificence of Persian character and culture. "Its spirit remained vast and indestructible," noted one textbook history; "Iran has always been much too firm and much too rooted to yield to a particular race or ... emir, khan, or conqueror. The realm of Iran has been the realm of culture, civilization and of language."[22] It is this perspective of nationhood, not directly contradicting Muslim teachings, that imbues Iranian thinking. "The post-revolutionary narrative, just like the Pahlavi predecessor, presupposes the existence of the Iranians as a unified group moving through history," concluded one scholar studying textbooks. "The post-revolutionary state has appropriated major parts of the Pahlavi historical memory with a view to elevating 'Iranianism' to the rank of a leading ideology."[23] "Iranians continue to nonchalantly refer to the *nezhàd-e àriyàyi* [Aryan race] and their alleged belonging to this family that would include Europeans. It figures prominently even in scholarly production," Reza Zia-Ebrahimi wrote. "Banal Aryanism," he continued, "is common in different aspects of daily life in Iran. It abounds in popular culture, literature, and symbolic repertoires. In fact, the Aryan discourse has become so entrenched in Iranian identity and self-perception that it is unconditionally reified."[24] Officially, however, it is not. Islamic identity is privileged over Iranian identity, even when the latter is acknowledged as an acceptable constituent of national identity, as President Khatami said on numerous occasions.

That inclusive spirit has not been evinced by Supreme Leader Khamenei, who has been wholly insistent on Islam's all-encompassing role as the nation's identity. This is a result in part of his deeply held suspicion of foreign influence. "If the culture, morality, beliefs and convictions of the enemies and aliens are spread among a nation, such a nation . . . cannot claim to be independent," he stated in 2000. "A human society can be considered independent only when it can immunize itself against the poisonous cultural waves created by aliens."[25] As Islam claims to be a universal religion (as does Christianity), a question lingers as to how to conceive of "nation"—its basic legal and political significance—if Islam is not merely its defining feature but its comprehensive cultural, social, and political reality.

However official Iran defines its national essence, "on a daily basis, Iranians are moving between spaces, both public and private, which are dominated by a particular political discourse."[26] The result is an Iran/Islam blended identity that combines several elements: a distaste or even revulsion regarding foreigners, foreign interference, and foreign cultural poisoning; the elevation of a distinctly Iranian character and culture above others; respect for popular sovereignty; and an unusually strong reverence for charismatic figures.

■ America's National Narrative

"We shall be as a city upon a hill. The eyes of all people are upon us," John Winthrop told his fellow settlers just before landing in the New World in 1630. It's a phrase that has become a standard of American self-identity. The borrowing from the Gospel according to Saint Matthew frames both the aspiration to divinity ("The Lord will be our God, and delight to dwell among us, as His own people, and will command a blessing upon us in all our ways") and what came to be known as American exceptionalism. This conceit is paradoxically both true and false: true in that the American experience is unique and powerful, a story lesson for the entire global community, and false in that many societies, nations, and cultures are exceptional (including Iran).

Those who insist on American exceptionalism typically invoke a more contemporary version of Winthrop—that America and Americans are uniquely virtuous and exemplary.

This is less identity than it is simple self-admiration, albeit in the idiom of Christian piety. Those observers underscoring American exceptionalism, such as Alexis de Tocqueville in *Democracy in America*—the first use of "exceptionalism" in this regard—were denoting the stark differences from European political development. The United States, less than fifty years old as a nation-state, was lightly populated on a vast continent. Political sovereignty for European-origin men of property was protected. Economic opportunity was open-ended for such men, and even those of lesser means. An indigenous population was at that time (1830s) and for decades thereafter subjected to genocide, and hundreds of thousands of African slaves would remain in bondage until 1863, long after Europe (even czarist Russia) had cast off the institution.

These characteristics were unique, giving rise in some accounts to an American creed of individualism and minimal government that also set the United States apart from other major powers.[27] As a set of ideas with global ambition, however, American exceptionalism is hardly unique. Tenets such as personal liberty, rule of law, democratic governance, and free markets have been promoted with some consistency on the world stage, and they represent Enlightenment principles that the British and French, among others, have long claimed to foster as well.[28] This liberal internationalism entwined by a set of values remains rhetorically powerful in US politics. It is not, however, a national narrative.

More convincing is an overarching story in which notions of exceptionalism are subsumed. That is the frontier myth that began with Winthrop's Puritans and has reappeared in the ensuing four hundred years in various forms, always with standard elements. The Puritans saw their presence in America as an "errand to the Wilderness," a civilizing mission in which the wilderness would be tamed, the savages native to the wilderness subdued, and a bounty reaped.

Puritan leaders saw this as no less momentous than the exodus from Egypt and the establishment of a New Jerusalem. Whatever its theological trappings, it became the main account of European (mainly English) settlement of the first thirteen colonies, one by which land acquisition and suppression of the Indians, often violently, constituted core reasons for making the hazardous and uncertain journey to the New World.

The frontier represented the aspiration of expansion, but it was also the nearly mystical place where the uniquely American character and worldview were forged. It is a place of freedom and natural richness, the vitalizing venue where democratic principles were shaped and practiced alongside the Protestant's individual relationship to God. The liberty and rewards this frontier offered were achieved by the fatal encounter with the savages. Cultural historian Richard Slotkin called this encounter "regeneration through violence"—not merely redemption or necessity, but nourishing the pioneers' mission by suppressing the one obstacle in their way: a continent filled with indigenous tribes. These ideas shaped nationalism in the nineteenth century particularly as the frontier became a dominant preoccupation of politics, commerce, and literature.

Across time, both the heroes who tamed the wilderness—Washington, Boone, Houston—and the yeoman farmer on the edge of civilization who cultivated land and virtue regarded the frontier as the vital site of their endeavor. And that frontier was ever moving west toward the Pacific Ocean. Slotkin, the main theorist of the frontier myth, explained: "The Myth of the Frontier is arguably the longest-lived of American myths, with origins in the colonial period and a powerful continuing presence in contemporary culture. Although the Myth of the Frontier is only one of the operative myth/ideological systems that form American culture, it is an extremely important and persistent one. Its ideological underpinnings are those same 'laws' of capitalist competition, of supply and demand, of Social Darwinian 'survival of the fittest' as a rationale for social order, and of 'Manifest Destiny' that have been the building blocks of our dominant historiographical tradition and political ideology."[29]

The pivotal, actionable constituent of the frontier myth is how the savages—the "Indians"—were regarded and how that cultural trope became embedded in national consciousness and behavior. From the early seventeenth century to the end of the nineteenth century, well more than half of the period of the European presence on the continent, the principal threat to white settlers were the indigenous tribes, and those 280 years witnessed endless rounds of Indian wars as the settlers moved westward. The Indian was a source of fear and fascination, but the operating ideology of expansion required that indigenous tribes be removed (by violence) or exterminated. That ideology, attributable to a young nation's hunger for land and riches, necessitated an elaborate set of justifications. "The Indian is characterized by his savagery, his closeness to nature and to animalism, his lack of a sense of private property and the related inability to recognize and respect Woman," wrote Slotkin. "His politics take the form of violence, which is directed to cruel and destructive ends."[30] Such sentiments, voiced and written repeatedly by a variety of American intellectuals, pastors, journalists, businessmen, and others, constituted a deeply held belief that went unchallenged by nearly everyone in the settlers' world, from Thomas Jefferson to Abraham Lincoln to Theodore Roosevelt.

At the same time, the wilderness had become a kind of paradisiacal imaginary in the Euro-American mind, once feared but gradually tamed, exploited, admired, and embraced (in Hegelian terms) as a culmination of human progress. Historian David W. Noble noted that this was a European invention, the notion of timeless space—timeless in that European class divisions and endless wars would be left behind and human liberty would finally be achieved in the vast, wild space of

North America. "The promised land, the West, where liberty would find her final home, was that space in North America populated by the descendants of English Protestants—the space destined to be the national landscape of the United States," wrote Noble. Nineteenth-century American historian George Bancroft, Noble observed, "could imagine one more exodus from east to west. West of the thirteen colonies and their long local histories, intertwined with European power, across the Appalachians, was 'Virgin Land.'" Achieving the goal of democracy would be the destiny of men who "crossed those mountains and became 'Americans.'"[31]

The emphasis on space had three consequences. The space was occupied by indigenous tribes, which in the Euro-American ideology obligated elimination. Second, the land, however expansive, was finite. The continental United States was "settled" and the frontier closed by 1890, according to the US Census Bureau, an assertion that stirred a crisis among intellectuals who located America's unique virtues of democratic development on the frontier. Third, this crisis of democracy stirred many of these same thinkers and political leaders to see expansion as a project to continue overseas.

Historian Frederick Jackson Turner famously articulated his frontier thesis in 1893 in response to the Census Bureau's assertion, a thesis that became gospel among many intellectuals for years to come. The frontier, "the meeting point between savagery and civilization," fairly defines the progress of American history, Turner argued, from hunter/trader to farmer to city builder, from east to west. The army made this possible by protecting settlers from the Indians. Characteristics forged on the frontier promoted rugged individualism and the democratic values that go with it: "That coarseness and strength combined with acuteness and inquisitiveness; that practical, inventive turn of mind, quick to find expedients; that masterful grasp of material things, lacking in the artistic but powerful to effect great ends; that restless, nervous energy; that dominant individualism, working for good and for evil, and withal that buoyancy and exuberance which comes with freedom—these are traits of the frontier."[32]

These ideas reflected what others were also thinking—that the end of the frontier was a civilizational crisis for America. Two of those, remarkably, were future presidents: Theodore Roosevelt and Woodrow Wilson.[33] Both had elaborated ideas about the centrality of the frontier and what might remedy the crisis of its closure, specifically with respect to the durability of democratic values. And both men, among others, saw the "errand to the wilderness" as a global endeavor. The American frontier may be closed, but elsewhere frontiers awaited the unique qualities of the American pioneer.

The first such overseas adventure was in the Philippines, occasioned by the war with Spain, where an easy US victory was followed by a long war for independence by Filipinos that was suppressed harshly by Presidents McKinley and Roosevelt; some two hundred thousand Filipinos were killed. "Applying the Frontier Myth to the imperial project begins with a metaphoric extension of Frontier categories to a new situation in which Asians become figurative Apaches and the Philippines become a symbolic equivalent of Boone's Kentucky or Houston's Texas," Slotkin explained.[34] The prize to some was China, and the Philippines was a stepping-stone. "The East is to be opened and transformed, whether we will or no; the standards of the West are to be imposed upon it," Woodrow Wilson, then a Princeton professor, wrote in the *Atlantic* in 1901. In classic imperialist and Orientalist language, he predicted that Americans would "teach them order and self-control in the midst of change; impart to them, if it be possible by contact and sympathy and example, the drill and habit of law and obedience."[35] (China continued to be an aspiration of American globalism for years to come and a destination of many Christian missionaries, but the political chaos preceding the Communist takeover in 1949 made it a forbidding venue for an American frontier.) The Philippines war created a template of sorts for foreign military involvement, although the United States would eschew the formal possession of territory that marked its presence in the Philippines until 1946.

The pattern was to see military adventurism as righteous and civilizing, the countries the US military invaded as a wilderness populated by savages, and a bounty to reap from the action. The elixir of American exceptionalism served to inebriate American political elites and allowed them to see their interventions not in the idiom of European imperialism but as something far nobler. Bringing democracy to the uncivilized nations was an idealism that is associated with Wilson particularly, and the sincerity of the sentiment did not mean that the frontier template was any less powerful. Wilson was, for example, the frequent trailblazer of US military intervention in Mexico, Central America, and the Caribbean, which American forces invaded thirty-five times in the first thirty years of the twentieth century,[36] largely to establish and maintain hegemony for economic gain while publicizing these ventures as democracy promoting.

While the two world wars did not overtly reflect the frontier myth, they did extend America's global scope and the righteousness of US involvement throughout the world. Following the Second World War, and partly in response to the policy of Soviet containment, the US government built a vast network of military bases throughout the world, with additional capability of power projection from the territorial United States and from its formidable sea-, air-, and spaceborne assets. Even today, some eight hundred US military facilities are based in seventy countries.[37] Actual military fighting took place in so-called Third World countries—Korea, Vietnam, Cambodia, Laos, Panama, Afghanistan, and Iraq most prominently, with dozens more covert paramilitary actions carried out by the CIA or small special operations teams.

In those wars—the "savage wars of peace," as one military analyst called them—the frontier myth is more visible. The world wars posed adversaries (apart from Japan) who were well-developed, white, Christian peoples whose states, while aberrant in important ways, fit into the contours of Western political development. Culturally, the adversaries were close cousins of predominant ethnicities in the United States, German and Italian most obviously, and to some extent Slavic. The Cold War pitted sides that were more ethnically diverse (China being a prominent antagonist along with the Soviet Union), but its defining feature—other than global security—was ideology, with defense of religion a bedrock principle for the United States and its allies. The almost biblical tone of the 1950 presidential memorandum, NSC-68—a key, early text of US response to Communism—clearly embraces that as a priority.

The venues for those "small wars" (which were not small in human costs, with millions killed in Korea and Vietnam, and many more millions displaced) can be seen in the idiom of the frontier as the "wilderness." Even the long-used descriptive term "the Third World" indicates such otherness. The wars were fought for varying reasons, but commonalities exist. Korea and Vietnam (as well as Cambodia and Laos) were partly about China. Afghanistan and Iraq were about the barbarity of terrorism. All the adversaries were depicted as savages who placed little value on human life. Most of the countries were considered to be bountiful in one way or another. Iraq is a major oil producer and sits next to oil giants Kuwait and Saudi Arabia. Afghanistan and Vietnam have strategic minerals wealth. The Korean War protected Japan and sustained American presence in East Asia. Even the 1989 invasion of little Panama was about its canal.

The elements of the frontier myth, then, were largely in place during the most active period of American globalism—the wilderness, the savages, and the bounty, more or less present in each case. The response to the 9/11 attacks and the 2003 invasion of Iraq featured much of the cowboys-and-Indians imagery and language in the debates about initiating hostilities.[38] The Iraqis, even those who were supposedly US sympathizers, were relentlessly depicted as uncivilized, and the Afghans even more so. The missions of Operation Enduring Freedom (invasion of Afghanistan in 2001) and Operation Iraqi Freedom (2003) can be glimpsed in the names of the campaigns. While the goal of the invasion of Afghanistan was hot pursuit of Osama bin Laden and the goal of the invasion of Iraq was disarmament of Saddam's weapons of mass destruction (WMDs), both were glorified in the familiar tones of freedom and democracy. They were, at root, errands to the wilderness.

Other historical, economic, and cultural forces were at work in shaping America's encounter with the rest of the world. Students of imperialism in its many manifestations recognize the United States' striving for hegemony in Latin America, East and Southeast Asia, and the Middle East in those familiar terms. One such perspective was that promulgated by Brooks Adams, an intellectual from the renowned Massachusetts family who grappled with the closing frontier anxiety of the 1890s and influenced Roosevelt and other political elites. Like Roosevelt and Wilson, he saw the world as America's frontier and argued vigorously for expansion of the American presence globally, including, notably, a keen hope of intervening in China. Adams and Turner, with their outsized sway with two US presidents and exceptionally durable influence in policy circles for decades to come, articulated the idea of the world as America's frontier as virtually no one had before or has since. They revealed American imperialism as a highly specific ideology that equated expansion with the ennobling features of the frontier. This differentiated US expansion from other notions of imperialism, such as white man's burden, great power prerogative, and Soviet Marxism, among others.

As with Iran's constitutional movement, the American narrative contains a root and branch of idealism, which has served as an alternative or adjunct to the frontier thesis during the past one hundred years. Typically associated with Wilson and his postwar advocacy of multilateralism, popular sovereignty, and democratic governance, idealism or liberal internationalism did significantly influence US foreign engagement from then on. It served as a key precedent for Franklin Roosevelt's global vision following the defeat of Nazi Germany and Imperial Japan.

This idealism informed the post-1945 world, in which American power was unmatched and its responsibilities pivoted on making a moral case for both anti-colonialism and anti-Communism. Certainly, the Wilsonian impulse was evident in all these undertakings. It did not necessarily contradict the frontier myth, but it was represented in a different way. The historian William Appleman Williams argued that the frontier thesis was evident in much of Franklin Roosevelt's foreign policy and in the Truman Doctrine, both of which envisioned (and enacted) an expansionist US role in the world on behalf of certain principles drawn from the American frontier experience. One could see the entire postwar liberal order, the Bretton Woods institutions particularly, as an embodiment of this thinking—that is, formal guarantees of freedom, liberalized trade, and an end to European domination of the global south.[39] Where Wilsonianism and the frontier thesis came into conflict, the prerogatives of frontier thinking seemed to prevail—in the wars in Korea and Vietnam, in the Cold War's treatment of the Third World, and particularly in the Middle East.

The cultural thrust of the global frontier—civilizational and superficially Christian—was always embedded in a nest of attitudes borrowed from Europe that was at once racialist and Orientalist. The racism is plainly visible in Theodore Roosevelt and Wilson and reflected long-held and persisting beliefs about white superiority. The Orientalist attitudes lend a slightly different cast to America's encounter with the global south. That is, Orientalism does not merely treat Asians (and others) as racially inferior to Europeans and European-origin Americans, but rather discovers a more complex relationship of fascination, seduction, and historical depth, as well as domination, subjugation, and backwardness—almost precisely the same relationship that the American frontiersmen forged with indigenous peoples.

The frontier favored financiers and traders perhaps above all. Turner's thinking explicitly regarded the frontier as a steam valve, a way to reduce the pressures created by class warfare in the metropolis of the industrial East. The idea of the frontier thus was promoted intentionally as a national narrative, hegemonic in Gramsci's sense—to produce certain economic outcomes—and this remains a key to the frontier myth's lasting viability. The extension of the frontier to Asia and Latin America was partially to reinvigorate the democratic soul of America, in Theodore Roosevelt's meaning, but was also a simple (if energetic) foray of capitalism's global reach. The errand to the wilderness was, after all, a search for bounty.

The American national narrative has hued closely to the frontier myth, now a story line lasting four centuries and intertwined with more conventional narratives of imperialism, racism, Orientalism, idealism, and economic exploitation.[40] What sets the frontier idea apart from other national narratives (Britain and France most obviously) is the romantic attachment to the life-giving dynamism of the frontier itself and the exalted role of violence in securing and regenerating its promise. Even as cultural sources of the American story diversify, the frontier remains a bedrock.

◼ Clashing Narratives and the Narrative Trap

Two nations, antagonistic to one another and with well-defined national narratives, find themselves—forty years after their relationship broke down—unable to escape the constraints those narratives impose on political leaders. The constraints are the individual narratives themselves and how expectations emerge on any particular issue, as well as how the two narratives are inherently in conflict with each other.

The American narrative, which is expansionist at its core and obligated to regard natives as savages in the lands where that expansion is pursued, clashes with the Iranian narrative, which is deeply suspicious of foreign intrigue and influence. Iran has been buffeted by Western imperialism for two centuries and regards "expansion"—even, for example, in the form of the global financial system—as another attempt at domination. More active measures, such as attempts at regime change or threats to take military action against nuclear facilities, reinforce Iranians' wariness. Indeed, the supreme leader of Iran and numerous political leaders regularly regard the United States as the "Great Satan." The reliance on the clergy in Iran for such broadsides in turn has convinced American elites that they are "mad mullahs"—savages—that deserve only contempt and possibly annihilation.

The two narratives nonetheless share some similarities. Both have difficulty accounting for ethnic and religious diversity within the country. Nationalism tends to embrace homogeneity and use a cudgel against otherness. For the United States, Black Americans, Hispanic Americans, and Asian Americans, as well as Catholics, Muslims, and Jews, have been on the outside looking in. For Iran, non-Persians face discrimination, particularly Kurds and the Baha'i. The narratives cope with the lack of "racial" or religious purity mainly thorough exclusion. Such an incomplete narrative not only leaves out a large portion of the population but also cannot adequately account for significant events in its history—for example, the Civil War in the United States, or longtime rule by Turkish monarchs in "Persian" Iran.

A second similarity is the role of violence. According to Slotkin, violence is central to the frontier myth, and "savage war" is its most consequential form. "Ineluctable political and social differences—rooted in some combination of 'blood' and culture—make coexistence between primitive natives and civilized Europeans impossible on any basis other than that of subjugation."[41] That subjugation was enforced by relentless violence, which the Puritans saw as regenerative: a recurring rebirth of uniquely American frontier ideals. Wars abroad had precisely the same quality, from the contrived Mexican-American War to the terrible swift sword befalling Hiroshima and Nagasaki.

The Iranian narrative's immersion in violence is mainly through martyrdom. The sacrifice of martyrs recurs frequently in the national narrative, particularly relating to Hussein and those likened to him. "Speaking to protestors against the [Pahlavi] regime, Khomeini here made references both to an Islamic brother and sisterhood and to the courageous spilling of blood 'on the same road as that of the Prophets, Imams, and their followers,'" recalled a scholar. "In so doing, he linked the present day act of spilling blood in protest of the Shah to a prophetic lineage of religious Muslim belonging and to the martyrdom of Hussein," which is a "material and transformative act. According to the late Ayatollah Mutahhari, for instance, the blood of the martyr is never wasted. Rather, it 'infuses fresh blood into the veins of society.'. . . It is a transfusion for a society 'suffering from anemia.' These statements make a direct link between the blood of the martyrs and the regeneration of (Islamic) society."[42] Martyrdom is routinely evinced in situations of social stress—the Iran-Iraq War, or the US shootdown of an Iranian passenger plane in 1988, for example—to condemn enemies or legitimate certain actions of the state.

Despite the emphasis in both narratives on violence and the spilling of blood, it is noteworthy that one typically celebrates the assertive use of violence while the other solemnly commemorates the victims of violence.[43]

The clashing qualities of the narratives enlarge the possibility of each side misunderstanding the other. It is often said, for example, that Jimmy Carter misread the Iranian street protests against the shah and that he (along with the US intelligence community) was taken by surprise by the rapid demise of the Pahlavi regime and the rise of Khomeini. In this, they misunderstood the Iranian national narrative and its implications for politics, and they failed to regard the limits of the

American national narrative as well. The American presence in Iran in the 1960s and 1970s was not a "civilizing" mission, but one of extending US power through a surrogate in the region, accompanied by belated, weak entreaties about human rights.

That period demonstrates one aspect of a narrative trap. The "trap" is evident when one country or both act excessively on the basis of their national narrative. Narratives, so often self-congratulatory myths, are poor guides to action in the international arena. Yet they exert exceptional influence over foreign policy decisions. The narrative frames discussion about virtually any consequential foreign involvement and is braced by years of cultural production, social practice, and political conventions. The cultural, social, and ultimately political power of these archetypal story lines can overwhelm other sources of decision-making, even including clear national interests. They can so contextualize decision-making that the people making those decisions are not fully aware of how biased their frames of reference are.

It is difficult to say with certainty whether the cultural framing and social impetus of national narratives shape decisions or help justify decisions made for other reasons. Economic self-interest, national security interests, global norms, interest group politics, and legal obligations, among others, have their say in these countries' foreign policy decision-making. We demonstrate, however, that the cultural impulses driving US-Iran relations are revealed through the narratives each country has constructed of itself, of the other, and of their relationship. This perspective taps into a still-nascent strand of constructivist thought in international relations theory that regards narratives as being constitutive of agents and structures in shaping world events.[44] These elements are informed and enlivened by "precedents and shared symbolic materials—in order to impose interpretations upon events, silence alternative interpretations, structure practices, and orchestrate the collective making of history."[45]

US-Iran relations cannot be understood outside of the shared experiences that have characterized, shaped, and determined them. Although these experiences have been narrated and understood in different ways, they have defined a continuing relationship that persists despite the absence of formal diplomatic relations since 1979. To understand the current predicament, therefore, one must understand the evolution of the relationship and unearth the myriad processes of differentiation and representation that, according to Ali Ansari, have brought us to "the threshold of a conflict that many accept but few understand."[46] The enmity that exists between the two nations today is handily grasped by the intimacy that preceded it—friendship precedes betrayal in the case of US-Iran relations. Yet, to the contemporary observer, it must seem remarkable that the now-great enemies were friends and stood shoulder to shoulder as staunch allies. As with any betrayal, however, the disputants lay claim to different interpretations of what led to their estrangement, resort to selective memory, and opt to omit facts that are inconvenient to the ruling elites. And so it remains in the mainstream American discourse that contemporary Iran, in the words of Secretary of State Condoleezza Rice, constitutes "an outpost of tyranny," while in the lyrical chants of the Iranian faithful at virtually every Friday prayer session America seems perennially destined to symbolize the "Great Satan."

Understanding what constitutes these kinds of social construction—how they come about, and what the stories tell us—enables us to comprehend more fully why nation-states act as they do, more fully than a calculation of interests does.

We posit a narrative trap in the US-Iran confrontation because the two national narratives operate mechanistically in relation to each other, as if designed to thwart progress toward normal state-to-state comity. Simply put, America's assertiveness internationally, pursued with all the trappings and rhetoric of the frontier myth, rouses a nearly

automatic reaction in Iran, deeply wary as it is of foreign encroachments and fiercely protective of its Islamic character. The tenor of this
wariness and protection is frequently heated and couched in language
that is alien to Americans, which fits the American perception of non-
rational impulses supposedly found in savages. This back-and-forth
fulfillment of the lowest expectations of each other can proceed for
years at a time, as it did during the Iran-Iraq War, during the Bush-
Ahmadinejad period, and then again during Trump's presidency. It is
not merely rhetorical, since the perception of threat can and does lead
to specific, hostile acts. Even when the narratives can be set aside, as
they seemed to be in the final stages of the negotiations that led to the
nuclear agreement in 2015, it takes very little for the narratives to return in full force. Nothing germane to the deal made it unravel, but
other events did (Iran's actions in Syria, US support for Saudi bombing of Yemen, and especially Trump's election), conforming to the expectations of the narratives each held about the other.

We can say with confidence that these narratives prevented in several cases the exercise of foreign policy according to national interests
alone. Given other challenges in the region, a more normal bilateral
relationship, even accounting for philosophical differences, would benefit both countries greatly in stemming violence in Afghanistan, Yemen, and Iraq; addressing the civil war in Syria; possibly enabling a
serious peace process in Israel/Palestine; and easing Persian Gulf tensions generally. The narratives also were a root cause of missed opportunities in the relationship, those somewhat unusual moments when
the United States and Iran seemed to be on the verge of diplomatic
breakthroughs. George H. W. Bush's invitation to a dialogue, the election of Mohammad Khatami in 1997, gestures to Khatami by Bill Clinton in his second term, the cooperation on Afghanistan state building
after 9/11—these events, among others, had the potential to lead to a
broader entente. That they did not so proceed was due in part—perhaps mainly due—to the grisly work of the narratives.

While it is not our purpose here to suggest how the two nations can extract themselves from the briar patch of their national narratives, it is at least noteworthy that other nations have succeeded in this regard—France and Germany, Korea and Japan, Argentina and Brazil, among others, though each circumstance is unique. Those countries, for all the bloodshed and animosity, share borders, culture, and interlocking economies. It is possible if not probable that the United States and Iran will never enjoy commonalities that help to overcome the animus of clashing narratives. The best we can do, perhaps, is to build a common narrative, a mutual understanding of what has happened to them and why, in order to move forward unimpeded by the singularities of their own reckonings with history.

The Fraught US-Iran Relationship, from Mosaddeq to Khomeini

2 In early 1980, three months into the hostage crisis that was crippling his presidency, Jimmy Carter took a question from a reporter at a press conference: "Mr. President, do you think it was proper for the United States to restore the Shah to the throne in 1953 against the popular will within Iran?" The question seemed to irk Carter: "That's ancient history, and I don't think it's appropriate or helpful for me to go into the propriety of something that happened 30 years ago."[1] What possible bearing, he seemed to be asking, could the actions of the Eisenhower administration have on the turmoil of today?

For many Iranians, of course, 1953 was far more than history. Memories of the Western-backed overthrow of Prime Minister Mohammad Mosaddeq touched sensitivities, not just for the regime but even for many of its opponents. Few Iranians would have had trouble drawing a causal line from that time to the Iranian Revolution, traversing a period during which US support for the shah profoundly deepened. In contrast, few Americans were even aware of the anti-Mosaddeq coup. Carter was one of the few, but his dismissal of its pertinence suggests that he, too, had not grasped the weight of its memory on Iran.

This book contends that the coup was one of a series of events prior to the revolution that helped to solidify public perceptions in both countries, which in turn molded leadership approaches to the relationship, even though neither side may have fully recognized the process or absorbed its significance.

■ From World War to Coup d'État

While World War II still roiled, policy makers in Washington had already begun to anticipate America's emergence from the conflict as the dominant world power. On the security front, planners mapped out strategies to prevent the rise of a new global threat. (There was only one contender—the Soviet Union.) Economic interests would be key, especially guaranteeing access to natural resources to fuel American industries and international markets for exports. They also foresaw a world struggling to recover from war and in desperate need of a helping hand—and only one great power with the means and humanitarian impulse to offer it. These intertwined concepts of threat and opportunity largely shaped the outlook of America's leaders throughout the coming Cold War.

Iran, which had played an unheralded but valued role in the Allied victory, turned out to be integral to the postwar stratagems of President Roosevelt himself. A few weeks after the 1943 Tehran Conference, Roosevelt wrote to his secretary of state to ask how to help the strategically placed country progress. "Iran is definitely a very, very backward nation," he declared. "It consists really of a series of tribes and 99% of the population is, in effect, in bondage to the other 1%." In the president's view, that made it ripe for uplifting. Roosevelt forwarded to the secretary, Cordell Hull, a plan he had directed his personal envoy to Iran to draft. The memo began, "It is the purpose of the United States to sustain Iran as a free, independent nation and to afford the Iranian people an opportunity to enjoy the rights of man as set forth in the Constitution of the United States and to participate in the fulfillment of the principles of the Atlantic Charter." For Roosevelt, the country was a petri dish. "I was rather thrilled with the idea of using Iran as an example of what we could do by an unselfish American policy. We could not take on a more difficult nation than Iran. I would like, however, to have a try at it."[2]

The country that for centuries (until 1935) had been known as Persia had recently impressed American planners as a vital interest, mainly because of its oil resources and long, shared border with the Soviet Union. As a key to the Near East, Iran after the war enjoyed added significance because of the presence of Western military bases, more oil fields abutting the Persian Gulf, and trade and transportation routes that needed defending from possible Soviet attack. By declaring the United States the guardian of the area, as the British edged closer to a decision to withdraw, American officials also hoped to project an image of strength and reliability.

Roosevelt was not alone in his vision for Iran. A year earlier, a State Department country desk officer wrote a memo that eventually found its way to the upper reaches of the agency. A young idealist, John Jernegan suggested Iran as a "test case for the good faith of the United Nations." The idea would be to showcase the United Nations' ability to balance "ambitions, rights and interests" that would be "fair not only to the Great Powers of our coalition but also to the small nations associated with us." The United States, he declared, was the only country capable of helping Iran fend off the machinations of the other great powers—Britain and the Soviet Union. The effort would take "disinterested American advisers" and "assistance of a material character," and "if railroads, ports, highways, public utilities, industries, are to be built, we can build them and turn them over to the Iranian people free of any strings."[3]

It was an optimistic time, as historian Bruce Kuniholm has since remarked, when "altruism . . . nicely coincided with self-interest." Both the president's special Iran envoy, Patrick J. Hurley, and Jernegan made pointed references to the Atlantic Charter. A document with personal meaning to FDR, the charter espoused principles of territorial integrity, respect for sovereign national rights, and equal access to trade. Observing it was not only a moral imperative, in Roosevelt's view, but also in America's "vital interest" to make sure that all members of the United Nations did the same. "The coincidence between idealism and self-interest did not appear self-serving to the president or to lesser officials charged with implementing American policy," Kuniholm notes.[4] Whether innate or acquired, this ability to elide these contradictory notions goes far in explaining American behavior—for example, the ability to rationalize a case of direct interference like the 1953 coup as purely unselfish.

American strategic concerns about Iran near midcentury were genuine. Years before the war, Britain had staked a commercial claim to Iran's southern regions, where it operated a hugely profitable extraction and refining industry. By 1944, Stalin was demanding his share, egged on by the leaders of Soviet Azerbaijan eager to reunite with their ethnic brothers across the border. In late 1945, the Kremlin established pro-Moscow "republics" within the Iranian provinces of Azerbaijan and Kurdistan. Annexation seemed a distinct prospect.

By now, Harry Truman was president. Generally unprepared in most people's eyes, he was at least more clear-eyed than Roosevelt about Soviet intentions. Fearful that Stalin would be tempted to intervene directly, as he had notoriously in Eastern Europe, Truman decided to preempt him in Iran. Earlier in the war, the Soviets, British, and Iranians had signed a treaty pledging the two outside powers to withdraw within six months after the end of hostilities. At the 1943

Tehran Conference, they repeated their promise. Britain eventually complied, but the March 1946 deadline passed with no movement from the Soviet side. Truman raised the rhetorical pressure on the Kremlin and encouraged Iran to take its case to the United Nations Security Council, a first for that body.

The crisis eventually ended, but only after intensive negotiations between Tehran and Moscow. The two sides signed an oil agreement in April 1946 and promised to pursue closer ties, at which point the Soviets finally withdrew their troops from Iranian territory. To everyone's surprise, above all Stalin, Tehran turned the tables on Moscow. Iranian troops swooped into Azerbaijan and Kurdistan, crushing the remaining, undefended pro-Moscow forces there, and the Majles, despite assurances to the Kremlin, rejected the oil deal. Moscow was left empty-handed. Yet Stalin chose not to respond with force, knowing it would risk a clash with the West.[5] The United States emerged as a hero. Not only had it faced down the Soviet menace and rid the country of an unwelcome British presence, it had defied expectations by not filling the void as a traditional colonial power would. It was the high point of US popularity in Iran.

Once the risk of Soviet aggression had receded, the Truman administration turned to other preoccupations. Over the next few years, one global crisis followed another—from Moscow's detonation of an atom bomb to the founding of the People's Republic of China to the Korean War. The influential policy statement NSC-68 from April 1950 articulated the prevailing alarmist conviction that "the assault on free institutions is worldwide now." When North Korean forces attacked the South, Truman's instinct was once again to see Iran and the rest of the region as possible targets of Communist intrigue. "If we just stand by, they'll move into Iran," he warned, "and they'll take over the whole Middle East."[6]

Soon, Iran would return to world attention, leading to a severe downturn in US-Iran relations that would color the Iranian narrative. The precipitating event was the nationalization of the oil industry in spring 1951. With major implications for both the Cold War and the global decolonization movement, the move touched off near panic in the West. The British, whose massive petroleum facilities had been the main target, immediately hatched plans to recover their principal overseas source of income through a combination of political and military force. The Americans worried more about keeping Communists from exploiting the resulting instability, which they expected to manifest through either a Soviet attack or internal subversion by the local Tudeh Party.

Spearheading the nationalization push was Mohammad Mosaddeq, a widely respected veteran politician with family ties to the Qajars, who had been appointed prime minister after the assassination of his predecessor, an opponent of nationalization. Mosaddeq's bold act made him a champion to his country but anathema in the West. Britain launched a vitriolic public relations crusade, which the media enthusiastically picked up. *Time* magazine named Mosaddeq its "Man of the Year" for 1951—though it was hardly a compliment. The article was a full-throated Orientalist tirade lambasting the "dizzy old wizard" as "an appalling caricature of a statesman" who had "put Scheherazade in the petroleum business and oiled the wheels of chaos." Projecting profound conflict in the Middle East, the editors called attention to "a hatred and envy" in the area that was "almost incomprehensible to the West." "The word 'American,'" they lamented, "no longer has a good sound in that part of the world."[7]

Truman's sympathies initially lay with Iran's nationalists as exponents of the global decolonization process. An early advocate of what would become modernization theory, he felt as inspired as Roosevelt to promote economic prosperity abroad. Two years after the Marshall Plan, he announced "a bold new program . . . for the improvement and growth of underdeveloped areas. . . . The United States is pre-eminent among nations in the development of industrial and scientific techniques. . . . I believe that we should make available to peace-loving peoples the benefits of our store of technical knowledge. . . . The old imperialism—exploitation for foreign profit—has no place in our plans. What we envisage is a program of development based on the concepts of democratic fair-dealing." Iran was to be an early recipient of this largesse, through the so-called "Point Four" program.[8]

Over time, pressures from the British and from American oil interests, on top of deteriorating political and economic conditions in Iran, led Truman gradually to harden his position. Local exigencies, as always in the Cold War, appeared to have global implications. Truman shifted to planning how to confront a growing Soviet threat.[9] But until the end of his presidency, he rebuffed pressures for drastic action, notably from London.[10]

The Eisenhower administration arrived with a different take on Mosaddeq in January 1953. The Cold War remained at the center of US strategic concerns, even though some of the president's counselors were close to Great Britain and Big Oil. These individuals also shared the general British condescension toward Mosaddeq and Iranians in general, shamefully reflected in terms such as "irrational," "volatile," and "childlike" that often appeared in Western newspapers.[11] Eisenhower never betrayed such crudeness, but he seems to have been unable to see how these attitudes might affect popular perceptions there. At a National Security Council (NSC) meeting early in his first term, he was generally mystified by the unfriendly behavior of foreigners the United States was trying to help. "The President said . . . it was a matter of great distress that we seemed unable to get some of the people in these downtrodden countries to like us instead of hating us."[12]

Increasingly, the dominant viewpoint in Washington was that the West needed to take decisive action to save Iran from itself. Truman had been prepared to go as far as deploying American forces, but only in response to an overt Soviet move. Eisenhower's policy innovations were to operate clandestinely, rather than assume the burdens of a military intervention, and to strike before the Soviets could act. Otherwise, the two leaders shared the same motive—to keep Iran out of Communist hands.[13]

Eisenhower and Winston Churchill soon gave their approval for a coup, and following weeks of joint planning with MI6, the Central Intelligence Agency launched Operation TPAJAX in August 1953. The plan involved persuading the shah to sign decrees replacing Mosaddeq, putting together a coalition of security forces, seizing control of key facilities, bribing Majles members, and paying mullahs and other organizers to gin up street crowds, all of which built on an extensive propaganda campaign designed to undercut Mosaddeq's popular standing. Mosaddeq foiled the initial plot after being warned in advance. But Kermit Roosevelt and his Iranian collaborators regrouped and, after a few days of frenetic, improvised activity, tried again. It was a mixed performance that benefited from miscalculations by Mosaddeq, but it managed to return the young monarch to the throne. In short order, Iran's political and economic circumstances stabilized and the shah found himself firmly in control. For the United States, the Communist threat had been exorcised, oil flowed freely, and a vital region of the world was made more secure.[14]

Over the years, the coup took on ever-greater political and rhetorical significance. As dissatisfaction with the shah grew in the 1960s and 1970s, the idea took root that the ouster of Mosaddeq, who quickly acquired folk legend status, had been a tragic turning point in Iran's political history, a moment when the country might have taken decisive steps toward democracy. Instead, the theory went, the sycophantic shah, with uncritical backing from the United States, set up a dictatorship that was ever more corrupt, self-serving, and toxic for the country. Washington was the power behind the throne that either failed or chose not to exercise its limitless influence on the shah to reform. After the revolution, the coup became part of the regime's narrative—no longer just a rallying theme for the shah's opposition. But Mosaddeq's role became glossed over as a result since he lacked the all-important credential for the revolutionary government of a devotee of political Islam. In his place, approved figures such as Aya-tollah Abol-Qasem Kashani, a politically active, senior cleric and rival of Mosaddeq, moved to the center of the story as the significance of "28 Mordad" became less about secular nationalism than about the familiar saga of foreign exploitation.

The full story is far more involved. A core reason for the coup's success was that a substantial cohort of the population sided against Mosaddeq and in favor of the shah, or at least in favor of what he rep-resented—the monarchy, anti-Communism, and stability. The notion that outside powers could have pulled it off without ample Iranian participation is simply not sustainable. Nor is the reverse—that Irani-ans themselves were solely responsible. It is also harder to make the hypothetical argument that Mosaddeq's ouster by itself stunted Iran's experiment with democracy. He was a hero to many, a politician of unusual personal integrity, even in British and American telling, but his premiership was far from unblemished. And he was in some ways an anomaly in a political environment that was byzantine, fractured, and corrupt. As for some prominent mullahs, the record of their role in 1953 is unflattering in the context of today's Islamic Republic. Aside from evidence that CIA agents at a minimum expected that payments they were distributing would end up in the hands of clerics to orga-nize street mobs, there is also documentation that senior ayatollahs Kashani and Behbehani sided against Mosaddeq in the coup.[15]

Reality, then, does not easily fit the contours of either of the Ira-nian narratives (pre- or post-revolution) that have grown out of 1953. The same is true of the standard American and British versions. The caricatures of Iranian primitive incompetence shared by Anglo-Iranian Oil Company executives and some British diplomats were grotesque. US Ambassador Loy Henderson's dismissal of Mosaddeq as a "lunatic" was hardly better. The other side of the narrative for US policy makers was their belief in America's calling to save Iran, which was presumed to be innately incapable of managing its own affairs. Both sides of this picture can be seen in the musings of State's chief officer responsible for Greece, Turkey, and Iran, which he shared with a colleague shortly after the coup: "My basic assumption is that we cannot avoid a responsibility to become involved in Iranian internal affairs.... I fear that refusal to interfere in Iran would not only be disbelieved but could be as dangerous as refusing to stretch forth a hand to help an unstable man walk along a precipice."[16]

■ The 1960s

For the next decade, Iran's government accepted that helping hand from its US patron, although the shah chafed at the implied inferior status. For both Tehran and Washington, the future looked upbeat. When a young economics officer named Bruce Laingen arrived for his first tour of duty in Tehran—twenty-six years later he would be among the hostages taken by Iranian revolutionaries—it was a few weeks after the coup and a "very optimistic period in terms of American interests," he recalled. The shah was still young and "malleable," and ready to ensure that the "policies of his government . . . would be responsive to American concerns." "The United States was a very large player in Tehran at that time. It was the player."[17] In time, the shah grew more confident, and his relationship with his American counterparts became more complex.

By the time John F. Kennedy took office in January 1961, Iran's long-term stability and prosperity had failed to materialize, despite infusions of US support. Popular unrest had bubbled up, and the shah, who had already tried cracking down, could not ameliorate it with the tepid moves toward liberalization he was comfortable with. Iran was not high on Kennedy's agenda because of the crises in Germany and

Southeast Asia, but the country was still considered strategically vital.[18] Besides, the architects of the New Frontier were keen to test out their theories of modernization on the Third World.

Kennedy's limited enthusiasm for taking on Iran was tempered further by a lack of confidence in the country's stability, the shah's ambitions, and, apparently, his personal views about the monarch (who had favored Richard Nixon in the 1960 elections). Choosing the most effective approach was also complicated by quarrels among advisers like Walt Rostow, a true believer in modernization, and NSC staff Middle East expert Robert Komer over practical implementation.[19] By early 1963, Iran's inability to resolve various challenges, in addition to pressure from Washington, led to the launch of the White Revolution. A step forward in terms of land distribution, women's suffrage, and other improvements, its political foundation was precarious—based on a farcical national referendum showing 99.9 percent approval and its association in the popular mind with the brutal suppression of major protests a few months later, in June 1963.

Kennedy's ambivalence toward—and ignorance of—Iran's circumstances showed plainly in some curious messaging to the shah during this period. After the sham referendum, he wrote that it was "gratifying" to know "that a vast majority has supported your leadership in a clear and open expression of their will."[20] He then effectively endorsed the shooting of hundreds of protesters in June by calling their demonstrations "unfortunate attempts to block your reform programs," adding that he was sure "such manifestations will gradually disappear as your people realize the importance of the measures you are taking to establish social justice and equal opportunity for all Iranians."[21]

Nevertheless, the shah never warmed to Kennedy. He called JFK's administration the "worst period." His connection to Lyndon Johnson was better, amicable even, thanks in part to their prior personal acquaintance. Johnson also attributed more value than Kennedy to what

Iran brought to the table. Not only was Iran a geographical barrier to Soviet aggression in the Middle East, but the shah was also an unabashed cheerleader for unpopular US policies on Israel, Vietnam, and other nettlesome issues. And his position on world oil markets was increasingly influential.

But the shah was also an irritant. His endless appeals for advanced weapons rankled one presidential administration after another. He seemed deaf to arguments that a huge arsenal was unnecessary, would drain resources from badly needed economic investments, and probably could not be absorbed by the military. Mohammad Reza also suffered from a nagging sense of disrespect. He carped about unfair deals compared to other American allies, about the attention Washington paid to the Arab states, and about the possibility of being tossed aside by his patrons. He once lamented to his old confidant, Kermit Roosevelt (then an oil company executive), that "his special relationship with his closest friend, America, is coming to an end" and that he was "tired of being treated like a schoolboy." To drive home his unhappiness, he repeatedly played the Soviet card, threatening to cozy up to Moscow because the US relationship had become a "one-way street."[22]

Each of these incidents relates to the question of the shah's independence (or lack thereof)—a feature that is central to his public image. He was acutely aware of the issue throughout his reign. "We are not your stooges," he insisted to Kennedy's secretary of state, Dean Rusk.[23] Nor was he fooled by "your great American 'liberals,'" he pronounced at another time, who wanted "to impose their way of 'democracy' on others."[24] The costliest incident of US intervention in that period was the imposition of the 1964 Status of Forces Agreement (SOFA). Standard wherever US military personnel are stationed, a SOFA defines their legal status in the host country. In Iran's case it evidently was broader than usual, giving Department of Defense (DOD) staff full immunity from Iranian laws including criminal statutes. This struck a bitter note in a country whose earlier rulers—the Qajars—had notoriously caved in to foreign dictates.

The issue exploded after Ruhollah Khomeini, already a senior ayatollah, gave a speech in which he called the shah an "agent of America" and then denounced the agreement in terms that evoked the American narrative: "The government has sold our independence, reduced us to the level of a colony, and made the Muslim nation of Iran appear more backward than savages in the eyes of the world!" He also included a personal taunt at Johnson that would prefigure standard post-revolutionary rhetoric: "Let the American President know that in the eyes of the Iranian people he is the most repulsive member of the human race today because of the injustice he has imposed on our Muslim nation."[25]

But the succeeding period saw a growth in the shah's self-confidence, along with a sense that Iran was on the road to modernization. The rise in oil revenues had much to do with both accelerating economic development and persuading observers of the country's greater stability. A by-product of this development was Iran's adoption of a more non-aligned foreign policy. Several factors contributed: the second Kashmir war in 1965, which exposed kinks in the United States' ability to protect a region under external threat; America's growing preoccupation with Southeast Asia at the expense of other regions; the Arab-Israeli conflict; and the gradual shrinking of Soviet global ambitions (and danger to its neighbors) as the Brezhnev era got underway. The resulting deliberate shift to a more independent international stance also had domestic motivations—the prospect of broadening Iran's sources of economic aid and trade, and the benefit for the shah of presenting himself as a staunch nationalist.[26] Mohammad Reza's shrewdness, willingness to support American interests, and sheer perseverance paid off in August 1967, when Johnson awarded him with a major arms deal that also marked a point of transformation for Iran from a client state to something approaching a genuine partner.[27]

■ Nixinger and the Nixon Doctrine

It was Richard Nixon and his secretary of state, Henry Kissinger, who were finally prepared to forge the kind of alliance and mutual support system the shah wanted so badly. The relationship among these three had more continuity with the Johnson administration than is sometimes appreciated. Like Johnson, Nixon was preoccupied by major foreign policy concerns over the course of his presidency—détente with Moscow, the opening to Beijing, the Middle East peace process, and above all an honorable exit from Vietnam. The shah once again had services to offer. The president's signature strategy, the Nixon Doctrine of 1969, whereby the United States could rely on regional allies to be the first line of anti-Communist defense, was made to order for Iran. Advanced weapons and respect were what was asked in return.

One major difference was that the new president and the monarch not only saw the world similarly but also, by their public accounts, shared a mutual admiration. Kissinger was effusive in his memoir: the shah was "that rarest of leaders, an unconditional ally, and one whose understanding of the world situation enhanced our own." Kissinger did not see him as dependent at all; rather, his closeness to Washington was a principled choice that required courage in the face of hostility from Moscow to the radical Arab states.[28]

Nixon was less impressed but still positive about Iran's ruler. (His 1,100-page memoir mentioned the shah only once—in the context of 1953.)[29] Two years into his presidency, Nixon did not yet have a firm grasp of the shah or his circumstances, relying on his ambassador to Tehran for insights. But Nixon saw that Iran had potential. The ambassador, Douglas MacArthur II, made a strong case. "Mr. President, between Japan and NATO Europe, it's the only building block we've got. It's small, it's sound, but it's progressive, and . . . above all . . . it's just about our sternest friend." The president agreed: "By God, if we can go with them, and we can have them strong, and they're in the center of it, and a friend of the United States, I couldn't agree more." Nixon wanted to be sure the shah understood that he had Washington's attention. "In all your conversations with him," he instructed the ambassador, "assure, very strongly . . . that he comes very high in our thoughts." As if to quell doubts about his own sincerity, Nixon added, "Besides that, it's true." "I know it's true, Sir," the diplomat replied.[30]

The relationship truly took off during Nixon and Kissinger's May 1972 visit to Tehran. By then, Nixon had clarified his thinking and was ready to go all in with the shah. Besides, he was drained from the groundbreaking Moscow summit (he flew directly from there to Tehran). Ignoring the advice of both his Department of State and DOD, the president approved a sweeping set of requests from the shah. Sophisticated fighter jets, munitions, and other equipment soon began to flow. Iran's defense budget ballooned from $1.4 billion in 1972 to $9.4 billion five years later. Military and security expenditures rose to 40 percent of the national budget. Ten thousand American advisers and trainers would soon descend on the capital city. In a further departure, Kissinger informed the secretaries of state and defense that the president had decreed that "decisions on the acquisition of military equipment should be left primarily to the government of Iran."[31]

Mohammad Reza did have more on his wish list. He wanted to be able to count on a generally positive reaction from Washington to his diplomatic and military forays around the region, which were designed in part to enhance his stature. In Iraq, for example, the United States went along with his cynical plan to prop up the Kurds as a foil in Tehran's perennial dispute with its neighbor. Domestically, the shah insisted that US intelligence and diplomatic personnel cut back on monitoring political developments and building contacts with the opposition. This, of course, had huge consequences in the lead-up to the revolution a few years later. But it was not unacceptable to Nixon and Kissinger by any means. Citizens' rights and freedoms were, for them, a purely domestic matter. How a local ruler chose to cope with his people was his concern, and the United States—paradoxically—should not intrude.

For Nixon, if the shah was not a paragon of democracy, he stood above almost every other potentate in the region. In his April 1971 meeting with Ambassador MacArthur, he revealed some startling views on the developing world: "Look, when you talk about having a democracy of our type in that part of the world, you've got—it wouldn't work, would it? . . . Look—let's look at Lat- let's look at Africa—this country [Iran] at least has got some degree of civilization in its history, but those Africans, you know, are only about 50 to 75 years from out of the trees, some of 'em."[32] The president was particularly admiring of Iran's ruler for having been able "to run, basically—let's face it—a virtual dictatorship in a benign way." The two leaders eventually warmed to each other, and for the shah the Nixon years were the high point of his relationship with the United States.

Nixon's disgraced departure after Watergate was a political and personal blow for the shah. President Gerald Ford did not have Nixon's grand strategic view and found less of value in keeping up a close relationship with Tehran. Kissinger did his best to rally US support for Iran among the reluctant voices in Ford's cabinet, and for the most part the Ford White House stuck with Nixon's general approach. But the affinity of the early 1970s was no longer there, in part because of heightened disputes over the shah's nuclear ambitions and perceived lack of restraint or concern for the position on rising oil prices. And while Iran was able to shrug off some of the new administration's unwelcome complaints, Ford and his team essentially returned to treating Iran more "as a client, rather than a partner."[33]

■ Carter: Avant le Déluge

Officials of the Islamic Republic reserve a special loathing for President Jimmy Carter. Part of his difficulties stemmed from his bad luck in taking office as the revolution was about to crest; to a substantial degree, his tenure was shaped by forces beyond his control. At the same time, he and his administration made some whopping missteps that made matters worse; however, his intentions were certainly no worse than those of his predecessors.

From a combination of personal principle and electoral strategy, Carter pledged a presidency that would disavow the amoral realpolitik of the Nixon/Ford administrations. Two core policies he touted were the promotion of human rights and the curtailment of US global arms sales. Rather than become caught in the East-West paradigm of the Cold War, the United States would work to bridge the North-South divide, emphasizing humanitarian aid to uplift impoverished societies rather than military programs to prop up dictators. Almost immediately, the realities of policy making and of Iran's centrality to American Middle East strategy (not to mention the appeal of billions in commercial revenues and the associated boost for balanced budgets and jobs) caused him to veer from his campaign platform when it came to Iran. His casual jettisoning of principle would dog him throughout his presidency, but it soothed the shah's initial apprehensions over the moralizing of a new president that seemed to be aimed directly at him.

During Carter's first year, 1977, the two leaders met twice, once in each capital, with each evidently impressing the other. The American administration took pains to signal its eagerness for smooth relations. US arms sales that year broke records thanks to the large consignments of advanced fighters and sophisticated Airborne Warning and Control System (AWACS) surveillance aircraft earmarked for Iran. However, snags developed, which the shah came to see as either a lack of US commitment or incompetence. Some problems were a function of the fickleness of American politics—Congress's obstruction of the AWACS deal, for instance. Others grew out of canyon-sized divisions within the administration—especially between Secretary of State Cyrus Vance and National Security Advisor Zbigniew Brzezinski—while still others were a function of simple ignorance about Iran.[34]

Few outside observers, and almost no one in the US government, foresaw the political earthquake about to destroy the monarchy. US embassy reports and CIA analyses through mid-1978 predicted a long reign for the shah. A small cadre of State Department analysts raised qualms in the fall, but senior policy makers stuck to past assumptions about the monarchy's stability, buttressed by assurances from the shah himself. Ambassador William Sullivan's unexpected and unwelcome cable in early November urging the White House to "think the unthinkable" came as a shock.[35] Paralyzed by the split among his advisers, the president commissioned an independent report by veteran diplomat George Ball.

Ball's eighteen-page analysis was far too late to make a difference, but it was nonetheless insightful. A cover note to the president clarified the stakes: "Iran is today the strategic center of the world." Ball went on to blame long-standing US policy: "We made the Shah what he has become. We nurtured his love for grandiose geopolitical schemes and supplied him the hardware to indulge his fantasies. Once we had anointed him as protector of our interests in the Persian Gulf, we became dependent on him." (This was the exact opposite of how most of the shah's Iranian critics saw him.) Ball's recommendations had more to say about America's affinity for intervention than about Iran. His main proposal was to "persuade" the shah to set up a Council of Notables to select a new government. But the list of "responsible opposition" figures was to be "carefully vetted" by the United States. Carter's reply confirmed the continuing tendency of US decision-makers to fool themselves about the impact of their actions. He declined to accept Ball's suggestion because "I cannot tell another head of state what to do."[36]

Carter's idea instead was to send Brzezinski to Tehran. This time Ball shot down the idea, calling it, "with all due respect, the worst idea I ever heard." Showing greater awareness of the optics of interference, Ball explained that Brzezinski's presence in Iran would "immobilize the Shah, since anything that he does after that will be regarded, Mr. President, as an action taken on your instructions."[37]

The revolution by then was inevitable—and just weeks away. Carter's atrocious timing led to some very awkward public moments. He chose New Year's Eve 1978 to toast the "great leadership of the Shah," just a year before the monarch would flee his supposed "island of stability." In September 1978, two days after the Black Friday massacre of demonstrators in Jaleh Square in Tehran, he sent a message of support—much as Kennedy had done in June 1963. The Palace immediately broadcast Carter's words, making Washington look complicit.[38] Brutality by the security forces was a feature throughout 1978, and each occurrence magnified the public's outrage. And while Carter did not send Brzezinski to Tehran, he acquiesced (at the urging of Brzezinski and the Pentagon) to a mission by a senior military officer, Gen. Robert Huyser, to assess the military and, in case of the collapse of the premiership of Shahpour Bakhtiar, possibly to encourage the army to undertake a coup. As Ball might have foretold, Huyser's presence became instant news in Tehran and managed to aggravate both the shah and the opposition.[39]

Near the top of most critiques of US performance in Iran was the failure to reach out to members of the opposition in later years. The shah famously forbade such contacts, and Washington obliged, with predictable consequences. From 1978 through 1979, policy makers debated whether to approach Khomeini, the leading symbol of resistance to the monarchy. The question reached the highest levels in Washington, but no order ever came down, or if it did, it was rescinded. As the regime disintegrated in January 1979, Ambassador Sullivan, who at one time had acceded to the ban on opposition contacts, was so livid that he sent an eyes-only cable to Cyrus Vance excoriating Carter: "You should know that president has made gross and perhaps irretrievable mistake by failing to send emissary to Paris to see Khomeini as previously agreed—I can not rpt not understand the rationale for this unfortunate decision."[40] Even General Huyser, who was still in Tehran, agreed.

The shah evacuated Iran—for the second time in his life—in mid-January 1979, and Khomeini returned from exile in triumph two weeks later, on February 1. The prevailing view among Khomeini's supporters has always been that the United States could never accept the revolution and worked ceaselessly to reverse it. The American declassified record indicates otherwise. US officials on the ground scrambled to understand the lay of the land after the shah's departure and to build ties to the new Provisional Government of Iran (PGOI). Chargé d'Affaires Bruce Laingen reported on one such meeting with Prime Minister Mehdi Bazargan in August: "We wanted to work with Iran, I told him, although we understood that it would take time and patience to develop a mutually beneficial relationship.... I said that I had been instructed to say that we were ready to help in any way possible that might contribute to Iran's stability and the well-being of its people."[41]

One problem was that the Americans limited their outreach to moderates. Very few meetings with hard-line clerical representatives occurred. The reasons were perhaps natural enough. There was a comfort level with the technocrats in the PGOI, who were mostly educated in the West and willing to interact, whereas the hard-liners were deeply suspicious of, not to say hostile to, Americans. Most abhorred the idea of a relationship with the patrons of the dictator they had just overthrown. The Americans also believed that the future belonged to the moderates: "We doubt the hard-line mullahs will be able to score a decisive and lasting victory over the secular elements," a senior diplomat informed the secretary of state in fall 1979. Sounding like a British oil man from the 1950s, he continued, "The clerics cannot themselves run a complex country and will be forced to seek help from Westernized officials."[42]

The moderates were skeptical too. Echoing a theme that Iranian officials would repeat often in later years, they complained that the United States had done nothing concrete to prove its good intentions. At the same August meeting, Bazargan told Laingen, "You have only given lip service to better relations and we have only heard promises from you." Where were Iran's promised spare parts, he asked, or badly needed help with visas? Ibrahim Yazdi, the foreign minister, was less cordial. Among other things, he criticized the American media—widely seen as shills for the government—for their coverage of the revolution. He admitted that Iranians had no basis for accusing them of "interfering in Iran's internal affairs" but insisted there was "a historical basis for ... suspicions." He recited a Persian expression to Laingen: "One bitten by a snake is then afraid of every black and white rope he encounters."[43]

The prime minister's parting comments were not as barbed, but Laingen thought they were worth reporting at length:

> Bazargan said he appreciated my views and assurances. He then told a story about how in the period immediately after WW II everything that happened in Iran, even a baby's crying, was blamed on British agitation. Later, during the time of Mossadegh, the U.S. enjoyed great prestige as a consequence of the good works Americans had previously done in and for Iran. But when Mossadeq was overthrown, Iranians began to blame everything that happened in the country on the U.S. just as they had once blamed the British. This perception may not be accurate, Bazargan said, but it is a reality to be dealt with. Accordingly, the U.S. must do something to back up its good intentions, to show that it is not agitating against Iran's interests.[44]

Just three weeks before all hopes of coming to terms crashed to earth, Laingen was still imploring the State Department to show a more positive attitude toward Tehran: "Specifically, we urge the Department to find ways publicly to say that we wish Iran well in putting its revolutionary objectives into forms and institutions that will command the support of all its people; that the U.S. has no interest in or intention of imposing any regime, monarchy or otherwise, onto Iran; that we have an abiding interest in Iran's integrity and independence; that American interests in access to Iranian oil are synonymous with Iranian interests in sustaining and financing its future industrial and agricultural development." Laingen even occasionally saw areas of commonality with the mullahs, in at least one case touching on a familiar American theme: "We should find opportunities as well to welcome revolutionary Iran's emphasis on Islam and its spiritual contribution to society as something that Americans understand and respect, given the way in which Americans also see things of the spirit as important to human endeavor."[45]

The November 4, 1979, seizure of the US embassy in Tehran, leading to 444 days of captivity for fifty-two Americans, nailed the lid shut on hopes for a rapprochement with the shah's successors. It also ended the chances for any "moderate" rule by steering Iranian politics in a radical direction that Khomeini and his circle quickly appropriated. The seeds were probably sown long before, but the proximate causes are clear. In May 1979 the US Senate adopted a resolution sponsored by Sen. Jacob Javits (D-NY) deploring continuing executions of former regime officials. Regardless of its merits from a human rights standpoint, it was taken by Tehran as brazen interference in Iranian affairs. After that, a State Department Iran expert said, the Iranians "refused to play ball."[46] Then, in October Carter decided to admit the shah to the United States for medical treatment for cancer. It was a politically fraught, even agonizing choice, but it was the spark for a group of mostly students to launch their plan to overrun what they would call the "Nest of Spies"— the sprawling US embassy complex in the heart of the capital. Asked later about their reasons, the organizers said it was to prevent another American coup to bring back the shah.

■ Ignorant Armies Clash by Night

A quarter century after the revolution, former State Department Iran expert Henry Precht observed that the two countries' troubled relationship could be summed up by a passage from Matthew Arnold's poem *Dover Beach*: "And here we are as on a darkling plane ... where ignorant armies clash by night." The key word, for Precht, was "ignorant." "If you master that word you understand the American point of view and you understand the Iranian point of view. You understand why we got into this problem and why we couldn't get out of it, not only the hostage crisis but the Revolution." Like many officials who grappled with Iran policy over the years, Precht developed an attachment to the country and valued the relationship. Far less typically, he freely admitted to feelings of guilt for failing to better understand his subject. "I don't think there is another country in the world that we've gotten so wrong, so consistently for so long a time as Iran. From 1953 [on], both inside and outside the government—and I include myself in that. Ignorance—profound, enduring—really characterized both sides."[47]

Indeed, the list of blunders by both countries is long. Neither side—at least at the leadership level—took the time to dive deeply into the history and culture of the other. This is hardly unusual, especially for great powers used to treating smaller states as pieces within a larger strategic picture. Of course, the shah devoted enormous energy to divining the interests and motivations of successive presidents, but he did so mostly in the service of his own narrow interests, and in the process he displayed less than a full grasp of American politics. The question in the context of this volume is, to what extent did each country's narrative—about itself and the other side—contribute to the misunderstandings, disputes, and crises that occurred?

On the US side, for the period from World War II to the revolution, a clear thread that ran through it was the sense of duty to improve the lot of less fortunate corners of the world. From FDR to Carter, every president expressed a desire to help Iran develop into a modern, progressive state. Bound up in that concept was the link in the minds of US officials, rarely officially questioned, between regional affairs and American global interests. In terms of the preferred direction of events, what was good for the United States was good for the locals. As stated, the self-serving quality of this presumption was rarely scrutinized at top levels of government. Nor (recalling Eisenhower's baffled comment to his NSC) did policy makers intuitively see that American policies that were assumed to be for local benefit might spark hostile responses. The diplomat in line to become ambassador to Tehran in 1979 recognized this problem years afterward. Responding to Precht's mea culpa, William G. Miller pointed higher up the political ladder: "The ignorance was on the part of our leaders . . . and that's one of the constructive problems . . . how do you get through to the leaders and convince them to abandon their prejudices?"

The Iranian side of the ledger is harder to document. It is also harder to generalize about the period of the monarchy because to speak of official Iranian perceptions of the United States is tantamount to speaking about the shah, given his domination over the government. But there is plenty of evidence of his need to harken back to the glories of the Persian Empire—from his regular references to Persian history and culture, especially when justifying major initiatives like the White Revolution, to the grotesque celebration of 2,500 years of Persian monarchy in 1971. His grand undertakings themselves betrayed a sense of self that rivaled past potentates. By some accounts, he came to believe, much like his American allies, "that it was his own manifest destiny to 'save' Iran."[48]

The events of 1979 should have been a wake-up call for American leaders to reexamine cherished beliefs about Iran. Instead, many US officials acted as if Iran's post-revolutionary conduct had occurred in a vacuum, with no historical antecedents. Jimmy Carter's dismissal of a reporter's question about 1953 as irrelevant exemplified this attitude. So did the reaction of Chargé Bruce Laingen to an incident while he was being held prisoner in Tehran. After rebuking a young guard over the illegality of seizing hostages, he was taken aback when his captor snapped that the United States had held his entire nation hostage in August 1953.[49] After the 1979–81 embassy saga and failed rescue attempt, policy makers saw little need to look further than those painful episodes, or to the gloating official Iranian reactions to them, to "understand" the nature of the Islamic Republic. Nor did many Americans make a serious attempt to examine the possible impact of their own actions and assumptions about the relationship.

As for Khomeini and his followers, available evidence makes clear that baked-in conceptions about America as a bad actor, based on a quarter century of the shah's rule, made it virtually impossible to see Washington as anything other than a permanent enemy to be reviled. The label "Great Satan" spoke volumes. Those assumptions stood in the way of any dispassionate look at the roots of American behavior (not to mention its manifest fallibility). Had they been attempted, such exercises might in turn have suggested ways to deal more constructively with the adversary. But that only occurred well after the ardor of 1979 had cooled.

The Iran-Iraq War

3 Virtually every city, town, and village in Iran features a cemetery, monument, mural, or other commemoration to those who perished in the conflict with Iraq from 1980 to 1988. The bitter contest that the regime refers to as the "imposed war" left few families untouched. To grasp its emotional and political significance, it would not be unreasonable to compare it to the combined effects of the American Revolution and Civil War.

During its eight-year course, the conflict sharply altered Iran's political direction. The emergence of a new existential threat was a harkening back to a history replete with instances of grave peril from outside. The country's leaders, not yet entrenched in power by fall 1980, used the threat to rally a divided population to defend simultaneously the nation and the revolution, whose fates immediately became intertwined. Urgent military needs justified the expansion of institutions such as the Islamic Revolutionary Guard Corps that were deployed to engage enemies abroad and opponents at home. All manner of extreme measures became acceptable in the name of protecting the homeland, eventually enabling the Islamic Republic of Iran to extinguish all serious domestic challenges and to establish an internal code of rigid adherence to religiosity that became a hallmark of the world's first modern theocracy.

At the same time, the Islamic Republic's choices and actions during the war created deeper problems for it internationally. Already a pariah after the 1979 US embassy seizure, the IRI faced worldwide censure for its counterinvasion of Iraq in mid-1982; its encouragement of martyrdom, with promises ranging from eternal life to household appliances; its "human wave" attacks; and its use of child soldiers. Iranian officials vigorously defend these actions in hindsight as being part of the exigencies of a war they did not seek and were ill-equipped to fight, and they countered Western outrage with charges of flagrant bias, inequitable treatment, and ignorance of Iran's circumstances—allegations that the record shows are not entirely without merit.

Of greatest consequence on the global level, the US-Iran relationship descended to new lows during the war, as both sides found more reasons to view the other with profound antipathy. Each major stage of the conflict contributed to the deterioration. A recurring phenomenon was the lack of understanding by either side of the other's motivations and actual role. In some cases, the big picture actually turned out to be fairly accurate, but the failure to appreciate more nuanced parts of the equation often complicated matters substantially. Nevertheless, experiences from the "imposed war" continue to the present day to provide both sides with a ready list of real and supposed grievances with which to condemn each other.

Invasion and Counterinvasion

Saddam Hussein's invasion in September 1980 caught Iran entirely off guard. The multipronged attack met only minor resistance and within days had made substantial inroads into oil-rich Khuzestan Province. Yet there were plenty of warning signs of an impending aggressive move by Baghdad. Centuries of rivalry and antipathy based on ethnicity, religion, and geopolitics characterized their relationship. The shah in 1975 had strong-armed the Iraqis to accept a new border with Iran that rankled Saddam, nominally the second-in-command of Iraq at the time. In the same year that the revolution engulfed Iran, Saddam formally took over the presidency.

What the ambitious new president saw to his east was a country in the midst of revolutionary changes that presented a potentially existential threat alongside an alluring opportunity. Khomeini was even more bitterly disposed against Iraq than the shah had been. The country's majority Shi'ite population and the presence of religious sites revered under Shi'a Islam made it an object of deep interest, amplified by the history of Sunni oppression and the secular Ba'athist philosophy of its rulers. Khomeini also had a personal history with Iraq, having been expelled from the country—by Saddam Hussein—in 1978, just a few months before returning to Iran at the head of the revolution. At the same time, Iran's chaotic political scene, the deep divisions within society, and especially the depleted state of the once-formidable military—now beset by purges and neglected hardware—made the Islamic Republic especially vulnerable, despite its advantages in size and power. The chance to seize control of the petroleum wealth of its western provinces, rescind the hated border treaty, and possibly even roll back the revolution itself was too tempting for Saddam.

To be sure, the Islamic Republic's leaders had plenty to distract them as they dealt with consolidating power and piecing society back together in their preferred image. In the months prior to the invasion, there had been terrorist attacks, a hostage rescue operation by the US military, and at least one major coup attempt with evident foreign backing. In April 1980, the Delta Force rescue effort ended in flames in the desert south of Tehran as a result of sandstorms and equipment failure, and in July Khomeini's followers brutally put down the uprising at the Nuzhih air base in western Iran. But the clerical regime was quick to conclude that these events were in reality part of a pattern with a single aim—defeating the revolution. The war would therefore acquire added significance as a rallying point for Khomeini to consolidate political control under the Islamic Republic.

In line with the leadership's general suspicions in Tehran, the assumption in fall 1980 was that the United States had been the hidden hand behind Iraq's aggression. A year or two earlier this would have sounded far-fetched. Baghdad had been a valued client of long standing for the Soviet Union. In the still-intense Cold War game of zero-sum relationships, local antagonisms fed into the superpower competition. Since Iran had been in the Western camp since 1953, Moscow's best option had been to ally with the next most powerful state in the region, Iraq. But the Islamic revolution turned the game board upside down. The United States was now out of the picture, leaving Iran theoretically free to align with the USSR. Cold warriors like Zbigniew Brzezinski, President Jimmy Carter's national security advisor, rushed to compensate for the "loss of Iran" by cozying up to Saddam Hussein, who had recently offended the Kremlin by attacking the local Communist party in 1978. Iran was the far bigger trophy, so all might have worked out for the Soviets, except that Khomeini had been uncompromising in his public and private statements on the subject, insisting that the new republic's policy would be "neither East nor West."

Contrary to Tehran's assumptions, the bulk of the evidence shows that the United States neither directed nor encouraged Baghdad to intervene. But the record is not without ambiguity. Jimmy Carter denied there had been anything approaching a "green light." Describing signs that cropped up as early as April 1980, he wrote in his memoir, "We had no previous knowledge of . . . this move."[1] Brzezinski also claimed ignorance, as have other US officials. Yet signs of an Iraqi assault had been building for some time. Almost a year earlier, the United States had been concerned enough to send an Iran expert from the Central Intelligence Agency to warn the provisional government in Tehran about the possibility. The envoy, George Cave, recalled later that there had been a "big debate among the big domes in Washington about if Iran and Iraq go to war ... what are the consequences for our strategic position in the Middle East."[2] Over the following months, the two neighboring states routinely engaged in artillery and aerial attacks against each other.

Eventually, American military intelligence detected sizable movements of equipment and troops toward the border, which it concluded was "in anticipation . . . of an invasion."[3] Just days before the actual intervention, US intelligence debriefed the former head of the shah's army, Gen. Gholam Ali Oveissi, an Iranian émigré general who had just been in Baghdad, where he had been told what was about to happen. The CIA put out an unusual warning to the president and his top national security advisers, informing them that "the intensification of border clashes between Iran and Iraq has reached a point where a serious conflict is now a distinct possibility."[4]

For the president to assert later that the United States had no information about a possible attack is therefore not accurate. In fact, in the same memoir, Carter implies that the timing of the ill-fated hostage rescue operation in April 1980 was partly based on the possibility of an Iraqi move.[5] But decision-making in a crisis is fraught with uncertainty, and the role that intelligence plays is far from dispositive in every instance. Policy makers are often quick to point out that reports from the field arrive constantly, and in fluid situations such as that between Iran and Iraq, the absence of key verifiable details, starting with a date certain for an anticipated event, makes preparing a response extraordinarily difficult. To put this seemingly inexplicable failure in perspective, it is worth recalling that Western governments had been unable to predict the Iranian Revolution, the US embassy takeover in Tehran, or the Soviet invasion of Afghanistan.

This is not to say there was no support at high levels of the US government for the Iraqi invasion. Brzezinski lobbied Carter on the need to oust Iran's revolutionary leader. "We need to consider military actions which contribute to his downfall," he argued in a memo to the president in late 1979—or at a minimum, a "covert political action designed to create an alternative to Khomeini."[6] Others undoubtedly quietly shared his view, especially after the hostage trauma. The attitude of virtually all Americans toward Iranians, a former senior diplomat recalled, was one of "almost universal hostility."[7] But at this stage, other concerns likely outweighed individual cases of schadenfreude. For one thing, concern for the safety of the hostages was paramount in Carter's thinking, according to his diary.[8] Common sense also dictated that war by definition would threaten long-standing priorities, including protecting oil routes through the Strait of Hormuz and promoting regional stability in the face of the perceived Soviet threat.

While Iranian suspicions of US complicity in the invasion do not hold up, the IRI's bitterness over the broad international failure to respond to Iraq's aggression are a different matter. It took eight days for the United Nations Security Council to promulgate Resolution 479, a relatively weak call for both sides "to refrain immediately from any further use of force" and find a peaceful resolution to the conflict. Iranians have often pointed out that the resolution contained no reference to Iraq's role as aggressor, nor the standard appeal to withdraw to the status quo ante, which would have required Iraq to vacate captured Iranian territory.[9] Western media reports explained the delay as part of an Iraqi and Pakistani attempt to bring in the Islamic Conference as a mediator. Meanwhile, and contrary to Iranian allegations, the United States at least officially registered its dissatisfaction with what it viewed as Baghdad's tactics aimed at consolidating its territorial gains.[10]

But as was the case throughout this period, American concerns were not over the injustice being perpetrated against Iran but over other superseding policy considerations. Both superpowers still implicitly saw Iraq as a Soviet ally, and each focused on whether Baghdad would gain from the situation—Moscow hoping time would play to Saddam Hussein's advantage, Washington fearing as much. In other words, the backdrop of the Cold War remained a potent factor, even the dominant element, in American calculations at this stage. The Carter administration and the US policy establishment, after all, were still reeling from the invasion of Afghanistan, a move most observers treated as an act of naked aggression and a direct threat to vital Western interests.

Also underlying the policy proclamations was the visceral outrage prompted by the recent embassy seizure. According to an American diplomat, "there was close to zero empathy for the Iranians anywhere in the U.S. government or even population." A senior CIA official went further: "We had a score to settle with the Iranians" for leaving the United States "paralyzed, humiliated, and frustrated. . . . I think the Iranians never fully grasped the depravity of the hostage-taking at the U.S. Embassy."[11] In other words, the Iranian sense of American hostility was hardly their imagination, but from the US perspective the IRI's actions were at the root of the matter.

Within weeks, Iraq's advance inside Iran had stalled, soon settling into a kind of stalemate. By early 1982, however, the initially unprepared Iranian forces had managed to turn the tables against the invaders, who had come in better armed and trained. By late May, with the recapture of Khorramshahr, the Iraqis had effectively been expelled from the country. Here, Khomeini and his advisers confronted the fateful decision of whether to sue for peace or press forward into Iraq. Saddam's forces were depleted and their morale low, whereas Iranian indignation remained pitched and the zeal among Khomeini's supporters for spreading the revolution to all corners of the Islamic world, starting with the conservative Gulf monarchies, was undiminished. The previous December had already featured a botched—but, for the West, worrisome—putsch attempt in Bahrain that was reported to be linked to Iran. Contributing to Iran's internal deliberations was the June Israeli invasion of Lebanon, where Shi'ites constituted the largest religious community, whose clerics had close ties to Iranian mujtahids. Within a week, a large contingent of Revolutionary Guards began to deploy to southern Lebanon, where they would help establish the formidable Hezbollah organization. By some accounts, Khomeini was not ready to confront the Israelis more directly, but Lebanon may have helped persuade him to go along with the majority of his advisers who pressed for going into Iraq. "The road to Jerusalem leads straight through Baghdad," he is quoted as saying.[12] On July 14, Iran's military declared the launch of a new offensive against Iraq.

Whatever claims to victimhood Iran had been making were nullified with that decision. The hostility toward the Islamic Republic that had led Western nations not to speak out or in any way help Tehran in the first eighteen months of the conflict now fed a sense of anxiety about what the future might hold—now that the mullahs had become the aggressors. US policy makers warned of the consequences of an Iranian victory. Days ahead of the assault, President Reagan was told by National Security Adviser William P. Clark that it would "create shockwaves throughout the Gulf and pose further dangers for US interests in the Middle East."[13] The consensus was that extraordinary measures were required. Therefore, in mid-July the CIA sent another envoy armed with alarming intelligence to the Gulf, much as they had done three years earlier, although this time, instead of Tehran, the destination was Baghdad. Thomas Twetten, a senior Middle East operations official, launched what would become a years-long process of providing battlefield data to the Saddam Hussein regime, with the sole aim of preventing an Iranian victory.

The exercise would leave many Americans with a poor taste. Undoubtedly lost on the Iranians was the fact that US officials loathed Saddam Hussein, fully aware of his brutality and odious behavior. But for all his sins, Saddam had signaled his openness to a better relationship with the United States, and US policy makers persuaded themselves that in return they would be able to squeeze commitments from Baghdad to curtail certain activities, notably the targeting of American interests. When it came to Iran, there was no such hope by mid-1982. To the contrary, the dominant mood in Washington was little short of dread at the prospect of an Iranian conquest of Iraq, which, in the words of a senior diplomat, might well lead to a "Middle Eastern Armageddon."[14] What was at stake was not just the idea of an unfettered anti-American theocracy bearing down on vulnerable US allies such as Saudi Arabia and the other Gulf monarchies but the possibility of the Soviet Union— still at the center of American strategic thought—exploiting the crisis in the heart of the world's most important oil-producing region.

The CIA's gift, the true value of which took time to sink in with an Iraqi intelligence service innately distrustful of the United States (another nuance Iranian officials probably never contemplated), was only one layer of assistance Washington provided. The new approach became known informally as the "tilt," but it was far more comprehensive than this made it sound. The first step was to take Baghdad off the State Department's list of state sponsors of terrorism, which removed legal barriers to other kinds of support. Commodity and agricultural credits soon followed, along with Exim Bank guarantees and approval for millions in trade deals involving aircraft, helicopters, and other dual-use materiel, despite the Reagan administration's claims of remaining neutral in the war.[15] While direct supplies of weapons were not on the list, the administration studiously averted its gaze while other countries—particularly the French, as well as the Egyptians and others— poured arms into Saddam's arsenals. "I don't think we paid any attention to it," former chief diplomat for the region Nicholas Veliotes acknowledged. Washington also helped by ensuring that shipping operations in the region were not blocked. On the other side of the ledger, the State Department, with personal backing from Secretary of State George Shultz, initiated Operation Staunch in late 1983, a worldwide campaign to keep Iran—already strapped by military sanctions—from obtaining weapons on the international gray market.

Diplomatic support for Baghdad was another significant step by the United States. The courtship featured a rare face-to-face meeting with the Iraqi dictator by presidential envoy Donald Rumsfeld in December 1983. Less than a year later, full diplomatic relations were established. In classified communications, American officials held out the hope that the United States and Iran might someday reconnect formally, but in the meantime every move, including putting Iran on the terrorism list in early 1984, seemed aimed at alienating and isolating the Islamic Republic rather than warming up to it.

■ Bloody Stalemate

Although definitive proof of impact is impossible to find, logic suggests that US intelligence and other support were important to helping Iraq survive the war. Iran had wrested the advantage but for years failed to achieve any major victories. American eyes in the sky showed the Iraqis where Iranians were massing their troops. Economic and financial aid boosted the country's sagging economy. Of course, Russian and French arms and tens of billions in direct grants and loans from the Gulf states were also critical. As a result of this combined assistance, Saddam's poorly led forces were able to slog through long periods of deadlock. Acts of desperation occurred on both sides, but it was the Iraqis who usually initiated them.

A particularly bleak chapter in the conflict was the so-called War of the Cities. First launched by Saddam in early 1984, the aim was to deliver a blow to Iranian morale by targeting vulnerable civilians and try to bring the Iranians to the negotiating table. (Tehran had steadfastly rebuffed the idea of talks since near the start of the war—another reason why the West was unsympathetic.) Iran instead retaliated with its own strikes on the Iraqi capital. Casualties were in the thousands, and the objective failed—no talks followed. A year later, Saddam tried again, targeting Iran's main urban areas—Tehran, Isfahan, Shiraz, and elsewhere. In so doing he violated an agreement that had been worked out to stop future such assaults. Another round of strikes occurred in July 1986, touching off a series of escalatory strikes by both sides lasting until September of that year. More assaults followed, sometimes in retaliation for an Iranian action or as a way to induce a reaction. Despite Iraq's repeated violations of past agreements, Iran often found itself being blamed in the West.

Targeting Iranian commercial interests was another feature of the conflict and a further sign of Iraq's desperation. Finding little success on the battlefield, Saddam decided to try to cripple Iran's main source of revenue—oil. The first attacks were against Iran's major petroleum facility at Kharg Island. It was widely assumed that Saddam's goal was to get Iran to overreact so that US forces would get drawn directly into the fighting. At first the tactic failed, but over time both sides started to treat noncombatant shipping as fair game, which raised the odds of a US response significantly.

Ironically, it was not an Iranian attack but an Iraqi mistaken hit on a US Navy vessel that brought the Americans directly into the shooting war. An Iraqi pilot flying a French-supplied Super-Etendard fighter jet misidentified his target and fired two Exocet missiles into the USS *Stark* in May 1987. To Tehran's chagrin, the United States publicly blamed the IRI—for having allowed the war to continue and creating the conditions that led to the incident. The Reagan administration debated internally how to respond, and even though officials were eventually satisfied that the Iraqis were entirely at fault, within a week they opted to guarantee safe passage for so-called neutral shipping through the Gulf. The operation formally commenced two months later. As many feared, it did not take long—just two days—for the first incident to occur that threatened to escalate the conflict. The event was the collision of the USS *Bridgeton* with a mine that was widely assumed to have been planted by Iran. In September, US Navy forces caught an Iranian vessel laying mines and opened fire on it. Much more dramatic clashes were soon to come.

■ Bizarre Interlude

In the midst of the war, an episode took place involving Iran, the United States, and even Israel that demonstrated that even bitter foes can find common ground. In the early 1980s, a string of hostage takings occurred in Lebanon at the hands of militants tied to Hezbollah. Several Americans were among the captives, some of whom had been taken by associates of Imad Mughniyah, a soon-to-be-infamous member of the Islamic Jihad Organization responsible for a spree of terrorist acts. Mughniyah's immediate aim was to trade hostages for the release of a relative who had been swept up by Kuwaiti authorities in connection with a series of bombings in that country in late 1983. Among the kidnapped Americans was the CIA's Beirut station chief, William Buckley. The hostages' plight struck a chord with Ronald Reagan, on both humanitarian and political levels, and he soon made it a top priority to gain their freedom.

American policy makers assumed that Hezbollah was under the direct control of Iran, in part because the IRGC had played such an important role in the organization's founding and because Iranians sat as members of its Shura. This provided a key part of the rationale for a team of US and Israeli officials (with the approval of both Reagan and Israeli prime minister Shimon Peres) to devise a plan to make American-made missiles available to Iran for use against Iraq in exchange for freeing the American hostages. Over the course of 15 months from late summer 1985 to early November 1986, the Iranians bought a variety of missiles and spare parts and in return negotiated with their Hezbollah partners for the release of the Americans. In the end, three hostages were freed, but three more were taken during the same period. When the deals were exposed following a leak to the media by an Iranian hard-liner who opposed them, the operation came to a halt. Despite its peculiarity and its ultimate failure, the episode offers some takeaways that are relevant to the broader history of US-Iran relations.[16]

The main conclusion is that despite their deeply held mutual aversion, the leaders of both countries understood that the other side could offer things of value that were worth negotiating for. A number of improbable variables had to fall into place for anything resembling success to occur, but the principle was implicitly accepted by both sets of players. Unfortunately, it became clear that mutual distrust had already poisoned each side's views of the other. Particularly for the American side, the unshakable assumption was that the Iranians could not be relied on. That in turn fed the notion that lying and manipulation by the Americans were entirely acceptable—which happened frequently. In fact, a careful review of the American record (which might be expected to show a bias against Tehran) offers no evidence of meaningful Iranian government duplicity. It was the Americans who provided a fabricated price list, authorized vast overcharges, and presented doctored intelligence about Iraq's order of battle—in addition to constantly misrepresenting other points of fact. The lead American operative, National Security Council staff member Oliver L. North, later boasted to Congress, "I lied every time I met the Iranians."[17] The only Iranian who consistently behaved dishonestly was the arms dealer chosen by the Israelis. (Both CIA and Iranian government representatives concluded he was a charlatan, and he was eventually removed from the operation.)

Domestic politics in both countries turned out to be another extremely important factor in the Iran-Contra affair, as it has proven to be throughout the post-revolution period. In this instance, fears among the leadership in both countries of being discovered led them to conduct the entire enterprise in secret, which was not sustainable. Parliament Speaker Akbar Hashemi Rafsanjani even feared for his life, until

Ayatollah Khomeini decreed that there be no recriminations for anyone involved. On the American side, Reagan's inner circle genuinely worried that he might be impeached, and several lower-rung participants faced serious legal difficulties for their roles. Finally, most observers and participants have since agreed on at least two basic points. One is that the operation was crippled by a woeful lack of understanding of the other side. The other is that the scandal that ensued delayed any prospect of pursuing closer bilateral ties for a considerable time.

■ Going Chemical

The most provocative development of the war period—and for the Iranians the most sensitive—involved Baghdad's resort to chemical weapons (CW). International norms have long established an absolute prohibition against their use, to which most nations subscribe. In 1980, the year the war started, negotiations began regarding the Chemical Weapons Convention, an agreement all but three states have since signed.[18] Yet when reports began to surface that Iraq had initiated attacks using mustard gas, sarin, and other substances, Iran argued vehemently for the global community to take action, but to little avail.

The first such reports from the Iranian side came in fall 1983. As usual, they approached the UN secretary-general with their complaint. Javier Pérez de Cuéllar had proven to be one of the few international organization leaders to pay heed to Iranian concerns—earning him considerable trust from Tehran. (By contrast, Iraq, supported in some form by every permanent member of the UNSC, addressed its concerns primarily to that body.)

The Iranian reports did not come as a surprise to American experts. Within days, the secretary of state learned from his chief of politico-military affairs that Iraq's CW use had been confirmed and that it was occurring "almost daily." Moreover, the secretary was told that Iraq had "acquired a CW production capability, primarily from Western firms, including possibly a U.S. foreign subsidiary." A cable to US diplomats in Baghdad a few days later shows that Washington was aware that Baghdad had been using "tear gas and skin irritants against invading Iranian forces quite effectively" since at least July 1982. Furthermore, "lethal chemical weapons" came into use "at the orders of Saddam" in October of the same year. And in summer 1983, Iraqi forces employed an unidentified "chemical agent with lethal effects."[19]

The publicity put the Reagan administration in an extremely uncomfortable position. The United States had prided itself on its principled stand on weapons of mass destruction, including chemical and biological weapons, and as the politico-military affairs director reminded his superior, American credibility on the matter was important for advancing the policy goal of curtailing the proliferation of such weapons. On the other side of the coin, however, was the competing priority of building up the relationship with Baghdad and, even more importantly, preventing Iraq from being defeated by Iran in the war. Clearly, Saddam Hussein had made the calculation that his forces were in desperate straits. Senior US policy makers were adamant that Iran not succeed and essentially fell back on justifications about maintaining "our strict neutrality in the Gulf war." There was also a collective shoulder shrug over "the low probability of achieving desired results."[20]

The most horrific episodes were yet to come. In late June 1987, the town of Sardasht in northwestern Iran suffered an attack involving mustard gas dropped using four 250-pound bombs. Two-thirds of the population of 12,000 was exposed, with effects lasting to the present time. Iranians talked about "another Hiroshima" and evacuated large cities for fear of expanding attacks. The assault thus had its intended effect. In the following spring came the infamous attack by Iraqi forces on their fellow citizens in the Kurdish town of Halabja with both mustard and nerve agents. The five thousand dead and seven thousand wounded included many Iranians.[21]

Those events became a stain on the reputations of several Western governments. Allegations about the United States providing weapons or precursors to Iraq have not been borne out by documents or testimony. But the story does not end well. US military personnel working with the Iraqis confirmed that American-provided targeting data—an outgrowth of the intelligence cooperation begun in 1982—was specifically used in the attacks of spring 1988.[22] The fact that the Americans may not have provided explicit instruction or direction does not absolve them of accountability.

Like a bad dream, the Iranians once again found themselves viewed by the outside world not as victims but as somehow blameworthy, alongside the Iraqis. A review of the evidence indicates either that it was manufactured or that extraordinary assumptions were made based on little more than presuppositions about Iranian guilt.[23] In hindsight, former top Middle East diplomat Richard Murphy lamented the too-easy temptation in official Washington to declare Tehran's culpability once rumors started to circulate about their employment of chemicals:

> There was palpable joy in some quarters over this. The feeling expressed was "Oh boy, this is great news. Now there is no need to even consider harsh measures to condemn or cut off the CW capability of the Iraqis. Let's put our energy into finding some evidence of Iranian use."
>
> Our view . . . was highly unbalanced. . . . You could even bring up the incredibly inhumane way the Iraqis treated their own soldiers. . . . But many people in Washington in those days were unmoved by facts like these. No matter what was said, the reply was: "Oh, the Iranians are much worse; in fact, the Iranians are crazy zealots."[24]

Former senior CIA operative Chuck Cogan had a similar reaction: "Looking back it is a disgrace that we supported an Iraqi regime that was gassing its opponent. I can think of no better term. It's just disgraceful."[25]

■ Final Acts

After years of brutal, World War I–style combat, the final stages of the war unfolded relatively swiftly. Over a roughly six-month period, a cascade of defeats and disasters for the Iranians finally persuaded Khomeini to end his crusade. The last major victory for Iran had been the capture of the important Faw peninsula in February 1986. Contrary to Tehran's fervent hopes, Iraq's strategic defeat there turned into a moment of reckoning for Saddam Hussein. Rather than convincing him to surrender, it became a long-overdue catalyst for organizational and strategic changes—something his American counterparts had been urging. He replaced his chief of staff and the head of combat tactics. New training techniques were adopted based on other countries' military manuals, and more sophisticated use was made of American-provided intelligence from satellites, such as building models of targeted areas for purposes of planning offensives. The Iraqis also became more adept at improving the equipment they had, rigging their French-supplied jets to increase the weapons payload, for example.[26] The Iranians later suspected that Baghdad's foreign patrons had a major hand in all this, most importantly boosting even further their supply of weapons. There is undoubtedly some truth to that.

The first blow to Iran in 1988 came with the revival of the episodic war of the cities. But this time there was a major change. The Iraqis had retooled their Soviet-supplied Scud-B missiles to overcome a basic geographical disadvantage. Baghdad is roughly 75 miles from Iran's border, putting it in easy reach of enemy missiles, whereas Tehran is about 250 miles from easternmost Iraq. Saddam's Scuds were therefore not nearly as effective as Iran's—until the Iraqis (with foreign help?) realized they could splice additional sections into the middle of each missile, thereby adding propellant, and lighten the payload. That innovation dramatically raised the lethality and terrorizing effect, and in February Saddam ordered the unleashing of his new "al-Hussein" missile against Tehran.[27]

Underlying Iranian concerns about this new development was the chilling realization that Iraq could easily arm its new weapon with chemical agents. This was the chief takeaway from Sardasht and became an immensely more urgent consideration after Halabja in March, just a few weeks after "al-Husseins" began raining on the capital. That nightmare scenario did not occur, but nerve agents played a critical role in Saddam's long-planned campaign to retake Faw in mid-April. Iraq's first major offensive since 1982 came as a complete shock, taking as little as thirty-six hours to rout the Iranians, who were forced to retreat across the border to the east. An internal CIA analysis called it "by far the biggest Iraqi victory since 1981."[28] Publicly, international observers reacted at first with admiration, crediting the Republican Guards with a "well-planned, well-executed operation in difficult terrain." Not long afterward, however, an American military adviser visited the battlefield and found hundreds of atropine injectors, proof of the use of sarin. It later came out that, before advancing, the Iraqis had launched aerial bombing and artillery strikes filled with sarin against Iranian placements. The result was demoralizing for Iran on three levels: they had lost a key strategic foothold, Iraq was surely buoyed by the win and would continue on the offensive, and Baghdad had again shown no compunctions about using chemical agents, raising Iranian fears of more devastating attacks on civilians.[29]

At virtually the same time that Iranian troops were retreating across Faw, the country's navy faced its own shattering setback. For months, tensions had been high as US warships implemented Operation Earnest Will, escorting reflagged tankers—though not those docking at Iranian ports—through the Gulf. No significant incidents had occurred since the September clash with an Iranian mine-laying ship, but on April 14, 1988, the USS *Samuel B. Roberts* suffered major damage after hitting a mine. Four days later, the US Navy struck back against Iranian oil platforms that had reportedly been converted to military outposts. According to US accounts, Iranian ships and aircraft counterattacked, resulting in further losses. The skirmish reportedly cost Iran half of its navy. This was the point, according to Majles Speaker Rafsanjani, at which "the U.S. entered the war against us," insisting long after the conflict that support for oil tankers was only "the pretext."[30]

The timing of the US response, dubbed Operation Praying Mantis—literally within hours of Iraq's assault on Faw—persuaded Iranian strategists that the two must have been coordinated, a conclusion they reportedly presented to Khomeini. But US records indicate that it was the hit on the *Roberts* that prompted the order to retaliate. At the same time, it is instructive to read the retrospective account of the US Navy air wing strike leader in order to understand how deeply the animus toward Iran ran among some Americans:

> As strike leader, I felt Operation Praying Mantis was more than just retaliation for the *Samuel B. Roberts* because it was also an opportunity to regain American national pride. America had been suffering Iranian humiliation beginning with their taking our embassy personnel hostage, the hostage rescue failure of Operation Eagle Claw at Desert One, and the more recent attacks and continuous harassment of oil tankers in the Gulf. America was portrayed as the "Paper Tiger" in large part because of these Iranian actions. Operation Praying Mantis gave the U.S. Navy the opportunity for America to regain credibility, and credibility is directly linked to restoring our national pride.[31]

The summer brought the final stage of the war to an end with Iraq's surprisingly easy seizure in late June of the contested Majnoun Islands, another direct blow to Iran's ground forces, and just days later the shooting down of a civilian airliner, Iran Air Flight 655. The captain and members of the crew of the guided missile cruiser USS *Vincennes* claimed they were in international waters during the incident (whereas they were actually in Iran's territorial waters), misidentified the Airbus A300 as a hostile F-14 jet fighter, and reported that it was descending as if to attack (although the ship's sophisticated tracking systems indicated otherwise). Yet the Navy concluded that all of these actions had been inadvertent. President Reagan's expression of regret over the "terrible human tragedy" was weakened by simultaneous assertions from the Pentagon that Iran should bear partial responsibility. "If a country is going to wage combat operations in a certain area and then send a commercial airline in the area during that," Chairman of the Joint Chiefs William Crowe remarked, "of course it's an accident waiting to happen."[32]

Iran's reaction reflected the belief that the shootdown had been deliberate. "We will of course in due course have our own response to the American crimes," an Iranian embassy official in London told a news conference the following day, adding that it would be an "appropriate and measured response to the magnitude of the crime."[33] Tehran soon approached the UNSC to ask that the United States be censured for its "criminal act." The fact that Captain Will Rogers later received the Legion of Merit for "exceptionally meritorious conduct" for the period from 1987 to 1989 and the consistent refusal of the US government to apologize for the tragedy (despite agreeing to pay $61.8 million to the victims' families) ensured that the incident would remain high on Tehran's list of grievances.[34]

■ Drinking Hemlock

On July 16, 1988, two weeks after the Iran Air shootdown, Ayatollah Khomeini sent a message to the Iranian people. It followed a flurry of top-level discussions among his aides, including Rafsanjani and IRGC head Mohsen Rezaie. The former had recently been appointed commander of the war effort, but his belief, in line with several of his colleagues, was that the conflict had to be brought to an end. Rezaie, respected and trusted by Khomeini, was essentially the lone holdout. Rafsanjani solicited a letter from the IRGC commander asking that he lay out what would be required for Iran eventually to win the war. The letter sought $4.5 billion over five years, which Rezaie estimated was 20 percent of the country's revenues (far less than Saddam Hussein was spending). He also proposed a broader military strategy to replace what he considered to be a politically based and shortsighted attempt to end the war as soon as possible. The seasoned bureaucrat Rafsanjani had the final word, however, since it was he who presented the letter to the supreme leader, who in turn accepted the view that Rezaie's request was unachievable.[35]

In his message to the country, Khomeini declared that the military brass had "readily conceded that the Islamic Army will not achieve a victory anytime soon" and that both military and political leaders agreed "that fighting the war is no longer in the national interest." Beyond the unaffordability of Rezaie's wish list, he acknowledged that "our recent military losses have given our people the impression that we cannot win the war anytime soon. . . . In addition to all these problems is the enemy's use of chemical weaponry against our cities and civilians." Stating his readiness to accept a cease-fire, he said, "I trust you know that this decision is like drinking hemlock for me. But I am only concerned with what pleases God." He closed by asking God to witness "that we do not reconcile ourselves to either the American or Soviet governments, and that we regard friendly relations with these superpowers and other great powers in this world to be contrary to the fundamental principles of our Islamic faith."[36]

The following day, President Ali Khamenei sent a letter to the UN secretary-general formally accepting Security Council Resolution 598, the July 1987 proposal for reaching a cease-fire. Khamenei explicitly mentioned the "shooting down of an airbus aircraft" by American warships as a sign that the conflict had "gained unprecedented dimensions." In addition to a cease-fire, the resolution called for each side to withdraw from the other's territory, exchange prisoners, hold peace talks, and establish an independent body to apportion blame for the war. The official announcement came on August 8, 1988, with the cease-fire to take hold on August 20. The Iraqi population reacted with jubilation, reportedly firing celebratory gunshots into the air for three days. The mood in Iran was far more tentative. A Teheran Radio commentary declared somewhat ominously, "Just as acceptance of the resolution was not tantamount to ending the war, implementation of the cease-fire will not close the file on the war either."[37]

Both the United States and the Islamic Republic came out of the war with even more negative perceptions of the other than when it began, and each side hastened to fit the conflict into their own story line on the relationship. US officials, like most observers, gave Tehran low odds of surviving the invasion at first, but they grudgingly changed that assessment as Iraqi forces found themselves ground down and forced to go on the defensive for most of the conflict. The Iranian decision to turn the tables and counterinvade in July 1982 opened the way for Iran's detractors to point the finger at them and encouraged fears of a regional conflagration of major proportions, fueled by the regime's presumed insatiable thirst for expansion—at the West's expense. There was also Iran's seemingly indefensible attitude on matters such as the resort to child combatants. Along with an unbending determination not to accede to negotiations, these patterns understandably colored the already-grim views of most American officials about the Iranian regime.

Representatives of that government compiled at least as ponderous a set of grievances against the outside world, particularly the United States, from the conflict. The global community's collective silence in the face of Iraq's unexpected attack in September 1980 and, worse, Saddam Hussein's repeated use of banned chemical agents fed into expectations, while also intensifying the sense of indignation and victimhood. Distinctions between Washington's actual role (e.g., no direct sales of weapons or provision of chemical agents to Iraq) and its presumed role were far too fine-grained to register. Each outrage was worse than the one before, with the loss of 290 civilian lives in the Iran Air disaster leading to the conclusion that the Great Satan would stop at nothing to destroy the Islamic revolution.

In the end, the prospects for finding common ground diminished dramatically as a result of the war and the attempts by each government to use it to bolster its own moral standing and denigrate the other. Another significant obstacle was the fact that neither side fully grasped the complex of historical and other factors that influenced the other's actions. Without that understanding it was impossible to assess causality evenhandedly, or explain actions that fell outside the expected range, much less come up with policy choices that could speak to the genuine concerns of the other party. This is why there was "palpable joy" at the prospect of finding proof among the rumors of Iranian use of chemical agents, instead of it occurring to the American side to ask what it might signify that Iran specifically chose not to go down that path despite possessing a CW capability. On the flip side, one wonders whether it ever occurred to Iranian decision-makers to acknowledge that their own actions and rhetorical condemnations of the United States might explain at least partially (if not justify) American behavior in response. Unfortunately, the Iran-Iraq War added deeper layers of distrust and anger to the relationship, making it even more difficult for anyone who might be inclined to break out of the mold of orthodox thinking.

And yet, the war did produce an attempt—one of the strangest on record—by each side to reach out to the other. The Iran arms-for-hostages initiative, one aspect of the Iran-Contra affair, required leaders on both sides who saw the undertaking as worth the heavy political risks. It also required a far deeper appreciation of the motivations, practices, and constraints affecting the other party. Moreover, without the existence of a domestic political environment that could handle a break with years of mutual hostility, even a more rationally framed approach probably would have been doomed.

The Iran-Iraq War

The relationship would have to endure more difficult times and evolving conditions before an environment more conducive to diplomatic engagement would emerge. But the war left the population exhausted and the country's infrastructure and economy shattered. That reality, plus the death of Khomeini, father of the revolution, less than a year after the end of hostilities, helped to clear the way for a more pragmatic approach to the rest of the world, one less encumbered by self-serving historical interpretations.

Rafsanjani and the Post-Khomeini Order

4 The first major leadership milestone in the post-revolutionary life cycle of the Islamic Republic of Iran arrived in the summer of 1989. Just a few months after the tenth anniversary of the revolution, on June 3, Ayatollah Ruhollah Khomeini, the supreme leader and founder of the *nezam-e jomhouri-ye eslami* (system of the Islamic Republic), died after suffering a series of heart attacks. Khomeini's death threatened to plunge the entire system into turmoil since so much of Iran's post-revolutionary politics and its institutions had been founded and shaped in his image. But even before his demise, given his advanced age and relative distance from the daily conduct of statecraft, it was (tacitly) understood that the burden of leadership would fall on one or a group of younger clerics in charge of various organs of the state. In fact, by the standards of revolutionary regimes, the ensuing succession process was relatively swift and trouble-free. The morning after Khomeini's death, the Assembly of Experts held an emergency session and voted 60–14 to elect Ali Khamenei as the next supreme leader of the Islamic Republic.[1] Initially, the assembly was divided on whether, especially given the dearth of qualified candidates, there should be a single person replacing Khomeini or a "council of leadership." Those arguing for the latter structure were in fact steadfast supporters of the regime and of Khomeini who believed that simply no one of his world-historical stature existed within the system.[2] But the proposal for a council of leadership was immediately voted down once the speaker of Majles, Ali Akbar Hashemi Rafsanjani, testified that in a private meeting in March 1989 between himself, "the Imam" (Khomeini), and Khamenei, the question of succession had been discussed, and that Khomeini had unequivocally pointed to Khamenei as his chosen successor.[3]

Khamenei's lack of requisite credentials to succeed Khomeini as the supreme leader was not only controversial among the members of the Assembly of Experts but also in violation of Articles 107 and 109 of the 1979 Constitution, still in effect at the time.[4] The Council for the Revision of the Constitution—which was convened on Khomeini's orders shortly before his death—sped up its work with a view toward reconciling the new political situation. The newly amended Constitution was completed on July 8, 1989, and was put up for a public referendum, alongside a new round of presidential elections (to fill Khamenei's vacated position) on July 28.[5] The changes were approved by an overwhelming majority, and Rafsanjani was elected president in a mostly symbolic contest.[6] Although different in temperament and background, Khamenei and Rafsanjani had both earned Khomeini's trust as loyal, but also pragmatic, servants of the regime, and their rise to the top ranks of the Islamic Republic underlined the resiliency of the system to friends and foes around the world. Of the two men, however, Rafsanjani was universally regarded as more worldly-wise and politically adept. Indeed, his critical role in swaying the Assembly of Experts in favor of Khamenei cemented his reputation as a Machiavellian operator gently shaping the interests of the regime, a position that sharply divided public opinion on him and his family throughout his career (he died in January 2017).[7] Khamenei, in contrast, cut a mercurial figure—dour and rigid in demeanor, trenchant in his defense of the regime, but no less interested in political positioning and power.[8]

The new order of rule after Khomeini's death and the revision of the constitution is sometimes referred to in political studies of post-revolutionary Iran as a form of "dual leadership." In reality, dual leadership was but a short phase that barely lasted to the end of Rafsanjani's first term as president. The Constitution of the Islamic Republic of Iran, based as it is on the principle of the Absolute Rule of the Jurist, simply invests much more power in the office occupied by Khamenei than it does in any other person or branch of government. Khamenei instantly became the commander in chief of Iran's armed forces, including the Islamic Revolutionary Guard Corps and the domestic Basij forces; through his political and religious appointments, he came to control the Guardian Council, the Judiciary, and the regime's public relations from the pulpits and through state media; and most significantly, the supreme leader's office oversees a vast complex of financial assets spanning religious and state foundations (*bonyads*) as well as social charities, which it deftly utilizes to cultivate and control networks of patronage across the political spectrum. Given the expansive constitutional prerogatives of the supreme leader, entry into the elected institutions of the state—most notably the Majles and the presidency—is effectively gatekept. As Rafsanjani and the reformists after him soon learned, Khamenei had every intention of fortifying his constitutional powers by discharging them against potential rivals with near-total abandon.[9]

◼ Reconstruction and the Struggle for Power

Khomeini's death marked the end of a most turbulent but also defining phase in the political development of modern Iran. In just ten years, the country was transformed from a secular monarchy into a

religious theocracy, the new regime's violation of diplomatic protocols and frequent resort to rogue tactics such as hostage takings and
political assassinations made it overnight into an international pariah,
a long and brutal war with Iraq sapped the country's resources and
severely damaged or strained its infrastructure, and the ruthless suppression of internal dissent initiated a "brain drain" that continues to
this day. Yet, under Khomeini's leadership, the Islamic Republic not
only defied numerous projections of its imminent demise but also
consolidated its grip on power despite concerted domestic and international efforts to shorten its life span. Significantly, it did so largely
by deploying a surprisingly effective dual narrative of resistance to
foreign pressures ("Neither East, Nor West, But the Islamic Republic!")
and collective resilience in the face of international isolation. The central challenge to Khomeini's successors, therefore, was how to maintain that narrative while forging a path out of international isolation
and economic malaise at home.

For Rafsanjani, the dual imperatives of postwar reconstruction and
economic revival served as ideal justifications for softening the hard
edges of revolutionary rhetoric that needlessly alienated potential regional and European trading partners. This shift was overwhelmingly
supported by ordinary Iranians and especially by business leaders,
who had come to lament the quite severe limitations on their movement and contacts with the outside world due to visa restrictions,
trade embargoes, and low to nonexistent foreign investments in Iran.
To address the wide scope of issues contributing to these limitations,
Rafsanjani convened "a cabinet of reconstruction" composed mostly
of Western-educated technocrats and practical-minded political operatives skilled at navigating the insider/outsider dichotomies within
the regime. His government soon announced a "Five-Year Development Plan" (1989–94) that set an annual target for real GDP growth at
8 percent and increases in public sector employment and infrastructure spending. Although the ambitious economic plans were reminis-

cent of Soviet central planning schemes that vastly expanded the power and size of state bureaucracies, the Rafsanjani government's proposals were in fact designed to gradually liberalize Iran's economy, which had grown heavily dependent on the state during the Iran-Iraq War.[10] It would not be until the onset of the "Second Five-Year Plan" in 1995, however, that the legal framework for the privatization of key industries would go into effect. As such, during the first term of his presidency, the size and power of state institutions in fact increased significantly.

A major aspect of this new trajectory was the expansion of the IRGC's (and to a lesser extent the Basij's) role in the economic reconstruction of the country. Initially, Rafsanjani had sought to integrate the IRGC and the Basij forces into the existing ranks of the national armed forces, having already formalized their ranks, offices, and uniforms. But at the direction of Khamenei their discretionary budgets and autonomy were preserved under the purview of the Office of the Supreme Leader. Most rank-and-file IRGC commanders resented Rafsanjani for his critical role in convincing Khomeini to end the war with Iraq and were deeply suspicious of him and his family's enterprising ways and ambitions. For his part, Khamenei exploited these fissures to distinguish himself as the ultimate vanguard of the *nezam*, thereby crafting and augmenting his own base of support independent of Rafsanjani's.[11] From the outset, therefore, Rafsanjani's reconstruction plans had to proceed in parallel to—and sometimes in conjunction with—the development of a shadowy, labyrinthine network of military, industrial, intelligence, and commercial enterprises that in time would function as an underground, controlled economy of their own.[12] During Rafsanjani's presidency, most of the latter stakeholders' powers were concentrated in the major state-controlled foundations (*bonyads*) established by Khomeini shortly after the revolution. The most powerful of these foundations, the Foundation for the Dispossessed and War Veterans (*bonyad-e mostaz'afin va janbazan*), was for nearly a decade run by one of IRGC's top commanders and a former defense minister, Mohsen Rafiqdoost, who turned the organization into a multibillion-dollar commercial behemoth.[13] Rafiqdoost and other directors of these foundations used their connections and enterprising pursuits to extract ever-greater rents from the private sector and the state alike. By the end of the First Five-Year Development Plan, direct payments to these foundations accounted for nearly 60 percent of the fiscal budget, according to official reports.[14]

Rafsanjani's government achieved greater success in the realms of social and educational policy, however. To stop the flight of intellectual and professional talent out of Iran, Rafsanjani reopened and expanded the network of tuition-free public universities that had been closed as part of the campaign to purge oppositional intellectuals from university faculties during the Cultural Revolution. Specifically, he founded the Islamic Azad (Free) University, which by the end of the 1990s grew to be the single biggest institution of higher education in Iran. The reconstitution of a viable higher education sector came at an especially critical time for the regime, just as the first wave of the so-called youth explosion was about to reach the university-level age group. By 1996–97, the share of university students had doubled that of pre-revolutionary levels, reaching approximately 1.2 million entrants.[15] In conjunction with these improvements, Rafsanjani's government also took deliberate steps to allow for more openness in Iran's culture industries. The restrictions on the production, distribution, and marketing of independent artistic works such as music, films, and publications were eased to a considerable degree, which helped to prepare the public sphere for the ensuing reformist era. As will be expanded on in the next chapter, Rafsanjani's appointment of Mohammad Khatami as his minister of culture and Islamic guidance would prove very consequential in the subsequent transformation of factional politics within the regime.

Indeed, the singular contribution of Rafsanjani's approach in this period was the infusion of dynamism and new ways of thinking into the conduct of governance, which the regime badly needed. The extent to which the impulse behind these changes was linked to attitudinal shifts and winds of change at the international level, moreover, cannot be understated. The period immediately after Khomeini's death also directly corresponded with the demise of the Soviet Union and the near-universal sense, at the global level, that the central tenets of Westernization—liberalism, capitalism, and democracy—were the new metrics for development, prosperity, and good governance in the near and far future. Setting aside both the illusory foundations of such feelings and their routine dismissal by Iranian leaders, the sudden implosion of the Soviet system and the growing attraction of the Western model to ordinary Iranians weighed heavily on the minds of Rafsanjani and his administration. In this regard, their pragmatism was born out of an urgent sense that economic revitalization and social dynamism were key to adapting regime institutions and public expectations to new realities.

The cumulative impact of such pragmatist policies could best be gleaned in the capital city, Tehran, whose mayor, Gholam-Hossein Karbaschi, was directly appointed by Rafsanjani. From 1989 to 1997, the city underwent a massive transformation (which continued apace for the next two decades) through major infrastructure improvements, various beautification and gentrification projects, a construction boom in shopping malls and private complexes, a raft of new private and public schools and university campuses, and the introduction of public transit routes, among other changes. These urban renewal efforts highlighted not only the dynamism of the Rafsanjani era but also its limitations, since hardly any of these decisions were made in consultation with the public.[16] Born out of necessity, pragmatism generated much-needed reorganization and revitalization in the domestic realm, which in turn helped to project a narrative of dynamism and flexibility to the Islamic Republic's detractors abroad.

■ A Push for Modus Vivendi in the Persian Gulf

On the foreign policy front, the central objective of the Rafsanjani presidency was to review, reestablish, and rearticulate Iran's strategic priorities in the Middle East, toward Europe, and vis-à-vis the United States. The impetus behind these efforts was clear enough: the Islamic Republic's growing support for extremist proxies in Lebanon and the Palestinian territories, its brazen assassination of dissident intellectuals and artists abroad, Khomeini's infamous fatwa authorizing the killing of the British novelist Salman Rushdie for his alleged blasphemous novel *The Satanic Verses*,[17] the mass executions of scores of leftist opposition activists in 1988,[18] and allegations about the regime's covert pursuit of weapons of mass destruction—the accumulation of these factors had nearly cemented an impression of the Islamic Republic abroad as a global pariah. Contesting and overcoming the prevailing narrative—especially in Western societies—about the Islamic Republic as a totalitarian, terrorist regime incapable of moderation and bent on regional domination (in Khomeini's terms, "to export the revolution from Tehran to Jerusalem") was not only critical for enhancing the regime's reputation in the international community but especially crucial for reviving Iran's economy and placing its national interests on surer footing.

At the regional level, Rafsanjani's chief objective was to improve Iran's relationship with Saudi Arabia. Shortly after his inauguration in 1989, Rafsanjani's foreign policy hands organized a conference at the Iranian foreign ministry's think tank arm, the Institute for Political and International Studies, which featured speakers from across the region, as well as Europe and the United States. Rafsanjani closed the three-day proceedings by rehearsing Iran's rationale for its actions, as well as the sense of grievance against Western powers behind them, but significantly also offered an olive branch to its Persian Gulf neighbors by explicitly rejecting any interest in pursuing regional hegemony and becoming a "policeman" (a role he implicitly accused Washington of grooming Saudi Arabia for). As he remarked,

> The policy approach that we recommend for governing the region is one which requires countries to cooperate and help solve each other's problems in an atmosphere of friendship and mutual understanding. Help one another in areas where they are deficient and utilize the resources and riches of the Persian Gulf together. If we take such steps not only will the countries of the region, but also many far away nations will be able to benefit from these divine gifts and God-given resources. There is no other alternative. Even if they decide to create a new policeman in the region, they will certainly turn toward the largest countries. If they collect all the countries around us, they will equal us in strength. There is no need for another policeman. We do not want to become the policeman.
>
> We should all reject this policy. Extending an invitation to foreigners does not solve anything. Foreigners do not come here for the sake of our people or our interests. They do not stay here and put up with the warm weather in this region, with all the problems of distance, logistics, and being away from their homeland so that we may live well. This is certainly not the reason for their presence. However, they can claim that they come here in order to establish peace and security, since this is the center of world energy and the future of the world is dependent on the Persian Gulf. Yes, this is a fact. If this is their reasoning, a better way would be for them to allow the people of the region to live in peace and understanding on their own. We should not try to provoke con-

flict. They should not bring about events such as the bloody incident in Mecca and the imposed war between Iran and Iraq.

Rafsanjani's remarks were reported on widely in the regional media and were warmly received by Arab leaders, for many of whom a stable relationship with Iran was also a top priority. Reconciliation with members of the Gulf Cooperation Council (GCC) was especially crucial for the Rafsanjani administration for two reasons: sale of its oil, and containing Iraq. Given Iran's overreliance on oil revenues for funding its reconstruction efforts, continued stability in the oil markets, coordination of production targets and pricing schemes with the Organization of Petroleum Exporting Countries, and security cooperation around the Persian Gulf were of utmost importance to the regime. To this end, Rafsanjani's guarantees of good citizenship were meant to reassure GCC members of post-Khomeini Iran's pragmatic turn away from earlier projections of revolutionary rhetoric and influence. Similarly, there was mutual interest between Iran and the GCC to contain Saddam Hussein's ambitions for regional domination (which superseded ethno-religious, sectarian, and even geopolitical affinities for him). Iran's recitation of Saddam's record of bellicosity and use of banned chemical weapons against Iranian forces and Kurdish populations framed Iran's part in the eight-year war with Iraq as a victim state's "Holy Defense" against an American-backed pariah.

Saddam's invasion of Kuwait in August 1990—which, with the sole exception of the Palestinian leader Yasser Arafat, was roundly condemned by all countries in the region—allowed Iran a special opportunity to not only demonstrate its solidarity with GCC members but also highlight the international community's hypocrisy. Iran's foreign minister Ali-Akbar Velayati pointed out the contrast between the United Nations Security Council's swift resolution strongly condemning Saddam's invasion of Kuwait and the same body's lackluster response (due to American reluctance) to similar aggression by Saddam in 1980 against Iran.[20] By strongly supporting all UN resolutions against Saddam in 1990 and expressing solidarity with its GCC neighbors, moreover, Iran was also able to apply pressure on Saddam to finalize outstanding issues related to the end of the war (e.g., the repatriation of Iranian prisoners of war, the payment of war reparations, and Iraq's formal acceptance of the terms of the 1975 Algiers Agreement). The latter strategy worked, as Saddam, facing a multinational military coalition, conceded to Iran's demands in a last-ditch effort to convince Iranian leaders to shed their neutral stance and support Iraq's incursion. Not only did Iran not change its stance, but Saddam's concessions—and the Rafsanjani government's help in securing the releases of Western hostages held by Lebanese Hezbollah—paved the way for the United Nations to officially declare Iraq as the aggressor in the Iran-Iraq War.[21] Rafsanjani's artful handling of Iran's position during the Persian Gulf War—dubbed "positive neutrality"—resulted in a triple win for the Islamic Republic: it neutralized and further contained an enemy in Saddam's Iraq, it improved its relations with GCC countries (notably with Saudi Arabia), and the bump in oil prices injected much-needed capital into economic reconstruction efforts inside Iran.

By the end of the Persian Gulf War, Iran had effectively entered into a détente with Saudi Arabia. Riyad and Tehran had broken off their diplomatic ties in 1988 after 275 Iranian pilgrims died in what the Islamic Republic labeled as "Bloody Friday" during the 1987 Hajj pilgrimage. But Rafsanjani's conciliatory gestures toward the GCC and the House of Saud led to the official restoration of diplomatic relations between the two countries on March 26, 1991.[22] The reopening of Iran's embassy in Riyadh in April was immediately followed by the Saudi foreign minister Prince Faisal Al Saud's visit to Tehran in June 1991, which paved the way for the resumption of pilgrimages from Iran— upward of 115,000 pilgrims were allowed by Saudi authorities to travel to Saudi Arabia.[23] The lack of any incidents at the subsequent Hajj pilgrimages allowed for senior diplomats from each side to build on the reset in relations. As a signal to the Saudis, Rafsanjani dispatched his son, Mehdi, and one of his trusted foreign policy advisors (and ambassador to Germany), Hossein Mousavian, to meet in person with Crown Prince Abdullah at his summer retreat in Casablanca, Morocco. Over these more intimate meetings, both sides agreed to expand economic and trade relations, deepen diplomatic ties through regular meetings and state visits, and form a joint security commission for reviewing issues of mutual interest concerning the Persian Gulf region and beyond.[24] Although differences over the Israeli-Palestinian peace process and Riyadh's close strategic partnership with the United States inherently limited the extent of cooperation between Iran and Saudi Arabia, the relationship would nonetheless remain steady under Rafsanjani until the 1996 bombing of Khobar Towers, in which nineteen American airmen died.

■ "Goodwill" Begets Silence

By the end of the 1980s, and especially after the embarrassment of the Iran-Contra affair, the United States had begrudgingly dispensed with the fanciful notion that the clerical regime in Iran could be overthrown through internal opposition. The election of George H. W. Bush to the presidency further cemented the position of "realist" national security thinkers and policy makers within Republican ranks, who, like their counterparts at the time in Iran, approached matters of statecraft with a sense of pragmatism. By the time it assumed office, the top priority of the Bush administration was securing the release of the remaining American hostages held by Hezbollah in Lebanon. In his inaugural address, Bush directly appealed to Iran for help with a transactional offer. "There are today Americans who are held against their will in foreign lands," Bush said, "and Americans who are unaccounted for. Assistance can be shown here, and will be long remembered. Good will begets good will. Good faith can be a spiral that end-lessly moves on."[25] In July 1989, Hezbollah hostage takers released video footage of Col. William Higgins of the US Marine Corps—who had been part of a UN observatory mission in Beirut—being executed by hanging. The images jolted the American public and put more pressure on the Bush administration to secure the release of the re-maining hostages.[26]

Bush and his team were encouraged by Rafsanjani's ascent after Khomeini's death and believed that Iran's leverage with Hezbollah leadership could be used to bring an end to a national nightmare for the United States. In what would become a reliable indirect channel to the Iranians, Bush reached out to Qaboos bin Said of Oman to act as an intermediary with Tehran. In a phone conversation with Sultan Qaboos, Bush expressed his hopes that "Rafsanjani might turn out to be more reasonable . . . , and we didn't want to mishandle our affairs if there might be a change in Iran." Bush continued by saying that his administration was "trying to be moderate, reasonable, and restrained," and he assured Qaboos that "we would use every diplomatic means we could."[27] The message was duly conveyed to Tehran, and just two days later Rafsanjani telegraphed Iran's response publicly during his Friday Prayers sermon at Tehran University: "I wish to say—I address the White House—that Lebanon has a solution; the freedom of the hostages is solvable. They have intelligent and manageable solutions." He added, "One cannot solve the issue with such bullying ways, with arrogant confrontations and tyranny. Come along wisely; we then will help you to solve the problems there so that the people of the region may live in peace and tranquility."[28] In response to reporters' ques-tions in the Oval Office the next day, Bush greeted Rafsanjani's concil-iatory gesture with cautious optimism: "I don't want to raise hopes beyond fulfillment, but there's reason to be somewhat encouraged. . . . When you see a statement that offers hope for the return of the hos-tages, I want to explore it to the fullest."[29]

To put matters on firmer ground, the White House enlisted the help of UN Secretary-General Pérez de Cuéllar to act as an intermediary between Washington and Tehran in resolving the hostage situation in Lebanon. After further strategizing with Bush's national security adviser, Gen. Brent Scowcroft, Pérez de Cuéllar immediately dispatched his trusted deputy, Giandomenico Picco, to Tehran with a quid pro quo offer from Washington. The specific terms of such a deal were deliberately left vague, but Rafsanjani soon made clear through his foreign minister, Velayati, that "the process of freeing the hostages could begin if the United States released 10 percent of the assets it had frozen after the seizure of the U.S. Embassy in Teheran [sic] in 1979." Velayati amended the demand a few weeks later at a UN meeting: "Washington also needed to make good on Reagan's promise to pay compensation for the victims of the Iranian Airbus shot down in 1988 by the [USS] *Vincennes*."[30] Picco's mission stalled for some time given differences in Washington over whether the United States should agree to the demands. Secretary of State James Baker was wary of appearing too eager to the Iranians, and at any rate he worried about the moral hazard of rewarding Iran for what should have been a humanitarian impulse in the first place—and especially in light of ongoing terrorism activities by Iran's operatives abroad. The hesitation in Washington allowed Tehran time to formulate a more expansive list of demands, which it delivered to Picco through its ambassador at the United Nations, Kamal Kharrazi: "The United States could release frozen assets; it could lift the embargo on the shipment of several hundred million dollars' worth of weapons bought and paid for by the shah before his ouster in 1979; it could provide support for the Algiers agreement, which the shah and Saddam Hussein had signed in 1975 to delineate the border between the two countries; and it could urge Saddam to withdraw the Iraqi troops who had continued to occupy a piece of Iranian territory since the end of the war."[31]

Iran delivered on its promise of leveraging its influence with Hezbollah leaders to secure the release of all remaining American and other Western hostages over the course of three years. The UN secretary-general's office, and especially Picco, played a critical role as an intermediary between Iran, Hezbollah, Syria, Israel, and the United States at critical junctures in the process.[32] After the release of the journalist Terry Anderson, the last of the American hostages in Beirut, on December 4, 1991, the Iranians nudged Picco and Pérez de Cuéllar about the arrangement with Washington. Rafsanjani had delivered on his end of the bargain, and now it was time for Bush to do the same. Indeed, as Picco vividly and painfully recounted in his memoir years later, Rafsanjani's "goodwill" gesture would not be reciprocated by Washington:

> Scowcroft had intimated at our first two meetings that the
> United States might have difficulty living up to its "promise"
> of three years earlier. Even so, I held out hope that the admin-
> istration would give me *something* I could take to the Iranians.
> Perhaps I was in denial: the idea that a word given would not
> be kept was unacceptable to me, since my credibility had been
> essential to the success of my work.... Scowcroft made it offi-
> cial in April [1992]: the timing was not propitious; there
> would be no gesture toward Iran anytime soon. Was it the
> upcoming presidential election? Perhaps. After all, could the
> incumbent risk looking soft on a country that still tarred Amer-
> ica as "the Great Satan"? Could he appear to pay off a govern-
> ment that had essentially taken over the U.S. Embassy in
> Teheran [*sic*] in 1979? Whatever the reasons, a three-year op-
> eration in Beirut built on a foundation of trust had suddenly
> turned to sand. Unwittingly—naively, as it turned out—I had
> misled an entire government.[33]

Feeling downcast and compromised, Picco felt an obligation to travel to Tehran and deliver the news in person to Rafsanjani, half-fearing the risks to his own personal safety. Rafsanjani's reaction—along with that of his advisor and translator, Mohammad Javad Zarif—was understandably indignant:

> "My government has had always good relations with you," he began. "We have known you for a long time. We have assisted you in Lebanon out of respect for the United Nations secretary-general. We have taken many political risks in our cooperation with you. Not everybody was in favor of such cooperation. Nevertheless, we went ahead. Since we engaged in this effort we have listened carefully to what you told us, including all the various assurances. You understand, Mr. Picco, that you are putting me in a very difficult position. In fact, it may be a very difficult position for both of us."[34]

Picco's anguished reflections are worth reproducing at length here since they capture the raw ingredients of distrust and enmity between Washington and Tehran. Despite President Bush's promise that "goodwill begets goodwill" in any measure of cooperation shown by Tehran, Washington still could not find a compelling rationale with which to overcome its deep-seated impression of the Islamic Republic as a terrorist regime bent on extracting concessions from the West through hostage takings, terror attacks, and disruption of regional peace and security. Indeed, this impression was not entirely unfounded. A chain of murders of prominent Iranian opposition leaders, artists, and intellectuals in European capitals by agents of Iran's Ministry of Intelligence—most notably, the 1991 stabbings of Iran's former prime minister Shapour Bakhtiyar, his secretary Kourosh Katibeh, and another prominent opposition leader Abdorrahman Boroumand in Paris—during the Bush presidency very much supported the impression of Iranian leaders as rogue actors.[35] Additionally, on March 17, 1992, a car bomb exploded outside of the Israeli embassy in Buenos Aires, killing twenty-nine people and injuring 250 others. The Iran-backed Palestinian Islamic Jihad group claimed responsibility for the explosion. The attack in Argentina—there would be another in 1994—no doubt hugely influenced Scowcroft's official rejection of Iran's demands for unfreezing its financial assets and allowing European companies to provide spare parts for Iran's aging airliners. As Bruce Riedel, a veteran of the Central Intelligence Agency who served as the director for Gulf and South Asia affairs at the National Security Council at the time (1991–93), noted later at a conference on missed opportunities in US-Iran relations, "I think there were two problems in 1992: one, it's an election year [in the US], and two, there is new Iranian behavior in the shape of murdering Bakhtiar and others in Europe. The perception in the White House—and I was there in 1992—was that what we were seeing was a change in the Iranian terrorist behavior from taking hostages to murdering exiles, and that we couldn't reward the change in Iranian behavior (that there couldn't be a halfway house on terrorism)."[36] The Bush administration's decision not to reciprocate Rafsanjani's goodwill gestures must also be properly contextualized in terms of the quite full foreign policy docket the administration had to contend with at the time. With the fall of the Berlin Wall, reunification of Germany, the dissolution of the Soviet Union, concerns over nuclear proliferation, Saddam's invasion of Kuwait and the ensuing Persian Gulf War, the Israeli-Palestinian conflict, and a host of other global priorities, achieving a modus vivendi with the Islamic Republic was simply not a top priority for the Bush administration. In fact, of utmost importance to the administration was the maintenance of American interests against hostile, revisionist regimes such as Iran's.

On September 17, 1992, three Iranian-Kurdish leaders and their translator—Sadegh Sharafkandi (secretary-general of the Iranian Democratic Party of Kurdistan), Fattah Abdoli, Homayoun Ardalan, and Nouri Dehkordi—were assassinated by masked gunmen at the Mykonos Greek restaurant in Berlin.[37] The killings fitted the pattern of earlier assassinations across Europe, which also included the 1989 slaying of Sharafkandi's predecessor, Abdul-Rahman Ghassemlou, in Vienna. German authorities, as well as Western intelligence agencies, immediately suspected Iran's intelligence agents to have been behind the attack. A German court ruling in 1997, after a three-year trial featuring testimony from 166 witnesses, concluded that Iranian leaders at the highest levels of government (including the president, the Office of the Supreme Leader, and Minister of Intelligence Ali Fallahian) not only had foreknowledge of the operations but in fact authorized them. Although the killings and later legal findings were not a vindication of the Bush administration's decision not to reward Iranian leaders for their role in the release of hostages, it nevertheless reinforced the narrative about the Islamic Republic as an outlaw regime not aligned with American interests.

■ Clinton, Dual Containment, and Khobar Towers

The election of a newcomer—and especially a foreign policy novice— as the forty-second president of the United States represented a shift in priorities both at home and abroad. Bill Clinton was largely elected on account of his promise to revitalize the American economy and to maintain its preeminence above emerging economies in the new era of globalization. This was to be a time of economic interdependence and of political harmony—peace through prosperity was to be the order of the day. Such was the change of outlook for the new administration that traditional foreign policy topics only received a vague mention in Clinton's inaugural address in 1993: "When our vital interests are challenged, or the will and conscience of the international community is defied, we will act; with peaceful diplomacy whenever possible, with force when necessary."[38] Indeed, with the dissolution of the Soviet Union, the Persian Gulf War, and American hostages in Lebanon all in the rearview mirror of American foreign policy, the Clinton administration shifted its focus to the major outstanding geopolitical issue of its time, the Israeli-Palestinian peace process, which was largely seen to be at the root of wider conflicts in the Middle East.[39]

With the Israeli-Palestinian peace process as the central focus of its Middle East policy, the Clinton administration sought to limit any possible interference by other states with a stake in the future of negotiations. This rationale formed the basis of a formal policy of "dual containment" toward Iran and Iraq, which sought to simultaneously contain threats to American interests in the region by these countries, but especially limit their interference with the Middle East peace process. The chief architect of this policy was Martin Indyk, a former director at the American Israel Public Affairs Committee and a senior official on the NSC in the Clinton administration. In a widely publicized speech at the Washington Institute for Near East Policy (of which he was the founding director in the 1980s) in May 1993, Indyk laid out the parameters of the administration's dual containment policy:

> The Clinton administration's policy of "dual containment" of Iraq and Iran derives in the first instance from an assessment that the current Iraqi and Iranian regimes are both hostile to American interests in the region. Accordingly, we do not accept the argument that we should continue the old balance of power game, building up one to balance the other. We reject that approach not only because its bankruptcy was demonstrated in Iraq's invasion of Kuwait. We reject it because of a clear-headed assessment of the antagonism that both regimes harbor towards the United States and its allies in the region. And we reject it because we don't need to rely on one to balance the other....
>
> When we assess Iranian intentions and capabilities, we see a dangerous combination for Western interests. Iran is engaged

in a five-part challenge to the United States and the international community. It is the foremost state sponsor of terrorism and assassination across the globe. Through its support for Hamas and Hezbollah, Iran is doing its best to thwart our efforts to promote peace between Israel, the Palestinians and the Arab states. Through its connections with Sudan, Iran is fishing in troubled waters across the Arab world, actively seeking to subvert friendly governments. Through its active efforts to acquire offensive weapons, Iran is seeking an ability to dominate the Gulf by military means. And, perhaps most disturbing, Iran is seeking a weapons of mass destruction capability including clandestine nuclear weapons capability and ballistic missiles to deliver weapons of mass destruction to the Middle East.

I should emphasize that the Clinton administration is not opposed to Islamic government in Iran. Indeed, we have excellent relations with a number of Islamic governments. Rather, we are firmly opposed to these specific aspects of the Iranian regime's behavior, as well as its abuse of the human rights of the Iranian people. We do not seek a confrontation but we will not normalize relations with Iran until and unless Iran's policies change, across the board. We are willing to listen to what Iran has to say, provided that this comes through authoritative channels. However, in the absence of dramatic changes in Iran's behavior, we will work energetically to persuade our European and Japanese allies, as well as Russia and China, that it is not in their interests to assist Iran to acquire nuclear weapons or the conventional means to pose a regional threat. Nor do we believe it is in their interests to ease Iran's economic situation so that it can pursue normal commercial relations on one level while threatening our common interests on another level. . . .

The necessity to act now derives from the fact that Iran's threatening intentions for the moment outstrip its capabilities. But this moment will not last for long. If we fail in our efforts to modify Iranian behavior, five years from now Iran will be much more capable of posing a real threat to Israel, to the Arab world and to Western interests in the Middle East. The opportunity to act now, on the other hand, derives from the fact that Iran is no longer a good commercial proposition. It is $5 billion in arrears on its short-term international loans and this figure is growing in leaps and bounds. Iran suffers from 30 percent inflation and 30 percent unemployment. In short, Iran is a bad investment in both commercial and strategic terms, not just for the United States but for all responsible members of the international community.[40]

Indyk's speech was notable for its clear formulation of American strategic priorities in the Middle East (i.e., Israel's security, US-Saudi alliance, and Western access to oil) and the clear articulation of how Washington's concerns about Iran's behavior and the nature of the Islamic Republic fit within those priorities. It was also curiously revealing in its partial approval of "Islamic government in Iran," but not necessarily of the Islamic Republic as a system. Indeed, as Indyk goes on to rehearse the familiar list of grievances against the regime's behavior in the region and "its abuse of the human rights of the Iranian people," the evocation of the grand narrative of the Iranian regime as a malign, illegitimate actor becomes strikingly clear. All the same, the speech also made it abundantly clear that the Clinton administration was willing to compartmentalize its grievances with Iran and leave the door open to possible communication and even cooperation around issues of mutual interest in the future.

There was, however, a danger in framing the policy of "dual containment" mostly in reference to Iranian malfeasance and bad faith. The characterization of Iran as a regional menace not only overlooked Rafsanjani's role in securing the release of American hostages during the Bush administration but also, according to one of Rafsanjani's key foreign policy hands at the time, Hossein Mousavian, ignored Iran's repeated signaling in this period that it would stay out of the peace process. In an exchange with Indyk at a critical oral history conference on this period, Mousavian, who was Iran's ambassador to Germany from 1990 to 1997, rebutted the basic premise behind the policy of dual containment:

> On peace process, the cornerstone of my suggestion was non-disturbance, non-interference. If the Arabs and Israelis could agree, we would stay neutral and we would not oppose; we would never recognize Israel, but we would not oppose. On the Persian Gulf security system, I told them that we are pre-pared for a regional cooperation system making every coordi-nation necessary with international bodies, whether this is NATO or the United Nations, to guarantee the healthy export of oil, non-interference in the internal affairs of countries in the Persian Gulf—a kind of cooperation like [the] OSCE [Or-ganization for Security and Co-operation in Europe]. It was discussed at the level of [German foreign minister Dietrich] Genscher and Rafsanjani, and Rafsanjani gave him carte blanche on this issue. Genscher was really surprised how pos-itive he [Rafsanjani] reacted on this issue. This was a compre-hensive package as far as [its statement of] the differences be-tween Iran and the US, Europe, and the West [when it came to] terrorism, weapons of mass destruction, peace process, and security issue in the region. But they [Western powers] didn't buy it.[41]

Undoubtedly, the shadow of chain killings of Iranian dissidents and intellectuals in Western capitals greatly impacted the reception of Rafsanjani's overtures on the issues recited by Mousavian in the ex-change with Indyk. The assassination of Iranian exiles, coupled with the death-laden rhetoric of clerical leaders in Iran—calling for Israel's destruction and vowing revenge on Western interests—and the regime's material support for extremist groups such as Hezbollah and Palestinian Islamic Jihad, reinforced the narrative of the Islamic Republic as a disruptive force and a state sponsor of terrorism.[42]

If this narrative had formed the backdrop to the Clinton administration's dual containment policy, it suddenly jumped to the foreground of US-Iran relations in the remaining years of the Rafsanjani presidency as a result of two major terrorist attacks—one against Israeli and the other against American overseas interests. The first of these was a suicide car bombing of the Argentine Israelite Mutual Association, a Jewish cultural center in Buenos Aires, on July 18, 1994. The attack killed eighty-five people and injured hundreds more, making it Argentina's deadliest terrorist attack to date. An offshoot of Lebanese Hezbollah, Ansar al-Allah, claimed responsibility for the attack, but Iranian agents and intermediaries were immediately suspected to have been involved by Argentine and Western authorities. It would be some time—not until 2006—before Argentine prosecutors would formally accuse the IRI of devising the attack and carrying it out through Hezbollah operatives.[43] A week after the attack in Argentina, a car bomb exploded outside of the Israeli embassy in London, resulting in thirteen injuries. Although the attacks did not appear to be coordinated, they nevertheless cast a spotlight on state sponsors of terrorism as the potential spoilers of the peace process.

The bombings put pressure on the Clinton administration to adopt an even tougher line on the Iranian government. In the absence of clear evidence of Iranian involvement in either of the attacks at the time, the administration issued only broad statements denouncing terrorism.[44] But over the course of the next year, the administration and a bipartisan coalition of lawmakers in Congress looked for ways to further contain Iran. One such action was the Clinton administration's forced cancellation of US oil giant Conoco's plans to develop two major offshore oil fields in Iran. The reportedly $1 billion deal between Conoco and the government of Iran was nullified on account of pressure by the White House and sharp criticisms by hard-line Republican lawmakers such as Senator Alfonse M. D'Amato of New York and Senate Majority Leader Bob Dole.[45] The deal would have been the largest foreign investment by a Western oil company in Iran since the 1979 revolution. It was formally canceled after President Clinton issued several executive orders prohibiting any American investments in Iran's energy sector. This action formed the foundation for a more comprehensive regime of sanctions that was passed by the US Congress as the Iran and Libya Sanctions Act (ILSA).

The passage of ILSA was preceded, and indeed hastened, by the second major terrorist attack on the Khobar Towers in Saudi Arabia, near the headquarters of the Saudi national oil company, Aramco, in Dhahran, where hundreds of US Air Force personnel were stationed. On June 25, 1996, a massive truck bomb ripped through the compound, killing nineteen US airmen and wounding more than four hundred others. The bombing sent shock waves through the Saudi royal family and government, as well as in Washington and across the Middle East. It was not immediately clear who was responsible for the attack, but subsequent investigations by Saudi intelligence, the CIA, and the Federal Bureau of Investigation (FBI) revealed that a Saudi branch of Hezbollah ("Hezbollah al-Hijaz") carried out the attack by smuggling explosives into the kingdom from Lebanon. The immediate aftermath of the attack nearly placed the United States military on a war footing, but in the absence of solid evidence clearly pointing toward a government or territory in the region, the risks of stumbling into a mistaken conflict outweighed the anguish of a slow investigative process. President Clinton formally tasked the director of the FBI, Louis J. Freeh, with investigating the bombing in cooperation with Saudi authorities—a flawed three-year process that yielded a long list of indictments of individuals linked to Iranian-backed organizations such as Hezbollah and formally holding the Iranian government responsible for the attacks. (The implications of the Khobar Towers bombing for US-Iran relations are explored in greater depth in chapter 7.)

The Khobar Towers bombing was a disappointing bookend to the Rafsanjani presidency, which had begun with the promise of improving Iran's relations with its regional neighbors—especially Saudi Arabia—and enhancing its international standing by presenting a more compromising and pragmatic side of the Islamic Republic. By the end of Rafsanjani's tenure, however, the Islamic Republic once again found itself isolated in the Middle East, under Western sanctions, and cast out as an international pariah by the United States. To be sure, Rafsanjani also succeeded in normalizing the Islamic Republic as a conventional regime capable of engaging in transactional relations with other states—not a fanatical theocracy on a millenarian crusade, but rather a religious republic chastened by the experience of war and the imperatives of reconstruction. Yet, in the final analysis, neither Rafsanjani nor his American counterparts were capable of reconciling these contrasting narratives to each other, and instead, in light of their respective priorities—regime survival for Rafsanjani, and American supremacy for Bush and Clinton—each side reverted to its own familiar shibboleths. Narrative prevailed over interests.

Khatami and the Possibility of Dialogue

5 The emergence of a reform movement in the mid-1990s was the first major opportunity for change in post-revolutionary Iran's internal politics and foreign relations. The significance of the movement lay in the organic composition of its leading champions and objectives. The former's record of service and fealty to the Islamic Republic lent the array of reforms advanced by them—for example, for a more pluralistic, transparent, and representative political system—a degree of authenticity that could not be dismissed by the ruling hard-line establishment as either an insidious Western plot or the work of pitiful "Westoxicated" intellectuals.[1] The advent of the reform movement also challenged conventional Western narratives about a rigid and uncompromising regime populated by anti-Western zealots and a repressed civil society ruled over by "mad mullahs."[2] The putative leader of the movement, Mohammad Khatami, was a soft-spoken, smiling, sartorially conscious cleric whose public speeches and demeanor stood in stark contrast to the archetypal post-revolutionary politician in the Islamic Republic.[3] To insiders and outsiders alike, Khatami's swift ascendancy to the presidency seemed especially surprising given how the Iranian electoral process was deliberately designed to produce expected, soporific results in favor of the status quo in every contest. Elections were meant to be an artifice in service of the *nezam* (system), not a popular check against its singular authority. New developments inside Iran challenged this dominant view.

Moreover, this period also coincided with the height of a triumphalist discourse in the West—and one especially shared by American policy makers—about the forward march of liberal democracy and human rights in the post–Cold War international order. This messianic narrative not only evinced in Western democracies a model of economic and political governance for the rest of the world but, relatedly, also posited a Manichean "clash of civilizations" between Western purveyors of liberal values and their Islamic and Confucian counterparts.[4] To exponents of these views, the sudden appearance of a grassroots movement for change and democracy inside Iran merely confirmed the universal yearning for Western models, while to their detractors, Iranian reformists' rise in fact testified to the possibility of a sui generis Islamic democratic model that more accurately reflected local traditions and aspirations. In time, the reform era would be remembered as an instance of civil assertion against arbitrary rule—a robust resistance that achieved more by way of exposing the limits of change in the Islamic Republic than by actually mitigating the authoritarian impulses and political structures of the regime. But in the global context of the late 1990s, the prospect of an alternative, more representative and less adversarial government in Tehran increasingly challenged the dominant view of the Islamic Republic as a monolithic, static, and uncompromising regime that is rooted in, and sustained by, antipathy toward Western values.

■ Khatami and "Second of Khordad"

Khatami's surprising landslide win in 1997 was a culmination of a series of ponderous microevolutions in political thinking and practice that gained momentum and organizational form after Khomeini's death in 1989. More than anything, Khatami's own public profile and career trajectory personified these steady changes. A son of a grand ayatollah, he was born in 1943 in Ardakan in the province of Yazd. He attained his bachelor's degree in Western philosophy from Isfahan University of Technology and a postgraduate degree in education at Tehran University, followed by clerical education in Islamic jurisprudence at the Qom Seminary. Prior to the revolution, Khatami headed the Islamic Center in Hamburg, Germany, which did not make him any less revolutionary, but it did shield him from imprisonment, torture, and the bonds of radical solidarity that were forged between some of the more conservative and hard-line supporters of Khomeini. From 1980 to 1982, Khatami served concurrently as a deputy in the Majles and the managing director of the Keyhan publications, followed by a decade-long tenure as the minister of culture and Islamic guidance (*Ershad*) in the cabinets of Prime Minister Mir-Hossein Mousavi and President Ali Akbar Hashemi Rafsanjani. Khatami was forced to resign his cabinet post in 1992 after he pushed back on the implementation of stricter censorship guidelines (for the Iranian film and television industry, mostly) favored by hard-line conservatives in the Majles. After his resignation, he was named the director of the National Library, where he remained until announcing his candidacy for president in 1997.

Khatami's early political résumé is noteworthy for the absence of any high-level executive postings and decision-making responsibilities typical of the regime's top brass up to the late 1990s. Although he had been involved with various revolutionary and post-revolutionary organizations and was a true believer in the ideals of the Islamic Republic (he was a proud member of the conservative Association of

Combatant Clergy), his mild-mannered temperament and philosophical dispositions directed his interests toward cultural pursuits. Over time, like many of his revolutionary contemporaries, Khatami's political passions became chastened by the authoritarian impulses and trajectory of a political system (*nezam*) that reduced the complexities of daily governance to arbitrary binaries: pious versus licentious, insiders (*khodi-ha*) versus outsiders (*gheyr-e khodi-ha*), martyrs versus infidels, friends versus enemies, and so on. This troublesome postrevolutionary trajectory, Khatami wrote in his resignation as the minister at *Ershad*, demonstrated the depths of "rigidity, inflexibility, and backwardness . . . [that acted as] the greatest plague on the government."[5] In a series of books and articles during his tenure at the National Library, Khatami elaborated on these worries, albeit in the allegorical doublespeak style of communication characteristic of nearly all public figures in the Islamic Republic.

Such hesitations aside, Khatami also fully subscribed to the notion that Islamic and Eastern cultures were under assault by Western modernity and materialism. Similar to other revolutionary-turned-reformist figures, he maintained a general suspicion of those perspectives that even remotely hinted at secular or liberal ideas.[6] To Khatami, the postrevolutionary lurch toward authoritarianism was not due to the marriage of Islam and politics, much less an indication of the predestined trajectory of the revolution. At issue, rather, was deviation from the true ideals of Islamic republicanism, which Khomeini's death in 1989 had exacerbated. The hard-line faction that had risen to power after Khomeini's death was intent on consolidating power around the person and institution of *vali-ye faqih* (supreme jurist, now led by Khamenei) and only granting symbolic and limited powers to the elected institutions of the state such as the presidency and Majles. With the Guardian Council vetting the revolutionary credentials of any candidate standing for elected office, the system was designed such that elected institutions of the state could not meaningfully check the arbitrary powers of either the judiciary or the Office of the Supreme Leader.

This problem was compounded by the precedence set by Khomeini during the first decade after the revolution. At that time, the institutions of government (both elected and unelected ones) were very much under the sway of Khomeini; if anyone serving in any organs of the government fell out of favor with him or disagreed with his injunctions, they would be summarily dismissed, which meant they could not stand for elective office ever again. As explained in the previous chapter, however, Khamenei clearly lacked the requisite theological credentials as Khomeini's successor, and so from the outset his appointment was as an act of expediency on the part of the Assembly of Experts in order to avoid any perceptions of a crisis of succession.[7] Khomeini's iconic status among the rank-and-file members of the regime owed much to his proven record against secular autocracy and as the founder of the Islamic Republic. Therefore, regardless of whether they disagreed with his views from time to time, most of the clergy revered his example and respected his decisions. The same courtesy could not be extended to Khamenei, of course—a fact too obvious to both Khamenei and his rivals. But whereas the latter—led by Rafsanjani—faced the burden of reconciling the arbitrary structures of power with the imperatives of reconstruction in the post-Khomeini era, Khamenei and his supporters focused their energies on cementing their hold on key powerful institutions (especially the Guardian Council and the judiciary), checking the ambitions of political rivals, and marginalizing any and all voices of dissent.

The ensuing factional competition between ultraconservative and pragmatist-conservative camps was mostly at the expense of Islamic leftist and progressive groups and dissidents, most of whom were either driven out of the country or consigned to nongovernmental centers and activities. This marginalization engendered a quiet rethinking of the unfulfilled emancipatory promises of the revolution among a cohort of reform- and liberal-minded intellectuals, journalists, and former technocrats.[8] In the early 1990s, the intellectual and political discussions between these individuals were mostly facilitated through cultural and economic publications such as *Kiyan*, *Ayin*, and *Iran-e Farda*, as well as in influential think tanks such as the Rafsanjani-supported Center for Strategic Research.[9] The recent collapse of the Soviet Union, followed by the forward march of pro-democracy movements across Central and Eastern Europe, weighed heavily on the minds of most participants. Yet while religious intellectuals such as Abdolkarim Soroush and Hassan Yousefi Eshkevari contemplated the possibility of democratic Islamic government (made possible through more pluralistic interpretations of Islamic doctrine), other figures such as the journalist Akbar Ganji believed that so long as any form of religious authority could override the popular will then no form of democratic government could be possible.[10] In the context of their times, these debates played an important role in creating a space for the contemplation of the basis of political legitimacy, civil and political liberties, social strictures, and open comparisons of other political regimes and outcomes with those of the Islamic Republic. In a relatively short span of time, they also crucially formed the very threads that wove together the fabric of a reform project. In the lead-up to the 1997 presidential elections a consensus had emerged that enacting reforms within the existing structures of the regime was indeed possible, especially if sufficient popular support could be generated in favor of an incremental program for change.

Although Khatami himself—given his overly cautious temperament—was not a direct participant in the fierce intellectual debates and political maneuverings that took place during Rafsanjani's second term, he was acquainted with many of the leading exponents of reforms and was eventually persuaded of the need for structural and policy changes.[11] But what he lacked in intellectual conviction, Khatami more than made up for through his retail political skills. As a pious, yet gregarious, cleric with a résumé mostly made up of cultural activities, he cut a worldly figure among otherwise dour and ascetic loyalists to the Islamic Republic. His command of Persian literary allusions and deft deployment of classical poetry endeared him to the general public, who had grown weary and even contemptuous of the routine use of Arabic (Quranic) words by regime officials. Through his travels to distant provinces and small towns, Khatami exuded an authentic aura of hope and progress. His message became one of renewal through change, which was precisely what a restive public wary of either continuity or revolution desired most at the time. As the election drew near, the symbolic and literal import of Khatami's candidacy became more difficult for a wide cross section of Iranian society, and especially the youth, to resist:

> What Khatami promised was an Iran where the government's voice would not ring out in silence. Civil society was a catch-phrase for all the recourse Iranian citizens lacked: an independent press, grassroots associations, political parties, checks and balances on power—even, for those who dared to hope for it, an independent judiciary that might enforce equality before the law and safeguard the rights and freedoms of individuals. He suggested such a future while wearing clerical robes and a black turban that marked him as a *seyyed*, or a descendent of the Prophet. He was not a radical figure. To vote for Khatami was to express the hope that the Islamic Republic had better days ahead of it, that the 1979 Islamic Revolution might yet be one of liberation.[12]

For their part, the conservative establishment was entirely aloof about the groundswell of support around Khatami's candidacy. They smugly assumed that a combination of public apathy and Khatami's relative newcomer status would work in favor of Khamenei's handpicked candidate, the speaker of Majles Ali Akbar Nategh-Nouri.[13] Their overconfidence proved to be a monumental miscalculation. On May 23, 1997, the political equivalent of an earthquake ripped through the Islamic Republic's clerical establishment as Khatami resoundingly defeated Nategh-Nouri with nearly 70 percent of the share of the total votes cast. Voter turnout was the highest in the history of post-revolutionary Iran, with 80 percent of those eligible participating.[14] Crucially, a significant portion of Khatami's share of the vote was cast by the youth (those under thirty years of age), which at the time accounted for nearly two-thirds of the entire population of the country.

Khatami's decisive victory also reverberated around the world. With masses of disaffected Iranians electing to exploit the existing channels of participation (i.e., a managed electoral process) to send a decisive message to the conservative elite about the need for change, conventional Western impressions of a passive and repressed society now had to be revised. As the *New York Times*, somewhat condescendingly, observed, "The vote showed Iranians that they have the power to influence their political structure, something many had come to doubt after generations of autocratic rule, first under the Shah and now under the Islamic Government. It also showed that people here no longer feel obligated to follow the direction of their political and religious leaders, a change that could have profound implications."[15] In fact, Khatami's surprising victory would become known as "The Epic of Second of Khordad," which referred both to the date of his election on the Persian calendar and to the loose coalition of student organizations, Islamic leftists, moderate clergy, women's groups, labor syndicates, independent journalists, and legal and intellectual institutions, among others, that ensured his win. Together, they mapped out a new political trajectory—and, with it, a new narrative—for a society hungering for change. Under Khatami, the narrative went, civil society could develop more freely, with social and economic liberalization forming the basis for a more open political sphere. In foreign relations, too, the Islamic Republic could possibly turn the page on a decade and a half of revolutionary fervor, enmity toward "arrogant powers" in the West (primarily the United States and Great Britain), and rogue behavior such as terrorism, assassinations and kidnappings, and mass executions of dissidents. Khatami could prove to be pivotal, even transformational—perhaps the Iranian Mikhail Gorbachev.

■ "Dialogue of Civilizations"

Khatami's election immediately improved Iran's regional and international standing. Encouraged by his campaign promises of international amity, regional Arab rivals and Persian Gulf countries welcomed the change of demeanor in Tehran and vowed to reciprocate in kind. In December 1997, at the eighth meeting of the Organization of Islamic Conference (OIC; later changed to Organization of Islamic Cooperation) in Tehran, Khatami called for the establishment of an "Islamic Civil Society" that would demonstrate the dynamism and plural constitution of "Islamic civilization" to the rest of the world.[16] In a preview of a theme that he would return to many times during his first term in office, Khatami urged a "dialogue among civilizations," by which he meant "for philosophers, writers, scientists and artists belonging to different cultures and civilizations to speak to one another, allowing truths to be better revealed and to grow through this exchange." Most significantly, Khatami concluded his remarks by directly addressing the possibility of engagement with the United States:

> Concerning dialogue with the United States of America, . . .
> I [have] raised the principle of detente in diplomatic policy.
> We have already begun this policy, and we have achieved total
> success in the region. We have also achieved much success
> throughout the world, the last case of which was the resolu-
> tion of problems between Iran, the European Union. . . . But

concerning the United States of America, I, first of all, pay my respect to the great people and nation of America. I hope to be able, in the not-too-distant future, to speak particularly with the people of America and about America; maybe before long.[17]

Roughly a month after Khatami's promise to directly engage the American public, he did so in a television interview with the veteran Iranian-British journalist Christiane Amanpour on CNN. The interview provided Khatami with the opportunity to present a softer side of the Islamic Republic to the American public and to signal his interest in political rapprochement to American policymakers. Khatami began with a long recitation of American history—from the time of Puritan settlements in New England to contemporary American society—to demonstrate his familiarity with the culture and political development of what he called "the American civilization." After offering a similar exegesis on Iran's civilizational development, Khatami made a pivot to cast the 1979 revolution in the same mold—in the scope and substance of its ideals—as that of the American Revolution. His call for a "dialogue of civilizations," he reasoned, was precisely meant to clarify the affinities between these two civilizational paths:

> In terms of the dialogue of civilizations, we intend to benefit from the achievements and experiences of all civilizations, Western and non-Western, and to hold dialogue with them. The closer the pillars and essences of these two civilizations are, the easier the dialogue would become. With our revolution, we are experiencing a new phase of reconstruction of civilization. We feel that what we seek is what the founders of the American civilization were also pursuing four centuries ago. This is why we sense an intellectual affinity with the essence of the American civilization.
>
> Second, there is the issue of the independence. The American nation was the harbinger of independence struggles, the

initiator of efforts to establish independence, for whose cause it has offered many sacrifices, leading ultimately to the Declaration of Independence which is an important document on human dignity and rights.

Finally, I should refer to the struggles of the Iranian people over the last two centuries which culminated in the quest for independence during the Islamic Revolution launched by Imam Khomeini. When Imam Khomeini launched the revolution, Iran was in a terrible condition. In other words, the Iranian nation had been humiliated and its fate was decided by others. You know that a remarkable feature of Imam Khomeini's struggle was his fight against capitulation which the Shah was forced to ratify making the American advisors immune from prosecution in Iran. This was the worst humiliation for our people. They rose up, fought for independence, and emerged victorious. Of course, the war of the revolution was one of words not weapons. We, therefore, endeavored to obtain a novel experience of religion and to gain independence. Both these features are salient in the American civilization and we feel close to them.[18]

Khatami's opening soliloquy on the abstract affinities between Iranian and American "civilizations" was meant to anchor the difficult matter of US-Iran diplomatic (non)relations in the much safer ground of societal-level understandings. This rhetorical device served a double purpose for Khatami. First, it enabled him to shift the perspective of the average American viewer away from the hostile flash points of America's dealings with post-revolutionary Iran. Political differences aside, Khatami was insisting, the Iranian and American publics have more in common than conventional perceptions allow. Second and most importantly, the abstract language of "civilizations" afforded Khatami sufficient political cover at home to shift the basis of relations with the West without seeming too obsequious or eager to establish official ties. After all, his outreach was meant to clarify that American policies, and not the American people, were the object of the Islamic Republic's enmity. He was improving the regime's image abroad, which would undoubtedly please the Iranian public, whose sentiments were mostly pro-American but also largely disaffected with the clerical establishment.

Khatami's headline-making comments, however, centered on the issue of the hostage crisis and the ongoing state-sanctioned use of anti-American slogans and imagery in Iran. "With regard to the hostage issue which you [Amanpour] raised," Khatami noted, "I do know that the feelings of the great American people have been hurt, and of course I regret it." He went on to contextualize the early years of the revolution and point out that ordinary Iranians' hurt feelings would also have to be taken into account. In response to a question about the persistence of state-sanctioned anti-American slogans and imagery on the airwaves and in Iranian cities, Khatami reiterated his point that "not only do we not harbor any ill wishes for the American people, but in fact we consider them to be great nation. Our aim is not even to destroy or undermine the American government. These slogans symbolize a desire to terminate a mode of relations which existed between Iran and the United States." Khatami then proceeded to address the possibility of diplomatic relations with the United States (which he distinguished from a dialogue between civilizations):

> In regard to political relations, we have to consider the factors
> which lead to the severance of relations. . . . There is a bulky
> wall of mistrust between us and the U.S. Administration,
> a mistrust rooted in improper behaviors of the American
> governments. As an example of this type of U.S. behavior, I
> should refer to admitted involvement of the U.S. Government
> in the 1953 coup d'état which toppled [Pahlavi-era premier

Mohammad] Mosaddeq's national government, immediately followed by a $45 million loan to strengthen unpopular foreign installed Government. I should also refer to the Capitulation Law imposed by the U.S. on Iran.... There must first be a crack in this wall of mistrust to prepare for a change and create an opportunity to study a new situation.... We are looking for a world in which misunderstandings can be overcome, nations can understand one another and mutual respect and logic govern relations among states. It is the right of every nation to stand on its principles and values and have the expectation of respect and dignity from others.[19]

On the topic of US-Iran relations, Khatami's response featured many of the familiar lines from the standard regime narrative of grievance against the US government. But, crucially, it also included new openings. By acknowledging the "wall of mistrust" between the two governments, Khatami let it be known that the core issue was about trust and confidence, not unbending opposition. What this implied was that any official diplomatic engagements must first be preceded by cultural and intellectual exchanges that demonstrated the goodwill of each society toward the other (hence Khatami's outreach at the level of a dialogue among civilizations). The primetime interview with CNN itself was a first step in this direction and was noted as such by many commentators and analysts in both Iran and the United States.[20]

If Khatami's gestures did not amount to a fully developed diplomatic approach toward the United States, they certainly proposed the possibility of a new narrative that could place the relationship on a more productive path. Khatami's "dialogue of civilizations" was a clever device carefully designed to undermine some long-standing misunderstandings and taboos parroted by reactionary hard-liners on both sides. In this sense, it was an olive branch disguised in a cultural initiative that deftly employed rhetoric and symbolism to elevate Iranian and American societies above the pettiness of their respective politics. The official American response to Khatami's overtures is explored in the next chapter, but it is important to underline here that "dialogue of civilizations" also served as a counternarrative to the "clash of civilizations" thesis that framed many policy discussions and academic forums in this period. As one scholar observed, "The communicative act of opening this dialogue created an international public sphere which had not previously existed, opening the potential for an alternative to the spiral of conflict and mistrust between the West and Islam."[21]

Conservative Backlash and the Limits of Reforms

The near-unanimous positive response to Khatami's landslide victory at both the domestic and international levels was initially greeted by the regime's conservative establishment with a mixture of public accommodation and private alarm. Publicly, the tone was set early on by Supreme Leader Ali Khamenei, who congratulated Khatami at his inauguration ceremony for earning the trust of the public but then proceeded to remind the public (and the world) of the unique accomplishments of the *nezam* up to Khatami's election: "What this popular and divine system—the Islamic Republic—accomplished in this country is both quantitatively and qualitatively incomparable with what was accomplished in this country before the Islamic Republic. This is the meaning of a system connected with spirituality and faith, a system that enjoys vast popular support, votes, passions, and assistance of the people, as well as faith and spirituality, brotherhood and coordination, reliance on God and faith in the occult."[22] Khamenei's speech was neither trenchantly hard-line nor dismissive of the election's result, but it was notably defensive in tone and resolute about the ostensible achievements of the Islamic Republic, a posture he would reserve for himself throughout Khatami's two-term presidency while releasing his surrogates to carry out the less dignified task of attacking and vilifying Khatami and reformists in Friday sermons and the pages of conservative newspapers.

In private, however, conservatives were deeply suspicious of reformist discourses on pluralism, civil society, and the possibility of Islamic democracy, which they regarded as a Trojan horse threatening their conception of Islamic government. Conservative antipathy toward reforms was—and still is—at its core about the relationship between Islam and *power*, and not merely, as some observers had hoped, about philosophical differences. At issue are questions about the power to interpret Islamic precepts and the further translation of those principles into instruments of state power. From the conservative standpoint, loosening the powers of interpretation to allow for divergent perspectives would inevitably result in the loss of pious authority, thus undermining the principle of supreme guardianship of the jurist (*velayat-e faqih*). Indeed, this was a principal objective of reformists from the outset: to challenge the very structure of power in the Islamic Republic. They did not seek to challenge the religious basis of the state, and most were proud revolutionaries who merely wished to redirect the state back on its intended liberationist, egalitarian, and justice-oriented path.[23] In fact, it was the reformists who viewed the conservatives as authoritarian Trojan horses who had usurped the instruments of power through rotten compromises, intimidation, and elimination of anyone who disagreed with them, and who carried out their arbitrary powers always in the shadows.

The main instruments for disseminating these lines of argument after Khatami's election were reformist newspapers, weekly magazines, public lectures, and, over time, online media platforms and websites. Alumni of earlier intellectual periodicals such as *Kiyan* and *Iran-e Farda* soon started their own broadsheets, perhaps most prominent of which in the early days of reforms were the dailies *Jame'eh* (Society) and

Sobh-e Emrooz (This Morning) run by erstwhile ardent revolutionaries.[24] The "new" media injected the public sphere seemingly overnight with a sense of dynamism and hope not felt since the early days of the revolution. New curiosities and lines of inquiry about issues both mundane and serious (e.g., divorce, dating, privacy, rights, Western culture) were now routine matters of discussion and correspondence in publications large and small. Parallel to these developments was the proliferation of satellite dishes across major cities in Iran, which provided alternative sources of news and entertainment from across the world. To millions of Iranians, programming from these outlets provided a window onto Westernizing trends in other parts of Asia, as well as in the Arab world, and to the ever-restive Iranian youth they functioned as an escape from the cumbersome nature of social and political life under the Islamic Republic.[25]

But the early days of the reform era were as much about collective release as they were about calls for public accountability and political change. The latter endeavors were primarily pursued by journalists and activists, many of whom were determined to take advantage of the brief period of legal relaxation of press laws to investigate the establishment's high crimes and misdemeanors involving the public treasury and even the brutal suppression of dissidents and intellectuals over the years. A rather prominent case in point around this time was the work of the investigative journalist (and former Islamic Revolutionary Guard Corps member) Akbar Ganji, who in a series of articles in *Sobh-e Emrooz* exposed and connected together a chain of disappearances, tortures, and murders of prominent Iranian opposition leaders, intellectuals, and other dissidents (between 1988 and 1998) by the regime's intelligence agents and at the direction of the highest political authorities in the Islamic Republic. Most infamously, Ganji implicated the former president Hashemi Rafsanjani—whom he referred to in the articles as "His Red Eminence"—and later pointed to his minister of intelligence, Ali Fallahian, as the "Master Key" in planning and supervising the murders.[26] As a major power broker during the first two decades of the Islamic Republic, Rafsanjani's name had become synonymous with graft, nepotism, and hypocrisy. To many reformist journalists, exposing Rafsanjani's Machiavellian ways was a first step toward dismantling a binary system of insiders and outsiders that many ordinary Iranians viewed as not that different from the arbitrariness and favoritism that characterized the Pahlavi regime.[27] The cumulative impact of these revelations on Rafsanjani and his family members cannot be overstated. In the year 2000, as reformist deputies swept to power in the Majles, Rafsanjani was publicly humiliated by only receiving 25 percent of the vote and barely winning the last open seat from Tehran. The results were embarrassing enough that Rafsanjani simply gave up his seat before he could be sworn in.

The wave of exposés and newfound public spaces for the expression of long-simmering frustrations with the regime—especially on university campuses—quickly ended the conservatives' patience with Khatami's government. In seeking to stem the tide of reforms and anti-regime populism, the conservatives controlled a powerful instrument in the judicial branch.[28] The local branches of the Islamic Revolutionary Courts, under the direction of arch-conservative "chief justices" Mohammad Yazdi and Mahmoud Hashemi Shahroudi, triggered an obscure constitutional provision that allowed for the censorship and closure of press organizations if either Islamic values or the public interest were threatened. Toward the end of Khatami's first term, the Special Press Branch of the judiciary in Tehran closed nearly 110 newspapers and handed out prison terms and financial fines to publishers, editors, and journalists. The closure of one particularly influential reformist newspaper, *Salaam* (Salute)—affiliated with the Association for Combatant Clergy—in July 1999 sparked the most widespread and longest demonstrations against the regime since the advent of the Islamic Republic. After nearly a week of protests, the dormitories of the University of Tehran were raided by plainclothes militiamen belonging to the Ansar-e Hezbollah branch of the Basij, which resulted in mass arrests of students and activists, as well as at least one death. The event, which became known by its location (Kouye Daneshgah) and the date on the Persian calendar (18 Tir [July 9]), marked the beginning of the conservative backlash against reformists, which over the course of Khatami's tenure would grow more violent and defiant.

The harsh crackdowns on the press, reformist groups, student activists, and dissidents exposed Khatami's limitations as a leader and operator inside the regime. He had been conspicuously silent during the protests—prompting protesters to chant "Khatami, Khatami, Where Are You?"—and when he finally spoke, he issued vague statements calling for public calm and the observance of the rule of law. Although Khatami's reticence at such crucial moments angered many of his supporters, who wished for him to more directly confront the judiciary and the Basij forces, it was ultimately a reflection of his weak position in the structure of power in Iran.[29] At the time of the protests, the senior leadership of the IRGC issued a stern warning to Khatami that placed the blame squarely on foreign powers and their naïve, Westoxicated domestic collaborators among the liberal and reformist ranks.[30] These widely publicized warnings to Khatami were meant to serve as a reminder of the ultimate instruments (IRGC) and source (the supreme leader) of coercive powers of the regime. Most ominously, however, they demonstrated the conservatives' complete lack of scruples in publicly threatening—and thereby dismissing—the authority of the elected institutions of the state. This contemptuous attitude toward reformists in fact gave license to some of the extreme elements in the security and intelligence ranks to take matters into their own hands and physically harm and intimidate prominent advocates of reforms. In March 2000, for instance, one of Khatami's senior political advisors, Saeed Hajjarian, who was also one of the leading architects of the Second of Khordad movement, was attacked by gunmen on motorbikes and nearly killed in plain sight (he was shot in the eye, leaving him severely paralyzed afterward). The attack was viewed as retribution for the landslide reformist victory in the February Majles elections that handed the reform coalition a robust mandate to institute meaningful changes.[31]

Although for a time the attempted assassination of Hajjarian rattled Iranian society and political establishment, it was in fact a harbinger of a more concerted and emboldened conservative reaction directed from the very top. The reformists' sweeping victory in the local and parliamentary elections garnered positive coverage and commentary in Western media, and even after the violent conservative reactions some analysts openly contemplated whether Khatami was indeed Iran's Gorbachev.[32] Predictions of the imminent collapse of the Islamic Republic and disquisitions about the future of democratic transition in Iran, however, were taken seriously by the conservative rank and file, who were determined to use it against Khatami at every turn to undermine the reform movement as nothing more than a soft coup designed by Western governments and "imperial" interests. Most dramatically, as if to underline the rationale behind the conservative backlash, Khamenei himself took up and directly addressed the comparisons with the Soviet Union under Gorbachev. In a televised address in April 2000, shortly after the assassination attempt on Hajjarian—and after a spate of newspaper closures by the judiciary—Khamenei framed the conservative reaction as a struggle against Western imperialism:

> Today, the issue of reforms is being brought up in the country, and it is one of the main issues. In other words, many individuals are talking about reforms or making efforts in this regard. But what are reforms? What is the best way to conduct reforms? What are the priorities of reforms? These are very important questions.
>
> Another important and relevant question is, what is the enemy seeking to achieve by giving special prominence to the

issue of reforms in Iran in its propaganda? What is the reason for the fact that the propaganda of certain international circles, which have never displayed any goodwill toward the Iranian people, has currently been focused on the issue of reforms in Iran? . . .

As someone who has dealt with various issues and political currents ever since the beginning of the revolution, I am quite familiar with politicians and their words as well as the motives behind the propaganda of the international media. Considering this experience, I have now reached the conclusion that the United States has devised a comprehensive plan to subvert the Islamic system. This plan is an imitation of the plan that led to the collapse of the former Soviet Union. The U.S. officials intend to carry out the same plan in Iran, and there are enough clues in their selfish and often hasty remarks made during the past few years indicating that they aim to do so.

However, the enemy has made certain mistakes in its calculations. I am going to elaborate on these mistakes, but this will not help the enemy to rectify those mistakes, since their main problem is their wrong knowledge about realities in Iran, which has resulted in their wrong planning. This is why all their plans about Iran always end in failure.

Regarding the mistakes that they have made, their first mistake is that Mr. Khatami is not Gorbachev. Their second mistake is that Islam is not communism. Their next mistake is that the popular system of Islamic Republic is not the dictatorial regime of the proletariat. The fourth mistake is that the integrated Iran is not like the former Soviet Union, which was made up of different republics. And their next mistake is that they have underrated the pivotal role of the religious and spiritual leadership in Iran.[33]

Khamenei's remarks are worth quoting at length here because they once again reveal the arc of his careful reframing of reforms as a necessary accompaniment of "the enemy's" (i.e., the United States, Great Britain, and other Western countries) grand designs to infiltrate the Islamic Republic and place it on the same trajectory as that of the Soviet Union before its sudden implosion. In essence, what Khamenei is ultimately inferring—through his many rhetorical questions—is that reforms would ultimately benefit Western interests more than they would the regime and the legacy of the revolution. This framing completely skirts the substantive grievances of reformists and their popularity among the public and instead forces the familiar binary of insiders versus outsiders that is at the very core of the conservative narrative of the revolution. In this way, Khamenei effectively absolved the violence of the IRGC, Basij militias, the revolutionary courts, and even plainclothes assailants of reformist figures, and he made it clear that henceforth the push for political reforms would be interpreted as attempts to topple the Islamic Republic.

◼ Twilight of the Reformist Narrative

The Khatami era presented Iranian society, especially the youth, with a pathway toward greater freedoms, political accountability, economic prosperity, inclusion, and coexistence—in short, with great hope. Yet no sooner had reformist efforts begun than they were systematically undermined and blocked at every turn by the public and shadowy arms of the conservative arbiters of power. By the time Khamenei reframed reforms as the "hidden plots" of Western powers, Khatami's agenda and coalition were effectively rendered enemies of the Islamic Republic. As the conservative judiciary and the security arms of the IRGC set about dismantling the Second of Khordad network of student activists, journalists, lawyers, writers and artists, and independent organizations, the two elected branches of the state—the presidency and the Majles—were exposed for their relative lack of power in the Islamic Republic. More importantly, the ferocity and extent of the conservative backlash also raised legitimate doubts about the possibility of any meaningful reforms within the existing constitutional framework. If the collective will of an overwhelming majority was to be rendered void and meaningless by a powerful minority, then what sense was there in participating in such a scheme at all?

Indeed, that is exactly what happened in 2005. Frustrated by the slow pace of reforms and especially discouraged by Khatami's timid and ineffectual leadership style (and those of other prominent reformists),[34] many Iranians stayed away from the polls in what seemed like a noncontest between the former president and head of the Expediency Council (charged with overlooking the conduct of the supreme leader), Rafsanjani, and the popular but nationally unknown mayor of Tehran, Mahmood Ahmadinejad. The latter, a former member of the now-ascendant IRGC, managed to successfully exploit the vacuum created by general feelings of apathy and disillusionment with the political process and defeat Rafsanjani, whose reputation, thanks in large part to the reformist press's early scrutiny of his postrevolutionary record, was in tatters. In time, however, Rafsanjani and his family would prove to be influential allies of the reformists, as the need for a more powerful coalition to counterbalance the unchecked powers of the supreme leader and the IRGC would become necessary.

The sudden emergence and then abrupt stifling of reforms fashioned a cautionary tale about the limits of change in a political system that only affords symbolic power to the elected institutions of the state. In this regard, the failures of reforms were less about the inability of reformists to leverage their popularity into a coherent agenda (although this was a major issue as well) than they were about the inability of Khatami and his allies to directly confront and counter the tested-and-tried binary narrative of the conservatives that reduced even the slightest of domestic considerations into a Manichean strug-gle against Western imperialism. Khatami was exceptionally success-ful at presenting a different side of the Islamic Republic to the world through his "dialogue of civilizations" initiative.[35] As the next chapter will demonstrate, during Khatami's tenure Iran's regional and interna-tional relations improved, especially its relations with some key West-ern European countries (even the Prince of Wales made a landmark visit to Iran in 2004). Crucially, it was through Khatami's travails that Western policy makers gained a better understanding of the multilay-ered dynamics of Iran's internal politics. In this respect, the ultimate meaning and power of Khatami's example may well have been the same as that of a future president of the United States, Barack Obama: the exception that proved the rule.

The Shadow of Khobar in Washington

Mohammad Khatami's election in late May 1997 surprised everyone, including the candidate himself. Virtually every observer had assumed that Supreme Leader Khamenei's pick, Ali Akbar Nategh-Nouri, would prevail. The country's foreign minister had given confident assurances that continuity would be the order of the day in Iran's foreign policy, no matter the outcome of the ballot.[1]

US officials pronounced themselves cautiously optimistic at first. Publicly, President Clinton found the results "interesting and ... hopeful," joining the generally upbeat international consensus. A few days after the election, Russian president Boris Yeltsin told Clinton he hoped the United States could "accord Iran better treatment." Clinton replied affirmatively, "if their policies change." He noted that the United States and the European Union had already agreed to set new "benchmarks to measure Iranian behavior" and insisted that Washington was "ready to talk," but "we have to be able to discuss the issues that divide us." Those issues had not changed for some time—Iran's support for terrorism, undermining of the peace process, and proliferation of weapons of mass destruction.[2]

Similar messages came from other allies. Israel's foreign minister, David Levy, welcomed Khatami's win, telling a Knesset meeting it might bring "a positive change to the entire region." Saudi Arabian leaders quickly conveyed official congratulations and hopes for the development of "brotherly relations" between the two countries. The emir of Qatar personally urged Clinton to ease up on the controversial dual containment policy. While other governments' reactions were also hopeful, many indicated they would have to wait and see whether and how the new president might try to change Tehran's international approach.[3]

Initial public statements by President Clinton and other officials accentuated the positive. Clinton used a press conference with British prime minister Tony Blair in late May to remark, "I have never been pleased about the estrangements between the people of the United States and the people of Iran," adding, "they are a very great people." The Americans clearly intended their signals to be read by Tehran, but from the very start the process was hampered by a lack of mechanisms as basic as a reliable channel of communication. When Yeltsin asked if Washington had sent a message to Khatami, he was told yes, but "only through our press spokesman." The Russian leader observed that this was not the same as a private message, which Clinton acknowledged, but he added, "Our relationship with Iran is complicated by the investigation into the Khobar bombing. Some evidence suggests Iranian involvement."[4]

For the rest of Clinton's presidency, despite genuine interest in both capitals for a rapprochement, the skeleton of Khobar would block the path of progress. Administration officials felt the need to call Tehran to account, while trying not to offend Khatami at the same time. Unfortunately, hard-line leaders in Iran accurately read the eventual American message as a direct assignation of their guilt. This was seen as a major insult and the crossing of a cultural red line for the IRI leadership, which demanded respect from the outside world above almost everything. The resulting failure to connect was not from a lack of effort, but the nature of those efforts and the disappointing outcome were direct outgrowths of the bombing itself, which built on previous negative experiences on each side.

◼ Clinton Takes the Lead

Recognizing the need for caution in approaching Tehran, senior American officials were nevertheless eager to move forward. The president himself drove the policy. Former senior National Security Council staff member Bruce Riedel described Khatami's election as "transformative" for Clinton.[5] After a first term characterized by deep wariness of Tehran's motives, the president made clear to aides that improving ties with Iran had risen several rungs on his foreign policy priority list. A routine cabinet reshuffle had brought in new agency heads who were more inclined to go along. Iran's media had taken note of the removal of "the two main anti-Iran cabinet members," Secretary of State Warren Christopher and Secretary of Defense William Perry, expressing the hope that their replacements (Madeleine Albright and William Cohen) would lead the way to improvements. Albright wrote later that both she and Clinton were "intrigued" from the start by the prospect of closer ties with Iran.[6]

One reason for refocusing on Iran was the state of the Arab-Israel peace process. Always the prize in Clinton's Middle East policy program, the goal of a negotiated deal between Israel and its key counterparts, the Palestinians and Syria, had suffered major setbacks prior to 1997 that had negated some significant victories. The assassination of Prime Minister Yitzhak Rabin in November 1995 and the election of Benjamin Netanyahu over Shimon Peres in May 1996 dealt severe blows to American policy after Clinton had personally spearheaded the diplomacy leading to the Oslo Accords of 1993 and 1995. For Assistant Secretary of State Martin Indyk, these were among the reasons the summer of 1996 marked a turning point for US Middle East strategy. Iran, Indyk and others concluded, had been significantly to blame for the virtual collapse of the peace process. Guiding, training, and arming its proxies, Hamas and Hezbollah, Tehran had enabled a series of rocket and suicide attacks against Israeli targets that played directly into the hands of committed opponents of the process such as Netanyahu. The regime's public celebration of Rabin's murder had been chilling for Clinton, who had viewed him as a mentor. If Khatami could be brought into the fold, or at least be persuaded to restrain Iran's radical allies, it might make all the difference in the broader region.

Khatami's arrival was also potentially a boon for the administration because of the breakdown of the dual containment policy. On the Iraq front, Saddam Hussein had proven an effective operator even within the grip of international isolation. Washington had never managed to win the full support of the majority of permanent members of the United Nations Security Council—France, Russia, and China—which, for political reasons and economic self-interest, had begun to peel off from the US lead by late 1996. Saddam Hussein had also managed to exploit the oil-for-food program, skimming billions in profits to help Iraq ease the burden of mainly US sanctions. Domestically, American public opinion was starting to cool on sanctions, which were seen as overly harsh, while Republican conservatives attacked the containment policy as far too soft.

As for Iran, allied protests had been mounting against the dual containment policy's punishment of companies that did business with Iran, especially in the lucrative areas of military sales and nuclear cooperation. Critics pointed out that while the policy might be hamstringing Iran's economy to a degree, it was also hampering Western trade, with few signs of crimping Tehran's WMD ambitions. The *New*

York Times in late 1997 quoted American policy makers describing dual containment as essentially a dead letter; they cited the requirements of the Iran and Libya Sanctions Act from the year before and the possibility of Iran's involvement in Khobar as the main obstacles to a more effective policy. Internal documents show that senior State Department officers working on the Middle East had already reached that conclusion a year earlier, even though Albright continued to promote the policy in public into 1997.[7]

In the weeks following Khatami's election, not much seemed different in Washington's approach, as the political environment initially remained distrustful. Clinton's occasional positive remarks were met with apprehension on the right. In July, some 240 House members from both parties called on the administration to stay strong on sanctions, and influential members warned the government not to be taken in by the seeming changes in Tehran. A month later, Clinton obligingly signed a new executive order expanding sanctions against both Iran and Libya.[8]

Behind the scenes, the White House was wrestling with the conundrum of Khobar. The president's goal was to rein in the Islamic Republic without having to retaliate against it in full for its suspected role in the attack. Intelligence officials came up with a creative approach—quietly outing to their own government the identities of dozens of Iranian operatives around the world. NSC counterintelligence expert Richard Clarke described it as a warning to Tehran: "We have just demonstrated what we can do to hurt you. If your agents continue to engage in terrorism against us, we will hurt you in ways that will severely undermine your regime."[9]

By the fall, the White House had decided that the best approach was to reach out to Iran's new leadership. To that end the State Department engaged the Swiss government, the designated intermediary between the two governments since the revolution. Albright's message via the Swiss was encouraging and featured a proposal to form teams on both sides to initiate a formal dialogue. (A basic lesson of the Iran-Contra fiasco had been never to rely on untrustworthy intermediaries.) She even named the American representatives—Under Secretary of State Thomas Pickering, Principal Deputy Assistant Secretary of State David Welch, and Special Assistant to the President for the Near East and South Asia Bruce Riedel. Their selection was a signal of US seriousness of purpose. But the Iranians never replied. Albright made several more public gestures, such as designating the notorious Mujahedin-e-Khalq opposition group a terrorist organization, which froze their assets and barred members from traveling to the United States. The Iranians appeared to react positively but then demanded stronger legal action. These tepid responses were a disappointment to Washington.[10]

But the picture brightened in the new year. In January, following a series of positive public comments by both presidents, Khatami agreed to give an interview on CNN. In a highly anticipated broadcast, he presented a strikingly different face to American audiences than they were used to from Iran's leadership. His relaxed demeanor, charm, and warm words about the American people and shared values resonated widely. He acknowledged the deep mistrust between the two governments and identified some of the root causes, ranging from the 1953 coup to the recent congressional appropriation of $18 million to overthrow the current regime. Significantly, he expressed regret about the Iran hostage crisis. While he said it was too soon for formal interactions—implicitly explaining the lack of reply to Albright's earlier message—his call for a "dialogue among civilizations" became a refrain for his administration's approach to the West.[11]

The administration focused keenly on the interview. CNN had confidentially invited officials to propose questions, which they did, including one on terrorism against Israelis, to which Khatami remarked, "We condemn every form of [terrorism] in the world." Indyk said later that Khatami had "batted it out of the park," delivering just the kind of signals the Americans were hoping for. In what would become a pattern, though, the reform-oriented president's statements were rebuffed by hard-liners in Iran, including the supreme leader himself, who called the United States "the enemy of the Islamic Republic [and] . . . Islam" and insisted that "we don't need any talks or relations with the United States." Some observers noted that he stopped short of criticizing Khatami personally.[12]

More positive signals were to come. Shortly after the CNN interview, Clinton played host to Palestinian Liberation Organization leader Yasser Arafat, who brought a letter from Khatami saying that, although he did not have great faith in the current peace process with Israel, if it produced terms acceptable to the Palestinians, he would not oppose it. This ran counter to Tehran's hostility to the US-led talks, which had been a core sticking point between Washington and Iran. The Arafat meeting also came just a month after Iran had hosted a summit of the Organization of the Islamic Conference, where conservative Arab leaders allied with the West emerged with a surprisingly favorable view of Khatami. Even Israel's Netanyahu showed signs of supporting a fresh approach to Iran. It was at this point that Albright concluded that "Iran no longer belonged to the same category as Iraq" and that "the time was right to move beyond dual containment."[13]

Over the course of 1998, numerous signals and fitful contacts followed. Clinton delivered messages to Muslims around the world over Voice of America in January and sent "Nowruz" greetings to Iranians in March. Senior US diplomats had close encounters with their Iranian counterparts on several occasions. In Davos, UN ambassador Bill Richardson found an opportunity to shake hands with Foreign Minister Kamal Kharrazi, while Albright planned to do the same with Kharrazi during Six plus Two talks on Afghanistan in September. The latter followed an incident in Mazar-e-Sharif, Afghanistan, in which the Taliban murdered nine Iranian diplomats. The Americans hoped it could provide some common ground between the two governments. But for some reason Kharrazi was absent from the September session and the Iranian side was represented by Deputy Foreign Minister Mohammad Javad Zarif. Embarrassingly, the American delegation mistook Zarif for the minister, revealing a stunning lack of familiarity about their counterparts.[14]

The event that most captured the public's imagination in this period was a competition between American and Iranian wrestlers. The match, held before cheering crowds at Azadi Stadium in Tehran, recalled Nixon and Mao's ping-pong diplomacy from the 1970s, which had helped thaw the ice between two historical adversaries. Afterward, Clinton pointedly invited the US team to the White House as a signal to Iran of the importance he attached to the occasion. At the same time the administration tried another diplomatic approach, sending Vice President Al Gore to Saudi Arabia in May, where he conveyed a message intended for Tehran that made plain Washington's interest in a rapprochement. In June, Albright went public with the same basic message, outlining a "road map" for improving bilateral ties in a major address at the Asia Society in New York. During the UN General Assembly meeting in September, Khatami took the initiative to declare that the fatwa against British author Salman Rushdie—a significant political barrier for the West—was "completely finished," after which Britain and Iran quickly announced plans to renew formal relations. Near year's end, the State Department removed Iran from its list of states involved in the narcotics trade.

But by now a pattern had been set. Seemingly, for every positive step taken by either side a countervailing event occurred, initiated by the other government or by critics in either country. It became common for the supreme leader, a senior figure of the Islamic Revolutionary Guard Corps, or even a foreign ministry official such as Kharrazi himself to counter statements by Khatami or one of his aides, often including a denunciation of the Great Satan. Khamenei routinely rebuffed suggestions that negotiations with Washington might be possible. Kharrazi sent contradictory signals at best, sometimes praising remarks by his American counterparts but just as often diminishing them. A constant refrain, even from Khatami, was that positive words from the United States were welcome but not enough—what were needed were actions. In fact, the signals coming from the United States, which included steady commentary from conservative members of Congress and right-leaning media, were equally mixed.

For the United States, developments inside Iran were another complicating factor. Actions taken by hard-line authorities against their own citizens, from closing reform newspapers to oppressing women and minorities such as the Baha'i, were regularly criticized by the outside world. As one example, stoning was the focus of an influential UN report in April 1998 that stirred universal condemnation. Western aversion toward Iranian behavior intensified over high-profile cases such as the death sentence handed down to a German businessman in early 1998 for allegedly having an affair with a Muslim woman out of wedlock—accompanied by a sentence of ninety-nine lashes for the woman accused. Adding to Western unease was evidence of dangerous regional ambitions, including the ongoing development of a nuclear program and continued testing of advanced weapons such as the Shahab-3 missile, designed in North Korea and able to reach Israel and Saudi Arabia. US assessments that the latter developments were mainly aimed at deterring Iraq, rather than threatening American allies, were largely ignored.[15]

Iran, too, found plenty of reasons to express outrage at the United States. Tehran resented being held up for international opprobrium as "the most active sponsor of state terrorism" by the State Department or being subjected to increased Persian-language broadcasting by the

Voice of America and Radio Free Europe. The regime saw these decisions as still more examples of political interference in its internal affairs. Worse, the ongoing American right-wing campaign against Iran—committing $18 million for covert operations in 1995, for example, or calling for air strikes, as Rep. Newt Gingrich did in 1998—cemented even further the conviction that regime change was Washington's ultimate goal. Hard-liners, including Khamenei, showed little sympathy when US citizens and facilities were the target of attacks, notably the embassy bombings in Kenya and Tanzania in August 1998. While the more pragmatic former president Rafsanjani condemned the bombings, the supreme leader lashed out at US retaliatory strikes in Sudan, calling them expressions of state-sponsored terrorism.

Meanwhile, American military deployments in and around the Persian Gulf loomed as a constant threat over Tehran. Iranian officials kept regularly updated on US force levels and composition out of concern that Iran itself might soon become a target. Ironically, much of the rationale for these intimidating moves, American officials said later, was defensive. The US Navy was indeed bulking up its presence in the Gulf, but largely to compensate for a parallel reduction in ground forces in Arab countries after Khobar. The Pentagon was itself on a high state of alert at the prospect of another terror attack and wanted to make sure US personnel were secure.[16]

Despite the distractions, both the US and Iranian presidents remained interested in better ties. American analysts recognized that Iran's leadership was riven with conflicts over not only relations with the West but also fundamental economic and social issues. Domestic politics in Washington, and even more starkly those in Tehran, were a persistent stumbling block for the objective of closer relations, as opponents tried to make political hay at every opportunity. Still, policy makers assumed that even though a major power play was underway in Tehran, the best thing to do was to keep reaching out to the so-called moderates.

Thus, as 1999 unfolded, the United States tried several more gestures, some of them quite concrete. In April, Clinton delivered what were reported to be off-the-cuff remarks at a White House Millennium Evening event that directly addressed a perennial Iranian grievance: "I think it is important to recognize that Iran, because of its enormous geopolitical importance over time, has been the subject of quite a lot of abuse from various Western nations." He acknowledged that Iran has "a right to be angry at something my country or my culture . . . did to you 50 or 60 or 100 or 150 years ago."[17] These were the most explicit words to date by a US president owning up to past acts against Iran. This was followed by a Treasury Department move to loosen restrictions on Americans' ability to travel to Iran and on Iranians' access to the United States. A few days later came an even more tangible step—a partial repeal of sanctions on food, medicine, and medical equipment. At the end of a busy month, the State Department released its annual terrorism report, which for the first time in years did not place Iran at the top of its list of state sponsors.

However, Iran basically dismissed these gestures. US diplomats had hoped Tehran would read the change to the terrorism list as a positive sign. Instead, the Ministry of Foreign Affairs condemned the State Department for including Iran at all. Kharrazi himself wrote off the sanctions shift as mainly intended to be "good news for American producers." (In fact, this was part of the White House sales pitch to critics.) He granted that he had seen "a change in . . . tone" but no "change in America's behavior."[18] As often happened, Washington seemed unable to make an offer or gesture without tethering to it some kind of offsetting feature to reassure domestic critics. For their part, the Iranians seemed either unable to grasp or unwilling to acknowledge that the Clinton administration also operated under sizable political constraints. Adding to the standard distractions during much of this period was the enormously draining scandal surrounding Monica Lewinsky and the presidential impeachment process.

The Shadow of Khobar in Washington

■ The Letter!

For the Americans, Iran's apathy was increasingly frustrating. As one senior official put it, Tehran "always seemed to be moving the goal-post." Still, the objective of harnessing the opportunity of the reformists' political rise seemed worth the effort. In mid-1999, the president decided to make his most direct pitch to the regime to date. By then, dual containment had run out of gas and the peace process was flagging. When Khatami himself came out in May in support of Palestinians opposed to the current effort, punctuated by personal meetings with Hezbollah leaders Mohammad Hossein Fadlallah and Hassan Nasrallah, it was clear to US officials that the policy was failing dramatically to contain the Islamic Republic.

Other factors also came into play—chiefly Khobar. In 1997 and 1998, *New York Times* columnist Tom Friedman wrote several pieces based on high-level leaks that pinned the blame for the attack on Iran and homed in on the White House's failure to hit back forcefully. In August 1998, he charged that the refusal to punish Iran had harmful consequences, including encouraging the recent embassy attacks in Kenya and Tanzania. The White House suspected that Friedman's source was Louis Freeh, director of the Federal Bureau of Investigation. For Freeh, Khobar had been "a call to action" for the bureau, and he grew increasingly at odds with the White House over what he saw as a lack of political courage to follow where the evidence might lead. Freeh's personal relationship with the president had also soured by then: "I'd fallen off the A-list at 1600 Pennsylvania Avenue," he noted in his memoir.[19]

By November 1998, the Saudis began giving FBI investigators more direct access to interrogations of Khobar suspects. And in early 1999 they turned over their accumulated evidence to Washington. The findings were stark, confirming for many in the intelligence community that senior Iranian officials, primarily from the IRGC and Ministry of

Intelligence, had been behind the attack. Freeh was persuaded by the evidence and became a persistent agitator for retaliation, even though he himself could say only that the new evidence made the case for Iranian authorship *"almost* beyond a doubt."[20]

Still, the groundswell for action by this point put the president and his national security advisor, Sandy Berger, in an extremely awkward position. Their predicament was complicated by a hard-line backlash against the reformists that was just reaching its apex in 1999. The intelligence community continued to monitor Iranian surveillance of American facilities around the world, a reminder that more attacks like those on the Khobar Towers might be in the offing. No Americans had been victimized for some time, but Iran's involvement with radical actors was plain. Within Iran, hard-liners were violently suppressing popular dissent, even murdering high-profile opponents, and anti-American rhetoric flowed. In this environment it was a risk for the United States to reach out, but Clinton (who still "really, really, really wanted" to find an avenue to Tehran, as an aide put it) opted to make at least one more diplomatic foray in order to fend off pressures for military action.

Clinton and his aides finally hit upon the idea to send a letter to Khatami, from one president to another. The intermediary chosen to take the message to Tehran was the foreign minister of Oman, Yusuf bin Alawi. Oman had an unusual history of good relations with both Iran and the United States, and Sultan Qaboos was eager to prove his value to both sides. Meeting in June outside Paris with Clinton's envoys, Martin Indyk of the State Department and Bruce Riedel of the NSC staff, the sultan (in a three-piece suit, heavy woolen coat, and wool hat, despite the heat) enthusiastically supported the plan and approved the letter's contents. Crucially, bin Alawi would also be asked to convey an oral message to the Iranian leader expressing Clinton's high personal regard and desire to achieve a closer bilateral relationship. The minister was instructed to deliver the message to Khatami alone, with no one else present.

The Shadow of Khobar in Washington

The text of the letter has since been made public through the Freedom of Information Act.[21] Although its aim has sometimes been described as being to encourage a political dialogue, it reads much more like an indictment. It begins, "The United States government has received credible evidence that members of the Iranian [sic] Revolutionary Guard Corps (IRGC), along with members of Lebanese and Saudi Hizballah, were directly involved in the planning and execution of the terrorist bombing in Saudi Arabia of the Khobar Towers military residential complex on June 25, 1996." The letter assures Khatami he is not being personally blamed since the bombing occurred prior to his election, but it points out that "those responsible . . . have yet to face justice for this crime."[22]

The only positive note in the text was the statement that the United States "has no hostile intentions towards the Islamic Republic of Iran and seeks good relations with your government." However, the letter immediately continues, "But we cannot allow the murder of U.S. citizens to pass unaddressed." It then demands "a clear commitment from you" to ensure that Iran abandons the use of terror and brings the perpetrators of Khobar to account—"in order to lay a sound basis for better relations."

The letter's authors insist that it was critical to make clear to Khatami that Khobar was a core concern for Washington that could not be dismissed, for a combination of political, legal, and ethical reasons. At some point, the White House's opponents were going to demand strong action. But since the military option had been explored at length—from cruise missile strikes to an all-out invasion—and found to be much too costly, the best way to deflect public criticism was to sound tough with Khatami.

This was why bin Alawi's oral message from Clinton to Khatami was so important. Its content is not entirely known, as noted. Beyond the partial accounts of US officials, the only available evidence is a disputed article from a Kuwaiti newspaper, *Al-Watan*, published a few days be-

Republics of Myth

164

fore the United States received Iran's formal reply. The article went into considerable detail about a purported series of meetings between Iranian and American diplomats to discuss Clinton's letter and larger message, as well as Khatami's reactions. Several claims in the article appear to be false and are certainly wildly at odds with American accounts. At the same time, many of the points attributed to Clinton track with what has since become known about his views and the political state of play during that period. For example, it mentions administration attempts to resist pressures from right-wing and so-called "anti-Iran" interest groups and the US desire for Iran to extradite certain "terrorists." Also interesting is the claim that the Iranians were shown satellite "photographs" and other materials documenting the presence in Iran of "terrorists and members of the Islamic revolutionary organizations and factions" from the region. Former US officials have described the article as "a complicated communication" but also point out that it is "full of invention."[23]

Shortly after the Paris meeting with the sultan, student demonstrations broke out in Tehran. The most serious in years, they forced bin Alawi to delay his visit until later in July. Upon arrival in Tehran, he was met by Khatami's car and driver, which he took to be a positive sign. But when he reached the meeting site, Foreign Minister Kamal Kharrazi was there to escort him to Khatami. He then stayed for the meeting. Bin Alawi pleaded that he had been told to speak only to Khatami, but the president brushed this off, forcing the Omani to deliver both the written and oral messages with Kharrazi present. This later struck Martin Indyk as significant, even decisive, in shaping Iran's eventual reaction. At the time, however, in bin Alawi's view the meeting went very well. Khatami read Clinton's letter and listened to the oral component before declaring encouragingly that he believed Iran could live with the overall import of the message. Bin Alawi reported the results to administration officials, who were duly pleased.

The Iranians did not formally reply for several weeks, however. This was the first bad sign. The second was that the message came not from

Khatami directly or even a high-ranking emissary but through a mid-level foreign ministry functionary assigned to handle communications with the Swiss, in their capacity as caretakers of US interests. The Americans' worst expectations were confirmed when the Iranian reply finally arrived—and was soon leaked to *Al-Watan*. The message took every allegation and statement about their own bad behavior in Clinton's letter and turned it around against the United States. They first flatly denied a connection to the bombing and slammed the United States for its baseless charges. They countercharged that the Americans had failed to bring wrongdoers of their own to justice—namely, the crew of the USS *Vincennes*, who had shot down an Iranian airliner during the Iran-Iraq War—and then, parroting the US demand, they insisted that Washington end its support for "terrorist elements and organizations," by which they meant the People's Mojahedin of Iran. Finally, repeating yet another US statement, the letter declared that the Islamic Republic bore no hostility toward the American people but would "vigilantly and resolutely defend" itself "against any threat."[24]

Some of those most directly involved on the American side said later they had very few expectations of the letter, but they were undeniably disappointed. Previous attempts via the Swiss, the Saudis, and the Six plus Two talks had produced nothing. Plus, there was recognition that both sides had "skeletons" that would not simply disappear. By most accounts the person most disheartened by the failure to open the channel to Khatami was Clinton himself.[25]

After so many prior false starts and dead ends, the Americans saw the Omani gambit as a "Hail Mary," and when it fizzled, the broad consensus was that the Khatami experiment had ended. Even so, the United States did not give up entirely. One more major public event was arranged—a speech by Secretary of State Albright in Washington to mark "Nowruz" in March 2000. Delivered before the American-Iranian Council in Washington, the address was an unreserved call for building a direct relationship between the United States and Iran.

The speech was notable in several respects. After admiring references to Iran's ancient civilization and its continuing importance as a nation, Albright stressed the existence of "much common ground between our two peoples." However, she said, various factors had thrown impediments in the way of closer ties. Among these were mutual perceptions "reinforced" by numerous objectionable Iranian policies over the years. "It is no secret that, for two decades, most Americans have viewed Iran primarily through the prism of the US embassy takeover in 1979," she said. But she acknowledged that the United States had also contributed to the problem and listed three instances: "orchestrating" the 1953 coup; backing the "Shah's regime," which had "brutally repressed political dissent"; and adopting a "regrettably short-sighted" policy toward Iraq during its war with Iran. "Neither Iran, nor we, can forget the past. It has scarred us both. But the question both countries now face is whether to allow the past to freeze the future or to find a way to plant the seeds of a new relationship."[26]

Aware of Tehran's calls for deeds beyond words, Albright announced three specific measures she hoped would provide a foundation for moving the relationship forward: a repeal of the US import ban on carpets and food products (such as pistachios and caviar), removal of constraints on personal and professional contacts, and the resolution of all remaining legal claims at The Hague.

The speech was carefully crafted to be a firm statement of encouragement "for a new and better relationship." Yet, once again, those intentions were derailed by language that inadvertently provoked indignation in the Islamic Republic. Not unexpectedly, the State Department's speechwriters had included references to Iran's bad conduct over the years and to the continuing presence of forces opposed to reform of the country's internal and external policies. While most proponents of rapprochement in Tehran still read the speech with favor, the player who mattered most—the supreme leader—was reportedly incensed by one phrase in particular: "Despite the trend towards democracy, control over the military, judiciary, courts and police remains in unelected hands." According to former foreign ministry official Hossein Mousavian, this was enough to reject the entire package, as Khamenei did in a blistering speech ten days later.[27]

In fact, his reaction had been predicted. NSC staff members who had worked on the draft for weeks flagged the phrase to the State Department as a deal breaker for Tehran but were told it would have to remain in the speech. Once again, the underlying problem was that any official US statement about Iran inevitably had more than one audience—the Iranians themselves and political critics at home. The Clinton administration was unable to find compromise wording that could satisfy both.

Over the remainder of Clinton's presidency, US officials continued to make positive public statements toward Iran, including Martin Indyk's speech at the Asia Society in which he declared that it was time for Iran and the United States, "two great nations," to engage directly on the basis of mutual respect.[28] The American side also tacitly allowed oil deals by companies such as Royal Dutch / Shell to go forward that should have triggered sanctions. And they authorized the sale of Boeing spare parts for Iranian civilian aircraft, a much-discussed topic in the media. In September 2000, Clinton made a point of sitting through the entirety of Khatami's speech to the UN General Assembly, and Khatami returned the courtesy. But these gestures were tempered by the administration's decision to block World Bank loans to Iran and to renew the 1995 executive order banning trade with Iran, as well as Congress's unanimous passage of the Iran Non-Proliferation Act. Developments inside Iran, meanwhile, continued to deteriorate, as exemplified by the arrest and trial of thirteen Jews on charges of spying for Israel, the serial shuttering of reform newspapers, and the attempted assassination of Saeed Hajjarian, an editor and personal friend of Khatami.

Khatami might have been delivering his first administration's epitaph in November 2000 when he made the following extraordinary statement: "I declare that after 3 1/2 years as president, I do not have sufficient powers to implement the Constitution, which is my biggest responsibility."[29] His foreign minister put his own stamp of disapproval on the outgoing Clinton administration, lamenting the lost "historic opportunity" for a breakthrough in bilateral ties.[30]

■ What Went Wrong?

Clinton's letter to Khatami was the culmination of a prolonged effort to build bridges to Iran. The takeaways from the experiences of both sides are instructive. To Clinton's credit, he was able to grasp the fresh opportunity offered by Khatami's election and willing to try to leapfrog the animosities and conflicting narratives of prior decades. But a number of impediments crippled their efforts. Among them was the problem of collective ignorance on both sides. Not to recognize another country's foreign minister by sight was merely embarrassing, but it was a major problem to be unaware that Iran's president did not have the power to take on such a risky initiative by himself. The Iranian side, starting with the supreme leader, was equally ignorant of American conditions, failing, among other things, to account for the inhibiting effects of domestic politics on the White House. Even within Khatami's circle of Western-educated advisers there was little sense of a need to clarify for the Americans the overarching difficulty of initiating direct talks. This would have mitigated the frustration and confusion that ultimately caused the Americans to stop trying.

Domestic politics has long been understood to be a powerful force in shaping foreign policy. Its impact on the Hail Mary letter was critical. The White House was determined to make one more leap in the direction of the reformists in Tehran, but the president's aides also were anxious to demonstrate to skeptics and critics that Clinton would not shy away from addressing the issue of terrorism head-on. That they hoped they could have their cake and eat it—by assuming Khatami could and would act on his own without sharing the letter with the rest of the leadership—was naïve, as its drafters now acknowledge. They argue that it was not outlandish to pose to Khatami the idea of holding the IRGC accountable since he had taken the initiative against the Ministry of Intelligence and Security of Iran after the assassinations of opposition intellectuals. But the Americans lacked sufficient insight to grasp that their accusations would invariably be taken as an indictment of the supreme leader himself and other top officials (much as Albright's statement about unelected hands did). Nor did they anticipate that Khatami's fellow leaders would view it as just another in a series of Western accusations, such as the 1997 German court ruling on the bombing of a Berlin restaurant, which blamed officials at the highest levels in Iran, or earlier American charges of Iranian chemical weapons use at Halabja in Iraq. Regardless of their validity, all of these cases had consequences for future political outreach because they were taken by the leadership in Tehran as unacceptable expressions of disrespect, a cultural artifact of centuries of foreign domination, whose psychological importance American negotiators would apparently grasp only years later.

Could either side have altered its approach and changed the outcome during the Clinton-Khatami era? Different possibilities have been considered. As far as the Clinton letter, an oral-only presentation by the Omani foreign minister might have helped, while holding a written version in abeyance if needed to reassure domestic opponents of the initiative. On a broader level, the United States might have come to the table with a "big offer"—such as significant sanctions relief—rather than a piecemeal approach, which Iranians had seen before.[31] This would have demonstrated seriousness and given the reformists something tangible to wave before the hard-liners. The Americans considered but rejected the idea on three grounds: it would have been unwise tactically without knowing they would get something of equal value in return; domestic critics would never have accepted a unilateral concession of any magnitude; and if sanctions were involved, the law would have required a change in Iran's designation as a terrorist sponsor.

According to Hossein Mousavian, sometime in 1997 officials in Tehran began putting together a major proposal to present to the Americans that would include concrete ideas for trade, cultural, and other components. The package stopped short of political measures such as establishing diplomatic relations because the supreme leader had designated that as a red line for Iran. Mousavian says that the Supreme National Security Council actually ratified the plan by consensus in 1999, even after the disastrous exchange of letters, but that Khamenei stepped in and rejected it, invoking a familiar logic—that to propose it to the United States after Clinton had accused Iran of complicity at Khobar would have been tantamount to an admission of guilt.

If the letter, as Mousavian asserts, had not made Khobar "the center of everything," Iran would have apparently been prepared to take a major step in the direction of rapprochement. If true, it is ironic that the Clinton administration's best hope for obtaining that very goal might have been a major reason for finally killing the possibility. Clinton's former top Middle East adviser on the NSC, Bruce Riedel, later responded to this scenario by saying that if Iran had presented such a comprehensive package, Clinton "would have moved heaven and earth" to make it happen.[32] Instead, it took more than a decade for both sides to decide that the stakes justified crossing their respective red lines.

Bush in the Khatami Era

7 Foreign policy was a low priority for George W. Bush when he came to office in January 2001. The subject broke through only sparingly in the presidential campaign, and he revealed few developed ideas about the direction in which he intended to take the country. His first major speech as president-elect on December 13, 2000, mentioned only that his approach would be bipartisan and involve a strong military. Elsewhere he promised a "humble" foreign policy. For insights, observers therefore often turned to an article published a year earlier by his future national security advisor. Writing in *Foreign Affairs*, Condoleezza Rice spelled out a classic realist's perspective centered around the "enduring national interest," a readiness to exercise power unstintingly in pursuit of that interest, and a resolve to resist the "reflexive appeal" of humanitarian and other "second-order" considerations, which she implied had marred President Clinton's policies.

Relying on Rice for insights into the new president's thinking made sense, as she was his most trusted confidant and tutor on foreign affairs. But predicting how policies might play out in practice would not be so straightforward. Bush's other senior aides, all of whom had strong personalities and sharply defined views, would frequently clash on the most basic issues. Secretary of State Colin Powell was considered a moderate who seemed closer to Rice on most matters. Their respective deputies, Richard Armitage and Stephen Hadley, had similar outlooks. Vice President Dick Cheney and Secretary of Defense Donald Rumsfeld, veterans of George H. W. Bush's administration, were far more hard-line and appointed committed neoconservatives to top posts. The hard-liners staked a claim to a values-based policy approach that included endorsing foreign interventions in the name of promoting democracy. To the surprise of many, Bush did not automatically defer to his father's former advisers. But his lack of depth on policy guaranteed that internal disputes would crop up, even on high-priority issues.

■ First Months

Iran ranked low on the priority list early on. Powell was asked about the subject in his Senate confirmation hearings. He acknowledged significant differences between Washington and Tehran but left the way open for "greater interaction" and "more normal or increased dialogue."[1] The State Department's Office of Policy Planning took up the question and by late January had circulated a paper to Powell and Rice that argued for engagement with Iran and highlighting areas of agreement between the two governments. But the idea did not gain traction, nor did an early paper written for consideration by the Joint Chiefs of Staff (JCS) that concluded that favorable demographics for reformers in Iran meant that political change was "simply a matter of time." Rumsfeld had a far more jaundiced view. He seemed more interested in the Islamic Republic as a military target than a political opportunity. Reviewing existing strike plans, he complained they were out of date and ordered new options for both retaliatory operations and a broader strategic campaign.[2]

Several factors explain the lack of high-level interest in Iran. To begin with, other priorities demanded attention. Iraq was a "festering problem" from the start, Rice noted later, and would soon become a "preoccupation," as would the Arab-Israeli peace process. North Korea, Latin America (Mexico was the president's first destination abroad), China, and Russia were other areas higher on the agenda. The administration's preference for taking a unilateral approach on most issues, exemplified by national missile defense and the Kyoto Protocol, aggravated strains with allies and required more time and attention.

The new team was also sensitive to the embarrassment experienced by previous American presidents after reaching out to the leadership in Tehran. Nothing had worked, they believed, raising serious doubts about whether the effort was worth the investment. Moreover, there was no meaningful political constituency at home pushing for improved relations. While some diplomats and even members of the uniformed military saw reasons to maintain contact with Iran's reformers, the Office of the Vice President and senior civilians at the Pentagon flatly distrusted the regime as a whole, which they hoped and expected one day to see toppled from power.

This suggests another contributing factor to the lack of policy focus on Iran: the enduring problem of unfamiliarity with Iran on the part of Bush and his cabinet, at the deputies' level, and indeed across much of government. Some inside the White House recognized that the deficiency went further than Iran. "While the president's foreign policy team collectively brought with them decades of experience," presidential envoy Zalmay Khalilzad has noted, "none of the principals and very few senior presidential appointees had a feel for the histories, cultures, and emotions that drove the politics of the broader Muslim world." Neither did the specialists, in Khalilzad's view: "This reality was compounded by the dearth of expertise within the permanent bureaucracy."[3] A core limitation, as Rice herself and others have since lamented, was the absence of direct diplomatic representation in Tehran since 1979 (and for years in Kabul as well). A predictable result was limited exposure to Iranian political culture and society, making it more difficult to reassess preconceptions initially formed in the dark days of the hostage crisis two decades before.

One pocket of interest in seeing an opening to Iran existed within the oil industry. Petroleum executives blamed sanctions for ceding lucrative business opportunities to the Europeans and Japanese. Hopes ran high that the new administration would share their outlook. After all, Bush was an ex-oilman and Cheney had been CEO of Halliburton before becoming vice president. In that role, he had criticized the Clinton administration for being "sanction-happy," and in the lead-up to the Iran and Libya Sanctions Act of 1996, he remarked, "The problem is that the good Lord didn't see fit to always put oil and gas resources where there are democratic governments."[4] As it happened, Iran's foreign minister, Sadeq Kharrazi, shared the hopes of Big Oil. He had been unhappy with Clinton's attempts at rapprochement and commented in January 2001 that the "transition of power" in Washington "presented an opportunity" for changes in US policy. In anticipation, he arranged for meetings with the heads of ExxonMobil, Chevron, and Conoco as the new presidency got underway. Iran's oil ministry was equally "encouraging" of major US oil companies, a Halliburton subsidiary noted, adding that the Iranian market offered "huge growth potential."[5]

But the president disappointed those expectations. When it came time to renew official measures against Iran, Bush, who tended to deride Clinton-era policies, supported them in this case. In mid-March 2001, he extended the national emergency declared in 1995, on the grounds that the Islamic Republic continued to "threaten the national security, foreign policy, and economy of the United States."[6] In early August, he renewed ILSA for the maximum five years.[7] Still, these actions did not amount to a coherent policy. The administration had promised a full review on Iran by June, but none emerged, as internal disputes played out for months and then years. Playing into the mix were a succession of both positive and negative developments on the ground, including Khatami's reelection and continuing signs of interest in engagement from Tehran, along with domestic crackdowns and other indications that hard-liners were still in control. Iran policy languished, as Bush was unwilling to bet on the reformers, but at the same time he was never fully comfortable with conservative calls to unseat the regime.

■ September 11

The terrorist attacks of September 11 did not immediately change Washington's approach toward Tehran. Instead, they unexpectedly opened a window for cooperation and created the potential for real breakthroughs beneficial to both sides. President Khatami's immediate public expression of "deep sympathy" for "the American nation"—one of the first by a world leader—and condemnation of the loss of innocent lives surprised Washington. According to Hossein Mousavian, it was an easy decision. The Supreme National Security Council (SNSC) held an emergency session—"one of the shortest meetings" it had ever had—leading to "a very, very rapid conclusion that Iran should immediately condemn [this] and ... cooperate with [the Americans] to pursue the terrorists." Khatami's statement had a dual purpose, Mousavian acknowledged: "There was a personal dimension to this tragedy," a desire to express genuine outrage, but also a sense that "we've got to fend off" the inevitable allegations that "Iran is part of it." Still, the message of condolence was by all accounts genuine. Rafsanjani soon followed, calling the attacks a "bitter human catastrophe." Even Khamenei allowed that "Islam condemns any massacre and the killing of innocent people," although he added that the United States could not escape judgment for its own actions.[8] The State Department thanked Tehran through the Swiss diplomatic channel.

Iran's supportive public statements led Powell to broach the idea of engaging with the Islamic Republic on the Sunday talk shows less than a week after the attacks: "We have serious differences with the government of Iran because of their support for terrorism. But they have made a statement and it seems to me a statement that is worth exploring to see whether or not they now recognize that this (terrorism) is a scourge on the face of the earth." He had already tasked his department to come up with a plan to get rid of Osama bin Laden that would include Iran, dangling the prospect of a strategic relationship with Washington as an inducement.[9] Simultaneously, others in the administration were drawing up very different plans. Notably, the office of Undersecretary of Defense for Policy Douglas Feith put together a PowerPoint for his superiors that labeled Iran a target in the war on terror. But that idea was shelved, at least for the time being, in part because of the practical military considerations involved and the growing inclination within the Pentagon for pursuing Iraq first.

A key factor in favor of working with Tehran was its close relationship with the Northern Alliance in its fight against the Taliban. The Alliance's charismatic leader, Ahmad Shah Masoud, had been assassinated just before 9/11. For Iran's part, hard-liners and reformists on the SNSC found rare consensus on whether to join America's war on terror—at least in next-door Afghanistan. Khamenei seemed to signal the opposite view, at least in public. Responding to Bush's admonition to the world—"Either you are with us, or you are with the terrorists"—the supreme leader insisted, "Iran will provide no help to America and its allies . . . in an attack on suffering, neighboring, Muslim Afghanistan." But Khamenei's rhetoric often masked undercurrents of regime thinking. Two days later, Rafsanjani flatly contradicted him: "Despite all our differences, we are willing to join the US-led coalition, under the umbrella of the United Nations"—as long as "America does not impose its own view." He could not have spoken so bluntly without the supreme leader's approval.[10]

After much discussion, the SNSC decided that collaboration was worth the risk. Washington was almost certainly going to strike anyway, so the thinking went, and Iran might derive significant benefits in its long-standing dispute with the Taliban, among them expanding its influence in the Muslim world and South Asia, and possibly improving its image in the West. According to Mousavian, the chance of a broader rapprochement was a factor. "Really, the idea, the hope . . . was in case of success, then this would become a pilot plan for further cooperation between Iran and the U.S. . . . to bring security, stability. . . . This was the mindset." Even the celebrated Qods Force commander Qasem Soleimani was in favor of working with the Americans. "The interesting issue was the positive reaction of the Revolutionary Guards," Mousavian remembered. "Qasem was one of the proponents of cooperating with the U.S., and if we didn't have his cooperation, it would never succeed at all. . . . The reality was, everything was in the hands of Qasem and the Revolutionary Guards, and the Qods Army, and he was really positive and hopeful." Ambassador Ryan Crocker, who headed several US diplomatic missions in the region during this period, confirmed this, recalling that an Iranian contact at the time "would tell me flatly that . . . Soleimani was running the policy" and that during a "brief window" after September 11 "even Soleimani thought that maybe we could do business together."[11]

Some officials in Washington also saw reasons for cooperating with Tehran. During the presidential transition, George Tenet, director of the Central Intelligence Agency, had advised that Iran and its proxies had an "extensive array of off-the-shelf contingency plans for terrorist attacks."[12] But at the time the United States was more focused on Al-

Qaeda, an entity also reviled by Tehran. In the months prior to 9/11, the Intelligence Community had forwarded a stream of reports to the White House about the threat from Osama bin Laden and his group—at least three dozen items made it into the President's Daily Brief, and the idea of exploring ways to confront a common enemy seemed logical.

For the next several months, out of the public eye, an extraordinary series of meetings took place between American and Iranian officials. The so-called Six plus Two group on Afghanistan (consisting of the country's six neighbors—China, Iran, Pakistan, Tajikistan, Turkmenistan, and Uzbekistan—plus Russia and the United States) had consulted regularly since 1997, occasionally providing a forum for brief interactions between top-ranking officials such as Madeleine Albright, Kamal Kharrazi, and Javad Zarif. After 9/11, the meetings took on greater significance. Neither Washington nor Tehran would officially concede that they had a broader purpose. In fact, opponents of the sessions, such as Paul Wolfowitz and William Luti at the Department of Defense and John Bolton at the State Department, would only acquiesce to them if they were limited to covering Afghanistan and did not involve high-level participants. Powell would publicly acknowledge only that "we have contacts with the Iranians at an interesting level, and we are receiving signals, and we will explore opportunities with them."[13]

Ryan Crocker participated in most of the sessions, including the key ones from September 2001 to the following May. Other participants over the next two years included Hillary Mann and Zalmay Khalilzad of the National Security Council staff. The chief Iranian intermediary for much of the period was ambassador to Afghanistan Mohammad Taherian, along with a deputy foreign minister and an Islamic Revolutionary Guard Corps general who served as a liaison with the Northern Alliance. All three reportedly had close ties to IRGC commander Maj. Gen. Yahya Rahim Safavi and to Khamenei. Future foreign minister Zarif attended the final three meetings. The two sides met either in Geneva at the Intercontinental Hotel or at various locales in Paris. The US side was impressed by the Iranians' professionalism, knowledge, and constructive behavior.[14]

The Americans were also surprised by the Iranians' eagerness to take joint action, pressing for military engagement at the very first meeting after 9/11. "The sweep of history and the geopolitics of the Middle East," they told Crocker, "made Iran and the United States natural allies." At the second session, in November, the Iranians produced a map of targets, which the Americans passed to Washington. Over time, the two sides consulted on the overthrow of the Taliban and dealing with Al-Qaeda members fleeing Afghanistan, agreed on the need for stability in the country, and consented to work together to form a new government in Kabul. The Iranians even offered the use of airfields and ports (rejected by the Americans) and protection for downed US pilots.[15] As part of a pattern that would reappear over the next several years, the Iranians made plain that they hoped for more from the United States, steering the talks to other sensitive topics, including Lebanon, Iraq, and terrorism. The State Department began to put together a set of proposals to pursue in case the idea gained traction, but evidently it went nowhere at the time. Even Deputy Secretary Armitage doubted that Tehran would ever agree to Washington's inevitable demands.[16]

In the wake of Operation Enduring Freedom, the question of Afghanistan's post-Taliban future came to the fore. Aside from Khamenei's intonations against America's pursuit of "colonial interests" and "dragging the world into a war," the atmospherics in October suggested growing acceptance of the idea of cooperation. A Majles commission proposed direct talks, while former IRGC commander Mohsen Rezaie publicly made a case for Iran's importance to resolving the situation. The media reported ongoing "quiet signals" between the two sides, including an agreement that Iran would conduct search-and-rescue missions for US pilots if needed and allow tons of US wheat to unload at Iranian ports for transfer to Afghan refugees. Western diplomats consulted with counterparts in Tehran, who told them the Americans had a right to punish the perpetrators and reportedly urged them not to "leave the job unfinished like you did in Iraq." A London-based Arabic newspaper printed that senior Lebanese Hezbollah figure Imad Mughniyah, linked for years to high-profile terrorist attacks, had been "persuaded" to leave Iran (although the FBI doubted it). Senator Arlen Specter, known for his vocal support for Israel, hosted Hadi Nejad Hosseinian, Iran's ambassador to the United Nations, for dinner with colleagues in a private Senate dining room.[17]

More positive signs surfaced in November. While in New York to attend the annual UN General Assembly sessions, Khatami gave a major interview to the *New York Times*, his first with an American publication since becoming president four years earlier, in which he rejected bin Laden's message and insisted that "the Moslem world in general wants peace." He garnered positive attention by implying more flexibility on the sensitive matter of the peace process, declaring, "Of course it is up to the people of Palestine themselves ... whatever all the Palestinians want must be accepted by the entire world." During the UN General Assembly session, senior US officials took further note when Kharrazi added impromptu condolences to his prepared remarks after a passenger airliner crashed near LaGuardia Airport. Kharrazi's aides made sure that Powell saw his handwritten addendum, and the two shook hands afterward. And when New York police detained an Iranian advance team after observing them with a video camera at the Midtown Tunnel and discovered some fifty passports in their van, a government spokesman waved it off: "The police and other agencies behaved in a very professional manner."[18]

■ The Bonn Conference

On November 13, Kabul fell to the Northern Alliance. Within twenty-four hours the United Nations passed Resolution 1378, calling for a conference of Afghan leaders to set up a transitional government. This was the immediate prelude to the most significant round of US-Iran talks since before the revolution. By late October, the Bush administration had begun preparing for multilateral talks that would determine Afghanistan's political future. Powell appointed State Department official James Dobbins, a veteran of post-conflict diplomacy in Somalia, Haiti, Bosnia, and Kosovo, to lead the US delegation. There was a consensus in Washington on the need to work swiftly to nail down a political solution while the Taliban was still reeling from the US-backed military assault. Most Iran hawks went along, given the stakes in Afghanistan.[19]

Later that month, Dobbins arrived in the former West German capital. The United States was a key driver of the conference, along with the United Nations, its nominal host. Dobbins and the United Nations' chief representative at the talks, Lakhdar Brahimi, had consulted about its makeup beforehand. Dobbins argued that all parties involved in the ongoing Afghan civil war should be included since they would have a stake in the outcome. Brahimi believed that the Afghans themselves should be the only participants. The solution was to invite all concerned to the venue, where they could consult with their factional allies on the margins, but only the Afghans would be in the actual negotiations.[20]

Shortly after his arrival, Dobbins received a message that members of the Iranian delegation wanted to meet. It was not a surprise since—armed with Powell's permission—he had previously asked Brahimi to let them know he hoped they could work together. The meeting took place late in the evening in Dobbins's hotel room. Mohammad Taherian, the diplomat who was part of the Six plus Two talks, expressed opposition to allowing exiled King Zahir Shah to head the new government and instead proposed Hamid Karzai. Dobbins had heard the same from the Pakistanis and their adversaries the Northern Alliance. His conclusion at the end of the conversation was positive: as far as

Afghanistan's governing structure, American and Iranian "objectives . . . were largely coincident."[21]

Dobbins had Powell's consent to speak to the Iranians, but he also understood that being far from Washington and mostly out of the glare of attention would allow him maximum discretion as the head of the US delegation. He was aided by the Muslim calendar: the Bonn talks coincided with Ramadan, so many of the guests waited until evening to take their meals. According to Dobbins, the Iranians chose to take a more flexible approach, adhering to a Shi'a practice of delaying the fast until they were back home from their travels. This meant that they and the Americans were sometimes essentially alone in the spacious dining hall at the conference venue. Early on, encouraged by German and Italian representatives, Dobbins arranged to have coffee and cake with the Iranians each morning, where they talked over the previous day's developments and what to expect next. The two delegations would then discuss things among themselves, "and then we'd go off and talk to the Afghans," Dobbins recalled. Most mornings the two sides "shared stories" and "built personal relationships," according to NSC staffer Zalmay Khalilzad, who credited the meetings with paving the way for resolving some of the issues raised at the conference.

On the second or third day, Brahimi circulated an initial draft of a concluding statement, essentially an interim constitution for the country, for comment by participants. Dobbins described what happened the next morning:

> I remember, I think Zarif must have gotten up earlier than the
> rest of us because he actually had read it by the time we sat
> down, and most of the rest of us had just thumbed through it.
> So he said he found one deficiency in this document and I said
> what was that? And he said, well, it doesn't make any mention
> of democracy and there's no reference to elections, which we
> want to be urgent—the Afghans to commit themselves to de-

mocracy and elections. So, at that point the Bush Administration hadn't discovered democracy in the Middle East, and I had no particular instruction, and so I agreed.

And then Zarif, with a certain twinkle in his eye, just pointed out that he was tweaking me. He said, also there's something else missing here ... there's no mention of international terrorism. Don't you think we should put a clause in this in which we can get the Afghans to cooperate against international terrorism? So I agreed to that, too, as a benign suggestion and eventually clauses of this sort I think were introduced into the document.[22]

There were no illusions that the Iranians and Americans shared each other's broader objectives or perspectives. Khalilzad said the Iranians would regularly protest when they thought the Northern Alliance was being pressured too hard. At one point an Afghan representative warned Dobbins that Zarif's team was being misleading about Iran's views on the constitutional process. Based on their rapport, Dobbins felt able to confront Zarif and insist that they needed to be in agreement not only in order to win an accord but also to ensure its implementation. According to Dobbins, "once I had that conversation, the problem went away and the next day, I talked to [the Afghan delegate] about this and he said 'yes, yes, the Iranians agree with you.' So, whatever the problem was, it was solved as the result of that candid but very polite discussion."[23]

For Dobbins, "the critical Iranian contribution" was yet to come. On the last night of the conference, a final stumbling block arose over the naming of ministers for the new government. The Northern Alliance wanted to be able to appoint more seats than other factions were willing to concede. At a late-night, multilateral session, various national representatives tried to persuade Younis Qanooni, leader of the Northern Alliance delegation, to trim his demands, but without success. Finally, according to Dobbins, Zarif took Qanooni aside for "no more than a minute," and when they returned Qanooni announced his willingness to agree to create two new ministries while keeping to the number of positions he had insisted on controlling. The result was a higher number of seats that other factions could appoint—and a breakthrough that led to the signing of the Bonn Declaration the following day.

The Bonn conference produced a new constitution for Afghanistan that included the crucial buy-in of the country's neighbors. It led to the election of a viable leader, Hamid Karzai, and provided a reasonable foundation for rebuilding Afghanistan's broken political structures. The two senior American delegates came away convinced that their counterparts from the Islamic Republic had played a significant part in each of these crucial advances, which benefited all sides. Dobbins reported the experience to Washington.

Several weeks later, another opportunity for cooperation—and signaling—arose at the Tokyo donors conference on Afghanistan, attended by representatives of sixty-one countries and twenty-one international organizations. On the first day, Iran set the pace by pledging $560 million to help with Afghan reconstruction, almost half of the $1.3 billion committed by the major Western donors plus Japan. As the event wound down, an Iranian diplomat approached Dobbins to inform him that Tehran was interested in pursuing talks on topics beyond Afghanistan. Dobbins said he was not authorized to do so himself but would pass the message along. Simultaneously, Sadako Ogata, a former UN high commissioner for refugees, passed a written message to Treasury Secretary Paul O'Neill, who was also in attendance, saying that the Iranians proposed a formal dialogue with the United States covering all matters in dispute. O'Neill passed the word to Rice and the State Department.[24]

While these attempts at building rapport were taking place, other American officials were pursuing an entirely contradictory line toward Iran. The driver of one such effort was Michael Ledeen, a conservative think tank analyst specializing in terrorism. In the mid-1980s, while a consultant to Reagan's NSC staff, Ledeen had pressed the president's national security advisor to take part in a new channel the Israelis were developing to explore contacts with elements of the Iranian government. The main intermediary in that initiative was Manucher Ghorbanifar, a notorious arms dealer whom the CIA had previously dismissed as a wholly unreliable source.[25] The White House nevertheless went along, resulting in the disastrous Iran-Contra affair, which almost crippled the Reagan presidency. Ghorbanifar was universally blamed for his deceitful conduct toward all sides.

Somehow Ledeen remained loyal to Ghorbanifar, and in the wake of September 11 he found a new opportunity to promote him as an inside source on Iranian terrorism. In late 2001, he contacted officials at the DOD and on the NSC staff and proposed a series of meetings. One senior official who proved receptive was Stephen Hadley, the deputy national security adviser, although Ledeen reportedly did not identify Ghorbanifar by name. Hadley had been on the staff of the Tower Commission appointed by Reagan in 1987 to investigate and draw lessons from the Iran-Contra affair; had he known that Ghorbanifar was involved, he presumably would have turned the proposition down flat. Instead, he gave Ledeen the go-ahead and then notified State, CIA, and DOD. Unaccountably, Hadley in turn failed to name Ledeen, whose own reputation in Washington was dubious. Deputy Defense Secretary Wolfowitz agreed to have his department coordinate, and that month two Pentagon officials, including one who was attending the Bonn conference at the time, set off discreetly to meet Ledeen's source in Rome.

For anyone familiar with Ghorbanifar's history, his presentation to the Americans would have immediately raised alarms. For example, he alleged that Iran had put together hit squads that it planned to deploy against US forces in Afghanistan, a claim almost identical to one he had made more than fifteen years earlier that led the CIA to issue a fabricator notice against him. Not surprisingly, in 2001, as he had during Iran-Contra, Ghorbanifar insisted the CIA be excluded from the discussions. He went on to sketch out for the Americans a plot for regime change that called for stoking popular unrest by, among other schemes, creating traffic gridlock in Tehran. He asked for $25 million to implement the plan.[26]

One of the two Americans present recommended against the operation to his superiors afterward, but both vouched for the usefulness of Ghorbanifar's information on the picture inside Iran. A senior DOD official therefore proposed to Wolfowitz that the meetings continue but that they be handled by the Defense Intelligence Agency. The Ghorbanifar channel might have persisted had the US ambassador in Italy not raised questions after meeting with Ledeen. Ambassador Melvin Sembler told the CIA's Rome station chief and evidently the State Department about his concerns; by February both the secretary of state and CIA director were demanding the channel be shut down. Armitage, another Iran-Contra veteran, recalled warning Hadley, "If Ghorbanifar sets one foot in an embassy, he'll be arrested. This is the man who almost single-handedly brought down the president's father, and you are responsible for having him feed us misinformation again. We knew then and we know now that he is an Iranian agent!"[27]

Dobbins later reflected on how the Ledeen-Ghorbanifar conduit might have impeded the quest to build mutual trust with Iran. "I only found out about this a year or two later, but in the U.S. Government, we were constantly saying, 'Well, the Iranians are playing a double game . . . they have intelligence agents that are doing things in Afghanistan that are . . . [the] antithesis of our interests. . . . And at the same time they were being cooperative. . . . These are not rogue elements. This is a concerted effort to deceive us.'" And yet the Americans could justifiably have been seen doing something very similar. "Here we had the U.S., who was at the one time cooperating with them, and senior

Defense Department officials who had actually been in the meeting in Bonn were then going to Rome to meet with, you know, violent opposition elements." It was possible Tehran had been aware of the Rome meetings, but perhaps not. If not, "would they have thought that this was a rogue American operation, which it was, or that we were playing a double game?"[28]

The Window Shuts

If the months immediately following 9/11 raised a few hopes for a new direction in bilateral relations, 2002 lowered them dramatically. Reports on the positive interactions in Bonn and later Tokyo percolated up to senior policy makers but failed to curb the prevailing distaste for cooperating with the Islamic Republic. By then, events had begun to unfold from Iran to the Gulf to Washington itself that ratcheted administration opposition to closer ties to new levels, pushing back the prospects to well into Bush's second term.

The new year began with yet another incident that seemed to paint Iran as a chronic bad actor. On January 3, Israeli forces intercepted the vessel *Karine A* in the Red Sea and seized its cargo of 50 tons of weapons. The Israeli government charged that its destination was the Palestinian Authority under Yasser Arafat and that the shipment had originated in Iran. The United States found Israel's arguments "compelling." Powell commented, "It is clear from all the information available to us that the Palestinian Authority was involved. . . . It's a pretty big smoking gun." According to Mousavian, the SNSC looked into the incident and came to the "very clear conclusion" that it was a "very well organized, orchestrated scenario by the Israelis" who wanted to "impede Iran-U.S. cooperation in Afghanistan."[29] Some in the State Department shared the same view initially, but to most observers the incident was hard evidence that Iran was still committed to backing international terrorists and sabotaging the peace process.

Hard-liners in the US administration used the episode to ramp up their case for terminating any warming trend with the Islamic Republic and clearing the path to regime change. A few days after the *Karine A* seizure, Rice distributed draft talking points for a new national security directive on Iran policy that was being prepared. The memo noted Iran's uncooperativeness in certain areas but indicated that the United States was ready to consult on "practical issues" related to Iraq such as weapons of mass destruction. The reaction at the DOD was alarm, according to a Pentagon historian. Senior aides complained to Rumsfeld that Rice's points undermined the objective to delegitimize the regime. Rumsfeld in turn wrote to the vice president, calling for the Geneva discussions to be terminated. Until then, the US diplomats involved had mostly been left to operate with few instructions, and it may have gotten back to the Pentagon that the scope of the talks had gone beyond Afghanistan. One day later, on January 10, President Bush reflected a harsher tone with Iran, publicly warning the regime not to interfere in Afghanistan, or "the coalition will deal with them." Soon, Rumsfeld had another opportunity to speak out at an NSC briefing, in which he opposed an opening to the regime. Instead, he advocated for siding with the Iranian opposition against a government whose collapse was seen as imminent and welcomed.[30]

The biggest blow to bilateral diplomacy in this period came at the end of January in President Bush's State of the Union address. Declaring it a US goal "to prevent regimes that sponsor terror from threatening America or our friends and allies with weapons of mass destruction," the speech lumped North Korea, Iraq, and Iran together into an imagined "axis of evil, arming to threaten the peace of the world." The administration saw the address as the "first opportunity for the president to set a new direction for our national security policy," Rice said afterward. But the formulation—which officials attributed to a speech-writer trying to produce a "great line"—only created confusion for observers everywhere and outrage in Tehran. Rice acknowledged that she and the president were "stunned" at the public focus on the "axis" phrase, although Bush made it sound like it was part of a strategy: "I doubt the students and the reformers and the liberators inside Iran were displeased with that. I made the calculation that they would be pleased." Against the backdrop of mounting pressures to take the war to Iraq—and even Iran—there was a rush to deny the implication of an alliance among the three states or the existence of plans to use force in every instance. "But, admittedly," Rice wrote in her memoir, "the harsh language suggested that negotiation was impossible." Even the neoconservative DOD official Doug Feith recognized the differences among the three cases. For example, unlike with Iraq, "when it came to North Korea and Iran, President Bush could *not* say that the United States had run the string on diplomacy, economic pressure, UN actions, or military operations short of war." Still, Feith praised "axis of evil" as a "seminal formulation."[31]

Predictably, Iran's leadership reacted with indignation, but also with growing anxiety about Washington's military intentions. Ayatollah Khamenei railed against "arrogant, aggressive, and hypocritical U.S. policies" and called Bush a man "thirsty for human blood." Officials from the foreign and defense ministries warned the administration against any attacks, saying they would be a "huge, irreparable mistake." The controversial Massoumeh Ebtekar, vice president for the environment and a former spokesperson for the 1979 US embassy hostage takers, called Bush's statement a "strategic mistake" that would only unite the population in the face of more unilateral American interference. According to Khatami policy adviser Hadi Semati, most of Iran's citizens agreed, viewing the speech as "a disrespectful way of characterizing Iran at a public forum." Contrary to Bush's claim, "The public anger was there."[32]

Ryan Crocker, who had recently been appointed the number two diplomat at the American embassy in Kabul, felt the impact of the address immediately. The next day, one of his Iranian interlocutors railed, "You completely damaged me." Worse, Qasem Soleimani had reportedly just told aides, "Maybe it's time to rethink our relationship with the Americans." Now, he was said to be "in a tearing rage. He feels compromised." Crocker lamented this turning point years later, telling a reporter, "We were just that close." From his vantage point, "one word in one speech changed history." The supreme leader and the influential Qods Force commander, he believed, simply "wrote us off." Mousavian largely confirmed this view: "Iranians, they got the message that the U.S. is not prepared to continue cooperation."[33]

■ Last Throes

Despite the blow, Crocker reported that "the talks did go on," although they were now more "stilted and non-substantive" and tended toward "an exchange of assertions, allegations, and denials." Much has been made about Bush's offensive language, which certainly had a negative effect, but references to the use of force more likely generated a stronger reaction in Tehran. After all, Iran had been demanding "Death to America" for decades. As Dobbins pointed out later, rather than Bush's phrase itself, "it was the American policy that flowed from the 'axis of evil'" that posed the more fundamental problem, "a policy of non-engagement and not taking up multiple offers." The Iranians deliberately missed the next Six plus Two session in Geneva in February, but they picked up again the following month. Semati credited Iran's continued interest to certain figures within the IRGC, who had taken away positive experiences from the Bonn conference. "They were still ready to go," and, more than any other players on the Iranian side, they had the "political capital to move the process in favor of engagement." But the atmosphere had clearly changed—"the heart went out of the negotiations," as Crocker put it—after senior US officials moved to close the channel down.

Notwithstanding the demands of Rumsfeld, Cheney, and their aides, it took until almost mid-2003 to achieve their goal. During that time, debates within the administration had continued with neither side able to hold sway. At the start of the first term, the aim had been to produce a review of the Clinton team's approach by early summer 2001. State's Policy Planning staff had churned out its first effort to Powell and Rice within weeks of the inauguration, laying out "essentially what we would do if we ever did talk to Iran," according to Lawrence Wilkerson, Powell's then chief of staff. But within the department, and even within specific bureaus, there continued to be "a lot of argument" and "controversy," Wilkerson said. "No-one could seem to come to a decision."

The Pentagon and Office of the Vice President were where the strongest voices opposing engagement with Iran could be heard. There, Iran was typically viewed through the prism of Iraq, the war on terror, or nonproliferation, and regime change was a constant theme in policy papers coming out of Feith's Office of Special Plans and other bureaus within the Office of the Secretary of Defense. Early on, the theoretical impact on Iran played into the rationale for ousting Saddam Hussein. A popular premise was that free elections leading to a representative government in Baghdad (and in Kabul) could produce demands for the same from unhappy Iranians, thereby further unsettling a fragile regime. Another claim was that a post-Saddam, majority-Shi'ite Iraq might help neutralize the Islamic Republic's regional influence by becoming an alternative rallying point for Shi'ism. (Najaf was seen as having a more exalted tradition than Qom, and Ayatollah Sistani held a higher religious rank than Khamenei, so the thinking went.) Yet another idea, subscribed to by the JCS, was that a newly empowered neighbor could put the mullahs in Tehran on the defensive and lead them to pull back support for terrorism or the pursuit of WMD. After Operation Iraqi Freedom, it became virtually an article of faith for administration hard-liners that the Islamic Republic was on the verge of collapse and that it would be morally wrong to prop it up or legitimize it through engagement. This made Rice's already ambivalent efforts to find consensus even more ineffectual.[34]

In mid-July 2002, events in Iran seemed to open a pathway for the administration. After a fresh round of demonstrations and the resignation of a respected cleric, Ayatollah Jalaleddin Taheri, whose blunt letter of criticism to Khamenei was published in a reform daily, President Bush issued a statement in his own name excoriating the country's "unelected" leaders and praising its citizens for demanding "the same freedoms, human rights, and opportunities as people around the world." Bush declared that the "future of Iran will be decided by the people of Iran" and promised that "they will have no better friend than the United States." The statement was widely overlooked in the West initially, although it sparked anger in the Islamic Republic. Eleven days later, the *Washington Post* wrote that a "policy shift" had taken place— that the administration had "abandoned hopes" of working with Iran's government reformists and would now focus on "appealing directly to democracy supporters among the Iranian people." Sources told the *Post* it was a victory for the NSC and the Pentagon in the wake of an "intense debate" that flared after the "axis of evil" pronouncement.[35]

In fact, the July 12 statement was entirely of a piece with a broader effort to define the administration's approach to the new world order that followed September 11. The State of the Union address presented the first opportunity to do so. Before the speech, Rice had prepped the media on the intended message: "America will take the side of brave men and women who advocate [democratic] values around the world, including the Islamic world." That point, of course, became lost in the blowback over the "axis of evil." A fuller elaboration would come in the September 2002 National Security Strategy (NSS), which enunciated the US commitment to "create a balance of power that favors human freedom" and reminded Americans "that we are ultimately fighting for our democratic values and way of life." Like the seminal Cold War policy paper its authors sought to emulate, NSC-68, the new strategy was based on a definition of the moral underpinnings of American policy, which pitted the United States, "sustained by faith in the principles of liberty, and the value of a free society," against the "enemies of civilization."[36] The NSS won praise as a fundamental reconfiguration of grand strategy, the first in more than half a century, but it also encapsulated a retreat to sweeping and comfortably familiar formulations of American identity and mission that justified seeing the world in good-and-evil terms and therefore precluded dealings with morally distasteful regimes. By incorporating these reflexive mindsets into official policy, the new approach buttressed subsequent rejections of promising Iranian overtures.

Still, the NSS did not finally settle the direction of Iran policy. Instead, it set off an internal debate about the feasibility of its proposals for dealing with North Korea and Iran, a debate that was still "roaring" at the end of the first term, according to Powell aide Wilkerson. The vice president, he recalled, generally held the stronger hand, in part because he was content to have no formal decision on an Iran policy because that contributed to his goal of "no talking, period." Cheney may not have focused on the fact that meetings with Iranians on Afghanistan had resumed after a short pause in 2002. Also, a new Track 2 initiative got underway late that year, initiated by several retired diplomats on the US side and primarily Zarif on the other. The Americans kept William Burns, assistant secretary of state for the Near East, informed, and over time the participants grew confident enough in the foundation they were laying to envision a future session where Burns and Kharrazi could announce formal plans for improving bilateral ties.[37]

Events nonetheless continued to raise obstacles. Planning for the impending war with Iraq was ramping up. Rumsfeld and his colleagues kept up the pressure internally for regime change in Iran. Eventually, Rice gave up on the languishing draft policy directive. A complicating factor was the August 2002 disclosure through the National Council of Resistance opposition group (of which the People's Mojahedin of Iran was a component) that Iran had secretly been operating a uranium enrichment facility at Natanz and another nuclear site at Arak. The revelation created a political stir in public, which made the case for dialogue more difficult, although Wilkerson claims it was nowhere near a "showstopper" for Powell, whose fundamental stance continued to be "We still want to talk."[38]

A more significant impediment during this period was the question of what to do about the Al-Qaeda forces that had filtered into Iran among the surge of refugees fleeing Afghanistan. The United States demanded more than once that Tehran turn them over, and sometimes Iran responded positively, as they did in January 2002 when they handed copies of two hundred passports of Arab refugees to the United Nations with assurances the holders either had been or soon would be deported. At other times, Tehran insisted they had placed hundreds of suspects under house arrest and complained that they could not be expected to police the entire border. The American side was not having it, however. Most officials assumed this was not the full story, and Washington reacted especially badly when it was strongly suspected that Abu Musab al-Zarqawi, the leader of Al-Qaeda in Iraq, was operating in Iran. The dispute would drag on for more than a year, both within the framework of private talks and in high-level public recriminations from both sides.[39]

The Geneva channel finally shut down in mid-2003. The tipping point was a series of truck bombs that exploded in the Saudi capital in May 2003, killing thirty-four, including nine Americans. US intelligence had picked up signals that Al-Qaeda elements in Iran were planning some kind of attack, prompting Ryan Crocker to fly to Geneva to intercede with his counterparts, but without result. Whether high-level circles in Tehran had been connected—the same question that arose after the Khobar Towers bombing—was not conclusively determined, but that was immaterial to the fate of the private negotiations. The Riyadh attacks played directly into the hands of opponents of engagement. The talks had survived numerous political shocks since fall 2001, continuing even after the Iraq invasion and through the end of combat operations.[40]

Finally, as often happened, the accumulation of developments on the ground fed into existing conceptions, building suspicions and making it impossible, for the time being at least, to sustain the argument for engagement. Rice's realist perspective, embedded in her vision for shaping Bush administration policy toward the world, became a victim of its own presumptions when it came to the Islamic Republic. The United States would not interact directly with Tehran for another three years.

The Iraq War and Its Consequences

8 The roiling confrontation that was US-Iran relations in the 1980s and 1990s was mostly about clashing interests, ideologies, and national narratives, but a number of ancillary players and events intensified it. These sideshows included the rise of the Taliban, 9/11, and the US war in Afghanistan; the long-brewing animus between Israel and Iran; and Iran's parlous relations with several Arab states, such as Saudi Arabia, but most consequentially with Iraq. Iran and Iraq became ensnared in a relationship of tangled loyalties and entwined religious history, but also of different strands of development and self-identity. There was nothing inevitable in their mutual animosity. Yet their sharply differing understandings of their own destiny brought them into lethal conflict, one that the United States played a role in constructing. That conflict then became a hurdle of its own in Washington-Tehran relations.

As noted earlier, the poisonous climate in the Gulf that provoked the Iran-Iraq War in 1980 continued through the next dozen years. Both states were at first weakened by the devastation of war, but they survived and continued to play their hands as before—Iran, the revolutionary Shi'a theocracy; Iraq, secular, authoritarian, and increasingly built on a cult of personality. Both oil rich, they maintained ambitions beyond their borders. In Iraq, such ambitions—for Saddam Hussein to be seen as the bold leader of the Arab world—soon manifested in the ill-considered invasion and occupation of Kuwait in August 1990, just two years after the conclusion of the war with Iran.

Iraq's action to assert its alleged right to its "nineteenth province," a move that seemed to be passively accepted by the US ambassador in Baghdad and was met in the first hours with a tepid response by President George H. W. Bush, soon became the focal point of global diplomatic attention and military preparedness. Notably, Iraq's occupation of Kuwait was preceded by a period of turmoil in the Organization of Petroleum Exporting Countries regarding oil production quotas and the price of crude oil: Iraq, suffering from the effects of the Iran-Iraq War, needed crude at $25 per barrel, but Kuwait (among others) continued to exceed its quotas, keeping the price at $14 per barrel. Iran agreed with Iraq in this increasingly hostile dispute.[1] The Bush administration seemed to view the imbroglio mainly as another instance of petrostates squabbling. When it became a military invasion, Washington was taken by surprise.

The surprise gave way quickly to a realization of the situation's gravity. Led by the United States (after British prime minister Margaret Thatcher insisted that Bush not "go wobbly" on the matter), Operation Desert Shield quickly mounted an enormous response, not least to protect the Eastern Province of Saudi Arabia, its primary oil-producing region and just miles from its border with Kuwait. Within days, airborne troops were deployed as a "line in the sand" to defend the Saudis, and the force was built up, with the participation of thirty countries and nearly seven hundred thousand US personnel, to eject Saddam's forces from Kuwait in Operation Desert Storm. From January 17, 1991, until the end of February, the US armed forces demonstrated astonishing prowess in subduing and essentially destroying the large Iraqi occupying force. Because of the broad cooperation in defeating Iraq, including many Arab states and the Soviet Union, President Bush declared, "What is at stake is more than one small country; it is a big idea: a new world order, where diverse nations are drawn together in common cause to achieve the universal aspirations of mankind— peace and security, freedom, and the rule of law."[2]

Not part of the Desert Storm coalition, Iran was officially neutral despite its bitter feud with Saddam Hussein. The war came at a time in which President Rafsanjani was attempting to renew relations with Saudi Arabia. To do so required some softening of its previously steadfast opposition to any superpower interference in the region, notably, Saudi Arabia and its strong ties to the United States.[3] The defense of the Saudi royal family by the enormous US deployment would gravely test Iran's diplomacy. As described earlier, Rafsanjani was also attempting another, less visible gambit—forging an opening with the United States by releasing hostages held by Hezbollah in Lebanon.

The war being only weeks in duration, there was little need for Iran to adapt its position of neutrality. Iran's most dramatic moment came with the escape of Iraqi fighter pilots and commercial pilots in late January 1991—a total of 132 aircraft were flown from Iraq to Iran, apparently to avoid being destroyed by the US-led coalition. There was some confusion about why the pilots took this unusual step, and some speculated that Iran was protecting the planes for Saddam. But Iran's ambassador to the United Nations, Kamal Kharrazi, assured US officials that Iran would not release the jets until the war was over. Iran confiscated the aircraft a year later. The Iranians also had nearly daily contact with the coalition, as Javad Zarif described, to avoid misunderstandings about military operations, although this included warnings not to use Iranian airspace.[4]

The Iraq War and Its Consequences

Of course, the destruction or crippling of Saddam's regime would benefit Iran, and there was no need for Iran to participate directly in the war to benefit mightily from the event. When the war ended, there were deleterious consequences, however. Saddam survived and wreaked revenge on the Shi'a populations of Basra Province. The Kurds in the north were attacked as well, though here Bush acted, somewhat tardily, to protect them, as the humanitarian disaster—hundreds of thousands fleeing into the snowy mountain areas of nearby Turkey and Iran—was a nightly television event worldwide. Unlike the perpetually beleaguered Kurds, the Iraqi Shi'as in the south gained no protection from the coalition. The US commander, Gen. Norman Schwarzkopf, had unaccountably permitted Saddam to retain enough armor and helicopters to carry out a sizable assault on the Shi'a, who rebelled at Bush's urging.

"We tried to get [Schwarzkopf] instructions, he tried to get instructions, but Washington was unable to provide instructions [for war termination], because they had no vision of what sort of peace they wanted to have follow the war," recalled Chas Freeman, US ambassador to Saudi Arabia at the time. "Of course, after the war, the absence of such a policy framework led to a fumbling and inadequate and greatly delayed response to both the Shia uprising in southern Iraq and the Kurdish uprising in the north." The dithering in Washington was due in part to concerns about Saddam being deposed and Iran gaining as a result, Iraq being majority Shi'a. "The Shia rebellion," noted Freeman, "which had some assistance from Iran, was the subject of great confusion."[5] Many thousands perished, and perhaps a hundred thousand or more fled to Saudi Arabia or Iran.

The episode left scars. The distrust toward US troops during the invasion and occupation of Iraq beginning in 2003 can be attributed in part to America's "betrayal" of the Iraqi Shi'a and their compatriots and coreligionists in Iran. Saddam's army—especially the Republican Guard Corps that the US military left intact—ran murderously through the southern towns and cities of Iraq, killing indiscriminately, hanging clerics in Shi'a shrines and mosques, and nearly exterminating the Marsh Arabs inhabiting the littoral at the junction of the Tigris and Euphrates Rivers.

Another major outcome of Desert Storm was the continuation of sanctions on Iraq. Sanctions were imposed to punish Saddam for the invasion of Kuwait and to contain his alleged program to build weapons of mass destruction (including nuclear, chemical, and biological weapons). The International Atomic Energy Agency implemented a rigorous inspection regime. Iraq had advanced significantly toward a WMD capability by 1991, but the war and the inspection regime halted and reversed that progress.[6] Sanctions were meant to oust Saddam, however, and it was increasingly clear that this objective was paramount. The sanctions were severe: no oil could be exported, and only essential foodstuffs and medicine were permitted in. Water treatment, sanitation, basic services such as electricity, and the like were affected. This deprivation appeared to be intentionally harsh. One report explained that "some targets, especially late in the war, were bombed primarily to create postwar leverage over Iraq." An official told a reporter, "Big picture, we want to let people know, 'Get rid of this guy and we'll be more than happy to assist in rebuilding. We're not going to tolerate Saddam Hussein or his regime. Fix that, and we'll fix your electricity.'"[7]

The sanctions regime continued until the next invasion of Iraq in 2003, and the twelve-year imposition of such scarcity had devastating effects. Up to five hundred thousand children died as a result of the sanctions, according to an authoritative study, a toll that Clinton's secretary of state, Madeleine Albright, declared was "worth it" to weaken Saddam.[8] (Subsequent studies placed the number lower, but still about twice the rate of mortality in comparable countries.) This kind of destruction leads to social dissolution and has powerful political effects, which in Iraq were centrifugal: Saddam began to lose control of the country outside of Baghdad, made peace with traditional local chieftains, and adopted more explicitly Islamic trappings to recover legitimacy. Apart from the human misery the sanctions caused, these impacts influenced the course of Operation Iraqi Freedom, the 2003 US-led invasion and occupation, and how Iran and the United States interacted in that theater during that decade.

■ Ambition in the Persian Gulf

The invasion of Iraq in March 2003 deposed Saddam Hussein, failed to find WMD of any kind, and left the country at the mercy of dozens of insurgent groups resisting the US coalition and often warring with each other. The misperceptions, failed governance, erratic provision of security, and tolerance of corruption and human rights violations by the American occupiers are well known. Amid this unfolding disaster, Iran played a significant role, one wholly enabled—however unintentionally—by the United States. The large Shi'a majority (60% of all Iraqis, with the remainder consisting of 20% Sunni Arab and 20% Sunni Kurdish) was bound to demand the lion's share of power. Not only had Saddam (a Sunni) repressed Shi'as throughout his reign, but those very victims of Saddam's wrath had formed several militias ready to exert influence, and many in the Shi'a power structure owed at least some allegiance to Iran. Grand Ayatollah Ali al-Sistani, the head of Iraq's Shi'a faithful, is Iranian. Ayatollah Mohammad Baqir al-Hakim, founder of both the Supreme Council for the Islamic Revolution in Iraq (SCIRI) and the Badr Brigade, emerged from years of imprisonment in Iraq and exile in Iran to become a major power figure right after the fall of the regime, although he was assassinated soon after. His younger brother Abdul Aziz al-Hakim, who also spent two decades in Iran, succeeded him and was prominent in Iraqi governance over the next several years. The "firebrand" Shi'a leader Muqtada al-Sadr, who led the

Madhi Army and became one of the most lethal resistance fighters against US occupation, came from a long line of clerics, some with Iranian lineage; he spent some years in Iran beginning in 2009 in religious study. Many others in the Shi'a opposition were exiled in Iran, and nearly all the major parties and organizations had strong links to Iran.

The Iraq War was, for America, not merely an effort to root out WMD or overthrow Saddam; it was also a war of occupation, opposed by a large majority of all Iraqis, and violently so by insurgent groups. Much was unexpected—the lengthy commitment of US troops, the fitful attempts at governance, and the horrifying human toll of several hundred thousand dead and as many as five million Iraqis displaced.[9] It was more intentionally a war with larger aims, a much broader scope than the villainous Saddam alone, and this did involve Iran. The involvement was not only the expats who were returned from Iran and supported by the Islamic Republic of Iran in their efforts to control Iraqi politics post-Saddam; rather, Iran always figured in US planning and rationales for Operation Iraqi Freedom. The quick toppling of Saddam's regime led to a certain bravado among the war's supporters in and out of government, encapsulated in a memorable conjecture by a British official close to the Bush team: "Everyone wants to go to Baghdad. Real men want to go to Tehran." The inveterate neocon Richard Perle invoked the spirit of the day when he proclaimed that with success in Iraq "we could deliver a short message, a two-word message: 'You're next.'"[10]

The threats were sometimes jocular, but the Bush Doctrine of preemption lent official license to them. After the September 11, 2001, attacks, the Bush administration fostered a policy of preemption against perceived threats to the United States and US interests abroad. The new doctrine, articulated in the 2002 National Security Strategy, stated that "our immediate focus will be those terrorist organizations of global reach and any terrorist or state sponsor of terrorism which attempts to gain or use weapons of mass destruction (WMD) or their precursors," and that the United States would deploy its exceptional military power in "identifying and destroying the threat before it reaches our borders." Further, the United States would secure the nation by "denying further sponsorship, support, and sanctuary to terrorists by convincing or compelling states to accept their sovereign responsibilities."[11] The doctrine is notable for its emphasis on preemption, and these points—state sponsors of terror, attempting to gain WMD or their precursors—could apply to Iran as easily as Iraq. Regime change for both was an official American pledge. Thus, the policy flourish of the Bush Doctrine that braced the invasion of Iraq was combat-ready for Iran as well, and this threat was never disowned by Bush or his subordinates.

Threat perception and preemption were only part of it. The war that commenced in March 2003, while focused on Iraq, was a vastly broader statement. The war was always intended by Bush's team to not only disarm Saddam of the alleged WMD—quite likely a contrived rationale for hostilities[12]—but also teach a lesson to recalcitrant Middle East authoritarians. The neoconservative impulse, after all, has been to use both US military power and diplomatic, economic, and cultural assets to generate a political transition, at least nominally democratic, in order to brace American interests. Bush articulated this in florid terms in the fall of 2003: "From the Fourteen Points to the Four Freedoms, to the Speech at Westminster, America has put our power at the service of principle. We believe that liberty is the design of nature; we believe that liberty is the direction of history.... Working for the spread of freedom can be hard. Yet, America has accomplished hard tasks before."[13] The use of the word "liberty" as a proxy for all Western values was doubtlessly a lance toward the authoritarians of the region, mainly Syria and Iran, as well as Saddam's Iraq. And "working for the spread of freedom"—American influence and interests—is a concise nod to the frontier ideology.

Defeating nuclear weapons ambitions and terrorism were the more tangible goals in the Persian Gulf. The administration was explicit with regard to Iran in those early years. "There are lots of ways to deal with these issues [of nuclear proliferation]," Condoleezza Rice, then national security adviser, told an interviewer in 2002. "We can try to deny weapons materials to hostile states. However, there may come a time when those efforts fail. And in the case of certain types of regimes, there may come a time when there is no other option than military preemption."[14] This concreteness blended with the more idealistic calls, as in George W. Bush's second inaugural address in 2005: "It is the policy of the United States to seek and support the growth of democratic movements and institutions in every nation and culture, with the ultimate goal of ending tyranny in our world." This blend continued to be served up throughout the Bush years: an ersatz Wilsonian idealism (the bow to democracy when the United States continued to support an array of authoritarians), the hegemonic assertion of values, and the global scope and fighting spirit of the frontier myth.

■ Intersections: Iraq and the 2003 Letter

Despite the grandiose rhetoric about democracy and freedom, along with nonproliferation and anti-terror policies, the Bush administration nonetheless had contacts with Iran during the war in Iraq. To some extent, the contacts built on earlier connections forged during the Clinton period and more directly as a result of the defeat of the Taliban in Afghanistan. These were in part the sort of "deconfliction" communications they had had during Desert Storm to avoid misunderstandings about US military operations. There were more fractious matters to address as well. In general, the six years of war under Bush had an undercurrent of hostility toward Iran, mainly because of Iran's support for Iraqi groups attacking US soldiers. Simultaneously, Washington was gradually reaching out to the "E3"—Germany, France, and Britain—as they begun their nuclear negotiations. Hence, there were two momentous encounters occurring at the same time.

The background for the fitful relationship in Iraq included Bush's "axis of evil" reference in the 2002 State of the Union address, even as Iran continued to be exceptionally helpful in stabilizing Afghanistan after the Taliban conceded power. For Bush, it may have been merely a rhetorical flourish by a speechwriter. For Iran, it signaled much more. "Politically, it was an odd thing to do," recalled Mohammad Ali Abtahi, a vice president from 2001 to 2004. "We helped overthrow the Taliban. Instead of opening a path for even greater cooperation, they turned to this slogan—the 'Axis of Evil.' That was Mr. Bush's biggest strategic mistake."[15] In fact, Iran's legendary leader of the Revolutionary Guard's Qods Force, Qasem Soleimani, met with Ambassador Ryan Crocker in Geneva in 2001 regarding Afghanistan, but the "axis of evil" speech ended their incipient dialogue. (He later tried to meet with Gen. David Petraeus regarding Iraq but was turned down.)[16]

A few months later, the National Council of Resistance of Iran, a group created by the anti-regime People's Mojahedin of Iran (MEK), announced that it had discovered a nuclear program in Iran that had not been known to the IAEA. The Iranians claimed they were declaring facilities in a timely and legal way, but the revelations stirred considerable controversy, only overshadowed at that time by the coming war in Iraq.[17] But the revelations nonetheless increased distrust.

US policy makers understood that a war toppling Saddam and the Ba'ath Party would benefit Iran. Iranian leaders understood this as well; Rafsanjani at one early point in the war told Muqtada al-Sadr that "it is better to work with American coalition forces, because it is a better situation now, without Saddam, and the best way for Shiites to show them that they can organize a government."[18] Several high-level Iranian officials told others in the region that they hoped US forces would stay in Iraq "for a while" to provide stability, and Foreign Minister Kamal Kharrazi noted that Iran would help quell militant Shi'a groups in Iraq if asked by the US-led coalition, but no such request ever came.[19] "It was the time which indirectly Iran was cooperating with the U.S.," recalled Hossein Mousavian, a prominent security official in Iran at the time. "The atmosphere was very positive between Iran and Washington. Saddam still was missing somewhere and Iran was looking to full collapse of the system in Iraq. Iran gave the green light to the Shia militant groups to cooperate on the ground with the U.S. army."[20]

The United States was willing to regard the likes of the Hakim brothers as legitimate interlocutors in the future of Iraq, knowing of their close ties to the Tehran regime and given the sizable Shi'a majority and the goal of deposing the Sunni elites that had been preeminent since the rule of the Ottoman Turks. But the Bush administration was no less wary of Iranian intentions. "After the ouster of Saddam Hussein in Iraq, Tehran and Washington again sought to cooperate to stabilize Iraq internally in the face of increasing terrorist and insurgent violence," Stephen J. Hadley, a top Bush security aide, recalled years later. "In 2004, U.S. and Iranian envoys held three meetings in Baghdad, two at ambassadorial level . . . Iran increasingly trained, armed, and aided Shiite extremists in Iraq and later Taliban militants in Afghanistan. Other engagement efforts had little merit or success."[21]

White House officials, led by Vice President Dick Cheney, were hawks on Iran, along with the Pentagon's civilian leadership—Donald Rumsfeld, secretary of defense, and high-ranking defense officials like Paul Wolfowitz and Douglas Feith. Whether there was ever an intention on their part to attack Iran militarily is questionable. According to a memo Rumsfeld wrote to the president in late 2006, given the "interference by Iran and Syria inside of Iraq and Lebanon, [and] rising concerns of Iranian nuclear and regional ambitions," Rumsfeld urged Bush to "counter subversive activity in Iraq by its neighbors, especially Iran, which seeks hegemony in the region."[22] Gen. David Petraeus, while commander of US forces in Iraq, told Congress that "it is increasingly apparent to both coalition and Iraqi leaders that Iran, through the use of the Quds Force, seeks to turn the Iraqi Special

Groups into a Hezbollah-like force to serve its interests and fight a proxy war against the Iraqi state and coalition forces in Iraq." Indeed, Petraeus scarcely mentioned any other sources of outside malevolence. It was all about Iran. "Foreign and home-grown terrorists, insurgents, militia extremists, and criminals all push the ethno-sectarian competition toward violence. Malign actions by Syria and, especially, by Iran fuel that violence."[23] But Iraqis, in many surveys, overwhelmingly blamed the United States, not Iran, for the extreme violence besetting their country.[24]

The State Department took a somewhat different tack. "You had controversy in State. And I daresay that in August of 2002, maybe even as late as December of 2002, we could not have put forth a coherent policy expectation vis-à-vis Iran," recalled Col. Lawrence Wilkerson, then chief of staff to Secretary of State Colin Powell. "It wasn't decided within State precisely what our policy should be. . . . Should it be really hard-core, or should it be moderate, or should it be a little soft here and a little hard there? No one could seem to come to a decision within the State Department in terms of what our policy should be with respect to Iran."[25] America's key diplomat in the Afghanistan talks, James Dobbins, commented, "I think Iran just wasn't on anybody's radar in this period. It wasn't a particular threat." But he also noted that "previous perceived Iranian transgression, Khobar Towers, the Beirut marine barracks, the bombing, et cetera, had deeply scarred individuals and led some of them to feel very passionately and very hostilely toward Iran."[26]

A telling case emerged in the form of an unsigned fax sent to the office of Assistant Secretary of State William Burns. Later to play a major role in the 2015 nuclear deal, Bill Burns was heading the Near East bureau, and he received this faxed message—apparently from Iran—warily. The letter it conveyed spoke of a potential grand bargain between the United States and Iran in which all issues separating the two countries could be resolved, including WMD, granting security guarantees, abolishing sanctions, refraining from supporting terrorist organizations, and working together on regional security, economic cooperation, and so on. The letter was astonishing in its scope and apparent concessions. Iran would stop military support for Hamas and Hezbollah, for example, and accept a two-state approach to the Israeli-Palestinian impasse. It would grant full transparency to the IAEA to assure that Iran had no nuclear weapons aspirations.

The letter came in May 2003, just weeks after the stunning (if short-lived) US-led victory in Iraq. Despite its potential importance, the US government essentially ignored it. The letter's provenance was unclear. It had come via the Swiss ambassador to Iran, Tim Guldi-mann; Switzerland represents US interests in Iran in the absence of normal diplomatic relations (including the absence of American dip-lomats). It was not obvious whether the proposals had the approval of the supreme leader, Ali Khamenei. There was little indication of who was making the proposal apart from Sadeq Kharrazi, the Iranian am-bassador to France and former envoy to the United Nations, nephew of the foreign minister, and a Khamenei relation through marriage. Family ties are important in Iranian politics, and such prominence should have indicated some importance to the fax. In any case, it was set aside.

The letter included several points about Iraq. It described US aims in Iraq as including "coordination of Iranian influence for actively sup-porting political stabilization and the establishment of democratic institutions and a democratic government representing all ethnic and religious groups in Iraq." It described Iranian aims as "pursuit of MKO [another acronym for MEK], support of the repatriation of MKO mem-bers, support for the Iranian claims for Iraqi reparation, no Turkish invasion of North Iraq, and respect for the Iranian national interests in Iraq and religious links to Najaf/Karbala." Such a set of ideas, if imple-mented, could have avoided much of the violence that Iraq suffered over the next several years.[27]

Deputy Secretary of State Richard Armitage was in the middle of the ensuing discussion about the fax. "We thought the Swiss ambassador in Tehran was so intent—and I mean this positively—but he was so intent on bettering relations between 'the Great Satan,' the United States, and Iran that we came to have some questions about where the Iranian message ended and the Swiss message may begin," he told an interviewer in 2007. Guldimann had provided a prologue to the "roadmap" proposal, in which he mused that according to one of the roadmap's authors the supreme leader agreed with "85%–90% of the paper." Both Sadeq Kharrazi and Javad Zarif, another of the coauthors, have confirmed that the supreme leader essentially approved the letter.[28] But Armitage was skeptical. Guldimann "has perhaps added a little bit to it because it wasn't in consonance with the state of our relations. And we had had some discussions . . . with high-ranking Iranian intelligence people, and nothing we were seeing in this fax was in consonance with what we were hearing face-to-face. So we didn't give it much weight."[29] It has subsequently been reported that the day before the fax arrived, Zarif was meeting with American diplomats Ryan Crocker and Zalmay Khalilzad in Geneva but didn't mention the proposal, feeding doubts in Washington about its authenticity.[30] Still, as Dobbins pointed out, it had all the appearances of a trial balloon and deserved probing.

The 2003 letter revealed perhaps more about Iranian decision-making than the American counterpart. The desire to reach out and put everything on the table was an extraordinary move. Whether or not the supreme leader assented to the details of the proposal remains something of a mystery, but by most observers' testimony, he allowed the effort to go forward. Zarif once claimed he had a draft copy of the letter with Khamenei's comments written in the margins. But the very sloppiness of the Iranian approach should have signaled to US officials—many of whom had been involved in Track 2 discussions—that the attempt at bargaining was hotly contested in Iranian ruling circles, and "exploring" or "testing" the issue with Iran was the prudent thing to do. "The political climate in Washington and the fact that always the United States wants us, the Iranian side, to understand the sensitivities and sensibilities of the US-Iran rapprochement, but does not want to give equal weight to what Iranian domestic political complexities suggest," observed Hadi Semati, an informal adviser to Khatami. "When this letter was being pushed around, the Revolutionary Guard were so much against any advance in cooperation with the U.S., even on Iraq. The idea of rapprochement always had a negative, significant opposition inside Iran in domestic political circles, national security circles."[31]

The episode indicates a latent inclination in the State Department to create a dialogue with Iran, if realized after the fact. Wilkerson recalls reading the fax and thinking that it was in effect the Iranian version of a State Department policy planning paper he had just seen. "We should have probed it," said Bill Burns of the letter years later. "Whatever its issues, that wasn't an argument against testing it. There was a lot of hubris in the administration at the time, after Saddam Hussein's overthrow. The general view was, they [Iranians] *should* be nervous. I'm skeptical that it would have borne a lot of fruit, but we should have tested it." Armitage, the one who buried the letter (which may never have been sent to the White House), still insisted on his and Secretary Powell's desire to talk to Iran, but he believed Iran wasn't sending clear signals that it wanted such discussions.[32] When Condoleezza Rice became secretary of state in 2005, she began to move slightly toward the view that the United States needed to engage.

◼ Conflict and Fitful Diplomacy

However apparent was the mutual aspiration for dialogue, the reality of warfare on the ground made those hopes untenable. Within months of the invasion, a full-blown Sunni insurgency had exploded against the Coalition Provisional Authority and newborn, post-Saddam Iraqi governance. The insurgency was actually many organizations—dozens—popping up against the US military particularly, but it soon became a sectarian conflict in which Shi'a militia were full partners. Muqtada al-Sadr's Mahdi Army was one of the more prominent antagonists, first against the occupiers and later in clashes with Sunnis and Hakim's Badr Brigade. He was involved in politics—notably, Nouri al-Maliki's ascension to prime minister is attributed to al-Sadr's patronage. His links to Iran were fragile, however; Iranian authorities regarded al-Sadr as a problem to be managed. The Badr Brigade, more openly cooperative with the occupiers, was active in the south, near Basra, a British responsibility. It was clearly linked to Iran, especially the Islamic Revolutionary Guard Corps.

There were many outside forces at work in Iraq—Saudis, Jordanians, Syrians, and Turks—in addition to Iranians, but it was Iran that generally earned Americans' scorn. Early on, the US head of civilian operations, Paul Bremer, warned in a June 2003 memo to Rumsfeld that "elements of the Tehran government are actively arming, training, and directing militia in Iraq," posing a long-term threat.[33] Meghan O'Sullivan, who was stationed in Baghdad early in the occupation and later was a White House adviser on Iraq, agreed that from 2004 to 2006 there was "a shift in Iranian behavior in Iraq, where Iran becomes … a very nefarious actor in Iraq, and an actor targeting US and coalition forces, actively supporting and training militants. … It seemed that Iran would be walking a very fine line, because Iraq was so close to being completely destabilized. By 2006, it's in the throes of a vicious sectarian war, where Sadr is our major antagonist in this war. What was Iran trying to achieve?"[34]

The mounting attacks on US forces included firefights, roadside bombings, assassinations, and kidnappings. A high-ranking US commander communicated to the Quds Force in 2007 that further attacks would be met by retaliation against their training camps in Iran. Perhaps due to that warning, said one report based on leaked US military documents, "the Quds Force has sought to maintain a low profile in Iraq by arranging for fighters from Hezbollah in Lebanon to train Iraqi militants in Iran or by giving guidance to Iraqi militias who do the fighting with Iranian financing and weapons."[35]

But the Quds Force and other Iranian players were prominent all the same. "We never denied our relation of very powerful ties with all Shiite groups, even Quds and Sunni groups," said Hossein Mousavian, who was head of the Foreign Relations Committee of Iran's National Security Council from 1997 to 2005. "We know the majority of Quds, they were in Iran before Saddam. They were supported with weaponry, financially. We never denied our links with them. This was our asset, this was our power in Iraq."[36] US leaders were increasingly wary of Iranian activities, and in late 2005 commanding general George W. Casey "ordered his staff to draw up contingency plans for a possible conflict with the IRGC and other Iranian operatives in Iraq, and tasked his staff judge advocate to determine whether the Quds Force could legally be declared a hostile force."[37]

As the violence spun out of control in Iraq, US authorities regarded the Sunni insurgencies as the primary threat to long-term stability in the country and concentrated political and diplomatic resources on bringing Sunni tribal leaders into the political process the United States fostered. This strategy to dampen Sunni outrage began in 2005 and, from Tehran's point of view, appeared to signal a shift of American favor toward the Sunni Arab tribes. It was around that time—though not necessarily related—that sectarian violence increased dramatically. The February 2006 bombing of the Askariya Shrine in Samarra, a holy site for Shi'a, set off a year of the worst violence of the occupation period, violence heavily involving US troops. More than eight hundred American troops were killed in both 2005 and 2006, a significant number from roadside bombings. American policy makers often attribute the increase in these bombings from improvised explosive devices (IEDs) mainly to Iran, as well as to other irregular forces in

Iraq, devices that became the most lethal threat to US personnel during the war, with thousands killed or losing limbs as a result of the blasts.[38] The searing violence of the war, which did not subside until 2008, cut many ways, not least into any US-Iran cooperation to diminish the lethality of conflict.

"Coming out of 2006—when America was very weak—into 2007, one of the many rationales for this shift in strategy was to send a message to the region about American strength," said O'Sullivan, speaking of the "surge" in US troops and support for the Sunni tribes to counter Al-Qaeda, the Iraq branch of which had become a powerful provocateur. "It was a very conscious signal sending, and with it not just a change in military strategy but a variety of other things. And one of them is maybe not hope but expectation that there's going to be a very serious engagement with Iranians, but there's definitely an openness to talk to the Iranians."[39] Zalmay Khalilzad, the US ambassador to Iraq for nearly two years beginning in June 2005 (following John Negroponte), recognized the need to speak to Iranians about the security and political dynamics of Iraq. From the beginning, he requested numerous times to speak with Iranians and was repeatedly turned down by his superiors in Washington. Finally, he caught Bush's attention in a teleconference and got permission. "Shia Iraqis were pressing me because they felt like they were in the middle, they wanted me to talk to the Iranians," he recalled. "The Shias were saying Iraq could be an area where Iran and U.S. could cooperate." This would have been Abdul Aziz al-Hakim, head of SCIRI and the Badr Brigade, who was very close to Tehran. "It seems the Iranians were also suspicious—maybe because of an issue raised with Bremer or Negroponte—that gave them reluctance. The foreign ministry apparently wanted to engage but they wanted the Supreme Leader's cover. Hakim saw the Supreme Leader and he may have said we can't trust them, we don't know their intentions. But Hakim got the authorization to go ahead."[40]

It still wasn't easy. Khalilzad helped arrange a meeting in late winter 2006 with Iranian diplomats through the Iraqi Shi'as, only to have it scuttled at the last minute by Cheney or Rumsfeld. "Condi was secretary of state. Colin probably definitely would have gone along; he had authorized Jim [Dobbins]. I don't think Condi was supportive. She wanted a big breakthrough." Wasn't this an obvious opportunity? "But it would be with me."[41] It wasn't the only time the Americans would not meet to discuss security in Iraq—an obviously common interest blocked by astonishing stubbornness given the level of violence.

Such behavior left Iraqis and Iranians shaking their heads. "After that, they played hard to get," Khalilzad recalled. Ryan Crocker, his successor, had two bilateral meetings that produced little. The Americans were back on their heels militarily and had lost leverage. In 2007, Condoleezza Rice attended a meeting of Iraq's neighbors and major states in Sharm el-Sheik, a city on the southern tip of the Sinai Peninsula in Egypt, to discuss an "International Compact for Iraq," a weak and short-lived UN effort to rectify the deplorable state of affairs the US invasion had caused. Rice recalled it as an occasion when she posed tough questions to Syrians and was ready to speak with the Iranian foreign minister, but only if Iran suspended its nuclear activities. The Iranian representative, Manouchehr Mottaki, President Ahmadinejad's first foreign minister, left the conference because, allegedly, he was offended by a female singer at dinner who was not appropriately dressed.

But there was little reason for Mottaki to discuss Iraq; the Shi'as had the upper hand, and the Americans had a losing hand. To make things worse, the Americans could not resist a confrontational attitude worthy of Ahmadinejad. "On one hand, while Americans come to us and say, 'Let's talk about the security situation in Iraq,' at the same time, Ms. Rice and [Secretary of Defense] Mr. Robert Gates go to Sharm el-Sheik and they announce that they want to sell $30 billion of arms to

Saudi Arabia, $13 billion of arms to Egypt, $30 billion to Israel," said Hossein Shariatmadari, editor in chief of *Kayhan*, the conservative Tehran daily. "What is their aim? They bluntly announce, in the words of Ms. Rice, that this is for your confrontation with Iran. Look, this shows that on the one hand they talk of negotiating, but they are after something else."[42]

One thing the Bush administration was clearly after was regime change: Rumsfeld recalled in his memoir that he dealt with Iranian militancy in Iraq with special operations raids, but also by aiding the "freedom movement inside Iran."[43] The Office of Iranian Affairs, a unit at the State Department under the direction of Dick Cheney's daughter, Liz, was one piece of that effort, supplying anti-regime elements inside Iran with resources to challenge the IRI's authority. It was a feeble, unproductive effort. "We are going to work to support the aspirations of the Iranian people for freedom in their own country," Rice told Congress in early 2006, and she was handed $75 million to do it.[44] Not only was the effort a flop, but most prominent Iranian dissidents also kept their distance, and many were exposed to charges of complicity. But the overt hostility and covert funding signaled anew to Tehran that the United States was intent on destroying their state.

■ Wages of War

Under such conditions, particularly ongoing Washington schemes to overthrow the IRI, it is scarcely surprising that Iranian diplomats were reluctant to engage over Iraq. Not only was the US government intensifying its regime-change subterfuge, but it was also isolating Iran on the nuclear issue by initiating new sanctions and rhetorically attacking Iran at nearly every public opportunity. As noted, Iraq was a "win" for Iran—the removal of Saddam and his Sunni henchmen, the rise of

Shi'a political power that was nurtured in Iran, and the US intervention humiliated by ragtag insurgents of every stripe. Support for the Shi'a militias by Iran was a small if symbolically important piece of that humiliation.

The American diplomats at the time wanted more engagement but only intermittently received permission from Washington to pursue it. Powell and Armitage expressed a desire to talk—"we've argued that we need to speak with our enemies perhaps even more than we need to speak with our friends," Armitage told an interviewer, "so we took the point of view that no matter how difficult relations are with any one country, we should not cut ourselves off from them, and we ought to talk with them."[45] Armitage did reach out to Zarif at the United Nations after a devastating earthquake in Iran in late 2003 to offer assistance, which was accepted, and this led to the expectation at the State Department that Iran might use this as an opening to begin a substantive dialogue. It did not. Conceivably, Iran did not seize that opportunity because the State Department had readily disregarded the May 2003 letter from Iran asking for a broad-ranging dialogue.

The Cheney-Rumsfeld wing of the administration was vigilant about preventing diplomatic engagement and remained so through Bush's eight years in the White House. The attacks on US troops in Iraq and Iran's nuclear program were often trotted out as reasons for this bumptious obstruction. But it was equally clear at the time that Iran was a perpetual target of neoconservative ideology, an example of authoritarian states that defied US hegemony, and it had, no less, brought the American government to its knees during the 1979–80 embassy hostage crisis. That blow to American prestige and power could not easily be overlooked by the US elite.

There was a mirror-image phenomenon in Iran. Hard-liners were adamantly opposed to any dialogue with the United States; this was evident particularly when the reformer Khatami came to office, and it intensified when Bush entered the White House. "Iran was ready for serious engagement but had not seen much if any reciprocity," recalled Hadi Semati, the Khatami adviser. "We went into a domestic cycle of conservative onslaught if you will. They pushed back. And now Khatami started his own agenda that again was not reciprocated."[46] Once the 2003 letter was ignored, even the most willing diplomats were discouraged. "After that failure, then everybody in Tehran had the feeling because of Afghanistan and because of this attempt, everybody had the feeling that there is no room to go further with Washington," said Hossein Mousavian.[47] These disappointments, and many to come, merely confirmed Iran's conservative narrative about the United States. "The Supreme Leader believes America doesn't want to negotiate to solve the problems that exist between us," the editor of *Kayhan* observed. "America wants negotiations just for the sake of 'negotiations,'" as a kind of show for other Islamic countries. "Therefore we are never in favor of pursuing negotiations with the United States."[48]

This mirror image of hard-liners and their mutually reinforcing actions are much remarked upon by Iran watchers in the West. In many cases, it would be hard to miss. The "axis of evil" reference, for example, was "not a slap in the face for Khatami, but a punch in the face for Khatami," according to Jack Straw, Britain's foreign secretary at the time. "The Iranians, I think, thought, 'Well, you know, Bush has announced that we're on the list.' So that was a major, major problem."[49] As noted earlier, the rejection of the 2003 letter and the "axis of evil" reference both came on the heels of cooperation on Afghanistan, so these rebuffs and insults were fodder for the conservative hard-liners, just as Ahmadinejad's wounding references to the Holocaust provided the anti-Iran lobby in the United States with a new story to tell.

The Iraq War tested the bilateral relationship more than anything had since the embassy hostage crisis more than two decades earlier. America encircling Iran—even while vanquishing two Iranian foes—

and the perceived threats to Iran were indeed existential. The Iran Quds Force's killing of perhaps as many as one thousand US military tormented American leaders.[50] Under these lethal and threatening circumstances, what may be most remarkable is that the relationship survived at all, and that more harm was not done. For during much of the war, the United States was engaged on the nuclear issue in negotiations; close allies, Britain in particular, who were part of the Iraq coalition could carry on more or less normal ties with Tehran; and the direct diplomacy that did occur, however apparently fruitless, was in the end a testament to the willingness of each country to connect with the other.

The failed diplomacy sat inert in the shadow of violence that was fueled by both sides. The wages of war were onerous because the war was so devastating to Iraqis. The war drew on all the frontier tropes, with endless references to "cowboys and Indians," savages, savage war, captivity narratives, tribalism, civilizational clash, Christian missions, and so on. The American news media treated dissent as suspect, insurgents as morally abhorrent, and civilian deaths (if mentioned at all) as consequences of those bad Iraqi actors, callously capable of decimating their own. Insurgents were frequently called "terrorists," particularly when they were foreign fighters. Much of this was reserved for Iraqis, but the emphasis on Iranians' insidious role was a strong subtheme throughout the war's most violent period.[51] In American eyes, it was difficult to discern the difference between Iraqi militants and Iranian saboteurs: the métier for both was violence, as was, indeed, that of US forces.

The obsession with Iran and its role in Iraq was omnipresent.[52] The use of violence was not confined to the Iranian side, but Tehran's decision to intervene so deeply (including material support for militias) revealed stark attitudes about violence. Its utility in "defending" Iranian interests, and particularly the state, was paramount. Undermining the US Iraq mission would discourage more adventurism by Bush. Violence was also symbolically powerful, a stinging riposte to the 1953 coup, support for the shah, the shootdown of the civilian airliner in 1988, and other indignities—often violent—visited upon the Iranians by the marauding Americans. It is no surprise that the Quds Force commander, Qasem Soleimani, was the most popular person in Iran until he met a violent end, killed by a US drone in Iraq in 2020.

The violence prompted violent rhetoric. Ahmadinejad was "an insane terrorist," said one newspaper editorial. A congressman called the Iranian leader's comments about Israel "an assault on civilized values and portends an attack on civilization itself." The IRGC's attacks in Iraq, the exposure of Iran's nuclear program, and Ahmadinejad's confrontational stance all came at the same time, and each upped the ante. Vice presidential candidate Sarah Palin, in prepared comments to a protest rally at the United Nations in 2008, called Ahmadinejad "oppressive and barbaric," accused him of "inciting genocide" (against Jews), and claimed that he "sponsors terrorists that threaten and kill innocent people around the world."[53]

The Iranian leader answered in kind. In his speech to the United Nations in 2008, he said that "a few bullying powers" spur the world's problems, and that "American empire in the world is reaching the end of its road." The United States was occupying Iraq to "dominate oil resources" while falsely "claiming righteousness."[54] That same year, visiting Baghdad, he said, "People have not seen anything from the foreign presence in this region but more destruction and division."

As the war dragged on and eventually involved the "Islamic State" jihadists—like an Indian tribe marauding and terrorizing the frontier settlers—the US involvement, meant to conclude in 2011, persisted through the ensuing decade. President Trump spoke of the US presence in Iraq as an opportunity to watch Iran, and he reacted harshly—threatening sanctions—when the Iraqi parliament demanded that the US military be withdrawn. Iraqi sovereignty itself was under US assault. It was increasingly apparent after thirty to forty years of attempting to control events in Iraq that the United States had created a neocolonial affect. Perhaps more than any other example, the national narratives vividly played out in Iraq with compelling force: America, expansive and filled with righteous ardor; Iran, slyly resisting foreign power. The script was written in hundreds of years of narration.

The Nuclear File under Bush 43

9 In August 2002, while Washington was riveted on the possibility of war against Iraq, a little-known group called the National Council of Resistance of Iran held a press conference in America's capital city to announce that Iran had a secret nuclear weapons program. The startling information, procured by one of the council's member organizations, the Mujahedin-e Khalq, contended that Iran had facilities to enrich uranium and to produce deuterium, or "heavy water," both of which are potential components of a nuclear weapons program. The revelations set off a slow-motion firestorm that drew the constant attention of the international community for more than a decade—all the attention it could spare, that is, given the war in Iraq, a war that was itself set off by false accusations about weapons of mass destruction.

The conjectures about Iran were headline grabbing, though the two facilities were known to US intelligence, and likely known to the

International Atomic Energy Agency as well. That the MEK was given the information to announce publicly was peculiar, possibly meant to rehabilitate a group—known to have murdered Americans in Iran in the 1970s and to commit other acts of terror—whose aim was the overthrow of the Islamic Republic of Iran. Once a secular leftist group, the MEK was banished by Ayatollah Khomeini after the Iranian revolution and dove headlong into cult-like, violent behavior. As it turned out, Iran *did* have a nuclear program with, according to the Central Intelligence Agency, weapons aspirations at that time.

It was possible to understand why. Saddam Hussein had attacked Iran and used chemical weapons in their deadly war in the 1980s. He was pursuing his own nuclear option, but Desert Storm put that to an end in 1991. Notably, the American government's constant accusations about Iraq's nuclear intentions may have fueled Tehran's determination to build a deterrent. And there was the constant undercurrent of threat *from* the United States, whose fantasy among many policy mavens from the mid-1990s onward was regime change in Iran, as well as explicit warnings from the Israelis. Iran has a sophisticated scientific culture, under the last shah had thousands of students trained at top American universities like MIT and Stanford, and had oil money to pour into military technologies if they wished to.[1] The motive and the means were vividly present.

The same CIA analysis authored in 2007 that asserted that Iran had a nuclear weapons program in 2002–3 also stated that such ambitions ended in late 2003.[2] But the MEK's clanging alarms set in motion a fervent attempt to prevent Iran from becoming a nuclear power. What followed in the next five years was complex, multiparty diplomatic maneuvering braced by coercive sanctions and the ever-present threat of military force. Along the way, there were missed opportunities aplenty, but the wrong players to take advantage of those openings held power in Washington and Tehran, men who subscribed to their national narratives and worst expectations about the other.

■ The Arms Control Industry

The idea of constraining the development and deployment of nuclear weapons began almost simultaneously with the onset of the atomic age at a test site in Alamogordo, New Mexico, in July 1945, less than a month before the atomic bombing of Hiroshima and Nagasaki. Efforts to prevent the Soviet Union and other powers from acquiring the devastating weapons proved elusive in the early years. It was also the most intense period of the Cold War, anti-Communist hysteria in America, Soviet expansion, and Chinese Communist triumph. Whatever their merits, proposals by Bernard Baruch and others failed to gain traction in the emotional maelstrom caused by Mao's victory in China, the war in Korea, and Moscow's "capture" of Central Europe. By the 1960s, however, some progress at the United Nations was taking place, including the introduction of resolutions by Ireland that led to the Non-Proliferation Treaty in 1968. The United States and the Soviet Union signed the Partial Test Ban Treaty in 1963, an accord motivated in part by the near miss of a nuclear war during the Cuban Missile Crisis in 1962.

There would be later, larger successes for arms control, the SALT and START treaties most prominently, as well as a number of other protocols and conventions.[3] What is striking about the salad days of the arms controllers is how both the United States and the Soviet Union—the two superpowers with by far the largest nuclear arsenals—adopted a process that was mutually recognizable as a serious commitment to diminish what was clearly a threat to the survival of civilization.

This process unfolded at the governmental level, both bilaterally and multilaterally. It was braced by an "industry" of sorts—thousands of analysts in universities, think tanks, and nongovernmental organizations—that was created with the explicit purpose of understanding adversaries more thoroughly, as well as the nature of the nuclear threat, the US-USSR rivalry, and the possible ways to resolve the nuclear dilemma. The largest epistemic community was American, but similar if smaller cohorts rose in the Soviet Union, the other nuclear powers (France, United Kingdom, China), and interested bystanders like Sweden and West Germany. The research, discussions, conferences, publications, and other intellectual products focused on the technical dimensions of nuclear weapons production, development and deployment of delivery systems like submarines and missiles, the effects of nuclear blasts, and the possibilities of defenses against nuclear attacks. Government labs like those at Los Alamos and Berkeley were oriented both to devising new and more effective weapons and, paradoxically, to the potential for controlling them in international treaties. The university centers undertook similar tasks, if at a smaller scale. Physicists and engineers would take up the technical challenges, while international relations scholars and game theorists would consider the strategic implications and devise ideas for deterrence and control. Nongovernmental organizations typically would inform and mobilize the public.

This has been going on since the 1960s, with its most active period in the 1980s. That the "industry" had a powerful impact on policy making is indisputable.[4] The combination of scientific élan, sound argument about national security interests, the articulated benefits of arms control, and the public's worries about nuclear war drove policy makers of all political ideologies to sustain and conclude arms control agreements of increasing scope and depth. What began as a moral outcry from the likes of Bertrand Russell and Albert Einstein, or game theory by the young Harvard professor Thomas Schelling, mushroomed into a remarkably robust, creative, and disciplined community of experts and activists. It withstood fierce backlash from conservatives worried about appeasing the USSR, fueled by fervent anti-Communism and the military-industrial complex. But the fact that the arms control community succeeded in achieving an impressive ledger of treaties, all of which worked reasonably well, marks one of the finer episodes of involvement by scientists and activists in international policy making.

This dynamic was successful in large part because of several factors that are relevant to the later US-Iran nuclear negotiations. There was, for example, an enormous investment by the US government in Soviet or Russian studies programs. Two generations of Russia scholars were trained, and many of them focused on Kremlin decision-making, military doctrine, and the like. Similarly, Washington nurtured generations of nuclear weapons experts, physicists and engineers mostly. As a result, a deep reservoir of knowledge was created about the US adversary and the prospect of nuclear war.

A second factor was arms control's essentially technical nature. Negotiations focused sharply on the technology—its capability and numbers, how deployments fulfilled different objectives of strategy, how a treaty could be verified by technical means (such as satellite monitoring), and what new technological inventions could thwart the goals of treaty making. Politics entered into negotiations only through the back door as an often-censorious national discourse. Things like human rights were never allowed to be part of negotiations, precisely because they were *not* technical and therefore engaged different and contested norms. Focusing on the technical dimension alone allowed parties with differing ideological outlooks and value systems to be partners in problem-solving. This abiding aspect of the arms control process angered constituencies intent on punishing the Soviets for their many human rights abuses. But it would have been virtually impossible to achieve both arms control and improved human rights.

A third feature of the glory days of US-Soviet arms control was its basic popularity. While the American right wing was constantly complaining about appeasement, its ultimate effect was attenuated because the steady momentum of negotiations rarely lost the public's favor, however wary the public sometimes would be. The growth of the antinuclear movement in the 1980s in particular stigmatized nuclear weapons, underscored the futility of the Cold War, and created political space for politicians to support disarmament. Even Ronald Reagan, the consummate anti-Communist, moved aggressively toward arms reductions when the Iran-Contra scandal jeopardized his presidency. The political space to do so had been carved out by the freeze movement and public intellectuals for several years before.

The fact that the United States and the Soviet Union maintained full diplomatic relations continuously from 1933 helped enormously. The Soviet ambassador was a frequent interlocutor for American elites, just as the US ambassador in Moscow explained the West's policies to Soviet leaders. The two countries maintained fairly robust trade during the entire period. And while too much can be claimed for cultural affinities, Washington and Moscow were operating from essentially the same playbook—the secularism, empiricism, and rationality fostered by the Enlightenment, albeit with the Russians using their Marxist-Leninist lens. But they did, at a fundamental level, understand each other. They both were born in secular revolutions, with compatible philosophical lineages, expansionist narratives that embraced imperialism (despite Lenin's insistence that capitalism, not Communism, was imperialist), and became continental hegemons before dominating a scattering of small countries overseas. American elites did not see Russia as a frontier to conquer (as they occasionally did with China), but the Soviets were often depicted in ways reminiscent of savages–violent, devious, and destructive of our democratic values.

The Cold War was thickly institutionalized, not only by the commitment to knowledge production but also by the training and orientation of the diplomatic corps, the intelligence services, the news media, trading companies, K–12 education, and the structure of military and economic alliances. It was a colossal undertaking, a fitful symbiosis of government and private actors, which reduced the East-West confrontation and the nuclear danger.

The response to the nuclear challenge by Iran benefitted from few of these factors at the outset. American policy makers were, as a whole, never knowledgeable about Iran, its 1979 revolution, the bitter effects of the Iran-Iraq War, or its wariness of Western intervention in its affairs. Washington was blind to the social forces that led to the 1979 uprising—indeed, the US government inadvertently aided it by helping the shah suppress the democratic process in the country for decades. From 1979 onward, the United States conducted its own cold war against Iran. Unlike the Soviet Union, however, Iran did not possess any weapons or military capacity to threaten the United States. Its human rights abuses, however deplorable, were no worse than those of many US allies, like Saudi Arabia or Egypt. Iran backed some politically violent groups, but nothing approaching what Moscow supported during the Cold War. There were virtually no academic programs in the United States to understand contemporary Iran. There was no epistemic community that bridged the various parties and institutions that could problem-solve together, in part because diplomatic relations had been cut off by Jimmy Carter and never restored. The two countries, moreover, operated by different cultural rules and their sharply differing national narratives: the flirtation with nuclear weapons by Iran fulfilled one of their narratives' bedrock values—defense against malicious outsiders, whether Saddam's Iraq or the United States. That flirtation also gave the Americans a reason to subdue the "savages," a necessary antecedent to domination of the oil-rich region.

Hence, the nuclear talks that would begin in 2004 with three European countries and be joined by the United States in 2006 were built on a rickety foundation. But if there is one thing the US government knows how to do, it's arms control. And the Iranians, with their keen sense of national interest and a formidable scientific capacity, became a worthy if reluctant partner.

■ Nuclear Ambitions of a Third World Country

Like many states aspiring to big-league status, Iran had long-standing plans to build an ambitious nuclear power program, beginning in the 1950s. The United States, swooning with Eisenhower's Atoms for Peace vision, aided this goal substantially. These ambitions were easier said than done. By the time the last shah was deposed, Iran's nuclear power program amounted to some contracts for uranium imports and a cadre of nuclear scientists and engineers, many if not most of them trained in American universities. A conventional nuclear power reactor was under construction near the southeastern town of Bushehr, supplied by Germany, but that work was suspended because Ayatollah Khomeini was initially opposed to nuclear development; it was completed with Russian help and fuel, producing electric power for the first time in 2011. It remains Iran's only nuclear power reactor.

From the late 1980s on, Iran invested heavily in a nuclear fuel cycle, signing extensive contracts with China, Argentina, Russia, and Pakistan for major pieces of that cycle—enrichment capability, uranium conversion, heavy water production, small but highly capable reactors, and so on. Fearing Iran's intentions, successive US administrations blocked several of those deals by putting pressure on the vendor governments. At the same time, throughout the 1990s the United States charged that Iran had a nuclear weapons program (or the burgeoning capability thereof) and could produce a weapon in seven to fifteen years; some estimates were even shorter, including those of Israeli intelligence.[5] Iran was indeed active around the world to acquire components of an expanding nuclear capability, so-called dual-use items that could be useful in a peaceful nuclear power complex or possibly in an effort to produce nuclear weapons.

The break in the cat-and-mouse games of the 1990s was the MEK revelation of 2002. As a signatory of the NPT, Iran had a right to a nuclear power program, and technologies like the Bushehr plant were allowed with the proper safeguards against diversion of fuel. The used or "spent" fuel of nuclear power plants is not easily convertible to the kinds of uranium and plutonium used in nuclear weapons. Iran would need several other sophisticated technologies, which were under the control of the IAEA, to work toward a nuclear weapon. Two of those kinds of facilities were exposed by the MEK press conference—a heavy water plant, named Arak, and an enrichment plant at Natanz. Iran was also constructing at that time a uranium conversion facility in Isfahan, in which mined and milled uranium is converted into a substance called uranium hexafluoride (UF_6), the stock for enrichment. The Isfahan plant had been properly declared to the IAEA.

The UF_6 is transported to Natanz or another enrichment facility, Fordow, near the city of Qom (coincidentally, the religious center of Iran); Fordow was under construction as a heavily fortified (largely underground) facility and discovered in 2009 by US intelligence. Enrichment, in which the UF_6 is "enriched" to yield more uranium 235, or U^{235}, is necessary for fission to occur in a reactor or an explosive. From 3 to 5 percent U^{235} is needed for power reactor fuel. Highly enriched uranium is necessary for bomb making, and typically weapons-grade is considered to be about 95 percent U^{235}. It is achieved by converting the UF_6 into gaseous form and then "spinning" out the U^{235} from the much more abundant U^{238} in thousands of centrifuges. The much purer U^{235} then can be fabricated into a solid metal for power reactors or weapons. All enrichment techniques were developed by the Manhattan Project in the United States during the Second World War.

The Arak heavy water reactor is a technology in which H_2, that is, hydrogen with two neutrons (in contrast to the more abundant single-neutron hydrogen), enriches U^{238} with those extra neutrons to produce plutonium, a weapons-grade material. Arak was under construction when it was revealed in 2002; it was meant to be operational by 2011 but was never completed.

The Iranians in 2002 and throughout the decade had and were expanding a very sophisticated nuclear production cycle. Largely compliant with IAEA standards, with some notable exceptions, the government insisted that it was going to declare Arak and Natanz within the time allotted to do so. The facilities were aimed, officials said, at producing electricity or medical isotopes or nuclear training and experiments, all allowable under the NPT. The question for the international community was whether the enrichment plant at Natanz was a component of nuclear weapons ambitions.

The assessment by the CIA published in 2007 held that Iran did have a weapons program early in that decade but had abandoned it by late 2003.[6] It said that Iran's program included "nuclear weapon design and weaponization work and covert uranium conversion-related and uranium enrichment-related work."[7] Why did Iran abandon these activities at that time? Many believe it was because of the Iraq War and Iran's fear that the United States would attack, using the same pretext as the invasion of Iraq—its alleged WMD. The 2003 fax from the Swiss ambassador would seem to conform to that interpretation. Whatever the cause for the program's discontinuance, the world's major powers needed to confront the proliferation threat as it was uncovered in 2002.

■ The Diplomatic Impulse: Europe First

The Europeans—Britain, France, and Germany—initially took the lead. Their concern predated the MEK press conference, because intelligence analysis had already by 2001 pegged Iran as having a nuclear weapons effort. "They knew that A. Q. Khan had supplied centrifuges and related technology to the Iranians, and they had reason to believe that some of those centrifuges had been tested by introducing nuclear material," said Peter Jenkins, one of Britain's negotiators.[8] Not all European Union (EU) countries agreed to this analysis, but by 2002 they were on board.[9]

What came to be known as the E3 process emerged from discussions among the three foreign ministers—Britain's Jack Straw, Germany's Joschka Fisher, and France's Dominique de Villepin. Diplomacy would not be the only option available to the West, just as it demonstrably was not in Iraq, where military intervention had not yet become the human catastrophe it soon would be. The Americans, not initially involved with the E3 officially but pelting them with criticism and demands behind closed doors, certainly maintained a military option to eliminate Iran's nuclear program. So did Tony Blair, the British prime minister. "What he said was, 'It wasn't on the agenda, but you couldn't take it completely off the table,' which I thought was dangerous, really dangerous," Straw recalled, explaining Blair's view. "Because he thought the only way the Iranians would shift is if they knew there was a threat of military action. My view was that this was only going to play to the hardliners in the Iranian system, that we weren't going to start a war with them unless they did something completely egregious, like starting a war with us."[10] Much of the intrigue around the MEK revelation had to do with Bolton's desire to get Iran referred to the United Nations Security Council in order to win a UNSC authorization for war against Iran. E3 diplomacy thwarted the American hawks' game.

The substance of the revelation was indeed alarming, however. More alarming, as the IAEA began to investigate, was how Iran hid many nuclear activities aimed at building a nuclear fuel cycle, one that could prospectively have aided a weapons program. Mohamed ElBaradei, the agency's head at the time, recalled in detail one after another subterfuge revealed by IAEA inspectors in 2003. Not only was there Natanz and Arak, which the Iranians told ElBaradei about in early 2003, but there was also evidence of testing enrichment techniques and other components, initially denied by the Iranians, including President Khatami.[11] ElBaradei's strong message to Iranian officials was that this deception and the specific activities (none of which proved the existence of a weapons program) had to cease.

These were the cards dealt to the E3, and the question for the Europeans was how to play them without the Americans upending the table. The three initiated action on Iran at the IAEA in Vienna in August 2003 that yielded a resolution supported unanimously by the Board of Governors the following month. It committed Iran to greater transparency and the Additional Protocol of the NPT, which allowed inspectors wider range to look at facilities not declared as part of the nuclear fuel cycle. The Europeans also insisted on a cessation of enrichment activities; the Russians agreed with most of what the E3 outlined, apart from cessation.

The reaction to the resolution inside Iran was turbulent. Hardliners wanted to reject the IAEA resolution, and some even urged a withdrawal from the NPT. The more moderate factions sought to find an acceptable way of cooperating without being accused of complicity with the international order. The demand for Iran to sign the Additional Protocol was particularly vexing. Ali Akbar Velayati, longtime foreign minister (1981–97) and key adviser to Khamenei, described the Additional Protocol as akin to the Treaty of Turkmenchai in 1828, which ceded much of the Caucasus to Russia and is "viewed by Iranians today as a betrayal and a black mark on their history."[12] But it was apparent that the IAEA Board of Governors was united in this demand, and Iran's choices were few.

Khamenei appointed Rouhani to be chief negotiator for Iran in October, and this brought new actions toward transparency. A breakthrough came, said one diplomat posted in Iran, with "Rouhani's successful attempt, in 2003, to get to the bottom of what Iran had actually done in the nuclear sphere. He forced through with (foreign) approval and support, the idea of coming clean internally." The effort was braced by a "crucial decision that Khatami took with Rouhani, to oblige different arms of the Iranian state to tell the Supreme National Security Council what they'd been up to, so that his negotiators wouldn't be blindsided in the course of the three negotiations."[13] The complexities of Iran's governing system notwithstanding, the Western powers were in some disarray too, not only because of the pestering from Washington, particularly John Bolton, but also because they could not agree on the definition of enrichment. ElBaradei had a narrow definition—when the UF_6 is fed into the centrifuges—whereas the E3 held out for a more expansive interpretation, namely, the entire effort to acquire and install any related technology.

The deadlock was serious, and the negotiating parties, who met in Tehran in mid-October 2003, were stubbornly holding to their positions—Iran, no suspension; E3, broad suspension. The meeting of directors general adjourned after an hour, and several of them met unofficially in a separate room at the foreign ministry's think tank, the Institute for Political and International Studies. They agreed on some measures but not suspension. The head of the E3 delegation, Stanislas de LaBoulaye of France, noted, "We were absolutely convinced that we could not narrow the definition of enrichment to only the introduction of fuel in the centrifuges. That you have to have in the definition of enrichment activities everything concerning the centrifuges. Like import of centrifuges. Installation and so on. Those were enrichment activities."[14] The issue was delayed for a conclave of the foreign ministers in Tehran a few days later.

The three Europeans—Straw, Fisher, Villepin—met with Rouhani at the Sa'adabad Palace, the sumptuous residence of the last shah, and focused sharply on the enrichment suspension issue. After days of haggling, Rouhani sought permission from Khamenei and Khatami to agree to a minimalist version of suspension, that which ElBaradei defined—the introduction of uranium hexafluoride gas into centrifuges. It was framed as a temporary, confidence-building measure. Iran signed the Additional Protocol, which the IAEA noted would lead to more extensive inspections, given Iran's past deception. This was known as the Tehran Agreement.

In the next few months, however, Iran balked at implementing their pledges, a pattern of evasion that vexed the nuclear authorities and major powers. It had failed to report all relevant activities in the flurry of the autumn 2003 diplomacy, even as it agreed to broader definitions of enrichment during the subsequent winter. The constant and nearly predictable behavior of not being completely cooperative while making authentically cooperative gestures characterized much of Iran's approach to the nuclear issue for a decade or more. At issue, apart from the pressure of domestic politics, was their keen desire to *not* be referred to the UNSC by the IAEA, a step that could lead to sanctions or worse. At the same time, the Europeans in particular were aware of US displeasure and renewed belligerency that characterized many Americans. The Iranians wanted to avoid steps that could lead to military action if at all possible, seeing to the west and east how trigger-happy America then seemed to be.

The central issue at stake throughout this period (and subsequently) was Iran's "right" to enrich uranium under the terms of the NPT. As a result, suspension of enrichment activities, whether under the narrow ElBaradei definition or the more inclusive scope wanted by the E3 (and the United States), was the core of the dispute. The back-and-forth between negotiators, often quite heated, revolved around this core and flared at every momentous meeting of the IAEA's Board of Governors, which included representatives of the United States and the E3.

One of the key moments of this initial phase of diplomacy concluded with what became known as the Paris Agreement in November 2004. The E3 had delivered a set of conditions and pressed Iran to accept them or face Security Council sanctions, and these conditions included a pledge to suspend enrichment activities broadly, including the testing and importing of components. But the Iranian negotiating team had a hard sell to Khamenei. He was prone to reject the Paris Agreement because of the demand for indefinite suspension. "Ayatollah Khamenei was extremely suspicious of the policies of the West toward Iran, the Persian Gulf, the Middle East, and the Islamic world," wrote Hossein Mousavian. "The supreme leader's rejection of the Paris Agreement came as a particular surprise to President Khatami and Dr. Rouhani. We found ourselves shocked, stranded, and stumped."[15] Personal appeals to the leader brought conditional approval to a temporary ban on enrichment. The agreement stated, "To build further confidence, Iran has decided, on a voluntary basis, to continue and extend its suspension to include all enrichment related and reprocessing activities."[16]

ElBaradei in his memoir related a conversation at the time with one of Iran's negotiators, Cyrus Nasseri, who explained that the presidential election in Iran the following year would be rooted in anti-US feeling and would strengthen the hard-liners, and as a result no permanent cessation of enrichment was politically feasible. "No Iranian politician would risk public disfavor by ending a program that Iran had endured so much to achieve."[17] The accord was treated by pragmatists in Tehran as a great victory over the United States in particular.

The Paris Agreement stipulated more negotiations to reach a permanent settlement of the issue, and Iran proposed in March 2005 to freeze enrichment at Natanz but complete a small pilot enrichment facility with five hundred centrifuges (expandable to three thousand) and a conversion plant. Their proposal was expansive, meeting many of the West's demands, but included a right to enrichment. This was the ever-present nettle between the E3 and Iran. The proposals from both sides included trade agreements and offers of various kinds of nuclear technology, including power plants, but enrichment was the single obstacle that the E3, under heavy pressure from Washington, could not hurdle. The fitful attempt to get to a permanent agreement was then disrupted by the election, in June 2005, of the mayor of Tehran, Mahmoud Ahmadinejad, as president of Iran.

■ Washington Steps In

"Our policy was we are besieged in the Oval Office, at Foggy Bottom, at the Pentagon by the issue of Iraq, which was growing worse and worse every day," explained Lawrence Wilkerson, Secretary Powell's chief of staff. "And we're going to let the Europeans deal with the challenge of Iran. And we're going to dispatch John Bolton or whomever we need to whenever it looks as if they might be doing something we don't like. Which was almost anything. And we're going to stop it. And we'll come revisit it sometime later."[18]

Wilkerson's summary is pithy but largely accurate. Bolton was turned loose in Europe to proselytize on Iran's nuclear weapons ambitions. His imprecations about Iran with the E3 were met with skepticism if not dismissal. Numerous cables from US embassies detail Bolton's relentless advocacy with foreign leaders to tar Iran and insist that it be referred to the Security Council. Nonetheless, the European diplomats tried to work with the Americans. "We kept the United States closely informed," recalled Peter Jenkins, Britain's ambassador to the IAEA. "And quite often when we were negotiating a resolution in the board of governors in Vienna, the British political director, John Sawers, would phone John Bolton . . . to sound him out on potential sticking points and, where possible, to carry the U.S. along with us."[19]

Bolton was less charitable toward the European effort, but he was not alone in setting off flares. Powell, for example, told reporters in November 2004 that Iran seemed to be working on an intercontinental ballistic missile that could, prospectively, deliver a nuclear warhead. (Experts discounted the assertion of an impending threat and were proved correct.) Bolton, who acknowledged "our campaign against ElBaradei" in his memoir, was far from a lone wolf, if something of an outlier in the State Department. Condoleezza Rice, who was Bush's national security advisor before being appointed secretary of state for Bush's second term, commented in her autobiography that Cheney and Rumsfeld were convinced that Iran (and North Korea) "would never make a deal and that any deal that could be made was not worth having. They made a reasonable case for toughening sanctions and isolation to lay the groundwork for regime change." She added that President Bush "was squarely on the hawks' side of the fence."[20]

Powell was mildly sympathetic to if wary about dialogue with Iran; he told ElBaradei that "feelings against Iran had remained very strong in the United States since the hostage crisis. Initiating direct dialogue would be difficult."[21] Despite their tendencies to side with the Cheney faction, Rice and even Bush seemed at least somewhat open to diplomacy. But little of that was pursued in the first two years of the imbroglio over Iran's nuclear ambitions. Rice and Powell only seemed to agree to let the E3 get as far as they could, using Bolton to guard against a too-generous deal with Tehran.

In many respects, this passivity was par for the course. The absence of problem-solving initiatives coming from the US government was consonant with America's general views of Iran, even without the additional burdens of Iraq. "There was deep distrust of what we like to call the mullahcracy," explained Thomas Pickering, a senior American diplomat who was undersecretary of state from 1997 to 2001. "What we saw as a theological leadership of a country where we had developed a huge theory and indeed practice in mistrust. We had the typical Washington disease of seeing everything through one optic, one prism. The prism only looked at Iran and never looked at us, and that prism only worked in a way that tended to allow the outside commentators and some of the insiders to adduce the most primitive and difficult motives for things that Iran was doing."[22]

Standing on the sidelines was not a viable option, however, at least not to Rice, who engaged immediately as secretary of state. Partly this seemed motivated by the perception that the E3 and ElBaradei would never be tough enough to overcome Iran's stops and starts toward enrichment. At the same time, she wanted to help repair US-European relations, at a low point after the run-up to the invasion of Iraq. The wartime catastrophe in Iraq likely exerted additional pressure—namely, that a military option to "solve" the Iran issue was not viable. Not only were the likely consequences of airstrikes on Iran's nuclear assets disastrous, but the American public had no more stomach for war, a sentiment that grew steadily from the invasion of Iraq through the remainder of the Bush years.[23]

Rice's idea of diplomacy, however, was coercive: negotiate on US terms—no enrichment allowed—and brandish the threat of referral to the UNSC if Iran refused those conditions. This was a tough path; she got pushback from Sergei Lavrov, the Russian foreign minister, but a 2005 National Intelligence Estimate still had Iran on a nuclear weapons path, and this was a powerful argument for the P5+1 to be firm and united. "Our general view was that Iran was fairly weak, was very much isolated, and that Iran did not have anything close to a unified decision-making process," explained Nicolas Burns, Rice's new under secretary of state for policy. "There were lots of different views in Tehran, we assumed, that would make it difficult for this negotiation to proceed. We obviously wanted to create an international coalition that would weaken the Iranians further. Restrict them. Contain them. And force them to abide by the requirements that they had signed up to in the IAEA and then to get the UN Security Council involved."[24] The Americans did not actually join the talks until June 2006, but they relied on the British and French to represent US views. Even with Rice's tentative steps toward engagement, the Bush administration remained hawkish, with Cheney and Rumsfeld opposed to any accommodation.

Not surprisingly, the E3 diplomacy finally fell with Ahmadinejad's election. The three made an offer to Tehran in summer of 2005, but it again insisted on a "no enrichment" condition, whereas the Iranians were already headed toward restarting the UF_6 conversion plant near Isfahan. Seven months into Bush's second term and at the beginning of the Ahmadinejad presidency, the efforts to slow or stop Iran's nu-clear development came to a halt. The diplomatic cupboard was not entirely empty; Rice was newly invested in the P5+1, a group that had four members with a recent history of intense negotiations with Iran and an inclination to find a resolution of the impasse.

The first year of Rice's tenure was turbulent, however. Iran in-formed the IAEA that it would begin enrichment in a small research facility—permissible under the NPT—in January 2006. The IAEA Board of Governors then referred the matter to the UNSC, a major step in the confrontation and a longtime objective of American hawks. In retaliation, Iran ended its adherence to the Additional Protocol. Be-hind the scenes, however, the new Iranian negotiator, Ali Larijani, asked ElBaradei to convey yet again a grand bargain-like entreaty to Rice, who seemed intrigued but continued to insist on a cessation of enrichment before talks could begin—a classic case of setting a condi-tion for negotiations demanding what that party sought to achieve in the talks.

An offer from the P5+1 was put on the table in June 2006, one that ElBaradei described as "quite generous," but it nonetheless demanded suspension of enrichment. The Iranians, as is their pattern, took their time replying, which US officials interpreted as a tactic of delay to fur-ther their enrichment program. They did expand enrichment that sum-mer, but the number of cascades of centrifuges brought on line were not technically significant. The offer accompanied a parallel threat, however—UNSC sanctions. "The Western notion of how to approach Iran was like going into a souk and offering the proprietor a fair sum for the desired merchandise but also threatening to burn down the shop if he didn't accept," ElBaradei recalled. "While the tactic might play well in a Clint Eastwood movie, it would be doomed from the start in Tehran."[25]

The process stumbled along that way, with Javier Solana, the EU foreign and security minister, doing much of the talking with Larijani.

Deadlines were missed, position papers quietly exchanged, back channels utilized, and threats publicly proclaimed. The Americans charged that negotiations weren't on track because Larijani "wouldn't show up" and accept the offer of suspension of sanctions for suspension of enrichment during the talks; they attributed that to the delaying tactic and disarray in Iranian decision-making. But Iran saw it differently. "Larijani gave a green light to Solana on the issue of timeout for suspension for suspension. But Larijani's argument with Solana was this: Suspension for how long? If you mean for one month, two months, three months, we are ready. Solana was not in a position to give him a time for suspension," explained Hossein Mousavian. "That's why Larijani couldn't show up." One Western diplomat, Mousavian claimed, said the suspension for negotiations could last ten years.[26]

The possibility of an agreement at that point rested on America's willingness to accept some, relatively token amount of Iranian enrichment and agree to security guarantees for Iran. But this was not to be, and in July 2006 the major Western powers, which had shown for three years both tenacity and patience, ran out of the latter and insisted on moving forward with a resolution demanding suspension in the UNSC. As ElBaradei pointed out, the resolution did not speak to an actual threat—the tiny enrichment activity at Natanz did not feed into a nuclear weapons program, and the UN action would prevent the IAEA from conducting inspections under the Additional Protocol. If one believed that Iran might be surreptitiously developing nuclear capability—which in fact was the basis of the UN action—then ending the possibility of intrusive inspections was aiding, even encouraging, opacity.

At the very same time, a "summer war" in Lebanon erupted, in which Israel bombed civilian areas for weeks in response to a Hezbollah provocation, a conflict that Rice bizarrely called "the birth pangs of a new Middle East." The United States supplied Israel with bombing munitions. At the same time, the war in Iraq was reaching new paroxysms of violence, with hundreds killed every day. The sense of calamity in the region was palpable, and thus the onset of sanctions applied to Iran for activities that were apparently legal appeared to many to be disproportionate. These crises created a deeply divided international community, with the West, including Israel, seeming to impose its will by force on the Middle East, sparking a turbulent atmosphere in which Iran could champion the "subaltern," protest the constant disrespect, and resist the commands of its adversaries.

Continuing diplomacy under such circumstances was strenuous. Pushback from within the Bush administration was powerful, moreover, even as the hawks were weakened by the disaster in Iraq. "How will engagement by the U.S. not be seen as a reward for Iranian intransigence?" Rumsfeld wrote in a May 2006 memo. "Negotiations with the U.S. would be seen by the world as out of context. We announce a decision to deal with them at exactly the moment they are killing U.S. soldiers in Iraq and when the U.S. has labeled them the leading sponsor of terrorism in the world." In a later memo to the president, he worried that "deterrence against a state led by a leader with religiously based millenarian ideology is, at the minimum, questionable," and that Iran could transfer a nuclear weapon to "non-state entities."[27] He opined, in a sentiment echoing Cheney, that the Iranians would never consent to diplomatic constraints on their nuclear program.

As a result, the Washington intervention in the fitful negotiations with Iran was always buffeted by the internal fragmentation of security thinking in the Bush administration and worst-case thinking about Iran, including the abiding belief that the "mullahs" would never deal in good faith. Even as Rumsfeld and much of his team left in disgrace after the 2006 midterm elections delivered a resounding rejection of Bush's Iraq tragedy, Cheney and other hard-liners remained. The Iran file, moreover, was no better than a distant third or fourth priority on the shambles of their foreign policy agenda. The formerly inviting frontier in Iraq had, for the Bush administration, ended dreams of "real men" going to Tehran.

■ Hard Lines and Accommodation in Tehran

For those in Iran's leadership who sought to come to a respectable agreement with the P5+1, the political dynamics at home were every bit as difficult as Washington's. A powerful conservative faction in the IRI's politics braced Khamenei's suspicion that the Europeans, much less the Americans, would never offer an acceptable deal. Cries of "treason" greeted steps like the temporary suspension and acceptance of the Additional Protocol. The 2005 election hinged in part on who could be a fiercer defender of the IRI and its autonomy; the E3's rejection of the 2005 nuclear offer from Iran and the suspension of enrichment were labeled during Ahmadinejad's campaign as the "failures of accommodationism."

Rouhani said in a 2012 interview that the decision to start the UF_6 plant in Isfahan that prompted the surprising referral to the UNSC achieved consensus among Iran's political elite. Such consensus building is needed in Iran's complex decision-making apparatus. Rouhani reportedly said that the heads of several key posts (foreign ministry, intelligence, defense, Khamenei's representative, and the Supreme National Security Council) met in 2003 and decided that a full nuclear cycle was the country's "red line," and that while temporary exclusions could be made, that full cycle—including enrichment—was the ultimate objective.[28] All their activity and diplomacy were geared to that decision. The nuclear file shifted to a higher bureaucratic level, with oversight transferred from the Iran Atomic Energy Organization to the Supreme National Security Council.

Observers agree that the Iranian public was (and is) supportive of achieving a full nuclear cycle but does not support a nuclear weapons program. Generally, the Majles seems to reflect that sentiment. The hard-liners have an advantage, however, in recognizing that public support for civil nuclear development can be seen as opposition to foreign control. The IAEA, the E3, and certainly any involvement by the United States to impose constraints on nuclear activities are viewed through that frame. Hossein Shariatmadari, the editor of the powerful daily newspaper *Kayhan*, wrote in November 2004, "What appears to be emanating from the whole affair [of negotiations] is the stench of giving in to illegal, illegitimate and excessive demands made by the European Union (EU) troika (read the U.S. and its allies)."[29] He advocated withdrawing from all treaty obligations. There is always a question whether *Kayhan*, closely aligned with Khamenei, is speaking for him.

Rouhani and others in government under Khatami and Ahmadinejad also readily accused the United States for any shortcomings in the outcome of the nuclear talks. In a long speech in 2005 explaining the nuclear negotiations to the Supreme Cultural Revolution Council, a religious body based in Qom, Rouhani was quick to blame the United States for forcing the E3 to "retreat from their commitments" and contended that a permanent agreement would have been reached "if not for American and Israeli pressures."[30] In a 2005 speech to the Open Society Institute in New York, Javad Zarif, Iran's UN ambassador at the time, charged that the United States was trying to torpedo the E3 negotiations and dealt with Tehran on a purely prosecutorial basis, that America was "obsessed" with Iran, and that it was this obsession that endangered security in the region.[31]

The atmosphere in Tehran for the nuclear negotiators—Rouhani, succeeded by Larijani—during the Bush years was fraught: talks needed to yield an outcome in which Iran's rights under the NPT were protected, which to them meant a full nuclear cycle for civilian purposes. Because of the multilayered decision-making process, they needed time to respond to E3 and P5+1 actions and offers. It was slow-moving machinery, possibly by design, but Western analysts and policy makers knew that this deliberative pace was how Iran proceeded. The pressure exerted by Britain and the United States in particular to expedite decision-making appeared in Tehran as just so much bullying, unreasonable demands masking unwillingness to compromise. This in turn made decision-making all the more difficult in Iran, because that pressure was seen, especially by the hard-liners, as unwarranted, aggressive interference in Iran's affairs. The more moderate officials, like Rouhani or Ahmadinjead's last foreign minister, Ali Akbar Salehi, then needed to manage both the internal political wrangling and the international dynamics.

This contrast in the expectations of deal making—not only the content but also the process itself—between the negotiators led to some missed opportunities. The Iranians were willing to limit the number of operating centrifuges and the level of enrichment to below 20 percent (consonant with civilian-only uses), but the P5+1 negotiators were unwilling to accept any enrichment. As this standoff held, Iran was installing more enrichment cascades. To the critics in the West, it appeared that Iran was stalling for time in order to expand its fuel-making capacity. This situation stirred calls for military intervention, particularly from Israel and pro-Israel and neoconservative voices in the United States, which in turn fed into Iranian fears of hostile foreign action.

This broader context informed Iranian decision-making during the ongoing negotiations with the P5+1. The referral to the UNSC caught many Iranian elites by surprise, but that then became the focus of their diplomatic efforts—to stymie the relentless move toward ever more stringent sanctions. In December 2006, the UNSC passed Resolution 1737, which punished Iran for not suspending enrichment, not permitting inspections, and proceeding with other nuclear-related activities by prohibiting transfer of any nuclear-related technologies or materials to Iran and imposing sanctions on individuals and organizations in Iran associated with the nuclear program.[32]

Iran attempted to reengage diplomatically by saying that the suspension of enrichment was a possibility if the negotiations could be returned to Vienna. New ideas on transparency were also discussable, but this gambit failed, and the UNSC tightened the noose in March 2007 by imposing sanctions on arms exports and loans to Iran, as well as further blocking individuals and companies from their foreign assets. Two weeks later, Ahmadinejad announced that Iran had joined the nuclear club by achieving a complete fuel cycle, a bit of triumphalism that had mixed reactions within Tehran's political elite. Some thought that it was a poke in the eye to the United States and would prompt the UNSC to harsher treatment; others applauded this celebration of a key national goal and saw it as a way to extract more "realistic" aims from the West. Iran's fuel cycle was now a fait accompli, they reasoned, and the talks could thereby focus on *how much* enrichment, not *whether* enrichment, would be allowable.

Iran's quickly expanding enrichment activity stirred rounds of diplomatic calls, memos, meetings, alliances, and probing to halt the seemingly inexorable tightening regime of sanctions. Solana, ElBaradei, and the foreign ministers and political directors of the P5+1, as well as Swiss, Swedish, South African, and other would-be helpers, threw themselves into the process. The issue blocking forward motion was always enrichment, while Tehran suggested some confidence-building measures and even a hint of enrichment suspension, which earned Larijani a rebuke from Ahmadinejad and finally led to his dismissal. ElBaradei had floated a "timeout" for both sides at the Davos world economic summit, an idea that enjoyed some favor but never took hold. The problem was not just the stubborn insistence of P5+1 on complete cessation of enrichment; Ahmadinejad was erratic in his handling of the nuclear talks, undermining his own envoy repeatedly and showing no flexibility on the spinning centrifuges. Other elites, including Rafsanjani and Khatami, were openly critical of the hard line, but with the presidency in the hands of the conservatives, they made no progress.

Larijani engineered a minor breakthrough by proposing a work plan with ElBaradei and the IAEA to resolve all outstanding issues regarding the nuclear program—all the things that seemed surreptitious or unexplained, even minor issues, because Iran's covertness was the primary cause for the P5+1 to sanction the IRI. Of course, Larijani had some difficulty convincing others in Tehran that such a pragmatic step was worthwhile when the United States and Britain were denouncing them on weekly basis.[33] But it was a way to move forward, however haltingly and in the face of hostility, when the formal negotiations weren't making progress. Much was cleared up gradually via the work plan, which involved IAEA inspectors on the ground in Iran and reporting to ElBaradei, who briefed the Board of Governors.

ElBaradei went to see the supreme leader in early 2008 to gauge the mood and potential flexibility of the ultimate decision-maker in Iran. He recalled in his memoir that Khamenei was well informed and showed some capacity for dialogue with the United States, but he was adamant about Iran's right to enrich uranium for civilian purposes, repeating the oft-heard line about nuclear weapons being antithetical to Islam. He told ElBaradei that "the real issue was U.S. anger over Iran's emerging role in the region" and that he was prepared to discuss such issues with the Americans.[34] But suspending enrichment was not on the table.

◼ The Final Throes of George W. Bush

President Bush had made a number of belligerent statements about Iran's program during his second term, possibly trying to recoup some leverage as the Iraq War continued to weaken his foreign policy credibility. Cheney had apparently urged Israel to bomb Iranian nuclear facilities, and Seymour Hersh reported that the US Special Forces had been inside Iran to scout bombing targets.[35] The US State Department and possibly intelligence agencies were at work to support anti-government forces inside Iran. So the atmospherics toward Iran in Washington remained stormy despite the mild attempt at diplomacy by Secretary Rice.

It persisted, moreover, despite a flurry of diplomacy by others. Many actors in this drama considered Iran's helpfulness in the effort to clear up past activities to be a strong assist in preventing new sanctions and returning the file to the IAEA, where Iran pledged more determined bargaining. Not all was resolved, however. At issue in 2008 was ElBaradei's statement to the IAEA Board of Governors that the Iranians were conducting, allegedly, "weaponization studies." The information came from documents on a laptop of an Iranian defector who claimed to be a weapons engineer, and the detail and breadth of the documents convinced many that Iran was continuing a weapons program that the CIA had just pronounced, with "high confidence" in its 2007 estimate, did not exist. This military dimension, while not illegal, fed into the narrative that Iran was hiding their true intention to build nuclear weapons. The complex intrigue behind this story, worthy of John Le Carré, persisted for years, even affecting the negotiations in 2013–14 leading to the nuclear deal. German intelligence finally determined that the information was passed on by the MEK and likely was not credible. It was nonetheless the basis for a new round of sanctions in early 2008.

The United States did finally allow for the enrichment reality in Iran's nuclear program. The P5+1 came along with a new proposal during the summer that offered a "freeze for freeze" deal in which no new sanctions would be imposed if Iran froze its enrichment expansion. The offer was the most generous made by the US-led powers and included a number of incentives such as civilian reactors. The offer necessitated an enrichment halt before negotiations, however, and the US representative at the IAEA declared that Iran had to respond within two weeks. Both conditions were nonstarters. The Iranians saw themselves in a strong position, with a fuel cycle complete and increasing numbers of centrifuges on line, and would await a new president in Washington.

The technical question that the nuclear controversy revolved around was whether Iran did indeed have a right to enrich under the terms of the NPT. (Unlike North Korea, Iran remained in the treaty regime; nuclear states Israel, India, and Pakistan never signed the treaty.) The treaty is somewhat ambiguous, but legal scholars generally regard Iran as correct in its interpretation of the NPT in this respect.[36] Six former ambassadors to Iran, led by the United Kingdom's Richard Dalton, declared that "nothing in international law or in the non-proliferation treaty forbids uranium enrichment," and that "in terms of international law, the position of Europe and the United States may be less assured than is generally believed."[37]

As Iran expert William Beeman explained, "The NPT treaty language is quite clear. In Article IV of the treaty it states: 'Nothing in this Treaty shall be interpreted as affecting the inalienable right of all the Parties to the Treaty to develop research, production and use of nuclear energy for peaceful purposes without discrimination and in conformity with Articles I and II of this Treaty.'" The ambiguity derives from the fact that the NPT never explicitly says that enrichment is a right, but it does say that research and development is.[38] States without nuclear weapons like Germany and Japan, among others, clearly endorse the interpretation that enrichment and reprocessing are rights under the treaty.

The United States has never recognized this right, but its application of this position has been arbitrary—denouncing and sanctioning Iran but not others who have taken this course of nuclear development. Iran's covert program and reluctance to comply with some IAEA or UNSC orders in effect formed the basis of those sanctions, not the language of the NPT. At the same time, the repeated precondition for talks—full suspension of enrichment—was frequently based on the US interpretation of the treaty. The impasse was conveniently structured for the United States (though largely self-defeating, given the progress of Iran's enrichment program) and frustrating for the Iranians, who invested a considerable amount of national pride in their nuclear achievements and insistence on their rights under international law.

Throughout the Bush period, this specific impasse about the NPT was drawn from each country's national narratives about the other. Iran was determined to be accorded respect after years of constant belittling by US politicians and opinion leaders. They resisted the P5+1 and its often strangulating sanctions as yet another example of foreign intervention and attempts at domination. Other countries' nuclear programs were not all treated as harshly, or at all—Israel, India, and Pakistan, as noted, were tacitly accepted as nuclear powers. The nuclear negotiations were, as a result, treated by Tehran as an aggressive, hegemonic move against Iranian sovereignty.

Elites in the United States viewed Iran's constant balking, delay, covertness, and rhetorical condemnations of the negotiating process as true to form, the form being cheating on or obstructing their obligations, while supporting terrorist activities in the region. "Diplomatic engagement on Iraq and Afghanistan went downhill" after 2004, former national security adviser Stephen Hadley wrote. "Iran increasingly trained, armed, and aided Shiite extremists in Iraq and later Taliban militants in Afghanistan . . . [and supported] other terrorist groups such as Hezbollah, Palestinian Islamic Jihad and Hamas."[39] The terrorism trope—as mentioned earlier, the contemporary substitute for "savages"—became standard, right-wing bombast even when Iran was negotiating in good faith. The issue at stake, however—nuclear weapons capability—dwarfed concerns about regional mischief making. The Al-Qaeda attacks of 9/11 often were cited in this regard: what if Osama bin Laden got his hands on nuclear explosives? This horrifying prospect was frequently conflated with the more prosaic tasks of arms control with Iran. The expectation, then, that Iran was a sly, deceitful actor with the ingrained mentality of a rug merchant opened the box of orientalist stereotypes that closely mirrored America's frontier myth. It has proved a resilient attitude.

Obama Enters

10 The 2008 presidential election was a bend in the American narrative. Not only did its outcome represent a transcendent shift in the American story (i.e., the election of the first biracial and cosmopolitan president), but also the manner in which that result had been delivered—via a trenchant repudiation of American leadership—signaled a departure from the increasingly cynical deployment of American values at home and abroad. Underscoring the significance of these changes was, of course, the improbability of it all. Writing shortly after the election, former presidential speechwriter and columnist Hendrik Hertzberg captured the sense of collective astonishment at the prospect of President Barack Hussein Obama thus: "Ten weeks from now, the President of the United States will be a person whose first name is a Swahili word derived from the Arabic (it means 'blessing'), whose middle name is that not only of a grandson of the Prophet Muhammad but also of the original target of an ongoing

American war, and whose last name rhymes nicely with 'Osama.' That's not a name, it's a catastrophe, at least in American politics. Or ought to have been." Instead, Hertzberg continued, "sixty-five million Americans turned a liability . . . into a global diplomatic asset, a symbol of the resurgence of America's ability to astonish and inspire."[1]

Indeed, to a world community increasingly weary of American unilateralism, Obama's ascendance to the presidency rekindled faith in international cooperation and, crucially, signaled the rejuvenation of multilateralism in dealing with pressing global issues.[2] A major gesture in this direction was candidate Obama's departure from bipartisan orthodoxy on the diplomatic isolation of America's long-standing enemies. Seizing the moment on his principled opposition to the 2003 invasion of Iraq and the handling of its aftermath, Obama had boldly argued for direct diplomatic talks with regimes in Iran, Cuba, North Korea, and Syria, *without any preconditions.* In the case of Iran, Obama argued that this new approach not only was necessary for stabilizing Iraq but also reflected an abject lesson in the utter futility of "regime change" as the focal point of American policy in the Middle East. As he explained to the *New York Times*, "I think it is important for us to send a signal [to the Iranian government] that we are not hellbent on regime change, just for the sake of regime change, but expect changes in behavior. And there are both carrots and there are sticks available to them for those changes in behavior."[3]

The foremost behavioral change was for Iran to halt the development of its nuclear capabilities, effectively foreclosing the possibility of any military dimensions to its active enrichment program in the future. Achieving this goal was, as the Obama campaign's general election policy platform noted, "a vital national security interest of the United States . . . [that] should start with aggressive, principled, and direct diplomacy—backed with strong sanctions."[4] Preventing Iran's path to nuclear weapons was to be a signature pursuit of the Obama administration's overall national security strategy toward a "nuclear free world," which it would seek to accomplish through existing diplomatic processes facilitated by European, Russian, and Chinese governments.

At around the same time that the Obama campaign was touting its policy of direct engagement with America's adversaries, a serious, if circumspect, effort was already underway at the Department of State to nudge senior Bush administration officials in the direction of a more proactive diplomatic approach toward Iran. The initiative was led by the incoming under secretary of state for political affairs, William J. Burns, who had just returned to Washington after a three-year post as ambassador to Russia. Shortly after becoming the highest-ranking foreign service officer in May 2008, Burns wrote a lengthy memo to Secretary of State Rice entitled "Regaining the Strategic Initiative on Iran." In the memo, he argued for a "new, long-term strategy" toward Iran that would "require calculated risk-taking on our part, applying pressure at as many points as we can, while simultaneously exploring creatively subversive ways to accentuate the gap between the regime's deeply conservative instincts and popular Iranian desire for normalization with the rest of the word, including the U.S."[5] At the core of Burns's intervention lay the imperative for the United States to "revive leverage over Iran," which had been squandered by a combination of strategic missteps in Iraq and short-term thinking about Iran. These mistakes had served to embolden Iran's behavior against American interests in the region and, crucially, handed Tehran a rhetorical advantage: "The regime has constructed a narrative which portrays Iran as the victim of implacable American hostility, increasingly gaining the diplomatic upper hand regionally and globally, with the American administration—not Iran—increasingly the isolated party." Perhaps anticipating the future Obama administration's approach, Burns advised, "Reviving significant pressure against Iran's nuclear program requires us to puncture that narrative."[6]

■ "Mutual Respect"

The official change in tone, if not yet narrative, of America's approach to Iran became evident immediately after Obama's election. In his inaugural address as the forty-fourth president of the United States, Obama offered new terms of engagement with the Muslim world "based on mutual interests and mutual respect," a clear departure from the Bush administration's binary approach—"You are either with us, or with the terrorists"—to the Middle East. Obama continued, "To those who cling to power through corruption and deceit and the silencing of dissent, know that you are on the wrong side of history, but that we will extend a hand if you are willing to unclench your fist."[7] The careful choice of words was meant to acknowledge the established patterns of official Iranian malfeasance both in its domestic affairs and around its nuclear activities, but also the promise of a way forward despite them. It is important to note that this change in tone was part of a general shift in American discourse toward the international community, which the new administration was keen to telegraph from the outset. In the same address, Obama envisioned a new course for America's foreign relations as an equilibrium point between the realistic pursuit of vital national interests and advocacy on behalf of universal ideals such as the rule of law and human rights.[8] Rejecting militarism and nationalistic bluster, he proclaimed that "our power grows through its prudent use; our security emanates from the justness of our cause, the force of our example, the tempering qualities of humility and restraint." The "Bush Doctrine" had officially ended.

The outreach effort to Iran gathered pace through a series of initiatives carefully crafted to convey the seriousness of the new administration in directly addressing issues of mutual concern between Washington and Tehran. On the eve of the Iranian New Year (Nowruz) in March 2009, Obama recorded a video message conveying his well wishes to the Iranian people and his hopes for constructive relations with the Iranian government. In a significant gesture of recognition, Obama addressed the ruling establishment as "the leaders of the Islamic Republic of Iran." Referring to the official post-revolutionary moniker was something the previous administrations had deliberately refrained from, lest it confer any measure of legitimacy on what they regarded as a rogue and unrepresentative regime. Acknowledging "serious [mutual] differences that have grown over time," Obama remarked,

> My administration is now committed to diplomacy that addresses the full range of issues before us, and to pursuing constructive ties among the United States, Iran and the international community. This process will not be advanced by threats. We seek instead engagement that is honest and grounded in mutual respect. You, too, have a choice. The United States wants the Islamic Republic of Iran to take its rightful place in the community of nations. You have that right—but it comes with real responsibilities, and that place cannot be reached through terror or arms, but rather through peaceful actions that demonstrate the true greatness of the Iranian people and civilization. And the measure of that greatness is not the capacity to destroy, it is your demonstrated ability to build and create.[9]

Obama ended his message by reciting a well-known verse by the famous Iranian poet Sa'di: "The children of Adam are limbs to each other, having been created of one essence." The reflective tone and constructive substance of the message surprised many observers of US-Iran relations at the time.[10] However, such encomiums were in fact not novel in the history of US-Iran relations. As referenced in earlier chapters, President Clinton dispatched similar messages on the occasion of Nowruz and Eid al-Fitr (marking the end of Ramadan) with the express aim of demonstrating respect to the Iranian people and signaling new possibilities to their leaders.[11] However, what made the American outreach different this time was the genuine possibility that such words could now be matched in deed and help transform the narrative arc of US-Iran relations (as had just happened in the case of Obama's own improbable election). The Obama outreach was not merely a policy preference but a reflection of an evolution in the American narrative.

The Iranian leadership greeted the Nowruz message with typical incredulity—but, crucially, not with indifference. In his own Nowruz address to the nation, Supreme Leader Ali Khamenei responded to the gesture from Obama by reciting a familiar catalog of American misdeeds against the Islamic Republic—for example, condoning Saddam Hussein's invasion of Iranian territory, supporting Iranian opposition and irredentist groups, and imposing political and economic sanctions, not to mention American imperial support for "unjust" regimes in the region. Overcoming these grievous episodes, Khamenei inveighed, required more than a change in tone and discourse. In a rhetorical tone characteristic of his public speeches, Khamenei retorted,

> What changed? Has your enmity toward the Iranian nation changed? What signs are there to support this? Have you released the possessions of the Iranian nation? Have you removed the cruel sanctions? Have you stopped the insults, accusations, and negative propaganda against this great nation and its officials? Have you stopped your unconditional support for the Zionist regime? What has changed? They talk of change, but there are no changes in actions. We have not seen any changes. Even the literature has not changed. The new US President, from the very moment of his official appointment as President, made a speech, and insulted Iran and the Islamic government. Why? If you tell the truth, and there are changes, where are these changes? Why can we see nothing? I would

like to say this to everyone. US officials should also know that the Iranian nation cannot be fooled, or scared.[12]

Despite the defiant tone and posture, Khamenei nonetheless ended his speech by noting that the Islamic Republic did not yet "have any experience with the new U.S. president and government." As such, he concluded, "We shall see and judge. You [the United States] change, and we shall change as well."

Khamenei's response, as many Iran observers at the time correctly noted, crucially left the door open for further gestures and confidence-building measures. For its part, the Obama administration seemed to have absorbed the lessons of previous missed opportunities by its predecessors and was able to look past the dismissive tone of Khamenei's speech by following up with concrete diplomatic steps. Following a policy review, on April 8, 2009, the administration formally announced that it would join the P5+1 (the five permanent members of the United Nations Security Council plus Germany) talks with Iran, dropping the precondition of Iranian adherence to UN demands prior to any such direct talks. Reinforcing this concrete policy shift, the following month Obama sent a secret letter to Khamenei emphasizing his commitment to resolve the standoff over Iran's nuclear program through diplomacy, and once again reiterating his administration's policy to not seek a change of regime in Iran.[13] Khamenei responded with a variant of his earlier public messages, which was mostly significant as a gesture itself: a willingness to engage directly in writing. Indeed, Khamenei's willingness to correspond directly with Obama was a historic exchange of views as a means of building confidence between the leadership of both countries, the first since the advent of the Islamic Republic. Seizing the significance of this opening, Obama wrote back with a concrete proposal for secret bilateral talks headed by the National Security Council staffer in charge of Iran, Puneet Talwar, and the top State Department diplomat, William J. Burns. The direct back-channel proposal demonstrated seriousness of purpose on behalf of the White House and placed the burden of engagement squarely on the shoulders of Khamenei and the senior Iranian leadership.

It must be noted that these targeted initiatives were parts of a comprehensive shift in policy toward Iran that was first envisioned and formulated within the State Department. It was mostly led by William Burns, who continued his position as undersecretary of state for political affairs under Secretary of State Hillary Clinton. Only three days after Clinton's confirmation, Burns dispatched a memo entitled "A New Strategy toward Iran" to Clinton, which plainly laid out the outlines of a new diplomatic approach commensurate with the national security priorities and outlook of the new administration. "Dealing with Iran," Burns noted, "will require enormous patience, persistence and determination. Deeply conspiratorial and suspicious of American motives, and riven by factions especially eager to undermine one another in the run-up to Iran's presidential election in June, the Iranian elite will be prone to false starts and deceit."[14] But much of that posturing, Burns wished to emphasized, was a requisite performative aspect of revolutionary political practices for domestic Iranian consumption. Defiance of the West—and especially the United States—was part and parcel of the revolutionary *raison d'être* of the Islamic Republic. A productive policy path would be one that looked beyond these rhetorical theatrics and instead both publicly and discreetly tested the regime's willingness to engage. Burns summarized the outlines of a new approach as follows:

> We should set an early tone of respect and commitment to direct engagement, however severe our differences. . . . [W]e should deal with the Iranian regime as a unitary actor, understanding that the Supreme Leader (not the President) is the highest authority. We have failed consistently in the past when we tried to play off one faction against another. . . . Iran

is a formidable adversary . . . but it is not ten feet tall. Its economy is badly mismanaged, with rising rates of unemployment and inflation. It is vulnerable to the ongoing sharp decline in oil prices, and to its dependence on refined petroleum products. It has no real friends in the neighborhood, distrusted by the Arabs and the Turks, patronized by the Russians, and suspicious of the Afghans. . . . [As such,] we need to be always conscious of the anxieties of our friends, as well as key domestic constituencies, as we proceed with Iran. . . . [W]e must make sure that the Administration speaks with one voice, and avoids the divisions which beset the last administration.[15]

In retrospect, the Obama administration's discipline and focus in preparing the ground for this shift in the early months of its first term are most impressive. President Obama's public and private messages to the Iranian leadership helped set the stage for more difficult in-depth discussions of the substantive issues at the heart of US-Iran enmity. But no sooner had the ink on the president's proposal for back-channel talks with Iran dried than internal Iranian politics threatened to completely upend the administration's new strategy.

■ Election Fraud and the Green Movement

Perhaps the most significant challenge posed to the Iranian regime by the Obama administration's new approach was the reconciliation of, on the one hand, Iran's repeated calls for respect and dignity by Western nations and, on the other hand, the suppression of basic rights and popular movements at home. The Bush administration's policy of regime change had provided the power elite led by Khamenei with a convenient cover to suppress calls for reform and stall the electoral progress of reformists in Majles and the presidency. By explicitly disavowing the policy of regime change, Obama had once again placed the burden of internal legitimacy squarely on the shoulders of Iranian leaders, thereby heightening the contradictions at the heart of the system of government in the Islamic Republic. The apparent shift in narrative in America, in other words, had the added advantage of puncturing the official regime narrative in Iran. Mahmoud Ahmadinejad's first term in office had demonstrated, with dramatic and mostly farcical effect, the careful construction of this narrative of grievance. Under its guise, the powers of the intelligence and security forces were consolidated at the executive level, further deepening the influence of the Islamic Revolutionary Guard Corps and their domestic networks of commercial and political interests in government. The combination of Ahmadinejad's misplaced anti-imperial populism in the face of changing Western narratives and the drastic shift in the Iranian domestic balance of power galvanized the Iranian public to reframe its own struggles for change and equal respect.

That change and reform were imperative was indisputable; however, what changes needed to be made, by whom and how, were not very clear. Within the reform camp, there were those who believed that a second chance at Khatami-era reforms would yield results; after all, they argued, the contrast between then and the sorry state of affairs now was stark in the minds of the elite and the public at large. Khatami himself initially endorsed the idea of a comeback, but after much vacillation and agony he withdrew his name from the race. Khatami's abrupt exist left the field open to the far less charismatic wartime prime minister Mir-Hossein Mousavi, whose candidacy had failed to attract much attention, let alone enthusiasm. Yet as the campaign got underway and Khatami and other prominent reformists threw their support behind him, Mousavi began to emerge as a serious contender. In this effort he was immensely helped by his more magnetic and spirited wife, Zahra Rahnavard, who would prove to be an indispensable political asset during the course of the campaign and after.

It is unclear exactly when green became the official color of Mousavi's campaign (the only other reformist candidate in the race, Mehdi Karroubi, had opted for red), but its meaning and symbolism were unmistakable in the minds of the Iranian public. Not only does the color green symbolize renewal, but it is also the color of Islam, and it is especially adorned by direct descendants and true followers of Prophet Mohammad. For his part, Mousavi managed to mount a very effective public relations campaign by capitalizing on the color green, coupled with his message of authentic change, and his first name, Mir-Hossein (Hossein being the name of one of the most revered figures in Shi'a Islam, who became a martyr by opposing the inauthentic, tyrannical rule of the Islamic caliph, Yazid). The Mousavi campaign was also very adept at using online media and social networking tools and communities to spread its message—indeed, so effective that it even captured the imagination of hundreds of thousands of Iranians outside of the country. After a series of unprecedented televised debates between the candidates in which Ahmadinejad all but self-destructed (he infamously brought along with him intelligence files on Mousavi's wife and accused Khatami, Rafsanjani, and Mousavi of teaming up against him in order to restore the status quo ante), there began talk of a "*mowj-e sabz*" (green wave) propelling the reformists back to power.

What took place next was nothing short of a badly orchestrated electoral coup. Within hours of polls closing (in which a whopping 85% of the eligible voters participated), the Interior Ministry (mostly run by former members of the IRGC) rushed to declare Ahmadinejad the winner with nearly 63 percent of the vote, an impossible feat given the latter's meager showings in virtually all public opinion polls in the days before the election and exit poll data compiled by Mousavi's campaign. Indeed, the final certified results were so skewed that even the conservative candidate and former wartime commander of the IRGC, Mohsen Rezaie, had to protest the final vote tally, which showed him with fewer than 2 percent support. The violent events and crackdowns in the ensuing days and months were among the first major world events to be broadcast and disseminated on social media, helping to register the transformative potential of such outlets as YouTube, Facebook, and Twitter. With their help, what was merely a "Green Wave" of support for Mousavi's candidacy quickly transformed into a full-fledged opposition "movement" across Iran and among the Iranian diaspora.

Many variables facilitated the emergence of the Green Movement and the regime's violent crackdown on it: the increasing political role of the shadowy but ever-present IRGC, responsible for engineering the electoral coup in favor of Mahmoud Ahmadinejad; the deepening of existing fissures among the clerical elite; a precarious and demoralized reform movement; the near collapse of the Iranian economy; the Iranian government's expanding military expenditures in the Middle East (at the expense of social welfare at home); the American about-face in international politics; and so on. But perhaps more than any other factor, the advent of the Green Movement was the direct consequence of the coming of age of a demographic explosion in Iran and the inability of the Islamic Republic to accommodate its basic social, political, and economic needs. This phenomenon, however, did not merely speak to a generational divide between an ever-restive youth population and a clerical establishment lacking in awareness and sympathy, but rather was a testament to the utter failure of Islamic governance to reconcile entrenched networks of unaccountable power and wealth with the general welfare and interests of the public. As such, the Green Movement represented the eruption of long-standing grievances against the ruling establishment—an indigenous struggle on behalf of civil and political rights of, by, and for a generation born into the Islamic Republic.

The Obama administration was initially slow and apprehensive in its official response to the election results and their aftermath. Mindful of potentially derailing the just-established back-channel talks with

Iran over its nuclear program and wary of undermining Iranian reformists, the White House did not publicly weigh in until three days into the ongoing nationwide unrest in Iran. In his first public remarks, Obama expressed his "deep concerns about the election" but also noted that "it's not productive, given the history of U.S.-Iranian relations, to be seen as meddling—the U.S. President meddling in Iranian elections." The protests, Obama continued, reflected "a questioning of the kinds of antagonistic postures towards the international community that have taken place in the past, and that there are people who want to see greater openness and greater debate and want to see greater democracy. How that plays out over the next several days and several weeks is something ultimately for the Iranian people to decide. But I stand strongly with the universal principle that people's voices should be heard and not suppressed."[16]

Obama's cautious reaction drew the ire of (neo)conservative commentators and was greeted with puzzlement and indignation by some human rights activists. The neoconservative commentator Charles Krauthammer slammed Obama's "abject solicitousness" in seeking "dialogue with a regime that is breaking heads, shooting demonstrators, expelling journalists, [and] arresting activists."[17] Many commentators also pointed to the awkward timing of Obama's tepid response, which came just a few weeks after his much-touted speech to the Muslim world in Cairo. In those remarks, Obama had made a point of urging Muslim societies to embrace pluralism, human rights, and democratic principles while affirming his own commitment to the noncoercive promotion of universal values.[18] As the clashes between peaceful protesters and the security forces across Iran increasingly turned violent and images of dead young Iranians were broadcast around the world, some wondered whether the Obama administration was overcorrecting the Bush-era policies by too bluntly placing interests above values.[19]

In fact, the Obama administration's response was fairly consistent with its stated policy of maintaining an equilibrium between interests and values in foreign affairs. In the Cairo speech, as in his inaugural address, Obama had envisioned a foreign policy agenda that, on balance, facilitated the *organic* development of democratic institutions and values, not their imposition through foreign pressure. As he underlined in his speech to the Muslim world, "So let me be clear: No system of government can or should be imposed upon one nation by any other. That does not lessen my commitment, however, to governments that reflect the will of the people. Each nation gives life to this principle in its own way, grounded in the traditions of its own people."[20] In reality, Obama's position on democracy promotion merely represented a shift in emphasis on pragmatism and away from messianism in dealing with the often difficult and complex process of democratic development. Whereas the Bush administration's "Freedom Agenda" emphasized a conception of democracy as a universal faith, Obama insisted on a vision of democracy as eternally beholden to contingency and shaped by context. The latter view does not mean that a liberal democratic great power such as the United States must shirk from championing democracy and human rights, only that the promotion of universal values must always be informed by practical realities and ethical obligations *in equal measure.*

That was, in essence, the justification Obama offered in defense of his cautious response to the post-election protests in Iran. In so doing, he was also keen to shed the image of America as the sole promoter of such values and instead compel the international community to work in unison in facilitating greater transparency, the rule of law, and human rights as the cornerstones of international legitimacy.[21] Obama offered a more considered iteration of this vision in his Nobel Peace Prize Lecture in October 2009, with the award having been bestowed on him solely on the basis of the promise of his compelling example and cosmopolitan narrative ushering in a similar era of universal cooperation and solidarity. In that lecture, Obama surprised many by eschewing idealism and instead reiterating the principles undergirding his ethical pragmatism. As he argued in a passage that surely had the continued overtures to Iranian leaders in mind, "The promotion of human rights cannot be about exhortation alone. At times, it must be coupled with painstaking diplomacy. I know that engagement with repressive regimes lacks the satisfying purity of indignation. But I also know that sanctions without outreach—condemnation without discussion—can carry forward only a crippling status quo. No repressive regime can move down a new path unless it has the choice of an open door."[22]

What the (mostly conservative) critics of the administration overlooked at the time were the new circumstances—geopolitical as well as domestic—that necessitated this shift in emphasis. The Bush administration's "Freedom Agenda" not only had failed in propping up democratic regimes in Central Asia and the Middle East but also had provided existing authoritarian governments such as that of the Islamic Republic with cynical justifications to label indigenous pro-democracy movements and human rights activists as Western collaborators and agents. The burden on Obama was thus twofold: to register the contextual basis of democratic development and to disprove cynical dismissals of democracy promotion as a tool of Western imperial statecraft.

In the case of Iran, the political context surrounding the post-election protests was especially important. The 2009 protests unearthed simmering tensions from within the clerical establishment, with some of the most senior dissident clerical figures, such as Grand Ayatollahs Hossein-Ali Montazeri and Yousef Saanei, and even the conservative-pragmatist former president Ali Akbar Hashemi Rafsanjani, openly questioning the election results and warning of impending tyranny.[23] This was an unprecedented crisis of legitimacy for the Islamic Republic, which many observers at the time surmised could plausibly lead to the emergence of a truly organic democratic beginning.[24] Aware of their historic opportunity, Green Movement leaders emphatically rejected any help or even expressions of solidarity from Western—and especially American—leaders and instead framed their struggle as the last-ditch effort to save the ideals of the revolution.[25] Moreover, in preelection debates and policy statements, both Mousavi and Karroubi had made it clear that their positions on Israel-Palestine, support for Hezbollah and other Shi'ite militia in the region, and the nuclear program would not be demonstrably different from those of previous Iranian administrations. Most importantly, they echoed and held fast to the long list of grievances against the United States. However, they rebuked Ahmadinejad's radical provocations, resented the increasing role of security forces in devising Iran's domestic and foreign policies, and were mostly wary of regional overstretch in Iraq and Syria.

Given the subtleness of these differences on Iran's foreign policy and the entrenched position of the supreme leader in the system, the Obama administration justifiably saw little reason that its major point of contention with the Islamic Republic—its expanding nuclear program—was going to be affected by a change at the presidential level. At the level of raw geopolitics, this was a cold calculation, indeed; but when considered next to Obama's approach toward democracy promotion, its operationalization into a policy of detached solidarity did not strain reason at the time, nor betray moral leadership. It could be argued, in fact, that leaving internal Iranian affairs to Iranians themselves gave the United States and the international community the upper hand in pressing their grievances against the regime's foreign and security policies.[26] The advent and eventual demise of the Green Movement in Iran presented the Obama administration with the first policy test of its evident pivot in narrative, and the president and his team held fast to principle with eyes firmly focused on the diplomatic effort to halt Iran's nuclear program.

■ Into the Nuclear Maze

The highest-level direct talks between Iran and the United States since 1979 took place on October 1, 2009, in Geneva. The meeting between the P5+1 and Iranian diplomats took place immediately following revelations by US, British, and French intelligence agencies that Iran had secretly built an advanced enrichment facility near the city of Qom. Although the Iranians protested that they had informed the International Atomic Energy Agency of the existence of the new site (named Fordow) on September 21, in a joint appearance on September 25 Obama, along with British prime minister Gordon Brown and French president Nicholas Sarkozy, insisted that Iran only made the declaration after the new facility had been discovered by Western intelligence. At the high-level October meeting, the head of the US delegation, William Burns, was instructed to use the new information as leverage to pressure the lead Iranian negotiator Saeed Jalili to accept a new scheme to supply the fuel for its Tehran Research Reactor in return for a portion of its 5 percent enriched uranium, which would roughly be equivalent to material needed for one bomb (the so-called "freeze for freeze" proposal). In their meeting, Burns warned Jalili, "in a straightforward tone, that the consequences of rejecting the proposal, especially in light of the Qom revelation, were certain to be substantially tougher sanctions."[27] Later in the same month, at a meeting organized by IAEA in Vienna, Jalili, after conferring with Tehran, rejected the swap proposal in principle and on technical grounds. This was a crucial missed opportunity for the Iranians, not only since it further unified the P5+1 and IAEA positions on more stringent next steps (e.g., sanctions) but also because it portrayed Tehran as either too rigid or too aloof to recognize the momentousness of high-level talks with Washington.

In reality, the swap deal was the victim of the crisis of legitimacy still brewing inside Iran in the aftermath of its presidential elections.

By the autumn of 2009, scores of Iranian reformists, students, political activists, and journalists affiliated with the Green Movement had been either thrown into jail, paraded through television screens in mass Soviet-style show trials, or else driven out of the country. The post-election convulsions had shaken the regime to its core, with many senior national security veterans on the fence about the efficacy of even tacitly lending support to any policy measure favored by Ahmadinejad. The pall of uncertainty hanging over the entire system made the prospect of a swap deal seem either an opportunistic move by Ahmadinejad to paper over the post-election divisions by delivering a major foreign policy win of his own or else a capitulation to Western demands after just one meeting with American diplomats as lead negotiators. Ahmadinejad's reformist and conservative opponents alike seized on these arguments in public statements and critical statements in the media, which likely pressured the supreme leader into rebuffing the swap deal.[28]

The rejection of the P5+1 deal also undermined Obama's outreach efforts since it played into the hawkish narrative on Iran—amplified by the Israeli prime minister Benjamin Netanyahu and Republican (and some Democratic) leaders in Washington—as a hardening authoritarian regime racing to acquire nuclear breakout capacity. Sanctions became an inevitability once Iran announced in early February 2010 that it had begun the process of producing 20 percent enriched uranium. At a meeting with European diplomats after this announcement, Netanyahu warned that "Iran is racing forward to produce nuclear weapons," further arguing that "what is required right now is tough action by the international community. . . . This means not moderate sanctions, or watered-down sanctions. This means crippling sanctions and these sanctions must be applied right now."[29] The campaign for robust sanctions also gained force in Congress as the Obama administration's own December 2009 deadline for diplomacy expired. On January 29, 2010, the Senate passed a sanctions bill on

Iran's gasoline imports, which put pressure on the administration to speed up its efforts for a comprehensive sanctions resolution at the UNSC.

Before securing sanctions at the UN, however, a last-minute diplomatic effort mounted jointly by Brazilian president Luiz Inácio Lula da Silva and his Turkish counterpart Recep Tayyip Erdogan aimed to rescue the swap proposal under slightly modified conditions. At a White House nuclear summit hosted by Obama in mid-April, the two leaders presented the Iranians with a new offer of shipping 1,200 kilograms of their supply of low-enriched uranium under IAEA seal to Turkey in return for fuel pads supplied by the P5+1. At the summit meeting, Obama and his national security team expressed their skepticism about the prospects of such a deal in the face of repeated Iranian hesitance and deception in the recent past. While the effort was clever in presenting Ahmadinejad and Khamenei with a face-saving option of reaching an agreement with budding populist leaders, it would be unclear what enforcement mechanisms these powers would resort to if the Iranians reneged once again. Moreover, since its rejection of the P5+1 swap proposal, Tehran had begun production of 20 percent enriched uranium, increasing its existing supplies to levels that would have required new offset terms for a swap to be viable.[30] Regardless, without any explicit objections from the P5+1 to such an effort, Brazilian and Turkish delegations arrived in Tehran a few weeks later to present Iran with their proposal.

On May 17, 2010, the "Tehran Declaration" was signed by all parties with great pomp and theater. The brief two-page declaration mostly reiterated the outlines of the proposal first pitched by Lula and Erdogan to Obama at the White House nuclear summit, but it was thin on the details of the exchange, which it conditioned on "the positive response of the Vienna Group (US, Russia, France, and the IAEA)."[31] Unbeknownst to the parties at the time, however, far from the possibility of a "positive response" anywhere on the horizon, the Obama administration had already secured the support of the Russian Federation and China for a sanctions resolution at the UNSC. Frustrated by Iranian backpedaling and deception on Fordow, the Russians had resolved to use Iran as a bargaining piece in their own diplomatic "reset" with the United States. They exploited this opening deftly, conditioning their support for a UN resolution on the lifting of US sanctions on Russian military units and the end to North Atlantic Treaty Organization expansion in Eastern Europe. Later on, Russian president Dmitry Medvedev agreed to cancel the delivery of the S-300 missile defense system to Iran, reportedly in exchange for the US canceling of a missile defense shield for Europe.[32] Similarly, China's worries around their access to Iranian oil were addressed through offers of increased shipments (to account for the falling Iranian supplies) by the United Arab Emirates and Saudi Arabia.[33]

With Russian and Chinese support secured, the UNSC Resolution 1920 was adopted on June 9, 2010, with twelve votes in favor, two against (Brazil and Turkey), and one abstention (Lebanon). The resolution placed severe sanctions on Iran's financial sector, effectively freezing Iranian banks out of international exchange systems. It also placed strict limitations on the sale of heavy arms to Iran by third parties and prohibited Iran from undertaking any activity related to its ballistic missile program. Other provisions included sanctions on IRGC-affiliated companies, frozen assets of forty individuals and organizations connected to Iran's nuclear program, and travel bans on specific individuals. For the sanctions to be lifted, the resolution called on Iran to "comply with the Safeguards Agreement with the IAEA, not undertake any further reprocessing, heavy water-related or enrichment-related activities or acquire commercial interests in other states involving uranium mining or use of nuclear materials and technology."[34] Ahmadinejad dismissed the resolution as "a used handkerchief which should be thrown in the dustbin."[35] In his remarks on the adoption of the UNSC resolution, Obama cataloged what he called a pattern of

Iranian "intransigence" and, notably, concluded with a reminder of the vulnerability at the heart of Iranian leaders' protestations:

> Saturday will mark one year from the day that an election captivated the attention of the world—an event that should have been remembered for how the Iranian people participated with remarkable enthusiasm, but will instead be remembered for how the Iranian government brutally suppressed dissent and murdered the innocent, including a young woman left to die in the street. Actions do have consequences, and today the Iranian government will face some of those consequences. Because whether it is threatening the nuclear non-proliferation regime, or the human rights of its own citizens, or the stability of its own neighbors by supporting terrorism, the Iranian government continues to demonstrate that its own unjust actions are a threat to justice everywhere.[36]

Obama's comments were instructive in terms of his willingness to exert noncoercive pressure on Iran, even at the risk of jeopardizing painstakingly procured yet still-delicate diplomatic capital during the first year of his administration. But his remarks were also curious in their reversion to the old narrative script about Iranian intransigence, roguish behavior, and authoritarian tendencies as ultimate obstacles in the way of a diplomatic breakthrough. He would repeat these themes again at the signing of the Comprehensive Iran Sanctions, Accountability, and Divestment Act, passed by Democratic majorities in the House and the Senate.

Understandably, a great deal of Obama's frustrations stemmed from the evident fact that Iranian leaders—especially Khamenei—seemed incapable of recognizing the unique momentum Obama enjoyed during the first year of his presidency to achieve a reasonably solid diplomatic platform for addressing a host of issues of mutual concern between Iran and the United States. This oversight not only had played directly into the hands of skeptics and hawkish leaders like Netanyahu, who were now arguing for even harsher positions, but also had introduced yet another layer of hurdles (i.e., sanctions) that now had to be negotiated prior to the resumption of talks on Iran's nuclear program. As such, the likelihood of events and third parties playing the role of spoiler was now much greater than before. Despite these misgivings, at the signing of the Iran Sanctions Act in July 2010, Obama reiterated his offer of diplomacy to Iranian leaders: "So, again, this is not a day that we sought—but it is an outcome that was chosen by the Iranian government when it repeatedly failed to meet its responsibilities. And the government of Iran still has a choice. The door to diplomacy remains open. Iran can prove that its intentions are peaceful. It can meet its obligations under the NPT and achieve the security and prosperity worthy of a great nation."[37]

◼ Testing the Back Channel

In defiance of the UN, American, and European Union sanctions, Iran continued to increase its nuclear activities by building more centrifuges and increasing its enrichment capacity at its Fordow and Natanz facilities, respectively. The sanctions had once again isolated Iran as a cause of concern and applied renewed pressure to its economy, but they had not actually succeeded in achieving the ultimate objective of such measures: halting Iran's progress toward a bomb. A major new opportunity revealed itself in late 2011 through the Sultanate of Oman, whose long-reigning monarch, Sultan Qaboos bin Said, maintained close ties with both the senior Iranian leadership and the United States. Having successfully secured the release of three American hikers who had been detained by Iranian authorities on suspicion of spying (based on unproven accusations), the Sultan and his trusted advisor Salem Ben Nasser Al-Ismaily presented the White House with the proposal for a direct meeting between US and Iranian diplomats in Muscat. The Omanis, like other Persian Gulf monarchies, were concerned about the prospect of escalation of hostilities between Iran and the United States, which they worried could break out into military confrontation, further destabilizing the region. But what made the offer especially enticing for American officials was the apparent endorsement by the supreme leader of Iran of unconditional talks with his own senior foreign policy advisor (and former foreign minister of Iran) Ali Velayati on outstanding issues between the two sides, but especially Iran's nuclear program.

A preliminary meeting was hastily arranged by Ismaily between a small Iranian delegation and the then director of policy planning at the State Department, Jake Sullivan, who was accompanied by the NSC staffer Puneet Talwar. Although the meeting focused on generalities and was mostly used by both sides to measure the level of interest of the other, it was an important exercise in keeping the channels of dialogue open. In time, it would prove to be an especially critical stepping-stone toward the resumption of comprehensive talks on Iran's nuclear program.[38] At the initial talks, the Iranian delegation made it clear that they sought an American recognition of their "right to enrichment," which is how the Islamic Republic had framed its undaunted expansion of its nuclear program at home and increasingly to the world community. Similarly, the Americans were insistent on registering to the Iranians the importance of confidence-building measures and concrete evidence of compliance with IAEA protocols in order to create room for good-faith negotiations. The airing of general grievances and potential stumbling blocks through this channel would prove to be an important release valve for both sides, away from and unaffected by the transactional gaze of other parties and potential spoilers.

Having tested and been reassured of the viability of the Omani back channel, both sides were cautious not to invest too heavily in the process in light of the evolving geopolitical crises in the Middle East—

the Arab Spring revolts raging across the region—and the upcoming American presidential election. With regard to the Arab Spring revolts, the Obama administration had struggled to maintain its desired equilibrium between noninterference and a policy of detached solidarity, as it had in the case of the 2009 protests in Iran. The collapse of long-standing autocratic leaders in Tunisia, Egypt, Libya, and Yemen, coupled with widespread destabilization of traditionally resilient regimes across the Arab world, overnight left a trail of failed or collapsing states in the region without any clear remedies or good options in sight. This new geopolitical backdrop introduced yet another labyrinthine layer of issues and practical difficulties that Iranian and American negotiators would have to manage and confront in parallel with the nuclear talks.

In 2008, Obama ran for and won the presidency on a platform of change and hope. Obama's own personal journey and improbable rise to the most powerful political office in the world shaped the narrative of his first term in office. Many changes across a range of domestic and foreign policy initiatives had indeed been introduced. But it was also the case that in many of these cases change was met with fierce resistance. Nonetheless, by maintaining an uneasy balance between realism and ethical obligations—that is, a genuine pragmatic equilibrium—the Obama administration had good reasons to hope that he had demonstrated sufficient goodwill to earn both a second term and a vote of confidence to stay the course on his agenda for change. Although Obama's comfortable reelection over former Massachusetts governor Mitt Romney was a confirmation that his message of hope and change was still resonant, the excited sense of seemingly limitless possibilities that accompanied his 2008 campaign was little in evidence. His second inaugural address perfectly exemplified this shift in lowered ambitions. Compared to his 2009 address, it contained only a small passage on foreign policy, which was as formulaic as it was abstract: "America will remain the anchor of strong alliances in every corner of the globe. And we will renew those institutions that extend our capacity to manage crisis abroad, for no one has a greater stake in a peaceful world than its most powerful nation. We will support democracy from Asia to Africa, from the Americas to the Middle East, because our interests and our conscience compel us to act on behalf of those who long for freedom."[39]

Rouhani, Zarif, and the Nuclear Deal

11 At the time of President Obama's second inauguration in early 2013, US-Iran relations had all but reverted to the status quo ante. Although officials on both sides remained open to diplomacy, their respective positions on Iran's nuclear program—that is, a recognition of the Islamic Republic's "right" to enrich uranium, and American-led sanctions on Iran's economy—made the prospect of a breakthrough increasingly difficult. In addition to the nuclear picture, the highly volatile geopolitical scene in the Middle East—in the aftermath of the failed popular uprisings across the Arab world—had locked Tehran and Washington into de facto proxy battles along sectarian divides. Daily reports and analyses of these entanglements gave the impression of a zero-sum struggle that often cast the Islamic Republic as a rising regional hegemon bent on upending a long-standing American-backed Sunni Arab order. In reality, Iran's increased support for its proxies was a symptom of a security dilemma forced on its leaders by the post–Iraq War geostrategic landscape that had just been augmented by antiauthoritarian uprisings across the region. Eager to fortify its allies and avoid isolation, the Islamic Revolutionary Guard Corps effectively took control of Iran's regional policy and poured in money and armaments to nourish their clients, especially in Iraq, Syria, and Yemen—failed and collapsing states all. Deeply resented by Sunni Arab leaders for its initial hesitance in the face of popular uprisings, the Obama administration also increased its intelligence and military support for its allies out of the fear that it might be drawn back into even deeper military engagements if massive power imbalances emerged.

With these geopolitical developments in the background, the rhetoric of Iranian and American officials increasingly featured familiar lines of argument. As Iran's firebrand president Mahmoud Ahmadinejad and Supreme Leader Ali Khamenei rehearsed their grievances against US hypocrisy, "imperial arrogance," and unjust sanctions, American officials blamed Iranian forces for destabilizing the region, engaging in pariah state tactics (hostage-taking, primarily), and nuclear malfeasance. Paradoxically, while the American discourse largely reflected the domestic pressures on the Obama administration by pro-Israel and pro-Saudi interests in Congress, the rhetoric of Iranian leaders belied public opinion and even factional politics inside Iran.

The harsh crackdowns after the 2009 elections that all but eliminated reformists from the political scene exposed major divides between radical and pragmatist elites in the conservative camp. The pragmatist faction, led by the former president and powerbroker Ali Akbar Hashemi Rafsanjani, was alarmed by the growing influence of the security establishment and weary of Ahmadinejad's mishandling of the economy and foreign affairs, which had been made worse in large part thanks to Ahmadinejad's anachronistic and alienating Third-Worldist posturing. Iran's foreign policy establishment—composed largely of Western-educated bureaucrats highly attuned to institutional politics

Rouhani, Zarif, and the Nuclear Deal

and policy debates in Western capitals—was a prominent and especially vocal wing of the pragmatist faction critical of Ahmadinejad. Senior members of this cohort openly worried about the possibility of missing a major opportunity to break the Islamic Republic out of isolation once and for all, and to possibly even normalize relations with Western powers, including the United States. To be sure, the pragmatist faction itself also did not lack for trenchant positions and rhetoric against purported American "bullying" and "untrustworthiness"; all the same, they regarded Ahmadinejad as being out of his depth on foreign policy and as especially feckless on the nuclear issue. To this group, if the Islamic Republic were to consolidate its regional gains in the post-Saddam, post–Arab Spring order, as well as possibly open its economy to Western investments and trade, then change would be imperative.

In the months preceding the 2013 Iranian presidential elections, the disparate domestic and international concerns preoccupying Iranian and American officials, respectively, paradoxically served to muddle the narrative of both sides. By shoring up United Nations Security Council support for economic and political sanctions against Iran, the Obama administration had succeeded in reassuring its regional allies that it could get tough on Tehran. However, the administration also underlined its commitment to diplomacy and bilateral talks after the appointment of John Kerry as the new secretary of state. As a senator, Kerry had been vocal about the need for building trust with Iranian officials and achieving a durable diplomatic agreement on Iran's nuclear program.[1] Together with national security officials in the White House, Kerry underlined the effectiveness of the sanctions while also acknowledging the fact that it was merely a temporary check on Iran's ambitions. On the Iranian side, no amount of defiant rhetoric about "resistance" or national resilience could override the reality that the Islamic Republic was facing perhaps the most acute crisis of social, political, and economic legitimacy since its founding. As such, although each side held fast to its customary grievances, the Obama administration's refusal to shut the door on diplomacy created a vital space for the exploration of new data points, milestones, and narratives. All that remained was an affirmative signal in the form of meaningful political change in Iran, which the 2013 presidential elections in Iran delivered in the most surprising manner.

■ Agent of Stability

On June 12, 2013, Hassan Rouhani, a technocratic cleric with a long résumé in national security affairs, became the seventh president of the Islamic Republic. Rouhani's resounding victory over his conservative rivals was unexpected and all the more astonishing because of the electoral engineering process that preceded it. Less than a month prior to election day, the Guardian Council—the body charged with vetting the qualifications of prospective candidates for political office in the Islamic Republic—had stunned the public and the establishment by disqualifying former president Rafsanjani's candidacy.[2] Although Rafsanjani's disqualification was unofficially justified (the Guardian Council does not have to justify its decisions to the public) on account of his old age in some conservative media outlets, the rejection was widely—and correctly—interpreted as a power move by Khamenei to prevent a major challenge to his near-absolute authority.[3] Since his public criticisms of other regime officials in the aftermath of the 2009 election, Rafsanjani's profile had undergone a remarkable transformation in the eyes of the public (and even in the judgment of some dissidents). He and his children were increasingly seen by reformists and centrist conservatives as the most optimal vessels for meaningful change in the leadership and direction of the Islamic regime. As a close and perhaps most trusted advisor to Ayatollah Khomeini, a former president and speaker of parliament, and the chairman of the Ex-

pediency and Discernment Council and Assembly of Experts, Rafsanjani not only possessed sufficient revolutionary credentials to challenge
the decisions of any institutional body in the Islamic Republic but
could also challenge the judgment and legitimacy of Khamenei himself.[4] His summary disqualification, therefore, was a deliberate act of
public humiliation designed to show that ultimate authority rested
with Khamenei and his office.

As with previous presidential elections, moreover, the Guardian
Council was also keen to approve the candidacy of at least one moderate and one reformist whom it deemed sufficiently harmless to the
chances of leading conservative hopefuls. In 2013, these included a
reformist former minister, vice president (under Khatami), and parli-
amentarian, Mohammad Reza Aref, and the pragmatic former parlia-
mentarian Hassan Rouhani,[5] who was known domestically and to
those outside of Iran mostly for his roles as secretary of the Supreme
National Security Council during the Rafsanjani and Khatami presi-
dencies and as Iran's chief nuclear negotiator with the European powers in 2003–5, respectively.[6] The remaining six candidates (out of nearly
seven hundred applicants) were well-known conservatives with close
links to both Khamenei's office and the IRGC: Gholam-Ali Haddad-
Adel (former speaker of parliament), Mohammad Gharazi (former oil
minister), Saeed Jalili (secretary of the SNSC and chief nuclear negotiator after Rouhani), Mohsen Qalibaf (former IRGC commander and
mayor of Tehran), Mohsen Rezaie (former IRGC commander), and Ali
Akbar Velayati (former foreign minister and chief foreign policy advisor to Khamenei). After Rafsanjani's disqualification, the stage had
been set for one of the two strongest approved conservative candidates—Jalili or Qalibaf—to win the poll.

But the qualification process provoked a huge popular backlash
against the audaciousness of the Guardian Council to engineer a conservative victory. The tacit imposition of yet another counterfeit process
after the last presidential election not only was brash but also seemed

especially sinister in light of the economic and political devastation Ahmadinejad's tumultuous tenure had wrought. Despite enjoying some of the highest oil revenues since 1979, under Ahmadinejad economic mismanagement, rampant corruption, and external sanctions had greatly damaged the country's fiscal and monetary health.[7] Between 2006 and 2013, the rates of economic growth and per capita income (19% and 10%, respectively) were demonstrably lower compared to those of the Khatami (37.5% and 24.7%) and Rafsanjani (27% and 11%) periods, and by 2012 the official inflation rate stood at nearly 30 percent.[8] Adding to these woes was Ahmadinejad's conspiratorial populism that constantly blamed "hidden forces" for his shortcomings, just as his own administration grew more nepotistic and unaccountable over time.

By the time of the 2013 elections, therefore, the public had little appetite for trenchant revolutionary rhetoric and sloganeering. Instead, it yearned for blunt acknowledgment of the country's myriad internal problems and the need for bold and practical solutions. None of the conservative candidates in the race could muster an authentic campaign message that approximated this vision. The reformist candidate, Aref, was very adept at contrasting the failures of Ahmadinejad and conservative parliamentarians with those of reformists during the Khatami era, but his relative marginality as a political player (and lack of personal charisma) rendered him implausible in the eyes of many voters. This left Rouhani as the only plausible choice for reformists and centrists alike.

Rouhani's profile as a national security technocrat with close ties to Rafsanjani and Khatami made him a palatable compromise for a restive public eager to resist an all-out conservative onslaught. But Rouhani's performance in a series of televised debates made it clear that he could indeed be an effective leader for stabilizing the system and rescuing Iran's economy out of international isolation. With barely a week left before election day, public polls shifted dramatically in Rouhani's favor after he challenged the twin pillars of conservative orthodoxy: pride in a "resistance economy" and inflexibility on nuclear negotiations in the absence of any workable alternatives. "It is all well for centrifuges to spin," Rouhani famously implored his rivals, "but it is also important that the country and the wheels of industry are spinning as well." Jalili in turn took Rouhani to task for his eagerness to please Western concerns over Iran's nuclear program during his time as Iran's chief nuclear negotiator, apparently unaware of the approval by a vast majority of ordinary Iranians for just such a diplomatic approach.[9] In response, Rouhani pointed out how "constructive dialogue" had in fact led to breakthroughs with European powers that were pivotal in shielding Iran from UN sanctions, international isolation, and even the threat of war.[10] Rouhani also used the debate platform to telegraph his sympathies with the victims of regime crackdowns after the 2009 elections, and he made ambiguous promises about working to secure the release of opposition leaders under house arrest in interviews and at campaign rallies.[11]

Prior to the debates, Rouhani's best chance was a strong second-place finish, in hopes of forcing a runoff against either Qalibaf or Jalili. However, his performance at the debates propelled him to clear frontrunner status in the campaign. In rebutting the conservative narrative of "resistance" while also avoiding any substantive comments—let alone commitments—on the imperatives of reform, Rouhani had succeeded in casting himself as a pragmatic moderate eager to chart a path forward—a realist not easily given to wishful thinking and dogmatism. The Rouhani campaign officially adopted the slogan *E'tedal* (moderation) and later combined it with the visual symbol of a key to signal that moderation was the key to Iran's future in both domestic and foreign affairs. Borrowing a page from Barack Obama's 2008 presidential campaign, Rouhani vowed that his would be a government of "Prudence and Hope," not of extremism. With that, the reformist candidate Aref was left with little choice but to drop out and endorse Rouhani's candidacy. Soon after, the Moderation and Development

Party (centrist), the Islamic Iran Participation Front (reformist), and the umbrella group the Reformist Front Coordination Council formed a united front in supporting his candidacy.[12]

In a wide-ranging and much-discussed (inside Iran) interview with the London-based Saudi newspaper *Asharq Al-Awsat*—strategically timed for publication on the eve of the election—Rouhani directly addressed his views on US-Iran relations, which were uncharacteristically detailed and conciliatory for a presidential hopeful in the Islamic Republic, let alone for a former national security official as cautious and historically timid as he. His response to the question "What steps can be taken to improve situation [*sic*] with the US? Do you support reestablishing ties with the US?" bears reproducing in full:

> The Iran-US relationship is a complex and difficult issue. A bitter history, filled with mistrust and animosity, marks this relationship. It has become a chronic wound whose healing is difficult but possible, provided that good faith and mutual respect prevail. In my view, the current state of affairs between Iran and the US cannot and should not remain forever. Extremists on both sides seem to be determined to perpetuate the situation of animosity and hatred between the two countries. However, common sense dictates a change in this trend with a view to opening a new chapter in this uneasy and challenging relationship to decrease enmity and mistrust.
>
> States can have differences of views on major international issues, but nevertheless remain civil towards one another and attempt, in the worst-case scenario, to narrow the differences through positive dialogue and interaction at any level possible under the circumstances. As a moderate, I have a phased plan to deescalate hostility to a manageable state of tension and then engage in promotion of interactions and dialogue be-

tween the two peoples to achieve détente, and finally reach to the point of mutual respect that both peoples deserve.[13]

Rouhani's written responses to the questions in the interview were clearly meant to signal his willingness to move beyond the stalemated public and back-channel talks with American officials. Most significantly, in a direct signal to the Obama administration, Rouhani reciprocated Obama's 2008 calls for "mutual respect" and "détente" through constructive diplomacy, albeit with the proviso that any progress ought to be measured by deeds.

On election night, Rouhani shocked the political establishment by scoring an outright victory with a nearly 51 percent share of the vote.[14] Equally shocking was the high level of turnout—at nearly 73 percent—which afforded Rouhani a robust mandate to govern and implement some of his major campaign proposals. Just three weeks prior to election day many pundits and political insiders feared a massive boycott of the elections due to the Guardian Council's clear attempt at engineering a favorable outcome for conservatives. Yet, quite improbably, Rouhani's candidacy had managed to turn the election into a test of wills between the conservative establishment and popular support.[15] The fact that the security establishment did not intervene in a similar fashion to that in 2009 to ensure a Qalibaf or Jalili victory was both a concession to majority will and a telling sign that a Rouhani presidency was not in any way a threat to the hierarchy and conduct of power in the Islamic Republic.[16] Moreover, a pragmatic approach to domestic and foreign policy was indeed a convenient and necessary shield for stabilizing economic conditions at home and fortifying Iran's national interests at a moment of heightened regional and international instability. Precisely because Rouhani enjoyed the support of a reform-minded electorate who nonetheless only expected modest changes ahead, he could be relied on to govern with only stability and prudence as measures of success in mind.

■ "Prudence" as Narrative

Rouhani wasted no time in assembling a cadre of seasoned technocrats and competent public servants in his "Government of Prudence and Hope." He set an American-style "First 100 Days" benchmark for stabilizing the economy and preparing the diplomatic ground for a major course correction in foreign and national security affairs.[17] Rouhani's own natural area of comfort was in foreign affairs. He was a member of the Supreme Defense Council and a deputy war commander (a civilian post) during the Iran-Iraq War (1983–85), was Ayatollah Montazeri's liaison to Islamic student associations in Europe (1983–85), and concurrently served as the secretary of the SNSC (1989–2005) and director of the highly influential Center for Strategic Research (1992–2000). The latter is a governmental think tank established by Rafsanjani for the purpose of nourishing conservative-pragmatist talent in national security affairs (many of Rouhani's cabinet appointments and advisors were CSR alumni).[18] Through these posts, Rouhani had established himself as a conservative-pragmatist in the mold of Rafsanjani: transactional by nature, moderate in temperament, but also fiercely devoted to the Islamic Republic. At the peak of Rafsanjani's power in the late 1980s and early 1990s, Rouhani was part of a small cohort of trusted hands that met with Bud McFarlane to negotiate the terms of the arms-for-hostages deal, helped with efforts to coordinate the end of the war with Iraq, and was a foremost advocate of deepening economic ties with Western European companies during the reconstruction period.[19] In constructing his own cabinet, therefore, Rouhani was particularly keen to call on experienced hands with roots stretching across those defining decades.

By far, the biggest star and most important talent in Rouhani's cabinet was the gregarious and polished senior diplomat Mohammad Javad Zarif, who was appointed as foreign minister. Untypical of a senior government official in the Islamic Republic, Zarif had attained his secondary and postsecondary education from schools and universities in the United States (his BA in International Relations at San Francisco State University in 1981, and his MA and PhD in International Relations at the University of Denver in 1984 and 1988, respectively).[20] Also unlike other high-ranking officials, Zarif had spent the majority of his life after the revolution in America as a diplomat at Iran's permanent mission to the United Nations in New York, first as deputy ambassador (1989–92) and then as ambassador (2002–7).[21] While at the United Nations, Zarif stood out for being decidedly more polished and well versed in the minutiae of domestic politics driving Western—and specifically American—policies on Iran. Although an ardent believer in the Islamic Republic, he projected a debonair sensibility that was in stark contrast to the gruff mannerisms and rigid sloganeering of most other Iranian diplomats posted abroad. Zarif's fluency in English and American culture also enabled him to cultivate a broad network of American interlocutors across the political spectrum in New York and Washington. The fruits of his efforts were on display during his five-year tenure as Iran's ambassador to the United Nations, when he met with Senators Joe Biden, Dianne Feinstein, Chuck Hagel, and John Kerry. As a profile of him in the *New Yorker* noted, "He may be the only person in the world who can telephone both Senator Dianne Feinstein and the Hezbollah chief Hassan Nasrallah."[22]

Zarif's personal qualities, diplomatic talents, loyalty to his country, and cultivated networks in the United States made him an ideal choice for foreign minister at a pivotal time in US-Iran relations. His appointment was greeted with a sense of relief and optimism in Western capitals by counterparts who had come to know him as a capable diplomat and a worthy adversary. But, predictably, Zarif and Rouhani were also dismissed by the Israeli government, Republican lawmakers, and pro-Israel groups in Western capitals as merely the smiling faces of an otherwise-menacing regime bent on erasing the Jewish state from the map. Shortly after the election, Israeli prime minister Benjamin Netanyahu warned that "the international community should not fall into wishful thinking and be tempted to ease pressure on Iran to stop its nuclear program."[23]

More than any other Iranian government, the Rouhani administration was attuned to the importance of narrative and public relations in rehabilitating the Islamic Republic's image after Ahmadinejad. The latter routinely peddled anti-Semitic conspiracy theories and notoriously hosted a conference questioning the existence of the Holocaust that featured a gallery of international racist and anti-Semitic speakers, including the former grand wizard of the Ku Klux Klan David Duke.[24] Repairing the damage wrought by Ahmadinejad required an unequivocal renunciation of anti-Semitism and public displays of respect for the Jewish faith that went beyond perfunctory gestures. Social media afforded Iranian officials an effective platform for just such an outreach. Both Rouhani and Zarif took to Twitter to extend their well wishes on the occasion of the Jewish New Year (Rosh Hashanah). Rouhani posted, "As the sun is about to set here in #Tehran I wish all the Jews, especially Iranian Jews, a blessed Rosh Hashanah."[25] Zarif's outreach on the Jewish New Year also marked his debut on social media, and it featured a revealing interaction with Christine Pelosi, a documentarian and daughter of the then House minority leader Nancy Pelosi. Pelosi responded to Zarif's New Year greetings by writing, "Thanks. The New Year would be even sweeter if you would end Iran's Holocaust denial, sir." Within an hour, Zarif responded with "@sfpelosi Iran never denied it. The man who was perceived to be denying it is now gone. Happy New Year."[26] The exchange provided Zarif with the perfect opportunity to signal the dawn of a new outlook and set the template for broadcasting the granular differences between the Islamic Republic's position on the Israeli-Palestinian issue and the respect for the Jewish faith. This approach would become an important blueprint for managing public expectations and even signaling differences of opinion within the Iranian government during the course of nuclear negotiations.

In addition to social media, Rouhani and Zarif also engaged prominent American and international media outlets to reiterate their commitment to diplomatic engagement and to telegraph reaching a compromise on issues of mutual concern between Iran and Western powers. In an op-ed in the *Washington Post*—strategically timed ahead of his visit to the annual meeting of the UN General Assembly in New York—Rouhani wrote, "A constructive approach to diplomacy doesn't mean relinquishing one's rights. It means engaging with one's counterparts, on the basis of equal footing and mutual respect, to address shared concerns and achieve shared objectives. In other words, win-win outcomes are not just favorable but also achievable. A zero-sum, Cold War mentality leads to everyone's loss." Rouhani's piece immediately caught the attention of the foreign policy community because of its directness and its avoidance of tired slogans or repetition of long-standing grievances, which had been the norm with previous Iranian leaders. Most importantly, it articulated the basis of the Islamic Republic's attachment to its nuclear program as a matter of identity: "To us, mastering the atomic fuel cycle and generating nuclear power is as much about diversifying our energy resources as it is about who Iranians are as a nation, our demand for dignity and respect and our consequent place in the world. Without comprehending the role of identity, many issues we all face will remain unresolved." In so doing, Rouhani hinted at outlines of a possible compromise that not only mitigated Western concerns but also recognized Iran's "demand for dignity and respect and our consequent place in the world."[27]

New Diplomatic Narratives

Rouhani's unexpected landslide victory and the ensuing change in the Iranian government's tone and approach to public diplomacy came as a welcome development to the Obama administration. The morning after Rouhani's election, President Obama wondered out loud to his national security team, "Why don't I send Rouhani a letter?" adding, "It's worth testing."[28] With that, the White House dispatched a congratulatory letter through intermediaries to Rouhani's office and proposed the possibility of direct talks on the nuclear front, and within weeks the administration received a positive response back. With the Omani back-channel option still open and the taboo of secret bilateral talks already broken, diplomats in both capitals could at long last proceed with substantive discussions about matters of policy without worrying too much about the optics of meeting with erstwhile enemies.[29] As Burns later reflected, "In hindsight, it was useful to have launched the secret channel while Ahmadinejad was still president and before Rouhani was elected. Had we waited until after the election, it might have appeared to the ever-suspicious Khamenei that we were fixated on Rouhani and neglecting the ultimate decision-maker."[30]

Rouhani's election also had given the supreme leader much-needed space in negotiations. Having a confident technocratic government as the face of the negotiating process with the United States afforded Khamenei plausible deniability in case the terms of a future agreement were not entirely to his liking or if public opinion shifted over time; alternatively, he would be able to take credit if the Islamic Republic emerged from the talks with a stronger hand. Khamenei's office also made a crucial concession to Rouhani by agreeing to move the nuclear portfolio from the SNSC to the Foreign Ministry, with Zarif as the lead negotiator. The change had the dual advantage of simplifying the byzantine and cluttered chain of decision-making and bringing more transparency to the process, a key Rouhani campaign promise.

With the diplomatic wills and bureaucratic processes aligned on all sides, Oman's Sultan Qaboos and his able deputies once again prepared the grounds for the resumption of secret talks in Muscat. A few weeks after Rouhani's inauguration on August 4, 2013, an Iranian delegation headed by veteran diplomats Majid Takht-Ravanchi and Abbas Araghchi met with Deputy Secretary of State Bill Burns and Jake Sullivan, who was at this point the national security advisor to Vice President Joe Biden. Ravanchi and Araghchi were both educated at Western universities and were fluent in English, which enabled them to interact more informally with their American counterparts and establish a solid rapport with them from the outset. Burns and Sullivan were immediately reassured by the competence and professionalism of the Iranian delegation but also noted that "they were no less committed to Iran, no less proud of the revolution, no less determined to show that they could hold their own in the diplomatic arena."[31]

The first round in September was mostly spent discussing the menu of issues that were to be addressed and how best to approach them in formal talks. The American team, led by Burns, had envisioned a "two-stage process" in which, in the first phase, Iran would immediately halt all activities related to its nuclear program in return for limited relief from nuclear-related sanctions. In the second phase of the talks, Iran would submit to intrusive international inspections regimes and forgo any pathways to a possible bomb in exchange for a comprehensive, long-term agreement on its nuclear prerogatives and the lifting of all nuclear-related sanctions. The first phase, then, would be an interim accord that would establish trust and mutually agreed-upon principles, as a precursor to the adoption of a comprehensive agreement in the second phase of talks. Ravanchi and Araghchi agreed to the two-phase approach given the enormity of issues on the table, even as they made clear that a formal recognition of Iran's "right" to enrichment would be a major sticking point for Khamenei and more skeptical principals in Tehran. Two weeks later, at a much-publicized address to a gathering of IRGC commanders, Khamenei signaled his openness to dialogue and compromise by calling on Iranian diplomats to demonstrate "heroic flexibility" in the resumption of talks with the P5+1. "I am not against appropriate and reasonable diplomatic initiatives," Khamenei declared, adding, "I believe in what was described years ago as 'heroic flexibility'. Flexibility is required in many areas; it is apt and there is nothing wrong with it. But a wrestler who displays flexibility for a tactical reason should not forget about who his rival is and his objectives. This is the main condition. Our diplomats should also know what they are doing, who their opponent is, and where they wish to attack."[32]

The combination of positive back-channel talks, Khamenei's nod to "heroic flexibility," and Rouhani's *Washington Post* op-ed generated a great deal of optimism about the prospects of a major breakthrough on Iran's nuclear program. It also raised the prospect of an in-person meeting between Rouhani and Obama at the annual meeting of the General Assembly at the UN headquarters in New York. Obama informed his advisors that he would be willing to meet with Rouhani on the sidelines, and Sullivan, after conferring with his Iranian contacts (presumably Ravanchi and Araghchi), confirmed that Rouhani would be willing to meet as well.[33] A hastily arranged plan was hatched to have the two leaders run into each other in one of the corridors outside of the General Assembly hall, without any cameras or journalists present, for an impromptu meet and greet. As Obama waited in a conference room adjacent to the UNSC, Sullivan received a call that Rouhani would not be showing up. The timing was not quite ripe for the meeting from Rouhani's perspective. The issue was not, as some analysts surmised, that shaking hands with the president of the United States would have been too politically costly for Rouhani, as he had both the popular mandate and the tacit support of Khamenei to pursue diplomacy with the United States; rather, the cold feet represented the stranglehold of the past—of layers upon layers of norms hardened into narrative—on the fast-shifting present. True to his conservative temperament, Rouhani preferred a gradual shift in narrative, not a hurried hop over thirty-six years of painful history via photo op.[34]

After the failure to arrange an in-person presidential meeting, Zarif and Kerry met on the sidelines of a P5+1 meeting at the United Nations, marking yet another major milestone: the first official meeting between the highest-ranking officials from each country since 1979. The meeting was mostly spent with formal exchanges of pleasantries and recitation of official positions on the nuclear file. The back-channel talks—which had shifted to New York City in the two weeks prior to the UN General Assembly meetings—afforded the principals on each side the space to focus on their respective public relations messaging during the UN meetings. In addition to a raft of interviews with American and international media, Zarif also delivered official remarks at the Council on Foreign Relations and the Asia Society, and he met with former officials and some members of the Iranian diaspora involved in Track 2 efforts. These efforts at public diplomacy were designed to counter the increasing pressure on the Obama administration by members of Congress—including some prominent Democrats—to bolster the existing regime of sanctions on Iran. In separate letters to Obama, prominent senators such as Charles Schumer (D-NY), John McCain (R-AZ), Robert Menendez (D-NJ), and Lindsey Graham (R-SC) argued against the lifting of any sanctions until the Iranian government committed to "meaningful and verifiable actions to halt its nuclear activities."[35]

Although the congressional pressure helped Obama's bargaining position, Zarif and Rouhani understood that rebuffing Obama was going to further strengthen the opponents of diplomacy with Iran. For this reason, they approached senior officials about the possibility of a phone call between Rouhani and Obama prior to the former's return to Tehran. The historic fifteen-minute phone call—the first between a sitting US president and his counterpart since the advent of the Islamic Republic—took place as Rouhani was being driven to the airport. The two leaders exchanged warm pleasantries and affirmed their commitment to continuing their dialogue on the nuclear issue. According to an accidentally leaked transcript of the call to the Iranian press, Obama also expressed his hope that a "breakthrough on the nuclear issue could open the door to a relationship between the U.S. and

Iran."[36] The phone call was a significant ice-breaking exercise in US-Iran relations, and in many respects it redeemed Obama's departure from the traditional script of American foreign policy that regarded engagement with hostile regimes as being tantamount to weakness and appeasement. Obama's extended hand was no longer being met with a clenched fist.

Having moved past the taboos, the task at hand was to arrive at a tangible interim agreement so that a formal process toward comprehensive negotiations could begin in earnest. Over the course of the next three months, the back-channel talks focused on the substance of an interim agreement, with the Iranian delegation determined to secure as much relief from economic sanctions as possible, and the Americans seeking to halt Iran's rapid progress on the enrichment front (by this point, according to intelligence estimates, Iran was weeks away from producing enough highly enriched uranium for several nuclear weapons).[37] The back-channel sessions in Oman surpassed both sides' expectations in their efficiency, breadth of discussions, and pace of progress. By the end of October 2013, a working draft featuring possible concessions by each side had been produced in time for a major ministerial-level meeting in early November between Iran and the P5+1 countries. However, it would be difficult for either side—but especially the United States—to explain to their counterparts in P5+1 why such progress had already been made without disclosing the existence of a back channel. The British already knew about the secret talks through their own intelligence contacts with Oman but had remained circumspect to ensure their success. As a courtesy, Obama had already briefed Netanyahu about the back channel at the White House back in September. The Israeli leader was already aware of the contacts as well, and he made it clear to Obama and his team that he viewed the back channel "as a betrayal."[38] Other leaders were briefed by Wendy Sherman, the under secretary for political affairs, and were generally supportive since they understood the momentousness of such trust-building processes in light of the history of US-Iran relations.[39]

The early November meeting of the P5+1 and Iran failed to produce an interim agreement, as Iran and the United States remained divided on the extent of sanctions relief (in unfrozen oil revenues) and suspension levels at various nuclear facilities, respectively. But these technical differences masked a more fundamental disagreement about Iran's *right* to enrichment under the NPT. The Iranians maneuvered exhaustively for the inclusion of language that acknowledged such an entitlement, but Kerry, along with his British, French, and German counterparts, stood firmly against it. In fact, neither the NPT nor any other arms control framework or regime stipulates any such rights for any state in international society.

For Zarif and other Iranian officials, therefore, insisting on the language of rights was a deliberate exercise in reframing its nuclear aspirations as a matter of equal treatment and respect for its sovereign rights. The rebranding also had the advantage of resurrecting nationalist grievances against a documented history of Russian and Anglo-American imperial bullying that had thwarted Iran's political development to the advantage of foreign powers. In many ways, Zarif was the ideal curator of this narrative. A high-ranking meritocrat in a regime operating mostly on patronage and nepotism, fluent in American-accented English and the art of diplomatic double-speak, and a proud nationalist, Zarif more closely resembled the hopes and aspirations of ordinary Iranians than most other officials in the Islamic Republic (including Rouhani). He skillfully made use of these attributes by regularly posting passages of verse by beloved national poets such as Ferdowsi, Hafez, and Sa'di on his social media accounts in the course of the negotiations leading up to the interim agreement, and his own communications to the public stood out for their directness and absence of any Quranic preambles, which are the template of official communication in the Islamic Republic.[40]

As the P5+1 talks in Geneva hit an unexpected snag owing to un-specified French objections to the draft text of the agreement, Zarif took the dramatic step of releasing a five-minute video message on YouTube to plead Iran's case on its rights and entitlement to equal treatment. The video began with shots of Zarif entering his office in the Foreign Ministry building, then facing the camera and asking, "What is respect? What is dignity? Are they negotiable? Is there a price tag?" He then launched into a presentation of his reframed narrative on the imperative of treating Iran with equal respect and dignity, which bears reproducing here in its entirely since at critical junctures in the negotiations leading up to the 2015 comprehensive agreement Zarif would resort to broadcasting a variation of this message via his You-Tube channel:

> Imagine being told that you cannot do what everyone else is doing, what everyone else is allowed to do. Would you back down, would you relent? Or would you stand your ground?
>
> We are all endowed with free will, with the ability to de-termine our own destiny. It's not about stubbornness, or the refusal to take into account the views of others. Free will is in our being, in our DNA. It has been the essence of the collec-tive demand of us Iranians for the past century. We have re-peatedly joined hands to stand up against tyranny, demanding respect for our free will. Iranians are no different from any other people on this planet we share. We expect and demand respect for our dignity. For us Iranians, nuclear energy is not about joining a club or threatening others. Nuclear energy is about a leap, a jump to deciding our own destiny, rather than allowing others to decide for us.
>
> For us, nuclear energy is about securing the future of our children, about diversifying our economy, about stopping the burning of our oil, and about generating clean power. It's about

the Iranian nation moving forward as an equal in a new realm defined by peace, by prosperity, by progress. What would you do if you were told this was not an option? Would you back down?

Rights are not granted, and since they are not granted, they cannot be seized. This does not mean that we have hit a dead end. There is a way forward, a constructive path, toward determining our destiny, to advance, to make progress, to secure peace, to go forward.

The choice is not submission or confrontation. This past summer our people chose constructive engagement through the ballot box. And through this they gave the world a historic opportunity to change course. To seize this unique opportunity, we need to accept equal footing and choose a path based on mutual respect and recognition of the dignity of all peoples. And more so, on the recognition that no power, however strong, can determine the fate of others; this is no longer an option. We all need a sober appreciation of our common destiny, our common challenges, and our common opportunities. We also need the conviction that imposition is not sustainable. A conviction that we cannot gain at the expense of others. A conviction that we either win together or lose together; that balance is key to success.

Honest dialogue and real confidence, this is all dependent on equal footing, mutual respect and common interests. But more so, on dignity for all. We promise this to our people and to the world and we always keep our promises. The Iranian people are determined to explore this path. Join us in ending an unnecessary crisis and opening new horizons. My name is Javad Zarif and this is Iran's message.[41]

The video was a noteworthy piece of propaganda. Although the irony of exalting the virtues of free will, rights, and equal respect was not lost on ordinary Iranians, who could not even watch Zarif's message on YouTube owing to the state's filtering of all social media platforms, the video was nevertheless effective in debunking Western public perceptions of Iranian officials as religious zealots bent on confrontation. More importantly, the message served as a reminder of the major qualitative differences between the Rouhani administration and the alternatives in Iran, especially since the supreme leader's website and social media accounts remained as hostile and uncompromising as ever.

Just five days after Zarif's public plea on November 24, the interim agreement, dubbed the "Joint Plan of Action" (JPOA), was signed by Iran and the P5+1. The preamble to the agreement acknowledged Iran's "right to nuclear energy for peaceful purposes" but also stipulated that a "comprehensive solution would involve a mutually defined enrichment program with practical limits and transparency measures to ensure the peaceful nature of the program."[42] As part of the agreement, Iran agreed to dispose of its existing stockpile of 20 percent enriched uranium and freeze its nuclear program for six months. In exchange, the P5+1 agreed not to place additional nuclear sanctions on Iran for six months and offered Iran limited sanctions relief totaling nearly $7 billion ($4.2 billion of which was Iran's frozen oil revenues in foreign banks). The stage was now set for tough negotiations toward a comprehensive deal.

■ The Nuclear Deal and Its Discontents

The JPOA opened the door to one of the longest, most complicated arms control negotiations in recent memory. The delicate and multilayered nature of the issues for resolution necessitated the inclusion of technical experts fluent in nuclear science, international law, and financial networks. On the American side, Sherman oversaw the work of these disparate groups, and Ravanchi and Araghchi did the same on the Iranian side. US Secretary of Energy Ernie Moniz and Ali Akbar Salehi, the head of Iran's Atomic Energy Organization—fellow MIT alums—supervised the technical teams and established a collegial spirit early on in the process. It was clear from the outset, however, that managing public expectations and neutralizing the opposition to the deal spearheaded by Netanyahu and some Arab states were just as important as hammering out the terms of a comprehensive agreement. Soon after the JPOA agreement was announced, Netanyahu denounced it as "a historic mistake," adding, "Today the world became a much more dangerous place because the most dangerous regime in the world made a significant step in obtaining the most dangerous weapons in the world."[43] Indeed, this would become a familiar pattern over the course of the roughly twenty months leading up to the signing of the formal comprehensive agreement, the Joint Comprehensive Plan of Action (JCPOA).

A major complicating factor in managing the interference by third parties like Israel in the talks was Iran's growing influence through its ever-expanding network of proxies across the Middle East. Although, by definition, the negotiations were exclusively an exercise in nuclear arms control, there was a great deal of pressure by allies of Israel, the United Arab Emirates, and Saudi Arabia; in the US Congress; and in European capitals to expand the scope of talks with Iran to include its support for sectarian groups and its ballistic missile program. The Obama administration, whether out of sheer folly or principled commitment to noninterference, had failed to contain the tide of chaos that continued to wash over the Middle East in the aftermath of the Arab Spring. The limited intervention in Libya had ended in a failed state there, Egypt had reverted to military rule, Yemen was in the grips of a civil war, and sectarian conflicts in Iraq and Syria had effectively led to the collapse of central authority and created a power vacuum that in turn helped spawn the Islamic State of Iraq and Syria (ISIS). The chaos engulfing the region created a security dilemma for Iranian leaders, who were determined to shape the emerging order to their favor, especially with regard to their strategic footholds in Syria and Lebanon. The Iranian regional strategy—devised and led by the shadowy commander of its elite IRGC unit, Qasem Soleimani (and not Rouhani or his national security advisors)—was a major headache for the Obama administration, which, on the one hand, had no interest in committing American troops to stabilize the region, but also did not wish to see the Islamic Republic emerge as a regional hegemon, on the other hand.

The latter topic had become an object of fascination in policy think tanks and among national security experts the world over throughout 2014–15. In a much-discussed interview with National Public Radio, former secretary of state Henry Kissinger observed with alarm that "there has come into being a kind of a Shia belt from Tehran through Baghdad to Beirut. And this gives Iran the opportunity to reconstruct the ancient Persian Empire—this time under the Shia label. From a geostrategic point of view, I consider Iran a bigger problem than ISIS."[44] Kissinger's intervention was representative of the rising chorus of voices that were fundamentally skeptical of Iran's intentions and unmoved by the Rouhani administration's charm offensive in the nuclear talks. To these critics, Iran's growing influence in the Middle East was being aided by the Obama administration's pusillanimity and unwillingness to take any steps that might foreclose the possibility of a nuclear agreement with Iran.

The bluntest expression of this criticism was made by Netanyahu in a dramatic address to a joint session of US Congress, in a blatant attempt to erode congressional support for any nuclear agreement with Iran. In a speech packed with references to the memory of the Holocaust and Iranian leaders' penchant for threatening the destruction of the State of Israel, Netanyahu pleaded, "I've come here today to tell you we don't have to bet the security of the world on the hope that Iran will change for the better. We don't have to gamble with our future and with our children's future. We can insist that restrictions on Iran's nuclear program not be lifted for as long as Iran continues its aggression in the region and in the world."[45] Netanyahu's address proved effective in galvanizing bipartisan opposition to a deal with Iran; it did so largely by dexterously appealing to the conventional perceptions of the Iranian regime prior to the start of diplomacy under the Obama administration. In effect, Netanyahu was asking American lawmakers and the public to reject the possibility of a new understanding with Iran since the essence of the Islamic Republic was hateful and would be impervious to change through diplomacy.

The merits and urgency of the other opponents' cases against a nuclear deal also rested entirely on arguments about the nature and historical track record of the Islamic Republic as a repressive, revolutionary regime bent on the destruction of Israel. A toxic combination of proven past duplicity on the hidden military dimensions of its nuclear program and lack of domestic accountability, critics noted, cast a long shadow over any agreement with the Iranian regime.[46] Acknowledging these worries while also reconciling them to the view that a comprehensive nuclear agreement would be a safeguard against future transgressions was the Obama administration's most daunting task—especially since opponents of the deal mounted a strong public relations campaign on social media and in traditional news and policy outlets.

Solving the nuclear puzzle required sensitivity to the underlying merits of each perspective—especially in light of the long history of enmity and mistrust between Iran and the United States. This is why, almost from the beginning of the diplomatic talks, Obama was careful not to seem either too unsympathetic to the genuine worries of his opponents about the nature of the Islamic regime or too eager a champion of a purely instrumental approach. In material terms, in order to allay the fears of Israel and Saudi Arabia that the US commitment to their security would be weakened as a result of the deal, the Obama administration furnished them with $38 billion and $115 billion in military aid, respectively.[47] In policy terms, Obama laid out his justifications for a balanced approach in an interview on National Public Radio:

> But this is a good deal if you think Iran's open to change; it's also a good deal if you think that Iran is implacably opposed to the United States and the West and our values . . . and the reason is this: My goal, when I came into office, was to make sure that Iran did not get a nuclear weapon and thereby trigger a nuclear arms race in the most volatile part of the world. And prior to me coming into office, we had seen Iran's program go very quickly and have a whole bunch of centrifuges reduce the timeline in which they could break out and obtain a nuclear weapon if they so chose. And because of the hard diplomatic work that we did internationally, as well as help from Congress, we were able to impose some really significant sanctions, brought them to the table.
>
> We're now in a position where Iran has agreed to unprecedented inspections and verifications of its program, providing assurances that it is peaceful in nature. You have them rolling back a number of pathways that they currently have available to break out and get a nuclear weapon. You have assurances that their stockpile of highly enriched uranium remains in a place where they cannot create a nuclear weapon. And that lasts not only for the first 10 years, but the inspections and verifications that are unprecedented go for another decade after that. Now, ideally, we would see a situation in which Iran, seeing sanctions reduced, would start focusing on its economy, on training its people, on reentering the world community, to lessening its provocative activities in the region. But if it doesn't change, we are so much better if we have this deal in place than if we don't.[48]

By conceding that there were serious dangers posed by Iran's nuclear program but also clearly laying out the costs and benefits associated with possible courses of action, the Obama administration in effect shifted the burden of proof to opponents of a negotiated settlement.[49] This strategy also had the crucial effect of exposing Iranian decision-makers to the formidable bipartisan opposition to any deal with the Islamic Republic if the opportunity to reach a deal with the Obama administration was passed up.

At the level of negotiations, too, the admixture of principled red lines and pragmatic concessions proved enormously effective. After a flurry of public relations maneuvers between April and July 2015, the final draft of the JCPOA was signed by Iran and the P5+1 on July 15, 2015. As part of the comprehensive agreement, Iran's nuclear program was subjected to the most extensive and intrusive regime of inspections to date, the Iranian government agreed to dismantle or convert possible military dimensions of its nuclear facilities (including the elimination of the heavy water reactor core at its prized Arak facility), Iran's enrichment capacity was reduced to benign levels, and the so-called "breakout time"—that is, the time needed to produce one nuclear bomb—was prolonged from two months at the time of the JPOA to one year for at least ten years. Critics were loath to admit it, but on each of these points Iran did in fact significantly compromise on the red lines set out by Khamenei. In the end, the United States and other world powers had achieved their primary objective: halting Iran's progress toward the weaponization of its nuclear program through diplomacy. Just prior to the formal signing of the JCPOA, Obama was asked by the journalist Thomas Friedman if there was a particular "Obama doctrine" that helped bring about the Iran nuclear deal. Obama's response just happened to be an apt summary of his approach to narrative as well: "We are powerful enough to be able to test these propositions [i.e., engaging long-standing enemies] without putting ourselves at risk. And that's the thing . . . people don't seem to understand. . . . You asked about an Obama doctrine. The doctrine is: We will engage, but we preserve all our capabilities."[50]

Although the JCPOA was merely an arms control agreement, the shifting contexts that helped produce it were decidedly more than just about managing Iran's nuclear ambitions. Its significance lay not merely in the triumph of a certain kind of diplomacy but in the transformative power of narrative. In just over two years, each side had cautiously set aside its well-worn slogans and conventional scripts in a good-faith quest for more constructive terms of coexistence. The change in the relationship was set in motion with Barack Obama's election and thereafter by his administration's steady and disciplined focus on placing diplomacy and dialogue above isolation and confrontation. The sustained shift in the American approach helped to convince Iran's paranoid supreme leader that perhaps a new outlook had dawned in Washington, and that the Islamic Republic had better respond with "heroic flexibility" of its own. The back-channel talks, too, were a crucial conditioning component of the shift in narrative. In the past, in the absence of discrete channels through which they could directly address their substantive differences, Iranian and American officials felt obliged to perform the roles that they thought were expected of them. Over time, these roles seeped into the subconscious of diplomats, spokespersons, journalists, policy experts, and even academics, disciplining their thinking and actions in ways that cohered with and reinforced the conventional narrative of the relationship. Hassan Rouhani's unexpected election and the subsequent elevation of an experienced and media-savvy foreign minister in Javad Zarif afforded the Iranian government the opportunity to reciprocate the Obama administration's differential approach in kind. The mounting pressure on the Obama administration by Iran's main regional rivals—Israel and Saudi Arabia—to mitigate rising Iranian influence across the Middle East tested the diplomatic discipline of leaders in both Tehran and Washington. But in the end, it fell to President Obama to once again summon the power of narrative on behalf of diplomacy and the possibility of a better future—a great accomplishment that in due course, alas, history would reflect as the exception that proved the rule.

Trump and Regeneration
through Violence

12 The summer of 2015 witnessed the completion of the negotiations on Iran's nuclear program and the entry of the eccentric businessman Donald Trump into the presidential race to succeed Barack Obama. The two events were not obviously linked but became so rather soon. For Trump decried the Joint Comprehensive Plan of Action before it took flight. He did so repeatedly throughout the ensuing campaign and as president, claiming that the accord failed to constrain Iranian militancy and cheating. In May 2018, he announced that the United States would withdraw from the agreement.

Whereas Obama's diplomacy appeared to be the culmination of slow but steady progress, Trump quickly relegated that effort to the status of an outlier. Trump's vitriolic criticisms of Iran and the nuclear deal conformed to the hostile sentiments toward Iran that much of America's elite had evinced for forty years. In this vein, the Iranian rulers were untrustworthy, uncivilized, and hell-bent on destroying the West (and Israel particularly) through religious zealotry and irrational violence. They were still the savages that always lurk in the wilderness and that we are meant to dominate.

Much of what Trump did in his years in the White House was seen as a personal rebuke to Obama, an objective clearly evident from the comparison of their inaugural crowds to the provision of health care to the Paris climate accord. This animus went far beyond the typical distaste for one's political opponents, soaked in racism and envy, but the hostility toward any accommodation with Iran was broad and deep. The entire Republican Party was dead set against the agreement. The neoconservatives in both parties had spoken longingly of invading Iran before the Iraq War became an untenable catastrophe, and gradually some neocons wormed their way back into government under Trump. The leader of the Democrats in the Senate opposed the JCPOA. The pro-Israel lobby prompted many members of Congress and other political elites to remain scathing toward Tehran.[1]

Because their personalities, knowledge, and styles contrasted so sharply, it was easy to regard Trump and his impulses as the exact opposite of Obama and his policies. In one sense, however, both were consistent with the frontier myth. Trump's reversion to name-calling, playing on people's latent prejudices about Muslim terrorists ("mad mullahs"), and similar derision was the more obvious in this respect. But the Obama administration (like its predecessor) treated the Iranian state as a pariah as well. It continued to heavily arm Iran's regional rivals. It supported the Saudi war in Yemen against alleged Iranian surrogates. It urged and provided covert support to guerrilla groups to overthrow Iran's key ally Bashar al-Assad. It weaponized the global financial system to punish Iran. The rhetorical assaults on Iran were scarcely muted.

The JCPOA itself could be seen in this light as endeavoring to tame the wily and violent adversary with a legal straitjacket enforced by international coercion (the sanctions most particularly). It recalls how the US government signed five hundred treaties with America's indigenous tribes, only to steadily degrade their rights to land but keep them bound to small parcels of those lands by force (while violating each of the pacts).[2] This line of reasoning holds that Obama's diplomacy—however important and preferable to war—was narrowly instrumental and did not fundamentally alter the American discourse on the legitimacy of the Islamic Republic of Iran. All the while, US intelligence agencies had concluded that Iran was not developing nuclear weapons.

Still, Trump's actions toward Iran and his administration's relentless attempts to isolate and diminish Iran were a distinct departure from Obama's approach. Regulation was supplanted by repeated threats, falsehoods, and confrontation. The renewed hostilities, moreover, seemed to have no end game apart from complete submission by the Iranian state or armed conflict.

■ The Trump Perspective

In manifold tweets and speeches, and as articulated by subordinates, Trump claimed that Iran was cheating on the JCPOA; poised to break out to a nuclear weapons capability; threatening neighbors and fomenting chaos in Syria, Yemen, Lebanon, and Iraq; and oppressing the Iranian people.

In his maiden speech as a candidate in June 2015, Trump mentioned Iran and the nuclear negotiation several times. (The speech was noted more for excoriating illegal immigration from Mexico, but he touched on many topics.) "Iran is going to take over the Middle East, Iran and somebody else will get the oil, and it turned out that Iran is now taking over Iraq. Think of it. Iran is taking over Iraq, and they're taking it over big league," he said. He called the nuclear deal, then still in the final weeks of negotiation, "laughable" and a "disaster." As a result of the agreement, he implied, "Israel maybe won't exist very long." He continued along these lines in tweets and speeches. "The #IranDeal is a catastrophe that must be stopped," he said via Twitter on August 11. "Will lead to at least partial world destruction & make Iran a force like never before."

His rhetoric became more refined and pointed in the coming months. His animus toward Obama was apparent, as he unfailingly described the JCPOA as poorly negotiated. But his words about Iran were familiar in American political discourse. His speech in October 2017, nine months into his presidency, in which he laid the ground-work for withdrawal from the agreement, spoke of a dictatorship, "fa-natical" and dedicated to terrorism, which has "spread death, destruc-tion, and chaos all around the globe." He linked the Tehran regime to Al-Qaeda, the Taliban, and other such violent groups. "We got weak inspections in exchange for no more than a purely short-term and temporary delay in Iran's path to nuclear weapons."[3]

Trump delivered a similar lashing in May 2018, when he announced that the United States would withdraw from the agreement. He claimed that Iran, with its "long reign of chaos and terror" and the "malign be-havior" and "sinister activities" of a "murderous regime" with "bloody ambitions," had tried to take America as a "hostage to nuclear black-mail."[4]

Most of the administration's policy team echoed his words in pub-lic. "The regime continues to play this council," Nikki Haley, US am-bassador to the United Nations, told the Security Council in October 2017. "Iran hides behind its assertion of technical compliance with the nuclear deal while it brazenly violates the other limits of its behavior, and we have allowed them to get away with it. This must stop." At the same time, the first wave of Trump advisers, including Secretary of State Rex Tillerson, Secretary of Defense James Mattis, and National

Security Adviser H. R. McMaster, all urged the president to remain in the agreement, citing the destabilizing potential of a withdrawal. Among those concerns was the impact of such a disruption on the European allies particularly, who were deeply committed to making the JCPOA work.

Trump's changing of the guard—firing Tillerson, Mattis, and McMaster, in effect—was wrought partly to pursue his more belligerent instincts, particularly toward Iran. With the April 2018 arrival of Mike Pompeo as secretary of state and John Bolton to be the national security adviser, a series of moves to undermine the arms control regime ensued quickly. Mainly negotiated with the Soviet Union, the agreements were honored to an important extent by the Russian Federation. By October of that year, the United States announced its intention to withdraw from the Intermediate-Range Nuclear Forces (INF) Treaty, a keystone agreement negotiated by Reagan and Gorbachev in 1987. (Russia was in violation of the INF Treaty but could possibly have been convinced to comply.) There was no movement to extend the strategic arms limitations accords that constrained intercontinental nuclear weapons capability. More than once, Trump openly questioned why nuclear weapons were not usable, and he endorsed plans to modernize the nuclear arsenal and develop a low-yield nuclear weapon that could tempt a president to use it.

Undermining the Iran nuclear deal could be seen as part of this pattern. It appeared all the more likely with the central role of Bolton, a longtime scourge of arms control.[5] Bolton not only led the charge against Iran, the INF Treaty, and strategic arms limits but also worked behind the scenes to undo Trump's flirtation with Kim Jong-un. The Iran deal certainly did fit into what Bolton once derisively called the "Church of Arms Control," but the Trump administration's animus toward Iran went much deeper than Bolton's distaste for legal limits on nuclear weapons. After all, Trump did try diplomacy with North Korea, and he had done so many favors for Russia that the Federal Bureau of Investigation opened a counterintelligence investigation into the president. Iran was different.

None of the other nuclear adversaries—Russia, China, and North Korea—earned the repeated rebukes from several Trump officials, if they earned rebukes at all. Nor did proliferators Pakistan and India, or those reported to be contemplating a nuclear weapons program, like Saudi Arabia and Turkey, receive public disapproval from the Trump administration. The brutal criticism of Iran was relentless. The president launched dozens of tweets and comments in speeches and interviews asserting that Iran was cheating on the JCPOA, that it was a horrible deal for the United States, and that Iran "is a vicious country that kills many people."

Pompeo gave several speeches that were aimed specifically at Iran and made the same points. Barely a month into his tenure at Foggy Bottom, Pompeo gave a scorching critique of Iran and the nuclear deal, claiming that Zarif and others were lying about not having a nuclear weapons program and continued to deceive. "The regime reaps a harvest of suffering and death in the Middle East at the expense of its own citizens," he told a receptive audience at the Heritage Foundation. He laid out twelve demands that Iran would have to accede to before US-Iran talks to replace the JCPOA could commence—few if any of which were remotely plausible for Iran to comply with, and some of which were based on false accusations.[6] Pompeo continued along these lines in other forums, including a speech in Cairo, Egypt, in January 2019 that was designed to draw contrasts with President Obama's speech in the same city in 2009. The contrasts were blighted with mischaracterizations of Obama's words and intent. "The good news is this," Pompeo said after belittling Obama's historic outreach to the Muslim world. "The age of self-inflicted American shame is over, and so are the policies that produced so much needless suffering." The apparent jab at Obama's reluctance to engage in Syria nonetheless brought attention to the ignition of chaos in the region, namely,

President George W. Bush's decision to invade Iraq. Most of the speech, however, was aimed at Iran's ayatollahs, who "spread terror and destruction throughout the world" through their "malign activity." He touted the formation of a Middle East Strategic Alliance—an "Arab NATO"—to counter Iran's "wave of regional destruction." (The author of the idea for the alliance was Mohammed bin Salman, the notorious crown prince and de facto ruler of Saudi Arabia.)

Bolton had an even longer history of vitriolic hatred of the Iranian elite. He had been calling for the regime's demise for years, perhaps getting his job because of his harsh views. In a memo to Trump in August 2017, Bolton asserted "Iran's significant violations" of the JCPOA and "unacceptable conduct." He then outlined a campaign to exit the nuclear deal and impose harsh and broad penalties on Iran. In an op-ed in the *Wall Street Journal* in early 2018, he called for ending the IRI altogether: "Recognizing a new Iranian regime in 2019 would reverse the shame of once seeing our diplomats held hostage for four hundred and forty-four days. The former hostages can cut the ribbon to open the new U.S. Embassy in Tehran." Invoking the captivity narrative (a common story of the frontier experience, in which white settlers were kidnapped by Indians) remains potent, particularly the "humiliation" suffered in 1979–81. After becoming the national security adviser, Bolton continued his jeremiad. In September 2018, he called the nuclear deal "the worst diplomatic debacle in American history" and warned, "According to the mullahs in Tehran, we are 'the Great Satan,' lord of the underworld, master of the raging inferno. . . . So, I might imagine they would take me seriously when I assure them today: If you cross us, our allies, or our partners; if you harm our citizens; if you continue to lie, cheat, and deceive, yes, there will indeed be hell to pay."[7]

The drumbeat echoed in conservative think tanks, news media, and members of Congress: Iran is dangerous, genocidal, devilishly guided by a strange creed, fomenting tribal warfare, stealing riches.

And while this line of disparagement was loud and persistent in Trump's Washington, it was playing from a script about Iran written over the course of forty years and on both sides of the proverbial aisle. The familiar contempt was heightened by Trump's "Muslim ban," the restrictions on legal entry into the United States that excluded people mainly from Muslim countries, prominently including Iran.

Even the border dispute—Trump's dogged hope to build a wall along the border with Mexico—got entwined with the chronic fears of terrorism from the Middle East. "There are instances that you can confirm that you know of terrorists that have tried to cross our southern border and we've apprehended them," Fox News host Sean Hannity cued Kirstjen Nielsen, secretary of homeland security. "Yes, Sean, and we've talked about the thousands—the thousands of terror watch list individuals," she replied in the January 2019 interview.[8] (The implication of this—that thousands of terrorists were crossing that border—was thoroughly debunked. It remains an evergreen accusation because it combines two deep fears—Islamic terrorists and a porous border.)[9] With Trump, Pompeo, and others repeatedly claiming Iran as the principal sponsor of terror in the world, a fear factor was introduced, or reissued, one that draws not only from the manipulated anxieties following the 2001 attacks but also from the frontier narrative (terrorists = savages) and how it has been adapted to US involvement in the Middle East.

Notably, the American public as a whole was not totally buying the fearmongering. The Iranian leadership has been unpopular in America ever since 1979, and consistently so. The support for the nuclear deal, however, was surprisingly strong even with that dislike and the perception that Iran poses a threat to the United States.[10] A CNN poll at the time of Trump's withdrawal from the accord in May 2018 showed that 63 percent of the public supported the deal and 29 percent opposed it, even as a large number (61%) believed that Iran was violating the terms of the JCPOA. Other polls showed less support initially but moderately growing support over time. A significant majority of the American public in all polling consistently opposed the Muslim travel ban.

Among the striking opinions reflected in the surveys is that Americans consider Iran to be a security threat and believe that the IRI is developing a nuclear weapon. In that same Gallup poll in May 2018, 85 percent said that Iran poses a very serious or moderately serious threat to the United States. How Iran can be construed in that way is a puzzle. The US military budget is thirty times greater than Iran's, and the technological edge is likely greater. No terrorist attack in the United States has been linked to Iran, apart from one alleged attempt to assassinate the Saudi ambassador in Washington. The other commonly held belief, that Iran was indeed developing nuclear arms or already had them, was surely an outgrowth of undisciplined talk even by those favoring the JCPOA and a concerted effort by opponents to misrepresent Iran's nuclear program.

As noted earlier, the Central Intelligence Agency estimated in 2007 and subsequently that Iran may have been working on a bomb program until 2003, when it abandoned the project and never initiated that pursuit again. How far along they were, or whether there were any remnants of the effort, have long been topics in dispute, but the assessment of US intelligence, reiterated under the Trump administration, is that the weapons aspiration has long been dormant. Still, many elites continued to suggest that Iran had a nuclear weapons program or could very easily break out to a weapon within a matter of months. Trump's assertions in this regard—such as his September 26, 2016, tweet, "Russia has more warheads than ever, N Korea is testing nukes, and Iran got a sweetheart deal to keep theirs"—were blunt. So was a statement issued by press aide Sarah Huckabee Sanders in April 2018: "These facts are consistent with what the United States has long known: Iran has a robust, clandestine nuclear weapons program that it has tried and failed to hide from the world and from its own people."[11] Publications like *Vox* and *Foreign Policy* were running articles that could be interpreted as suggesting similar claims, to say nothing of the right-wing media. And politicians often spoke of the JCPOA stopping Iran's nuclear weapons program, when it had not pursued that option for a dozen years.

Most startling among Trump's statements and those of his underlings were the intermittent threats of war. The starkest threat came after Rouhani had said that America "was playing with the lion's tail" in withdrawing from the JCPOA and publicly voicing the possibility of military action. Trump retorted on twitter, "To Iranian President Rouhani: NEVER, EVER THREATEN THE UNITED STATES AGAIN OR YOU WILL SUFFER CONSEQUENCES THE LIKES OF WHICH FEW THROUGHOUT HISTORY HAVE EVER SUFFERED BEFORE. WE ARE NO LONGER A COUNTRY THAT WILL STAND FOR YOUR DEMENTED WORDS OF VIOLENCE & DEATH. BE CAUTIOUS!" Time and again, Bolton had spoken or written about military strikes on Iran's nuclear and command facilities. Pompeo said often that Iran should not test America's military might. And at a Warsaw meeting organized by the State Department, Israeli prime minister Benyamin Netanyahu said that the purpose of the gathering was "war with Iran."[12]

■ What Is Old Is New

No wonder the American public believed that Tehran was nuclear-ready. The notion that Iran had nuclear weapons or nearly did fit the "savages" trope: lying, cheating, dangerous, armed, irrational, and seething with anger and revenge at Euro-American crusaders. Trump and his cohort certainly reverted to these characterizations shamelessly, even as the International Atomic Energy Agency inspected and reported that Iran was observing the terms of the JCPOA faithfully.[13] "Iran remains below the limits set on key nuclear activities and continues to cooperate with IAEA monitoring and verification activities," one report stated more than three years after the JCPOA was signed. "As with prior reports, the IAEA noted that inspectors have had access to all sites and locations in Iran they needed to visit."[14]

The White House and its allies in the news media and think tank world were having none of that. Charges of covert programs, cheating in various ways, and hiding program elements on sites not accessible to the inspectors were rife in the relentless right-wing assault on the accord. The JCPOA's "failure" to punish Iran for regional political and military activities, which arms control agreements rarely if ever do, was a common theme for Trump and special interest groups such as United Against Nuclear Iran or the Foundation for the Defense of Democracy.

The Trump position on Iran was forged in a climate that included his personal animus toward Obama but was broader, fitting patterns of rhetoric and ideology familiar in American politics. Certainly, his references to Iran vividly conformed to frontier thinking. More was in play than simply the frontier myth, however. As many observers have noted, the support for Trump in the 2016 election was likely a reaction to social and cultural changes in America, as well as the middle class being stuck in economic doldrums for forty years. The striking social and cultural changes included same-sex marriage, increasing immigration of "brown" people, rising demands from and status for women, decline of mediating institutions (such as newspapers), and the sharply rising cost of higher education, among others. The fragmenting nature of the internet, a key source of information both authentic and "fake," added to a societal cacophony.

In this atmosphere, Trump's rhetorical style triumphed. His predilection for symbolic utterances, in contrast to straightforward informational speech, is especially noteworthy. The communications theorist James Carey calls this ritual communication: the "highest manifestation of communication [is] not in the transmission of intelligent information but in the construction and maintenance of an ordered, meaningful cultural world that can serve as a control and container for human action." Trump's repeated themes—make America great again, keep brown immigrants out of the country, build up the military, distrust the news media, America alone, et cetera—are the stuff of his messages to the public, and he also conveyed these ritualistically through his rallies and tweets. Again, Carey pinpointed the significance of this: such ritual communication "creates an artificial though nonetheless real symbolic order that operates to provide not information but confirmation, not to alter attitudes or change minds but to represent an underlying order of things, not to perform functions but to manifest an ongoing and fragile social process."[15]

In this light, it is easier to see Trump's constant falsehoods about Iran and the nuclear deal as rewarding his audiences' biases with the comforting notion that US military strength and resolve will punish the ayatollahs for their deceit. Iran was important not only because the JCPOA was Obama's triumph but also because it served as a focal point during the 2016 campaign for Trump to satisfy another frontier attitude—to show his toughness toward the savages, a need that only Iran seemed to afford him. Iran's fractious history with (and previous subservience to) the United States, its oil, its appeal to political Islam, and its appearance of fanaticism all fit the bill.

Contrast those features with North Korea—which actually did possess nuclear weapons and threatened close US allies. Partly this was circumstantial, with Trump believing he could woo Kim Jong-il and in turn being deceived, but partly it reflects long-standing geostrategic realities. While North Korea was dangerous, with its nukes and totalitarian regime, it was nested in a fairly stable environment, with surrounding powers basically in agreement regarding containment. The Middle East presented a different set of challenges. Not only was there not a China, Japan, and South Korea in close proximity, but it was also a region in turmoil for decades that involved Iran directly. It was roiled by religion, petroleum politics, abiding ethnic rivalries, the legacy of colonialism and failed socialism, nuclear weapons (Israel's), and war, often wars involving America. At root, however, Trump's reasons for targeting Iran likely stemmed from its Islamic militancy, the lingering trauma of the embassy takeover of 1979–81, and Obama's diplomacy to secure the nuclear deal, and all of those reasons were encouraged by neocons and the Israel lobby. Those elements were absent in the case of North Korea, and later dustups (as with Venezuela) paled by comparison.

The rhetoric aimed at forwarding these views is not always straightforward. As the philosopher Albert O. Hirschman outlined decades ago, reactionaries often make their points indirectly, particularly so when a policy they oppose is popular. He described three ways this was done in American politics. The first, what he called the *perversity thesis*, is when "they will endorse [the policy], sincerely or otherwise, but then attempt to demonstrate that the action undertaken in its name is ill-conceived . . . [and] that this action will produce, via a series of unintended consequences, the exact contrary of the objective that is being pursued." In the case of Iran's nuclear ambition, Trump would say that diplomacy to stop a weapons program was laudable, but Obama's "one-sided" concessions would actually make it easier for Iran to build a bomb. (The latter claim was objectively false.) Hirschman calls the second way the *futility thesis*, which asserts "that the attempt at change is abortive, that in one way or another any change is or was largely surface, facade, cosmetic, hence illusory, as the 'deep' structures of society remain wholly untouched." For people like Bolton and Pompeo, the IRI could not be reformed; it had to be destroyed. Further, the JCPOA would be a failure because of the structural flaws (corruption, oppression, jihadism) in the Iranian revolutionary state.

The third gambit of reactionaries that Hirschman describes is the *jeopardy thesis*—that a new reform "would mortally endanger an older, highly prized one that has only recently been put into place. The older, hard-won conquests or accomplishments, so it is argued, are still fragile, still need to be consolidated and would be placed in jeopardy by the new program."[16] For Trump, the old, admirable order was that of sanctions and threats to Iran, a relentless taming of the mad mullahs in word and deed. The JCPOA implied a level of cooperation, certainly the lifting of most sanctions, and actually productive diplomacy. This wimpy surrender, in the Trump cohort's view, had emboldened Iran to be ever more active in the region (Syria, Lebanon, Yemen, Iraq) and was producing deleterious consequences.

The pro-Israel groups clustered around the American Israel Public Affairs Committee, one of the most effective lobbies in the United States, demonstrate how the rhetoric of reaction works. Mark Dubowitz, who heads the Foundation for the Defense of Democracies, used the perversity thesis in arguing that Bolton and Pompeo were undermining the JCPOA, whereas the agreement should be "fixed." The United States, he argued in a 2018 op-ed, "needed to convince our three key European allies—France, the UK and Germany—to reach a new understanding on the nuclear accord's most glaring deficiencies." Demanding a new deal, as Dubowitz knew well, would scuttle the JCPOA and result in no agreement, as Iranian political leaders repeatedly said. Danielle Pletka of the American Enterprise Institute made essentially the same argument and unrealistically supposed that the Europeans would go along.[17]

"The pact itself has failed to change Iran's violent vocation," wrote Pompeo in 2018. "Normal states do not attack embassies and military installations in peacetime; fuel terrorist proxies and militias; serve as a sanctuary for terrorists; call for the destruction of Israel and threaten other countries; aid brutal dictators such as Syria's Bashar al-Assad; proliferate missile technology to dangerous proxies; conduct covert assassinations in other countries; and hold hostage citizens of foreign nations."[18] This futility thesis (also asserting falsehoods) appeared prominently when skeptics considered the ten- and fifteen-year provisions of the JCPOA, arguing that the deal at best only slowed Iran's nuclear aspirations.[19]

By contrast, the jeopardy thesis was never fully embraced by the pro-Israel lobby owing to dissatisfaction with US policy, which has sought since 1981 to contain and coerce Iran rather than roll back the revolution and the IRI. Still, elements of the latter strategy were present through these four decades: sanctions particularly (the harsher the better), political isolation, and unremitting rhetorical condemnation. Surreptitious support for Iranian subversives and covert operations, while small in scale, were also part of the mix. These initiatives were in effect the regime-change policy, whether acknowledged or not. The JCPOA put all that on hold, even as Iran's acquiescence to the terms of the accord seemed to prove that pressure was effective.[20] Michael Rubin, a strong advocate of maximum pressure, noted at the time of Trump's violation of the JCPOA, "The nuclear deal was never meant to be a 'get out of jail free card' on other Iranian malfeasance. The United States should wage economic warfare against Iran's ballistic missile program and use all available means to disrupt Iranian terrorism."[21]

The reactions of the pro-Israel lobby to the JCPOA stood in a long line of criticism of Iran that predated its flirtation with nuclear weapons. In the 1990s, AIPAC worked hard to pass the Iran and Libya Sanctions Act, largely a reaction to Iran's support for Hezbollah. It proceeded toward regime-change promotion, and the discovery of Iran's nuclear program in 2002 and a president amenable to aggressive words and deeds had AIPAC and US leaders feeding from the same trough.[22] It is no less striking that the Iran nuclear deal, which actually did stoutly constrain any Iranian intention to threaten Israel with nuclear capability (real or not), would prompt the lobby to claim that a more effective deal could be negotiated, and, amid all the bombastic vitriol directed at Tehran, this was the Trump administration's supposed position as well.

■ Iran Responds

The election of Trump and his immediate threats to Iran and the nuclear deal spurred predictable reactions in Tehran. The so-called hardliners bluntly stated that the nation's moderates, including President Rouhani and Foreign Minister Zarif, had erred grievously by trusting the Americans. When the United States did withdraw from the JCPOA in May 2018, Rouhani was back on his heels. Calls for his resignation rang out. Khamenei, always a skeptic of any rapprochement, said, "You heard what worthless things the American president said last night," referring to Trump's announcement of the withdrawal. "He lied up to maybe ten times and he threatened the state and the nation. . . . We accepted the JCPOA, but they continued their enmity with the Islamic Republic." The matter of trust was a frequently voiced lament. Trust was betrayed, and the natural reaction in Iran's hard-line leadership was never to trust again.

Formally, Iran would remain within the confines of the deal, Rouhani insisted, as long as the Europeans, China, and Russia would abide by their obligations. The E3 were particularly crucial to make it work. This tenuous trust in Britain, France, and Germany was also scorned by the supreme leader, but the deal held for most of the Trump presidency, if just by a thread.

As the Trump administration continued its "maximum pressure" campaign—new, biting sanctions in particular—a level of social turbulence unseen since the revolution gripped Iran. Late in 2019, widespread protests broke out in working-class neighborhoods and towns in Iran ostensibly over a gasoline price hike, itself occasioned by the US sanctions. The protests spread quickly as they transformed into calls for overthrowing the IRI and were met with shocking violence by the Islamic Revolutionary Guard Corps. The number of protestors killed is estimated at between 500 and 1,500. Khamenei called the uprising a plot by foreign enemies, "a very dangerous conspiracy." The head of the IRGC, Hossein Salami, echoed the supreme leader, saying, "The aim of our enemies was to endanger the existence of the Islamic Republic by igniting riots in Iran."[23]

A month later, a new outburst of street protests followed the accidental downing of a full passenger jet departing from Tehran. It was linked to a singular act of violence by the United States when a drone was used to assassinate Qassem Soleimani, the legendary head of the Quds Force of the IRGC, in early January 2020 in Iraq. The link supposedly was hypervigilance by an air defense unit due to the murder of Soleimani. Many conspiracy tales circulated in Iran regarding the protests (even some attributing the organizing of riots to conservatives hoping to embarrass Rouhani), but the uprising of autumn and winter altogether signaled growing dissatisfaction with the government, particularly by youth who saw the JCPOA as an opening that would change their isolation and bare economic existence.

At the same time, Iran's compliance with the nuclear deal became untenable in domestic politics. The conservatives were fully committed to undermining it. Europeans were not doing enough to salvage it, particularly the provisions allowing humanitarian goods to be sold to Iran, which became an acute violation as the coronavirus hit Iran with deadly force. With deliberate caution, Iran gradually violated the terms of the JCPOA. "Iran's heavy water stockpile, number of installed centrifuges, LEU stockpile, and LEU uranium-235 concentration, exceed JCPOA-mandated limits," said a June 2020 summary report. "Tehran is also conducting JCPOA-prohibited research and development activities, as well as centrifuge manufacturing, and has also begun to enrich uranium at its Fordow enrichment facility." LEU is low-enriched uranium, and indeed none of the violations brought Iran significantly closer to having weapons-grade nuclear material. The violations were staged as open defiance. They appeared to be designed to underscore America's more consequential violation, as well as the Europeans' failure to provide for the promised economic benefits of compliance.

"In the eyes of [conservatives], the JCPOA experience proved that diplomacy will not result in any major economic transformation for Iran, and that concessions only benefit the West," wrote Ellie Geranmayeh, an analyst with the European Council on Foreign Relations. Predictably, the US actions—including the scuttling of the nuclear deal, renewed sanctions, and attacks on the nuclear facilities, in addition to killing Soleimani—merely strengthened what she describes as the two camps of hard-liners, the Principlists and the securocrats. The "strategic patience" counseled by the "modernizers"—Rouhani and Zarif among them—could not readily be sustained in a climate of near war. The parliamentary elections of February 2020, in which many reformists and modernizers were disqualified by the Khamenei-dominated Guardian Council, swept conservatives into the Majles in overwhelming numbers and made Mohammed Bagher Ghalibaf, a former IRGC commander, speaker of the assembly.

The effect of the sanctions on Iran's economy was powerful. In the reckoning of the World Bank, Iran's economy slipped 4.7 percent in 2018 and 8.2 percent in 2019 but was projected to recover somewhat in 2020 and 2021, even to achieve positive numbers in 2021. Oil production and exports are also down markedly. However, Geranmayeh notes, "some supporters of the resilient economy model do not even believe that sanctions have hit Iran's economy as hard as modernizers claim: a clutch of hard-line Principlists have accused Rouhani of exaggerating their impact in order to try to reopen negotiations with the U.S." Trump's intermittent and suspect calls for negotiation were routinely dismissed as long as sanctions were imposed. Iran's reaching out to China for major trade cooperation was one strategy of coping, though conservatives were wary of coming under the influence of yet another global powerhouse.

When Israel and the United States engineered a series of attacks on nuclear facilities and other industrial assets in 2020, Iranian officials at first denied that such attacks were happening, likely to avoid the appearance of weakness, particularly with respect to Israel. Just as it had done after Soleimani's killing, Iran retaliated in Iraq, firing missiles at US bases.

Iran issued an arrest warrant naming Trump and thirty-five others for the killing of Soleimani, but INTERPOL, not surprisingly, refused it. The toothless response to that assassination and other aggressive behavior by the United States probably reflected necessary patience and a growing hope that Trump would lose the 2020 election, ushering in not just a Democrat but one strongly associated with the nuclear deal and bringing back many advisors who similarly supported the agreement. A number of incidents, real or perceived, could have stirred more militant responses from Iran but did not. Despite its typically heated rhetoric, actual kinetic retorts were few and mild. At the same time, some diplomatic feelers appeared. Former president Ahmadinejad, for example, wrote to Saudi Crown Prince Mohammed bin Salman in 2020 to seek a diplomatic solution to the war in Yemen, which had become a humanitarian disaster several years before and showed few signs of abating, thanks mainly to Saudi aggression. Zarif was peripatetic in trying to repair regional tensions and court powerful world players. With oil prices suffering, Iran was actively trying to open doors to trade and lower hostilities, though its commitment to Assad remained a sore point in many capitals.

Iran's adeptness at appearing the victim to Trump's capricious and irrational hostility earned it guarded sympathy among Europeans particularly, not least because the case was strong, according to the IAEA, that it was in full compliance with the JCPOA and had been shortchanged economically. The weakness of the state in the face of domestic unrest was clearly something of acute concern, and the tepid responses to provocations from the United States and Israel may be explainable in that context—forceful rhetoric, but unforceful actions. The usual fissures in Iran's political elite reappeared quickly and remained an enormous burden on the Rouhani government, as the supreme leader followed his suspicions and strengthened the hardliners. The culmination of Khamenei's caution—braced, no doubt, by Trump's behavior—was visible in the 2021 presidential election, in which no reformists were allowed to run and the winner was the hardliner Ebrahim Raisi, who might succeed Khamenei as supreme leader. Most viewed his election as a plus for the nuclear deal—namely, that hard-liners would accept it with Raisi as president[24]—but improved relations with the United States were unlikely under Iran's new leader.

The ongoing irony of conservative anger in each country bolstering that in the other continued unabated.

■ Return to the Wilderness

Trump's rhetorical bullying, tightening sanctions, and intermittent military actions continued throughout his term. Symbolically and actually, it came together in January 2020 with the assassination of Soleimani. Trump openly saw this as his bin Laden moment, and amid his impeachment shame the spectacular act of violence was perhaps intended to serve as an antidote.

The assassination provided a revealing drama. In disclosing the assassination, Trump said that Soleimani "made the death of innocent people his sick passion." He claimed that US policy and actions would deliver the future to the peaceful people of Iran, not "the terrorist warlords who plunder their nation to finance bloodshed abroad." Pompeo apparently convinced Trump to murder Soleimani as part of the maximum pressure campaign against Iran. Iraqi officials were miffed about the rising level of violence on their soil and demanded withdrawal of all US forces from Iraq. This earned a threat from Pompeo that the United States would impose sanctions on Iraq if such a demand—actually approved by Iraq's parliament—persisted. The scuffle demonstrated again the American attitude about this particular wilderness and seemed like a real-time affirmation of Iran's depiction of US imperialism.

The four years of Trump's animus toward Iran marked a mild but significant departure from the eight years of Obama's coercive diplomacy. If anything, Trump returned the United States to the hostile attitudes of previous presidents. Obama's willingness to concede some ground (mainly to do with uranium enrichment) in exchange for enhanced security enacted through the JCPOA appeared to be the outlier since the Iranian Revolution. Trump's return to the default position of seeing Iran's leadership as irrational, violence-prone jihadists was more extreme than any of his predecessors, however, at least in his speeches and tweets. Carter was politically victimized by the revolution and the hostage taking but remained rather restrained in his depictions of Khomeini and his followers. Reagan adopted a line consistent with his overall foreign and military policies, namely, tough words and sanctions and support for Iraq in its war with Iran, but no direct attempt to bring down the IRI. (He also pursued the weird episode resulting in the Iran-Contra scandal, which provided weapons to Iran.) George H. W. Bush opened a little to diplomacy but never followed through. Clinton signed the ILSA, threatened war with Iran over the Khobar Towers bombing, but softened in response to Khatami's election. Bush 43 and his neocon advisers were consistently hostile to Iran, though some intermittent episodes of tough-minded diplomacy, particularly on the nuclear file, did occur.

By comparison, Trump was unrelentingly hostile and never engaged in diplomacy. Compared with, for example, Bush 43 advisers, Pompeo was more belligerent and actively tried to undermine Iran's state. A telling episode occurred in the spring of 2020, when the coronavirus was severely damaging Iranian society; Pompeo put the onus on the IRI (even as Iran had fewer cases per capita than the United States did) and via sanctions made it nearly impossible for other countries to provide medical assistance to Iran. By contrast, the United States assisted Iran in recovering from a devastating earthquake in 2003, during the Bush 43 administration, and again in 2012 under Obama. True to form, Supreme Leader Khamenei accused America of using the coronavirus as a biological weapon against Iran.

Whatever the details, the political leadership of both countries reverted to the forty-year depictions of each other from the day Trump took office. While violence was relatively mild in this period, it was persistent, and threats of violence escalated. Several assassinations and subterfuge, allegedly carried out by Israel but approved by the United States, occurred with increasing frequency in Trump's tenure. The harshness of official pronouncements from both sides intensified. The claims of breaking norms and treaties proliferated. There was no genuine attempt at diplomacy. Trump's clear aversion to war, based on its likely political repercussions, perhaps saved the confrontation from sizable military hostilities.

The most notable gesture of restraint on Trump's part was an episode in June 2019 when Iran shot down a US spy drone. Trump and his advisers (Pompeo and Bolton) were about to order an attack with a limited strike on three military targets that likely would have caused 150 fatalities, which is what convinced Trump not to proceed, according to his own testimony.[25] Similarly, Iran attacked or aided an attack on Saudi oil facilities the following September, disabling a sizable amount of Saudi oil capacity and reducing worldwide production by 5 percent. No retaliation came. In part, this restraint may have been in the service of oil markets, which were already volatile.[26]

While not actually launching a major war against Iran, Trump's rhetoric was extremely bellicose, sanctions were a form of violence against the Iranian people, and numerous covert actions were ongoing. The sanctions alone, tightened time and again under Trump (and previous presidents), had a profound impact on daily life and survivability. The increase in mortality as a consequence of the sanctions has never been measured, but taking Iraq and the 1991–2003 period as a guide, the numbers must be significant.[27] There had been kinetic attacks on Iranian allies, such as militias in Iraq, and Israeli attacks on Iranian assets in Syria. The constant barrage of threats from Washington was very much in keeping with Trump's reliance on violent images and exhortations in other corners of his presidency and campaigning. "Defined in terms of populism, strongman politics, and identitarianism," wrote one scholar, "Trumpism employed emotional evocations of violence—fear, threats, hatred, and division—which at times erupted into physical displays of aggression."[28] Assaults on Muslims in the United States surged after Trump's election, as did hostilities toward immigrants. Experts agreed that Trump's use of violent talk, including threats, gave permission to dormant racists to take action.

Whatever Trump's reasons for his errand to the wilderness, it demonstrated how states easily revert to their national narratives and consequent behaviors. Trump had no strategic reason to inflame relations. Iran was not violating the JCPOA. Its assistance to the Houtis in Yemen was minor. Its backing Hezbollah in Lebanon was nearly forty years in the making, and, in any case, Hezbollah had long before established itself as a legitimate political organization in Lebanon. The civil war in Syria had extensive Iranian complicity, but Iran was no more significant than several other players, including Russia and Saudi Arabia. While Trump and Pompeo constantly cited Iranian regional misbehavior as reasons to disrupt the nuclear pact, such considerations (as well as human rights) had never seriously threatened arms control treaties the United States had negotiated before, nor seemed to affect Trump's offers to North Korea.

One might be skeptical about Trump embracing the frontier myth, attributing his actions to his well-established racism instead. His animus toward Obama explains quite a bit when it comes to Iran. The JCPOA was arguably Obama's greatest foreign policy achievement, and Trump's overturning the accord was, in this account, solely based on his ferocious and racist dislike toward his predecessor. His travel ban revealed a dismissive and possibly racist attitude toward Iranians generally. The sanctions alone would result in early death of thousands of ordinary Iranians, another callous response that at least implies racism. While it cannot be documented, these attitudes may have guided Trump's actions, but the official reasons for the "maximum pressure" policy rested much more clearly on the national narrative. The "terrorists" were violently attacking throughout the region, cheating and lying, unwilling to accept civilizational values—this depiction delivered time and again without the slightest admission of the violence and disruption America had forced upon Iraq and its neighbors. Even at the end of his presidency, Trump threatened to attack Iran for no apparent reason other than sheer, violent malice.

All the elements were there: the depiction of Iran's leaders as savages and Iran's policies as savagery, the angling for regime change that would enrich American energy corporations, and the constant, ambient threat of violence. In fact, the sanctions visited violence upon the Iranian people directly. All these tropes were kept alive during Obama's time in office, sometimes by Obama's aides, more often by prominent journalists, neocon leftovers, and the Israel lobby. In political salience, however, they were fading. What is remarkable about Trump's presidency is how quickly he revitalized these pillars of the national narrative. Their revitalization was due not to some covert cleverness in Trump but to the sheer resilience of these narrative elements in the American story.

Biden Lingers

Joe Biden's election in November 2020 was viewed by pro-JCPOA advocates as a game changer. Not only was he vice president during Obama's eight years in office, but he also repeated numerous times during the 2020 campaign that he would rejoin the agreement upon entering office.

His first nine months in office, however, in some respects reproduced the policies of the Trump presidency. At this writing (October 2021), Biden has not only stalled the reentry of the United States into the JCPOA but also broadened the aims of American dialogue with Iran about the scope of the pact. Matters such as ballistic missile development and Iran's militant activism in the region became relevant to JCPOA renewal. The Biden team, led by Secretary of State Anthony Blinken and special envoy Robert Malley, also talked publicly about extending the length of the nuclear restrictions in the pact.

"We have an interest in getting Iran back into that nuclear box," Blinken told a House committee in March 2021. "Think of it this way: We have fundamental problems with Iran's actions across a whole series of things whether it is support for terrorism, whether it's a ballistic missile program that's increasingly dangerous, whether it's destabilizing actions throughout the region. An Iran, with a nuclear weapon or with a threshold capacity to have one is an Iran that's likely to act with even greater impunity when it comes to those things."[29] Most prominently, the Biden administration seemed to reject "going first" by lifting sanctions imposed by Trump and insisted that Iran return to full compliance with the deal before the United States would act—despite Trump having made the first move to undermine the pact.

Whatever happens to the nuclear agreement, the first nine months of the Biden administration and Iran's reaction to it were a familiar refrain, as if both were reading from the national narrative script. This was true under Obama, and certainly true during Trump's time in the White House. That Biden feels constrained to act first, and to act boldly enough to revive the agreement, is remarkably revealing. It indicates that, JCPOA or not, the United States and Iran will cling to their narratives, and that the narratives still guide politics and policy.

Conclusion
Narratives and National Interests

 As we wrote earlier, "Two nations, antagonistic to one another and with well-defined national narratives, find themselves—forty years after their relationship broke down—unable to escape the constraints those narratives impose on political leaders. The constraints are the individual narratives themselves and how expectations emerge on any particular issue, as well as how the two narratives are inherently in conflict with each other."

The expansionist American narrative, the frontier myth, leapt overseas with the acquisition of the Philippines at the end of the nineteenth century, and it has insinuated itself into virtually every major foreign engagement since then. It has been particularly potent in America's ventures in the global south, with its hallmarks of personal freedom, Christian virtue, market economics, and Western or American hegemony in global politics. That so many of those engagements involved organized violence was also reflective of the frontier impetus, in which the local savages posed the greatest threat to the flowering of frontier values.

The Iranian narratives, that of the secular Cyrus/Aryan myth and that of Imam Hussein's sacrifice, both regard foreign encroachments as the greatest threat to the national (Persian) prerogative, namely, to its autonomy, unity, and identity. The Islamic narrative stresses resistance through martyrdom, and thus violence is both a central part of the story and a mode of actual resistance.

These narratives framed the highly charged events that have marked the US-Iran relationship since 1953. The overthrow of Mosaddeq, the US support for the oppressive reign of the last shah, the enforced isolation of the Islamic Republic of Iran, the support for Saddam Hussein in the Iran-Iraq War, the excruciating sanctions imposed for nearly four decades, the false accusations about Iran's compliance with the 2015 nuclear agreement and Trump's withdrawal from that deal, the killing of General Soleimani—these actions, among many others, exemplified America's attempt to control, subdue, and undermine Iran. In America, Iran's post-1979 leadership was depicted as irrational, "mad mullahs," violent and deceitful, the very embodiment of the savage. The embassy hostage taking of 1979–81 remains the symbolic apogee of this depiction, confirmed subsequently by acts of terror in Berlin, Buenos Aires, Lebanon, Saudi Arabia (Khobar Towers), and Iraq.

The Iranians saw the United States as intent on dominance, a virtually seamless successor to British imperialism. The United States saw Iran as a terrorist state, exhorting others to violent, political Islam. These perceptions were based at least partially on observable fact, but the confirmation bias of the national narratives powerfully reinforced these perceptions. To quote Ronald Krebs again (see chap. 1), dominant narratives "set the boundaries of what actors can legitimately articulate in public, what they can collectively (though not individually) imagine, and what is politically possible."

One need not look only at the low points of the relationship to see how these narratives exert influence. The most cooperative period since 1979 was the conclusion of the Joint Comprehensive Plan of Action, the nuclear deal completed in 2015. On its enactment, President Obama said, "We have no illusions about the Iranian government, or the significance of the Revolutionary Guard and the Quds Force. Iran supports terrorist organizations like Hezbollah. It supports proxy groups that threaten our interests and the interests of our allies—including proxy groups who killed our troops in Iraq. They try to destabilize our Gulf partners. But Iran has been engaged in these activities for decades." There was not the slightest hint of the United States seeking a normal relationship with Iran. Indeed, Obama supported actions in the region to thwart Iran, including increased military aid to Israel and support for the Saudi assault on Yemen and supposed Iranian proxies. The JCPOA was in all respects a narrow technical agreement—an important one, to be sure—that did not disrupt American attitudes toward Iran. And many Iranians rightly saw the sanctions and ultimate deal as another imposition, another case of blatant foreign meddling. Rouhani (and, of course, Khamenei) agreed to the restrictions only because the sanctions were creating genuine deprivation. It is worth noting that American political leaders starved indigenous tribes to force them to go placidly into reservations, and that same mentality guided the Iran nuclear deal and especially its aftermath.

The explanations for the behavior of states in the international arena typically hinge on interests, and this "realist" account provides additional clarity toward understanding the US-Iran relationship. America's interests over a long period of time since Mosaddeq's ouster had been first to create a friendly regime that would be a bulwark against Soviet expansion and, after 1979, to contain and possibly reverse the radical Islamist regime ushered in by Ayatollah Khomeini. Throughout those nearly seven decades there were two pillars of US interests in the region, namely, the control of oil and support for Israel, in addition to the global objective of containing the Soviet Union. Virtually every major US action conformed to those interests. Iran, too, has consistently pursued its interests. It has sought to create networks of proxies throughout the region, build alliances with certain states (Syria and post-Saddam Iraq), and resist with this "strategic depth"— violently at times—encroachments by the United States and its allies.

In what ways, then, can national narratives be said to shape behavior if interests are so clearly at work? The two—interests and narratives—do not obscure or cancel each other. Interests, after all, are significantly the outgrowth of narratives, seeded and nourished by the durable myths, legends, and habits of mind that narratives and the broader political culture provide. Consider why the United States could come to see "vital interests" in places like Iraq, Yemen, Saudi Arabia, or Iran. The vital interests, particularly vital security interests, grew from the global role the United States had assumed gradually in the twentieth century, most comprehensively after the Second World War and the diminution of the British Empire. The *longue durée* of postwar American globalism can be seen as the world's richest and most powerful country assuming its proper role as a great power. It can also be seen as a posture of generosity. At root, however, it is a conscious project to bring a certain order to the chaos of a war-torn, impoverished, and contentious world, and to do so with military power, free trade, and political coercion—precisely the attitude that Euro-American settlers imposed on the continental frontier. Oil is one of the rewards, and Israel is an outpost. Markets, Christian virtue, and a fervent rhetorical preference for democratic values (though casually enforced) mark the ventures into both Indian territory in the eighteenth century and Muslim lands in the twenty-first.

Discernible interests are also derivative of Iran's national narrative. The stories of betrayal in the Karbala Paradigm have taught generations of Iranians that foreign devils lurk, seeking to dominate the

Persian nation. Among those interlopers are Sunni Arabs, Turks, and others. This encompassing idea of resistance to malign foreign influence and control is a genuine, secular interest, and not unique to Iran. Hence, the interests that have led Iran since 1979 to seek strategic depth in Assad's Syria, the Houtis in Yemen, and Hezbollah in Lebanon, among others, draw from centuries of foreign domination, their culture suppressed or disrespected, their autonomy denied.

The cold construction of interests is scarcely consistent for either country. America's thirty-to-forty-year involvement in Iraq, with costs in the trillions of dollars and more than one million lives, cannot by any measure be described as a rational choice. The attempts to engineer regime change in Iran are similarly unwise given what we know about the sheer unpredictability of succession. Iran's foreign policy is beset by an irrational hatred of Israel and the history of the Jewish people—Holocaust denial in particular. Iran's belief in its own specialness, due to its long history, prompts a need for respect in the global arena that is largely irrelevant to the actual conduct of international relations. Thus, for both countries, cultural predilections that are drawn from the national narratives often overwhelm even an austere calculation of interests.

These culturally driven preferences can also be glimpsed in the obsessiveness each country exhibits toward the other. The United States is posed as the villain in the Friday prayers of IRI leaders, in conservative media, and so on, far more frequently than any other threat. Likewise, American political culture obsesses about Iran like no other adversary. Neoconservatives and the Israel lobby drive much of this, but the broader political culture is receptive and indeed replicates this obsession routinely. It mirrors, to some extent, the obsession Euro-Americans felt toward indigenous tribes until well into the twentieth century—not only attacking them militarily, stealing land, and forcing them on to reservations, but also insisting on "educating" their children in schools that aimed to "kill the Indian and save the man." In

Iran, the present-day mania about the United States is a replica of many Iranians' obsession with British control, dating back to the mid-nineteenth century. The Iranian focus on the Great Satan is even written into its constitution.

■ The Narratives in Action

We can look at each traumatic encounter of the two countries as drawing from and simultaneously nourishing the narratives and the political identities they construct. The overthrow of Mosaddeq has been for Iranians a uniquely representative act by the United States and Britain—malign foreign influence, in spades. (Never mind that many if not most clerics supported the coup d'état.) In Washington, removing Mosaddeq was in keeping with the worldwide containment of Soviet influence. As was so often the case in the Cold War, the local, "backward" populations hardly counted in the superpowers' calculations. The coup was also a means to control oil. The quarter century of the shah's subsequent reign featured US-supported repression and the elevation of Iran to the status of a US surrogate power in the region. That period also witnessed increasing American presence in Iran as the shah implemented his controversial and ill-fated White Revolution, which was mainly land and social reform. The shah's persistent attempt to be America's junior partner in the region never took root in Iran, not only due to his disconnectedness from "the people" but also because of the alien quality of that goal to the nation's political culture.

The seizure of the US embassy in Tehran in November 1979 by Iranian radicals is the signature event in Americans' perception of Iran. This and the "mad mullahs" that came to power months before fulfill the expectation of savages in this wilderness. This perception, buttressed by the indiscrete fulminations of Ahmadinejad, among others, has never really diminished among Americans. For those Iranian revolutionaries who held embassy employees hostage, the embassy—a "nest of spies"—symbolized American imperialism. The 444 days of the crisis remain a vivid piece of each country's narrative.

Everything since then seems to fit the narrative pattern. The Carter administration gave the green light to Saddam's invasion of Iran, and the Reagan administration supported Saddam during the Iran-Iraq War with vital resources—real-time intelligence for targeting, economic supports, military equipment, and political legitimacy. Reagan downplayed Iraq's use of chemical weapons and reflagged oil tankers from Iraq to protect them from Iranian saboteurs. Khomeini persisted with a bloody war of attrition in the name of Shi'a Islam. In Lebanon, seemingly unrelated turmoil in 1983 brought two devastating bombings against the US embassy and a contingent of marines that were attributed to Iranian-backed terrorists. In 1988, an Iranian passenger airliner was shot down by a US ship, killing nearly three hundred passengers, in what Iran saw as a deliberate act.

The period of Rafsanjani's presidency (1989–97) was marked by some hope of a US-Iran dialogue—hopes dashed perhaps by Operation Desert Storm soon followed by the collapse of the Soviet Union, both preoccupying President George H. W. Bush. Whatever the reasons for this missed opportunity, the Iranians committed a number of egregious acts of political violence, including the assassination in Paris of the last reformist prime minister before the revolution. In the United States, sentiment against Iran remained strong, and indeed President Clinton signed the Iran and Libya Sanctions Act in 1996. Regime change also became an explicit objective of the United States. ILSA passed the House of Representatives on June 19, 1996. Six days later, the US military complex in Saudi Arabia, Khobar Towers, was victim to a powerful truck bomb. Iran denied a role in the bombing, but Clinton nearly ordered a retaliatory attack.

The Khatami period brought considerable expectations of a warming of relations, but internal opposition and durable old suspicions prevented much substantive progress. The 9/11 attack and the take-down of the Taliban occasioned another opportunity for a rapproche-ment of sorts at the Bonn conference and afterward, but the new Bush administration was unable to shed neocon illusions of transforming the region. The "axis of evil" reference in Bush's State of the Union speech in 2002, coupled with the run-up to the Iraq invasion, poi-soned the atmosphere. President Khatami made a somewhat desper-ate entreaty in a 2003 fax to the US State Department, following the invasion of Iraq. It was ignored, not least because American policy makers were flush with success and possibly envisioned pushing the frontier into Iran.

Iraq turned out to be harder to tame than the Wild West, in part because Iran could make it so. Through militia leaders beholden to Tehran, the IRI killed hundreds of US military personnel, fought a gory civil war with Sunni militias (in which US forces were often involved), and ultimately won political control. It did not completely expel US forces, but it seems destined to outlast them. A similar dynamic is at work in Afghanistan, though there Iran is less active. Both places were venues of the clashing narratives, with Americans insisting they were bringing higher civilizational values and Iranians insisting that the American objectives were about political and economic control.

The Obama administration seemed to bring a different attitude toward the dysfunctional relationship, but little actual progress was made until Rouhani was elected president in Iran in 2013. The nuclear negotiating then became earnest, with an interim deal made in late 2013 and the final JCPOA signed in 2015. On the surface, the agree-ment seemed to have overcome four decades of mistrust. And to some extent, it did. As noted earlier, however, the narrow technical achieve-ment did not change the basic dynamic of each country's outlook and behavior. The temporary triumph of global norms on nuclear prolifera-tion, however important, did not bleed into other hot-button issues— Iran's support for Hezbollah, Assad's reign of terror in Syria, Houtis in

Yemen, or various militia in Iraq—nor did it affect America's fulsome support for Israel's abuse of Palestinians, its partnership with the Saudis in their war on Yemen, intermittent backing of militant actors in Syria trying to defeat Assad, and so on. The agreement stood, for a time, as an example of how the two countries could cooperate, but there were examples aplenty that they would remain at odds, often violently so. The JCPOA underscored diplomacy's utility, but diplomacy is only useful if exercised.

What we call the narrative trap seemed to exert itself on these many occasions, even at the peak of diplomacy's success. That the US government could revert to the defining hostility of the relationship so quickly after Obama departed the White House is the most vivid case of this exertion. Identities that were and are fundamentally at odds with each other and had been constructed over decades if not centuries were not going to be transformed or dislodged suddenly by a single arms control agreement. Narratives shape not only identities but also expectations, and the expectations in this relationship are nearly always ones of confrontation, suspicion, hidden motives, and ill intent. The difficulty returning to the JCPOA after Biden became president looked like a textbook case of expectations—cultural and political—driving the negotiations. When expectations are so deeply rooted, they can *cause* behavior by elites that reinforces the stereotypes and strongly shapes policy.

◼ Missed Opportunities

The nuclear agreement does raise the question about missed opportunities. So many opportunities were apparently squandered in the US-Iran relationship that it begs an explanation. A missed opportunity is present when both parties see an opening to create constructive dialogue or even a change in policy that accommodates the other, but that opening closes for some extraneous reason. Among those reasons are domestic spoilers, black swan events, intentional sabotage, misreading of the opportunity, or an inequality in response—one party urgent, the other casual or even neglectful—which dooms the possibility of moving the relationship in a positive direction. Reversion to the narrative can also obstruct an opportunity.

In this case, the missed opportunities appeared during Operation Desert Storm and Operation Iraqi Freedom, in which some dialogue proceeded; the beginning of George H. W. Bush's presidency, in which some promises of dialogue seemed to be made but never occurred; the entire Khatami period, which did witness some small progress but never fulfilled the apparent opportunity; the Bonn conference, which did involve constructive, joint problem-solving on Afghanistan but did not proceed further; the advent of the 2003 fax; the nuclear negotiating process, culminating in the JCPOA; and military operations to defeat ISIS in 2014–18.

The misses came from both sides, and, notably, many were rooted in each country's narrative. The reason that domestic spoilers—pro-Israel and neocon actors in America, hard-liners in Iran—can be so effective is that they play on old grievances that have been spun from the narrative. For example, the Trump retreat from the nuclear deal was paved with the old trope of cheating and deception by Iran, charges made frequently during the negotiations and immediately after it was concluded. Savages are inherently untrustworthy. In Iran, the Khatami presidency was stymied immediately by hard-liners, and one of Ahmadinejad's campaign slogans in 2005 disparaged Khatami's policies as a "failure of accommodationism." The conservatives' fear of American influence in Iran was based on, or at least coincident with, their national narrative.

One of the most obvious antidotes to missed opportunities is to have full diplomatic relations. In virtually every case of missed opportunities, the lack of a direct, reliable channel was fatal. The 2003 fax is perhaps the most glaring example, in which Washington policy makers could not discern the authenticity or seriousness of the grand bargain offered by Iran. The Khobar Towers bombing is another such example. Angry letters were conveyed, but an actual discussion about evidence, motives, and the like would never take place. In the absence of ordinary diplomacy, the national narratives actually gain more relevance and power.

Missed opportunities appear, then, to be outgrowths of miscommunication, or no communication. There are different modes of communications—the news media; social media; private, official, and back channels; among others—and all are used in diplomacy. Each can serve somewhat different purposes, including deceit, propaganda, delay, and so on, but each can also constructively revive and build a productive relationship. What seems clear from the history of US-Iran relations since 1979 is that officials' public statements tended to reflect the national narratives, whereas private communications (especially the back channel via Oman that set the parameters for the JCPOA) do not, at least not as overtly. The spoilers and others on the sidelines tend to heighten the narratives' themes about the other. This simple scheme suggests that more private conversations would be productive, but in the US-Iran case the need for a back channel was occasioned by the absence of formal diplomatic ties. Private channels cannot be institutionalized; they are by nature intermittent and designed for a specific purpose. But opportunities for improved relations do not necessarily occur in a form easily advanced by a back channel. Even when such a channel exists, as it did when the UN envoy Giandomenico Picco was ferrying between the Bush 41 team and President Rafsanjani, the opportunity can fail, as it did then when the Americans failed to come through with their implicit promises.

There are many channels of communication that are unofficial, and these are used often. The news media is one such channel, though it is public and therefore used mainly for propaganda. Khatami did use an interview with CNN to invite more dialogue, but it was an opportunity that the Clinton team did not fully appreciate. So-called Track 2 diplomacy creates channels, and there have been many such efforts in the US-Iran relationship. Pugwash, the venerable organization of scientists, convened many meetings between Americans and Iranians, among others, to discuss the nuclear situation. Track 2 is limited by how many influential people participate and how well it is oriented to problem-solving. Official Iran's aversion to contacts with Americans limited what this mode of interaction could accomplish.

The communications between the two countries, regardless of the mode, were hampered by the essentials of the national narratives, apart from the private discussions that had a specific purpose— JCPOA, deconfliction during the invasions of Iraq, rebuilding Afghanistan. That those dialogues could not blossom into a more comprehensive discussion about the relationship itself was a failure of political will. It was also a consequence of cultural bias, a lack of appreciation for the narrative lens through which the other sees. Opportunities were often missed as a result.

■ One Narrative

Our goal in this book is not only to explicate how national narratives exert influence over state behavior but also to construct a single narrative of the US-Iran relationship. To do so thoroughly would require years of interviews and surveys and other data gathering efforts, and even as the project from which this book was produced has gathered significant amounts of information, it would take even more to center and complete such a single narrative. It is further complicated by the fact that Iran remains a largely closed society, and research by outsiders in Iran is difficult.

Still, we have produced what we believe is a fair account of the relationship in an effort to produce that one narrative. Such a narrative—a history—is possible, if always incomplete. And it provides several worthwhile insights:

- Both Iran and the United States have purposefully avoided engaging with each other in normal and constructive ways.

- Both Iran and the United States consistently see each other in their national narrative terms and express those sentiments routinely in public media.

- For Iran, America looms large and menacing, its primary adversary; for America, Iran is one of several challenges in the region, albeit a significant one. This imbalance has consequences, not least the cavalier application of sanctions by the United States.

- Violence is a constant presence in the relationship. For Iran it is the violence that imperialists always visit upon the oppressed, or would-be oppressed; for America, it is the violence of terrorism, the savage in the wilderness.

- Brief moments of opportunities to improve the relationship have failed owing to both an absence of a structure, such as diplomatic ties, to take advantage of such moments and the negative influence of the national narratives.

- Spoilers in both countries play a large role in preventing better ties, and they do so by emphasizing the stereotypes of the other developed in each national narrative.

- National interests guide policy making in most cases. But interests are in part derived from long-standing attitudes fostered by the national narratives. At times, state actions are untethered to interests and clearly emerge from political culture shaped by the narratives.

- Policy failures, such as the US invasion of Iraq or Iran's hostility to Israel, tend to reinforce the narratives as both explanation for the failure and post hoc justifications for the policies.

- The nuclear deal of 2015 demonstrates how the two countries can "do business" on technical matters without improving relations overall, another effect of the national narratives.

- National narratives, while deeply rooted in hundreds of years of history, are replenished and activated by recent events, such as the overthrow of Mosaddeq and the seizure of embassy hostages in 1979.

Our one, major recommendation is for both nations to work toward normal diplomatic relations. So much of what we describe as missed opportunities and other dysfunctionalities comes from the rather rote responses in the news media when crises beset the relationship. Direct communication can strip away some of the routine references derived from the narratives that prevent useful, joint problem-solving. We have seen how quiet, back-channel talks can produce good results. Formal diplomatic ties would enable such problem-solving. That the United States could maintain diplomatic relations with the Soviet Union for fifty-eight years should disabuse the notion that one cannot have such relations with an adversary. Iranian reluctance to normalize relations is particularly self-defeating considering the ease with which the United States has isolated and sanctioned Iran.

A second recommendation is to organize an open-ended commission to consider the historical grievances that beset the relationship. A truth and reconciliation commission populated by former policy makers, a range of experts, some current legislators, and so on, could build trust simply by recognizing that both countries have erred often in dealing with the other. The therapy of acceptance, respect, and common interests could go a long way toward repairing the trauma of the many actions that have been harmful.

Diplomatic relations and a truth and reconciliation commission work only as much as political leaders will utilize them positively. It goes without saying that mechanisms succeed only when political will allows them to. And that elusive quality of political will is enabled or disabled by the national narratives that quietly shape it. Mobilizing public support, countering spoilers, reaching out effectively to the other—all of these require political will that is braced by a new narrative, a detour from the old crippling narratives, which is enabling, respectful, and true. It is a detour worth taking, and constantly renewing, for years to come.

Notes

1 The Narrative Trap

1 "The convergence of capitalism and print technology on the fatal diversity of human language created the possibility of a new form of imagined community, which in its basic morphology set the stage for the modern nation. The potential stretch of these communities was inherently limited, and, at the same time, bore none but the most fortuitous relationship to existing political boundaries." Benedict Anderson, *Imagined Communities: Reflections on the Origin and Spread of Nationalism*, rev. ed. (Verso, 2006), 46.

2 Steven Pincus, "Nationalism, Universal Monarchy, and the Glorious Revolution," in *State/Culture: State-Formation after the Cultural Turn*, ed. George Steinmetz (Cornell University Press, 1999), chap. 6. Pincus argued that English nationalism grew in a public sphere independent of the state. Anderson described an official nationalism, typified by czarist Russia, which was another notable phenomenon. It "can best be understood as a means for combining naturalization with retention of dynastic power, in particular over the huge polyglot domains accumulated since the Middle

Ages, or, to put it another way, for stretching the short, tight, skin of the nation over the gigantic body of the empire." Anderson, *Imagined Communities*, 86.

3 Anthony D. Smith, *Nationalism: Theory, Ideology, and History*, 2nd ed. (Polity, 2010), 30–31.

4 Ernest Gellner, *Nations and Nationalism* (Blackwell, 1983), 124–25.

5 Isaiah Berlin, "The Bent Twig: A Note on Nationalism," *Foreign Affairs*, October 1972, https://www.foreignaffairs.com/articles/1972-10-01/bent-twig.

6 As Berlin states,

> The central doctrines of the progressive French thinkers, whatever their disagreements among themselves, rested on the belief, rooted in the ancient doctrine of natural law, that human nature was fundamentally the same in all times and places; that local and historical variations were unimportant compared with the constant central core in terms of which human beings could be defined as a species, like animals, or plants, or minerals; that there were universal human goals; that a logically connected structure of laws and generalisations susceptible of demonstration and verification could be constructed and replace the chaotic amalgam of ignorance, mental laziness, guesswork, superstition, prejudice, dogma, fantasy, and, above all, the 'interested error' maintained by the rulers of mankind and largely responsible for the blunders, vices and misfortunes of humanity.

Isaiah Berlin, *Against the Current: Essays in the History of Ideas*, 2nd ed., ed. Henry Hardy (Princeton University Press, 2013), 1.

7 Berlin, *Against the Current*, 12.

8 Berlin, *Against the Current*, 13.

9 Ronald Krebs, "How Dominant Narratives Rise and Fall: Military Conflict, Politics, and the Cold War Consensus," *International Organization*, October 1, 2015, 813.

10 It is worth noting that two other famous protests against foreign taxation of commodities led to revolutions: the colonial American Tea Party in Boston in 1773, and the Salt March (Satyagraha) organized by Mohandas K. Gandhi in India in 1930. Both were protests against imperial power, leading to independence from Britain. The tobacco protest in Iran was about foreign domination and the monarchy's complicity in it.

11 Reza Zia-Ebrahimi, "Self-Orientalization and Dislocation: The Uses and Abuses of the 'Aryan' Discourse in Iran," *Iranian Studies* 44, no. 4 (2011): 466.

12 The Aryan discourse was shaped significantly by Orientalists in Europe, and the link to Nazism was vivid. In the 1920s and 1930s, considerable cross-fertilization among intellectuals and political operatives promoted the Aryan myth as both a foundation narrative of Iran and the ideological framework of Hitler's movement. They shared, among other elements, a complete disdain for the Semitic races and exaltation of Aryan superiority. Of course, in Iran these attitudes never converted into the psychotic murderousness of the Nazis.

13 Talinn Grigor, "Recultivating 'Good Taste': The Early Pahlavi Modernists and Their Society for National Heritage," *Iranian Studies* 37, no. 1 (March 2004): 20.

14 Grigor, "Recultivating 'Good Taste,'" 40.

15 "Editorial: Notre But," *Le journal de Teheran* 1 (March 15, 1935): 1, quoted in Grigor, "Recultivating 'Good Taste,'" 40.

16 Ali al-Taie, review of "Iran as Imagined Nation: The Construction of National Identity," by Mostafa Vaziri, *Digest of Middle East Studies* 5, no. 3 (Summer 1996): 55. "The Farsi language itself 'possessed no national homeland, and its speakers had never searched for a national homeland in modern times . . . ' Nevertheless, the Orientalists, together with the functionaries of the Pahlavi regime of Iran, expended great efforts to make the Farsi language and Iran sound synonymous. The different ethnic groups have been required to learn the national language, but not their own native languages, in order to develop and identify with the new national consciousness" (55).

17 Charlotte Curtis, "First Party of Iran's 2,500-Year Celebration," *New York Times*, October 13, 1971, https://www.nytimes.com/1971/10/13/archives /first-party-of-irans-2500year-celebration.html?searchResultPosition=1. There are many accounts of this most expensive party, including a BBC documentary. Six hundred dignitaries attended (though not President Richard Nixon; he sent Vice President Spiro Agnew instead). One Iranian minister complained that all food and wine served (except caviar) was French, including 25,000 bottles of *premier cru* wine; "if we have 2,500 years of glorious civilization, he asked rhetorically, why then can we not

serve them 'Persian' dishes like *kabab kubideh* or even *ab-gusht.*" Abbas
Milani, *The Shah* (Palgrave MacMillan, 2011), 322.

18 The Aryan myth has been roundly debunked as wholly contrived by European—particularly German—Orientalists. Iran has long been ethnically
mixed, a mixture of Arabs, Turks, Mongols, Kurds, etc., as well as Persians.
The continuity of culture is also contested by this ethnic mix; for example,
Farsi was not widely spoken throughout much of Iran's history. (Even the
Cyrus Cylinder was written in a dialect of Babylonian.) Given the com-
monness of human migration over the course of many centuries, this ethnic variety is unsurprising.

19 Michael M. J. Fischer, *Iran: From Religious Dispute to Revolution*, 2nd ed.
(University of Wisconsin Press, 2003), 27. Muharram is the month of Hussein's death.

20 This remains a powerful slogan. "'Everywhere is Karbala, every month is
Muharram, and every day is Ashura,' a phrase first coined by the intellectual Ali Shari'ati and adopted later by Khomeini as a banner of the Revolution. The slogan is a reminder of Hussein's sacrifice, of the Revolution, of
the Iran-Iraq War, and the continual Islamic/nationalist fight against
Western Imperialism." Rose Wellman, "Regenerating the Islamic Republic:
Commemorating Martyrs in Provincial Iran," *Muslim World* 105 (October
2015): 568. Ashura marks the day of Hussein's death.

21 Fischer provides another look at this dilemma, namely, during the uprising
following the apparently fraudulent reelection of Ahmadinejad in 2009:

> The Green Wave has effectively mobilized the Karbala Paradigm, the
> Shi'ite paradigm of struggle for social justice, against the government,
> although the government has not given up its own claims to that nar-
> rative.
>
> It is important to note, however, that the Green Movement has
> appropriated the Karbala Paradigm differently than during the 1977–
> 79 revolution. The differences are critical indices of the changing
> structure of the public sphere. The secular "left" factions of the 1977–
> 79 revolution either did not fully appreciate the eschatological discur-
> sive power of Shi'ism, or they wanted to consign it to the past. The
> Green Movement instead has skillfully deployed the Karbala Para-
> digm, turning it in a nonfundamentalist direction and contesting the
> state's capture of its discursive power. In 1977–79, the Karbala Para-

digm was used as a mobilizing device by the religious factions of the revolution to inject morality and social justice as the goals of politics; today it is the "secularists" who are using the Karbala Paradigm to claim both politics and morality from the assertion of monopoly control over interpretation of Islam by clerics and their allies and followers, an interpretive control that is explicitly antidemocratic and antirepublican. The latter view politics and democratic or republican forms as merely plebiscitary affirmation of decisions by a patronage state based on the control of oil and the key economic sectors, and on a new elite of war veterans and their clerical allies.

Michael M. J. Fischer, "The Rhythmic Beat of the Revolution in Iran," *Cultural Anthropology* 25, no. 3 (2010): 513–14.

22 From H. Anvari and H. Javardi, *Farsi*, a second-grade textbook; quoted in Haggay Ram, "The Immemorial Iranian Nation? School Textbooks and Historical Memory in Post-revolutionary Iran," *Nations and Nationalism* 6, no. 1 (2000): 77.

23 Ram, "Immemorial Iranian Nation?," 80, 82.

24 Zia-Ebrahimi, "Self-Orientalization and Dislocation," 447, 471–72.

25 Ayatollah Seyyed Ali Khamenei, *The Cultural Viewpoints of the Leader of the Islamic Revolution of Iran* (Center for Cultural and International Studies, Islamic Culture and Relations Committee, 2000), quoted in Shabnam Holliday, "The Politicisation of Culture and the Contestation of Iranian National Identity in Khatami's Iran," *Studies in Ethnicity and Nationalism* 7, no. 1 (2000): 35.

26 Holliday, "Politicisation of Culture," 40.

27 Seymour Martin Lipset, *American Exceptionalism: A Double-Edged Sword* (W. W. Norton, 1996), introduction.

28 Stephen Walt, "The Myth of American Exceptionalism," *Foreign Policy* 189 (2011): 72–75. See also Godfrey Hodgson, *The Myth of American Exceptionalism* (Yale University Press, 2009).

29 Richard Slotkin, *The Fatal Environment: The Myth of the Frontier in the Age of Industrialization, 1800–1890* (University of Oklahoma Press, 1995), 15. This is the second volume in Slotkin's trilogy. The first is *Regeneration through Violence: The Mythology of the American Frontier, 1600–1860* (University of Oklahoma Press, 2000), and the third is *Gunfighter Nation: The Myth of the Frontier in Twentieth-Century America* (University of Okla-

homa Press, 1998). The books were originally published by Atheneum in 1973, 1985, and 1992, respectively.

30 Slotkin, *Fatal Environment*, 301.

31 David W. Noble, *Death of a Nation: American Culture and the End of Exceptionalism* (University of Minnesota Press, 2002), 4.

32 Frederick Jackson Turner, "The Significance of the Frontier in American History," presentation to the American Historical Association, Chicago, July 12, 1893, 15. Also available at http://www.wwnorton.com/college/history/america-essential-learning/docs/FJTurner-Frontier_Significance-1893.pdf.

33 It is no small coincidence that Theodore Roosevelt's racialist ideas emphasized the superiority of the "Teutonic race"—Germans, mainly—as well as the "Aryan race." "His typology of human races is derived from the linguistically based theories of Aryanism and Teutonism, which held that one common racial ancestor or master-race is the root of all those peoples whose languages belong to the Indo-European family and that in some races (that is, the Teutons) the line of inheritance runs truer." Slotkin, *Gunfighter Nation*, 43. It is noteworthy that Kermani was nurturing similar notions about Iranians' Aryan lineage at about the same time.

34 Slotkin, *Gunfighter Nation*, 53.

35 Woodrow Wilson, "Democracy and Efficiency," *Atlantic* 87, no. 521 (March 1901): 289–99.

36 Stephen G. Rabe, "Historic Patterns of Intervention: U.S. Relations with Latin America," *Latin American Research Review* 23, no. 2 (1988): 206.

37 David Vine, "Where in the World Is the U.S. Military?," *Politico*, July/August 2015, https://www.politico.com/magazine/story/2015/06/us-military-bases-around-the-world-119321. The number of bases, what constitutes a base, etc., are notoriously difficult to state with precision.

38 Susan Faludi's *The Terror Dream: Myth and Misogyny in an Insecure America* (Atlantic, 2007) is an excellent analysis of the reliance of the debate on frontier myth rhetoric, with an emphasis on gender analysis.

39 William Appleman Williams, "The Frontier Thesis and American Foreign Policy," *Pacific Historical Review* 24, no. 4 (November 1955): 379–95.

40 The durability of the frontier myth is found not only in foreign interventions but also in domestic politics and culture. Cowboys-and-Indians references still abound. The literary structure of the hero remains intact, mainly for television and movie entertainment, in the avenging individual working

outside an apathetic or corrupt system. Slotkin shows exhaustively the appearance of the frontier themes in late twentieth-century American pop culture. The frontier myth, moreover, will redound in sometimes unexpected ways. For example, the debate over gun control that erupts after mass shootings pits bereaved families and liberal sympathizers against the National Rifle Association (NRA) and conservatives. The latter's position is nearly a perfect reproduction of some elements of the myth of the frontier: the gun, gun violence, and gun ownership are held as expressions of personal freedom, a hedge against tyranny or other threats, and a font of social and political empowerment. In the words of the head of the NRA, the gun and its urtext, the Second Amendment, are rights "not bestowed by man, but granted by God to all Americans as our American birthright." After a high school massacre in Florida took seventeen lives in February 2018, the right wing widely promoted the idea of arming teachers, a kind of vigilante force of gunslingers (which the public opposed in a national opinion poll by only a 50%–44% margin). The reasons for keeping open the sale of assault weapons typically revolve around "threats" posed by "illegal immigrants," groups like the Salvadoran gang MS-13, or, even more far-fetched, terrorist groups like ISIS (Islamic State of Iraq and Syria)—that is, the new savages of the frontier. One could argue that gun culture, as an expression of masculinity, autonomy, etc., also constitutes a narrative trap insofar as it has blocked preventive, national legislation to curb America's extraordinary level of gun violence, much of which afflicts gun owners and their families.

41 Slotkin, *Gunfighter Nation*, 10.

42 Wellman, "Regenerating the Islamic Republic," 568.

43 Note that Christian martyrdom was important to the development of Christianity, especially in its early centuries. It remains a powerful political tool in places like Northern Ireland, where Catholic, anti-British militancy is often roused by reference to martyrs to the cause of independence. Christian symbols and ideas have infused the frontier myth as well, but violence as a mechanism of mobilization and justification is much more often the assertive mode of attacking savages rather than the passive mode of celebrating martyrs.

44 Hidemi Sugamani, "Agents, Structures, Narratives," *European Journal of International Relations* 5, no. 3 (1999): 365–86. See also Geoffrey Roberts, "History, Theory, and the Narrative Turn in IR," *International Studies Review* 32, no. 4 (2006): 703–14.

45 Richard K. Ashley, "Foreign Policy as Political Performance," *International Studies Notes* 13 (1988): 53; quoted in Ted Hopf, "The Promise of Constructivism in International Relations Theory," *International Security* 23, no. 1 (Summer 1998): 179.

46 Ali M. Ansari, *Confronting Iran: The Failure of American Foreign Policy and the Next Great Conflict in the Middle East* (Basic Books, 2006), 2.

2 The Fraught US-Iran Relationship, from Mosaddeq to Khomeini

1 President's press conference, February 13, 1980, The President's News Conference | The American Presidency Project (ucsb.edu).

2 President Roosevelt memorandum to the Secretary of State, January 12, 1944, footnote 68 in *Foreign Relations of the United States* (hereafter *FRUS*), 1943, vol. 4, *The Near East and Africa*. See also "General Patrick J. Hurley, Personal Representative of President Roosevelt in Iran, to the President," December 21, 1943, Doc. 440 in *FRUS*, 1943, vol. 4, *The Near East and Africa*.

3 Memorandum by Mr. John D. Jernegan of the Division of Near Eastern Affairs, January 23, 1943, Annex to Doc. 366 in *FRUS*, 1943, vol. 4, *The Near East and Africa*.

4 Bruce R. Kuniholm, *The Origins of the Cold War in the Near East: Great Power Conflict and Diplomacy in Iran, Turkey, and Greece* (Princeton University Press, 1980), 160.

5 For the fullest account of this early Cold War episode, see Jamil Hasanli, *At the Dawn of the Cold War: The Soviet-American Crisis over Iranian Azerbaijan, 1941–1946* (Rowman & Littlefield, 2006).

6 "Subject: President Truman's conversations with George M. Elsey," June 26, 1950; source: G. M. E. notes of June 26, 1950.

7 *Time*, January 7, 1952.

8 Harry Truman, "Inaugural Address," January 20, 1949, Inaugural Address | Harry S. Truman (trumanlibrary.gov). "Point Four," so named because it was the fourth item in Truman's "program for peace and freedom," was an early precursor of the US Agency for International Development, established by President John F. Kennedy.

9 Truman's concerns are apparent in State Department, "First Progress Report on Paragraph 5-a of NSC 136/1, 'U.S. policy regarding the present situ-

ation in Iran,'" Top Secret Memorandum, March 20, 1953. In January 1949, Truman also approved plans to demolish petroleum facilities across the Middle East, including in Iran, in order to keep the oil out of Soviet hands in case of an invasion. See Steve Everly, "U.S., Britain Developed Plans to Disable or Destroy Middle Eastern Oil Facilities from Late 1940s to Early 1960s in Event of a Soviet Invasion," National Security Archive Electronic Briefing Book no. 552, June 23, 2016.

10 See, e.g., memoranda of two meetings at the State Department with British officials in late 1952, in National Security Archive Electronic Briefing Book no. 601, August 8, 2017.

11 A larger sampling can be found in Ervand Abrahamian, *The Coup: 1953, The CIA, and the Roots of Modern U.S.-Iranian Relations* (New Press, 2013), 98–99. The smears of Mosaddeq were worse.

12 NSC meeting, March 4, 1953.

13 See Mark Gasiorowski and Malcolm Byrne, *Mohammad Mosaddeq and the 1953 Coup in Iran* (Syracuse University Press, 2004), chap. 6, esp. 201–26.

14 For related declassified documents, see *FRUS*, 1952–54, vol. 16, *Iran, 1951–54*, 2nd ed. (US Government Publishing Office, 2018), and various National Security Archive Electronic Briefing Books featuring key internal CIA histories (https://nsarchive.gwu.edu/project/iran-us-relations).

15 See, e.g., "New Findings on Clerical Involvement in the 1953 Coup in Iran," National Security Archive Electronic Briefing Book no. 619, March 7, 2018, https://nsarchive.gwu.edu/briefing-book/iran/2018-03-07/new-findings -clerical-involvement-1953-coup-iran.

16 Doc. 345, *FRUS*, 2018.

17 Interview with L. Bruce Laingen, The Association for Diplomatic Studies and Training Foreign Affairs Oral History Project, January 9, 1993, https:// cdn.loc.gov/service/mss/mfdip/2004/2004lai01/2004lai01.pdf.

18 See generally James A. Bill, *The Eagle and the Lion: The Tragedy of American-Iranian Relations* (Yale University Press, 1988), chap. 4.

19 Roland Popp, "An Application of Modernization Theory during the Cold War? The Case of Pahlavi Iran," *International History Review* 30, no. 1 (March 2008): 76–98. Rostow's theories were put on the map by his book *The Stages of Economic Growth: A Non-Communist Manifesto* (Cambridge University Press, 1960).

20 Quoted in Popp, "Application of Modernization Theory," 92.

21 Quoted in James Goode, "Reforming Iran during the Kennedy Years," *Diplomatic History* 15, no. 1 (1991): 27.

22 George Carroll to Hubert Humphrey, "Conversation with Kermit Roosevelt," *FRUS*, 1964–68, vol. 22, *Iran*, Doc. 163, 299–300.

23 Department of State, Memorandum of Conversation, "Last Formal Conversation between Secretary and Shah: State Visit to Washington, April, 1962," April 13, 1962, in *FRUS*, 1961–63, vol. 17, *Near East, 1961–1962*, 611.

24 Bill, *Eagle and the Lion*, 137.

25 See the discussion in Roham Alvandi, *Nixon, Kissinger, and the Shah: The United States and Iran in the Cold War* (Oxford University Press, 2016), 24–26. For Khomeini's full remarks on SOFA, see *Islam and Revolution: Writings and Declarations of Imam Khomeini (1941–1980)*, trans. and annot. Hamid Algar (Mizan, 1981), 181–88.

26 Shahram Chubin and Sepehr Zabih, *The Foreign Relations of Iran: A Developing State in a Zone of Great-Power Conflict* (University of California Press, 1974), 5–7.

27 See Andrew L. Johns, "The Johnson Administration, the Shah of Iran, and the Changing Pattern of U.S.-Iranian Relations, 1965–1967," *Journal of Cold War Studies* 9, no. 2 (Spring 2007): 64–94; see also Claudia Castiglioni, "No Longer a Client, Not Yet a Partner: The US-Iranian Alliance in the Johnson Years," *Cold War History* 15, no. 4 (2015): 491–509.

28 See Henry Kissinger, *The White House Years* (Little, Brown, 1979), 1258–62.

29 Richard M. Nixon, *The Memoirs of Richard Nixon* (Grosset & Dunlap, 1978), 133. (By comparison, Romanian dictator Nicolae Ceausescu rates several mentions.)

30 Nixon and US Ambassador to Iran Douglas MacArthur II, April 8, 1971, Conversation no. 475-23 (RC 458-2), Nixon Presidential Materials, Tapes, Chronological Review, First Release (October 1999; February–July 1971), transcribed by Jim Hershberg and Malcolm Byrne. (The *FRUS* transcription differs in several places.)

31 See this quote and general discussion in Bill, *Eagle and the Lion*, 201–2.

32 Nixon-MacArthur, April 8, 1971.

33 See the discussion in Alvandi, *Nixon, Kissinger, and the Shah*, 128–30.

34 An illuminating example was a White House briefing about Iran by CIA director Stansfield Turner in late 1978 that touched on Ayatollah Khomeini, at which point a senior official asked, "What's an Ayatollah?" Gary Sick at

conference, "The Intervention in Afghanistan and the Fall of Détente," hosted by the Norwegian Nobel Institute, organized with the National Security Archive, Lysebu, Norway, September 17–20, 1995, transcript, 50.

35 William Sullivan, cable, "Thinking the Unthinkable," November 9, 1978.

36 George Ball testimony in "Relations in a Multipolar World," Senate Foreign Relations Committee hearings, November 6, 1991, 29.

37 George W. Ball, memorandum for the president, "Issues and Implications of the Iranian Crisis," December 12, 1978; George W. Ball, *The Past Has Another Pattern: Memoirs* (W. W. Norton, 1982), 461.

38 Jimmy Carter toast to the shah at state dinner in Tehran, December 31, 1977, Tehran, Iran Toasts of the President and the Shah at a State Dinner | The American Presidency Project (ucsb.edu).

39 Robert E. Huyser, *Mission to Tehran* (Harper & Row, 1986); see also Edward C. Keefer, *Harold Brown: Offsetting the Soviet Military Challenge, 1977–1981* (Office of the Secretary of Defense, 2017), 291–97.

40 William Sullivan, cable, Eyes Only for the Secretary, "USG Policy Guidance," January 10, 1979.

41 Bruce Laingen, cable to State Department, "Meeting with PM Bazargan," August 12, 1979.

42 Harold Saunders, Briefing Memorandum to the Secretary, "Policy toward Iran," September 5, 1979, Secret/Sensitive. As scholar Chris Emery has pointed out, one reason US approaches did not gain more traction was the fact that mere association with US officials made Iranians vulnerable to political attack. Chris Emery, *U.S. Foreign Policy and the Iranian Revolution: The Cold War Dynamics of Engagement and Strategic Alliance* (Palgrave MacMillan, 2013), 196.

43 Bruce Laingen, cable to State Department, "Meeting with PM Bazargan," August 12, 1979.

44 Bruce Laingen, cable to State Department, "Meeting with PM Bazargan," August 12, 1979.

45 Bruce Laingen, cable to Secretary of State, "Yazdi in New York: Where Now?," October 12, 1979.

46 Charles Naas, quoted in Bill, *Eagle and the Lion*, 285.

47 Henry Precht at the conference "The Carter Administration and the 'Arc of Crisis': Iran, Afghanistan and the Cold War in Southwest Asia, 1977–1981," organized by the National Security Archive and the Cold War Interna-

tional History Project (Woodrow Wilson International Center for Scholars), July 25–26, 2005.

48 Ali M. Ansari, *Modern Iran*, 2nd ed. (Routledge, 2007), 177.

49 Bruce Laingen, interview by Malcolm Byrne, July 25, 2005. Also cited in
Stephen Kinzer, "Inside Iran's Fury," *Smithsonian Magazine*, October 2008,
http://www.smithsonianmag.com/travel/inside-irans-fury-11823881/.
Laingen apparently did not remember the same lecture from Prime Minister Bazargan in August 1979.

3   The Iran-Iraq War

1 Jimmy Carter, *Keeping Faith: Memoirs of a President* (Bantam, 1982), 506.

2 George Cave, remarks at Iran-Iraq War conference, 8–9; George Cave, interview with the authors, Washington, DC, May 10, 2003.

3 Matthew J. Ferretti, *The Iran-Iraq War: United Nations Resolution of
Armed Conflict*, 35 Vill. L. Rev. 197 (1990). Available at http://digitalcom
mons.law.villanova.edu/vlr/vol35/iss1/3, 198–200. For US observations,
see Defense Intelligence Agency cable, "Title: Iraq Goads Iran," April 9,
1980, 05:33 Zulu.

4 Alert memorandum, "Iran-Iraq Conflict," dated September 17, 1980, with
cover note from Stansfield Turner to National Security Council, "Iran-Iraq,"
same date. A much-remarked-upon piece of evidence from the time is a set
of talking points for Ronald Reagan's secretary of state, Alexander Haig,
from April 1981 following a visit to Saudi Arabia. The notes include the
following: "It was also interesting to confirm that President Carter gave the
Iraqis a green light to launch the war against Iran through [Saudi Crown
Prince] Fahd." While it appears intriguing, several former policy makers
who served under both Reagan and Carter questioned the assertion on a
number of grounds. See the discussion in James G. Blight et al., *Becoming
Enemies: U.S.-Iran Relations and the Iran-Iraq War, 1979–1988* (Rowman &
Littlefield, 2012), 64–67, 260–62.

5 Carter, *Keeping Faith*, 506. The former president insists that the United
States had no "previous knowledge of nor influence over" the Iraqi move.

6 Brzezinski, memorandum for the President, "SUBJECT: NSC weekly report
#122," December 21, 1979. Several other recently declassified records ex-

pand on this sensitive topic; see *Foreign Relations of the United States, 1977–80*, vol. 11, pt. 1, *Iran: Hostage Crisis, November 1979–September 1980* (US Government Printing Office, 2020).

7 Former ambassador David Newton, quoted in Blight et al., *Becoming Enemies*, 165.

8 Entry for April 10, 1980, quoted in Carter, *Keeping Faith*, 506.

9 United Nations Security Council Resolution 479, "Iraq–Islamic Republic of Iran," September 28, 1980, http://unscr.com/en/resolutions/479. For a sample Iranian reaction, see Foreign Minister Javad Zarif's interview with *Frontline*'s Martin Smith, February 20, 2017, https://www.pbs.org/wgbh/frontline/article/the-frontline-interview-mohammad-javad-zarif/.

10 Bernard D. Nossiter, "U.N. Council Delays Appeal on Gulf War," *New York Times*, September 28, 1980.

11 David Newton and Charles Cogan, quoted in Blight et al., *Becoming Enemies*, 181, 121.

12 Transcript of Iran-Iraq War conference, organized by the National Security Archive and hosted by the Cold War International History Project of the Woodrow Wilson International Center for Scholars, July 19, 2004, 38. Ironically, the phrase was later picked up by American neoconservatives who anticipated that regime change in Iraq in the early 2000s would lead to a transformed Middle East. See https://thinkprogress.org/pnac-fpi-road-to-jerusalem-runs-through-baghdad-tehran-82c80e16219d/.

13 Clark to Reagan, "An Iranian Invasion of Iraq: Considerations for US Policy," ca. July 10, 1982.

14 Richard Murphy, quoted in Blight et al., *Becoming Enemies*, 108.

15 Malcolm Byrne, "The United States and the Iran-Iraq War: The Limits of American Influence," in *The Globalization of the Cold War: Diplomacy and Local Confrontation, 1975–1985*, ed. Max Guderzo and Bruna Bagnato (Routledge, 2010), 119–36. Insight into regional expert thinking within the State Department on the question of tilting toward Iraq is contained in Nicholas A. Veliotes and Jonathan Howe, "Iran-Iraq War: Analysis of Possible U.S. Shift from Position of Strict Neutrality," Information Memorandum, October 7, 1983.

16 See Malcolm Byrne, *Iran-Contra: Reagan's Scandal and the Unchecked Abuse of Presidential Power* (University Press of Kansas, 2014).

17 See Malcolm Byrne, "Long before Trump, Oliver North Was Incredibly Dishonest—and Beloved," *Newsweek*, May 17, 2018.

18 Egypt, North Korea, and South Sudan are the holdouts.

19 State Department, memorandum from Jonathan T. Howe to the Secretary, "Iraq Use of Chemical Weapons," November 1, 1983; State Department, cable to Baghdad Interests Section, "Background on Iraqi Use of Chemical Weapons," November 10, 1983.

20 State cable, November 10, 1983. See also generally the candid reminiscences of former State and CIA officials on this subject throughout Blight et al., *Becoming Enemies*.

21 Richard Stone, "Seeking Answers for Iran's Chemical Weapons Victims—Before Time Runs Out," *Science*, January 4, 2018.

22 Among many published accounts, see Shane Harris and Matthew M. Aid, "Exclusive: CIA Files Prove America Helped Saddam as He Gassed Iran," *Foreign Policy*, August 26, 2013.

23 The record would eventually show that the Iranians had manufactured certain substances, but they later declared them and never utilized them. See Joost R. Hiltermann, *A Poisonous Affair: America, Iraq, and the Gassing of Halabja* (Cambridge University Press, 2014), 157–65.

24 Murphy, quoted in Blight et al., *Becoming Enemies*, 107–8.

25 Cogan, quoted in Blight et al., *Becoming Enemies*, 110.

26 Gen. Aladdin Hussein Makki interview in Kevin M. Woods et al., *Saddam's Generals: Perspectives of the Iran-Iraq War* (Institute for Defense Analyses, 2011), 133–45; janet M. Lang, interview with the authors, June 24, 2009; Gen. Tarfa in Woods et al., *Saddam's Generals*, 99. According to Gen. Majid Rashid al-Hamdani, US satellite data were important for planning attacks. Hamdani interview in Woods et al., *Saddam's Generals*, 82.

27 Bruce Berkowitz, "What's a Scud?," *Air and Space Magazine*, May 2003, https://www.airspacemag.com/history-of-flight/whats-a-scud-4510864/. The Iranians believed that the USSR provided Iraq with the more advanced Scud-C variant, which had a longer range. See "Rafsanjani on the Conduct of the War," interview with Aftab News Agency, June 21, 2008.

28 Office of the Director of Central Intelligence, "Persian Gulf Situation Report," April 20, 1988.

29 Jim Muir, "Iraq's Swift, Stunning Victory . . . ," *Christian Science Monitor*, April 26, 1988; Harris and Aid, "Exclusive"; interview with Lt. Gen. Ra'ad Majid Rashid al-Hamdani in Woods et al., *Saddam's Generals*, 48.

30 "Rafsanjani on the Conduct of the War."

31 RADM Arthur N. "Bud" Langston (USN, Ret.), "Operation Praying Mantis: An Enterprise Combat Mission," Naval Historical Foundation, April 14, 2017.

32 Richard Halloran, "The Downing of Flight 655," *New York Times*, July 4, 1988.

33 Mohammed Basti, Iranian Embassy London, July 4, 1988, excerpted on Cineflix, Air Crash Investigation documentary series, "Mistaken Identity," October 19, 2005. For a critical analysis from a former US military officer's perspective, see Lt. Col. David Evans (USMC, Ret.), "Vincennes: A Case Study," *Proceedings Magazine* (US Naval Institute), August 1993, vol. 119/8/1,086, https://www.usni.org/magazines/proceedings/1993-08/vincennes-case-study.

34 See Fred Kaplan, "America's Flight 17: The Time the United States Blew Up a Passenger Plane—and Tried to Cover It Up," *Slate*, July 23, 2014. See also Michael Crowley, "Four Good Reasons Why Iran Doesn't Trust America," *Time*, October 15, 2013. Shortly after the shootdown, Vice President George H. W. Bush unwittingly captured the befuddling attitude of many senior US officials when he told a campaign audience, "I'll never apologize for the United States of America—ever—I don't care what the facts are." C-SPAN, August 5, 1988, https://www.youtube.com/watch?v=10qatUWwIeg.

35 Mohsen Rezaie, former commander of the IRGC, interview with *Baztab* magazine, September 28, 2006; see also "Rafsanjani on the Conduct of the War."

36 Ayatollah Ruhollah Khomeini, Letter to the Iranian People Regarding the End of the War, July 16, 1988.

37 Quoted in Alan Cowell, "Cease-Fire Takes Effect in 8-Year Iran-Iraq War," *New York Times*, August 21, 1988.

4 Rafsanjani and the Post-Khomeini Order

1 Fourteen members of the assembly voted for Grand Ayatollah Mohammad-Reza Golpayegani, who met the criteria of *marja'iyat* (source of emulation) laid out by the constitution at the time.

2 For an excellent summary of fast-moving political developments around Khomeini's death, see Mohammad Ayatollahi Tabar, *Religious Statecraft: The Politics of Islam in Iran* (Columbia University Press, 2018), 198–204.

3 Interestingly, the event that had occasioned the meeting was Khamenei's delivery of a letter of dismissal, at the behest of Khomeini, to Grand Aya-

tollah Hossein-Ali Montazeri, who was the designated successor to the leadership of the Islamic Republic. The leading architect of the concept of *velayat-e faqih* (rule of the jurist), Montazeri became a vocal critic of Khomeini's suppression of dissent and approval of the mass killing of dissidents at the hands of the regime's henchmen. As his criticisms became public, Khomeini took swift action to marginalize Montazeri and cast him as a heretic, an approach savagely continued under Khamenei's leadership. For more on Montazeri, see Sussan Siavoshi, *Montazeri: The Life and Thought of Iran's Revolutionary Ayatollah* (Cambridge University Press, 2003); on Montazeri as a dissident-cleric, see Abbas Milani, "The Good Ayatollah," *Foreign Policy*, February 11, 2010, https://foreignpolicy.com/2010/02/11/the-good-ayatollah/.

4 See the Constitution of the Islamic Republic of Iran (1979), https://irandataportal.syr.edu/wp-content/uploads/constitution-persianislamic-republic-of-iran.pdf.

5 Most significantly, the new constitution eliminated the position of prime minister, delineated division of powers between the three branches of government, and concentrated more power in the Office of the Supreme Leader (with key political, military, and judicial appointments directly appointed by him). The new draft also created a Supreme National Security Council directly reporting to the president (modeled after the US NSC). See the text of the revised constitution at https://irandataportal.syr.edu/wp-content/uploads/constitution-english-1368.pdf.

6 He received 94% of the vote over a relatively unknown candidate, Abbas Sheybani. It is important to note that turnout was low (54.6%) by later election standards. See Mehrzad Boroujerdi and Kourosh Rahimkhani, *Postrevolutionary Iran: A Political Handbook* (Syracuse University Press, 2018), 90.

7 He was nicknamed "the shark" by the public for both his inability to grow a beard (which was the norm among the senior clerics in the regime) and his smooth but cunning ways to blur the lines among self-, national, and regime interests. For a brief profile of Rafsanjani's post-revolutionary political career, see Haleh Esfandiari and Shaul Bakhash, "The Long Career of Ali Akbar Hashemi Rafsanjani," *Atlantic*, January 8, 2017, https://www.theatlantic.com/international/archive/2017/01/rafsanjani-iran-khamenei-khomeini/512507/.

8 As Karim Sadjadpour notes, "The fundamental differences between the two men were also reflected in their families. Khamenei grew up the son of a poor cleric in the Shiite holy city of Mashad, and each of his four sons became clerics. Rafsanjani's family were pistachio merchants from the sun-soaked southeastern province of Kerman, and his three sons became businessmen. Khamenei's reputation for asceticism prolonged his political longevity, while the fortunes allegedly amassed by Rafsanjani and his children brought about their political demise." Karim Sadjadpour, "Sons of the Iranian Revolution," *Atlantic*, January 9, 2017, https://www.theatlantic.com/international/archive/2017/01/rafsanjani-khamenei-iran/512540/.

9 Said Amir Arjomand captures the nature of the rivalry between Khamenei and Rafsanjani in the early years after Khomeini's death well: "The political positions they took were increasingly determined by the constitutionally defined vested interest of the office they each held, rather than their personal will. . . . Admittedly, the rules of the power struggle were not yet fully and clearly set, but the Leader turned out to be the better player in both constitutional and routine politics." Said Amir Arjomand, *After Khomeini: Iran under His Successors* (Oxford University Press, 2009), 37.

10 As economist (and former Pahlavi-era minister of finance) Jahangir Amuzegar noted at the time,

> Through a series of Majlis laws and cabinet decisions, the private sector is now asked to participate in non-strategic manufacturing, social services, transportation, tourism, and trade. One-fourth of state-owned enterprises have become candidates for privatization. Free trade zones have been established at Qeshm and Kish islands. The new strategy of "economic adjustment and reforms" aims at the establishment of a market mechanism for determining the prices of goods, foreign exchange, and money; privatization of non-strategic industries now under government control; deregulation of cumbersome bureaucratic rules; and reorganization of state machinery in the service of marketization. The policies designed to achieve some of these objectives relate to tax laws, import-export regulations, accounting procedures, exchange system, and monetary and banking guidelines. The ultimate goal is to enhance people's participation in economic activities and decision making, and reduce state controls.

Jahangir Amuzegar, "The Iranian Economy before and after the Revolution," *Middle East Journal* 46, no. 3 (Summer 1992): 413–25.

11 For a comprehensive investigation into the financial and commercial power of the enterprises and assets collectively controlled by Khamenei and IRGC commanders, see the report by the Reuters organization "Assets of the Ayatollah: The Economic Empire behind Iran's Supreme Leader," *Reuters*, November 11, 2013, https://www.reuters.com/investigates/iran /#article/part1.

12 In Rafsanjani's first term, as Amir Arjomand has noted, "Of particular importance was the growth of the engineering arms of the IRGC, known as the Seal of the Prophets (*khatam al-anbiya*) Headquarters, which greatly extended the IRGC's economic empire into construction, transportation, and the oil and gas sectors." Amir Arjomand, *After Khomeini*, 60.

13 As a profile of the entire operation in the *Atlantic* noted at the time, "the Foundation of the Oppressed, as the largest holding company in an oil-producing country of about 65 million people, has gargantuan amounts of real estate, cash, and other assets. It is a state within a state. . . . It was more impressive than any government ministry I saw in Tehran." Robert D. Kaplan, "A Bazaari's World," *Atlantic*, March 1996, https://www.theatlantic.com /magazine/archive/1996/03/a-bazaaris-world/304827/.

14 See Wilfried Buchta, *Who Rules Iran? The Structure of Power in the Islamic Republic* (Washington Institute for Near East Policy, 2000), 73.

15 Amir Arjomand, *After Khomeini*, 64.

16 See Kaveh Ehsani, "Survival through Dispossession: Privatization of Public Goods in the Islamic Republic," *Middle East Report* 250 (Spring 2009), https://merip.org/2009/03/survival-through-dispossession/.

17 The Japanese and Turkish translators of Rushdie's novel, as well as his Norwegian publisher, were all assassinated, and many of his associates in Muslim societies also had to go into hiding. On the Rushdie affair and its aftermath, see Kenan Malik, *From Fatwa to Jihad: The Rushdie Affair and Its Aftermath* (Melville House, 2010); for Rushdie's reflections on the fatwa and its impact on him, see Salman Rushdie, "The Disappeared," *New Yorker*, September 10, 2012, https://www.newyorker.com/magazine/2012 /09/17/the-disappeared.

18 For a comprehensive accounting of the massacre, see Geoffrey Robertson, *The Massacre of Political Prisoners in Iran, 1988: Report of an Inquiry*

(Abdorrahman Boroumand Foundation for Human Rights in Iran, April 18, 2011), https://www.iranrights.org/library/document/1380/the-massacre-of-political-prisoners-in-iran-1988-report-of-an-inquiry.

19 R. K. Ramazani, "Address by Ali-Akbar Hashemi-Rafsanjani, the President of the Islamic Republic of Iran," November 22, 1989, translated from Persian by Jubin Goodarzi, published in *Middle East Journal* 44, no. 3 (Summer 1990): 458–66.

20 After the invasion of Iran in September 1980, Velayati noted, it took the UNSC six days before the issuing of any resolutions, and even then the body failed to demand the immediate withdrawal of Iraqi troops from Iranian land. FBIS-NES, September 25, 1990, 59.

21 In his report to the Security Council on December 9, 1991, the UN secretary-general Javier Pérez de Cuéllar conspicuously noted that "even if before the outbreak of the conflict there had been some encroachment by Iran on Iraqi territory, such encroachment did not justify Iraq's aggression against Iran—which was followed by Iraq's continuous occupation of Iranian territory during the conflict." The statement was interpreted by Iranian leaders as tantamount to a full vindication of Iran's grievances against Iraq and an indictment of the Western powers' support for Saddam's regime. See "Iraq Blamed for Starting Iran War," *Washington Post*, December 10, 1991, https://www.washingtonpost.com/archive/politics/1991/12/11/iraq-blamed-for-starting-iran-war/9c12d9a5-298a-4a54-a6e4-c70a0177f709/.

22 For an overview of Iran's foreign policy approach toward its GCC neighbors, see R. K. Ramazani, "Iran's Foreign Policy: Both North and South," *Middle East Journal* 46, no. 3 (Summer 1992): 393–412.

23 As a goodwill gesture, the Saudis also allowed some Iranian pilgrims to partake in political demonstrations against "pagans" and "heretics." See Ramazani, "Iran's Foreign Policy," 399.

24 Dilip Hiro, *Cold War in the Islamic World: Saudi Arabia, Iran and the Struggle for Supremacy* (Oxford University Press, 2018), 147–51.

25 George H. W. Bush, "Inaugural Address," Washington, DC, January, 20, 1989, https://avalon.law.yale.edu/20th_century/bush.asp.

26 Israel Defense Forces avenged Col. Higgins's killing by assassinating the cofounder of Hezbollah, the cleric Abbas al-Mussawi, on February 16, 1992.

27 Memorandum of Conversation, President George H. W. Bush and Sultan Qaboos, "Telephone Conversation with Sultan Qaboos of Oman," Confi-

dential, August 3, 1989. Retrieved from the National Security Archive at https://nsarchive.gwu.edu/dc.html?doc=6585710-National-Security-Archive-Doc-06-Memorandum-of.

28 Bernard Weinraub, "Iran's President Offers Help in Hostage Crisis," *New York Times*, August 5, 1989.

29 Weinraub, "Iran's President Offers Help." The State Department spokesperson, Margaret Tutwiler, projected the same sentiment but amended it with the standard admonition of Iran for its support of terrorism: "President Rafsanjani's remarks appear to be moderate and are therefore encouraging.... Any improvement in relations between us will be contingent on Iranian willingness to act responsibly in the world arena, to include efforts to resolve the hostage issue once and for all by producing the release of our hostages, and by also making it clear that they have turned away from support of terrorism."

30 Giandomenico Picco, *Man without a Gun: One Diplomat's Secret Struggle to Free the Hostages, Fight Terrorism, and End a War* (Crown, 1999), 114.

31 Picco, *Man without a Gun*, 118.

32 See Picco, *Man without a Gun*, chaps. 8–17.

33 Picco, *Man without a Gun*, 3–4.

34 Picco, *Man without a Gun*, 6.

35 The so-called chain murders of opposition leaders lasted until 1998 and were blamed on rogue elements within Iran's Ministry of Intelligence. See the next chapter for more on this episode. For a brief overview of the killings, see Mohammad Sahimi, "The Chain Murders: Killing Dissidents and Intellectuals, 1988–1998," *Tehran Bureau*, PBS, January 5, 2011, https://www.pbs.org/wgbh/pages/frontline/tehranbureau/2011/01/the-chain-murders-killing-dissidents-and-intellectuals-1988-1998.html.

36 Bruce Riedel comments at a session of the critical oral history conference entitled "U.S.-Iran Relations during the Iran-Iraq War, 1980–1988," Musgrove Conference Center, St. Simon's Island, GA, December 12–14, 2008. For more context, see James G. Blight et al., *Becoming Enemies: U.S.-Iran Relations and the Iran-Iraq War, 1979–1988* (Rowman & Littlefield, 2012), chap. 7.

37 For a nonfiction account of the killings, see Roya Hakakian, *Assassins of the Turquoise Palace* (Grove, 2011).

38 William J. Clinton, "First Inaugural Address," Washington, DC, January 20, 1993.

39 As Martin Indyk, director of the Near East and South Asia affairs at the NSC at the time, relayed to us later,

> I think the most important part of the environment there [in 1993 at the White House], was that it really wasn't about Iran—sorry to tell you that, but it wasn't—it was about making peace in the Middle East. When Clinton came into the White House, the Soviet Union had just collapsed and therefore its position in the Middle East had just collapsed. Saddam Hussein's army had just been kicked out of Kuwait. Iran had already lost the Iraq-Iran war for all intents and purposes. All of the Arab states and the Palestinians had been in direct negotiations with Israel for 6 months before Clinton came into office. And Yitzhak Rabin had been the Prime Minister of Israel with a mandate to make peace and take risks for peace is what he told Clinton in their first meeting. So it was our view, very much the President's view, that there was a huge opportunity here. Warren Christopher, the Secretary of State, had gone out on his first trip—the first trip he made—to the region, came back and reported to the first National Security Council meeting that there was a real chance to make peace and the President should invest his energies in this.

Martin Indyk comments at a session of the critical oral history conference entitled "Khobar Towers," Musgrove Conference Center, St. Simon's Island, GA, April 8–10, 2011.

40 Martin Indyk, "The Clinton Administration's Approach to the Middle East," Soref Symposium, Washington Institute for Near East Policy, May 1993, https://www.washingtoninstitute.org/policy-analysis/clinton-admini strations-approach-middle-east.

41 Hossein Mousavian comments at a session of the critical oral history conference entitled "Khobar Towers," Musgrove Conference Center, St. Simon's Island, GA, April 8–10, 2011.

42 The US State Department first designated Iran as a state sponsor of terrorism on January 19, 1984. See "State Sponsors of Terrorism," Bureau of Counterterrorism, US Department of State, https://www.state.gov/state-spon sors-of-terrorism/.

43 The case has been an especially sordid affair in Argentina, resulting in the mysterious murder of the chief prosecutor of the case, Alberto Nisman, and calls for the prosecution of the former Argentinian president Cristina Fernández de Kirchner. See Dexter Filkins, "Death of a Prosecutor," *New*

Yorker, July 13, 2015, https://www.newyorker.com/magazine/2015/07/20/death-of-a-prosecutor.

44 See President Clinton's joint statement with King Hussein of Jordan and Israeli Prime Minister Yitzhak Rabin, "3 Leaders Angered by Terrorist Attacks," *New York Times*, July 27, 1994, https://www.nytimes.com/1994/07/27/world/3-leaders-angered-by-new-terrorist-attacks.html.

45 Paul Richter and Robin Wright, "Clinton Kills Pending Iran-Conoco Deal," *Los Angeles Times*, March 15, 1995.

5 Khatami and the Possibility of Dialogue

1 To be sure, stylized versions of both arguments were leveled against reformists throughout this period. "Westoxification" (*gharbzadegi* in Persian) is a storied Iranian postcolonial lament against the condition of having been struck by Western ideas and mannerisms. The most prominent version of the argument was put forward by the midcentury Iranian intellectual Jalal Al-e Ahmad in his book *Occidentosis: A Plague from the West*, trans. R. Campbell and intro. by Hamid Algar (Mizan, 1984).

2 See William O. Beeman, *The "Great Satan" vs. the "Mad Mullahs": How the United States and Iran Demonize Each Other* (University of Chicago Press, 2005).

3 As Laura Secor has observed, Khatami "had a different kind of face, and with it he presented a different face for Iran. Khatami's was open and good-humored, quick with a smile so spontaneous, it seemed to erupt for every occasion. He had the appearance of a favorite professor—the sort of face that looked familiar, even if you had never seen it before. Where Khomeini's imposed, Khatami's invited." Laura Secor, *Children of Paradise: The Struggle for the Soul of Iran* (Riverhead Books, 2016), 151.

4 See Francis Fukuyama, *The End of History and the Last Man* (Simon & Schuster, 1992); and Samuel P. Huntington, *The Clash of Civilizations and the Remaking of World Order* (Simon & Schuster, 1998).

5 "Full Text of Khatami-Ardakani's Resignation Letter," *Keyhan-e Hava'i*, July 29, 1992, FBIS-NES-165, August 25, 1992. See also Daniel Brumberg, *Reinventing Khomeini: The Struggle for Reform in Iran* (University of Chicago Press, 2001), 198.

6 As Khatami emphatically conveyed in an interview prior to his landslide victory in the presidential poll, "I believe that a true human being who believes and has accepted Islam cannot be a liberal.... [Whereas] liberalism is based on man's wants, wishes, and his materialistic needs, [Islam focuses on] the spiritual and ethical improvement of man." "Khatami Interview on Elections," *Jomhouri-ye Eslami*, February 25, 1997, FBIS-NES-97-047; quoted in Brumberg, *Reinventing Khomeini*, 228.

7 In reality, though, the political jockeying after Khomeini's death was very much a multipronged crisis of political and spiritual crisis. For more, see Said Amir Arjomand, *After Khomeini: Iran under His Successors* (Oxford University Press, 2009), 36–55.

8 Among the more prominent voices were Abdolkarim Soroush, Mohammad Mojtahed-Shabestari, Saeed Hajjarian, Mohsen Kadivar, Akbar Ganji, Ezatollah Sahabi, Abbas Abdi, Mostafa Tajzadeh, Abbas Abdi, Alireza Alavi-Tabar, and Hassan Yousefi Eshkevari.

9 For a comprehensive historical account and exegetical retelling of the currents of thought emerging out of the so-called Kiyan Circle, the Center for Strategic Research, and the Ayin Circle, see Eskandar Sadeghi-Boroujerdi, *Revolution and Its Discontents: Political Thought and Reform in Iran* (Cambridge University Press, 2019), 46–48, 136–86, 207–40. For a concise overview, see Mohammad Ayatollahi Tabaar, *Religious Statecraft: The Politics of Islam in Iran* (Columbia University Press, 2018), 214–22. For an assessment of these views in relation to liberal democratic principles, see Hussein Banai, *Hidden Liberalism: Burdened Visions of Progress in Modern Iran* (Cambridge University Press, 2020), chap. 4.

10 Soroush and Ganji (writing under the pseudonym Hamid Paidar) presented their respective views in the pages of *Kiyan*. See Abdolkarim Soroush, "Hokumat-e demokratik-e dini?" [Religious democratic government?], *Kiyan* 3, no. 11 (1993); and Hamid Paidar, "Paradox-e Eslam va Demokrasi" [The paradox of Islam and democracy], *Kiyan*, 4, no. 19 (1994).

11 However, despite the consensus around the imperative for reforms, not everyone was convinced that Khatami was the right choice for leading the cause. As Secor recounts from an interview with Mostafa Rokhsefat, the editor of *Kiyan*, "Khatami was not the man for the job. To stand up to Khamenei required strength, know-how, and, above all, conviction. Mostafa did not see these qualities in Khatami.... Khatami was not, Mostafa

argued, a reformist. He was intellectually confused; he vacillated in politics because he vacillated in his heart." Secor, *Children of Paradise*, 155.

12 Secor, *Children of Paradise*, 157.

13 The Guardian Council had also approved the candidacy of two other conservative candidates, the much-maligned former minister of intelligence Mohammad Reyshahri, and the deputy head of judiciary and member of the Guardian Council Seyyed Reza Zavarehi.

14 For the full results of the election, see Mehrzad Boroujerdi and Kourosh Rahimkhani, *Postrevolutionary Iran: A Political Handbook* (Syracuse University Press, 2018), 91–92.

15 Stephen Kinzer, "Moderate Leader Is Elected in Iran by a Wide Margin," *New York Times*, May 25, 1997.

16 Khatami's speech was especially well received by Arab leaders, who made sure that the final text of the OIC's Tehran Declaration noted their confidence that his chairmanship would lead the OIC "in the most able and constructive manner, further enhancing the role and participation of the Organisation in international affairs, in accordance with the purposes and principles of the OIC." "Tehran Declaration," The Eighth Islamic Summit Conference, Tehran, December 1997, http://ww1.oic-oci.org/english/conf/is/8/8th-is-summits.htm#Tehran%20Declaration.

17 "Khatami's Speech to OIC—Excerpts from Iranian TV," *BBC World Monitoring*, December 9, 1997, http://news.bbc.co.uk/2/hi/world/monitoring/39530.stm.

18 "Transcript of Interview with Iranian President Mohammad Khatami," *CNN*, January 9, 1998, https://www.cnn.com/WORLD/9801/07/iran/interview.html.

19 He went on to challenge American media's depiction of the Iranian government as a sponsor of terrorism, and he pledged that "if I learn of any instance of such assistance to terrorism, I shall deal with it, so will our Leader, and so will our entire system." He further reaffirmed Iran's commitment to the Non-Proliferation Treaty and denied the existence of any military dimensions to Iran's nuclear energy program. See "Transcript of Interview."

20 For instance, while an editorial in the *New York Times* lamented Khatami's familiar complaints against American policy toward Iran, it nonetheless reminded its readers that "changing the tone of Iranian rhetoric about the

United States is itself an achievement, and Mr. Khatami may have gone as far as he could for now, given the resistance of Iran's supreme leader, Ayatollah Ali Khamenei, to better relations with Washington." See "President Khatami Addresses America," editorial, *New York Times*, January 8, 1998.

21 Marc Lynch, "The Dialogue of Civilizations and International Public Spheres," *Millennium: Journal of International Studies* 29, no. 2 (2000): 307–30.

22 Ali Khamenei, "Remarks on the Occasion of the Inauguration of the President," Tehran, Iran, August 3, 1997, https://farsi.khamenei.ir/speech-con tent?id=2847. Translated by Iran Data Portal, Syracuse University and Princeton University, https://irandataportal.syr.edu/declaration-on-the -occasion-of-the-inauguration-of-the-president.

23 The fundamental loyalty of many prominent reformists to the revolution was also either overlooked or underappreciated by many of their lay supporters, many of whom wished for the gradual replacement of the Islamic Republic with a more liberal and secular democratic form of government altogether. See Ali M. Ansari, *Iran, Islam, and Democracy: The Politics of Managing Change* (Chatham House, 2009), chaps. 6–10.

24 *Jame'eh* was established by Mohsen Sazegara, a cofounder of the IRGC, shortly after the revolution, and *Sobh-e Emrooz* was founded by Saeed Hajjarian, who was instrumental in setting up the regime's intelligence and security apparatus soon after Khomeini's return to Iran. For more on the intellectual and political journeys of these men and their fellow travelers, see Sadeghi-Boroujerdi, *Revolution and Its Discontents*, chaps. 6 and 7.

25 On satellite dishes as a political battleground, see Rudabeh Pakravan, "Territory Jam: Tehran," *Places Journal*, July 2012, https://doi.org/10.22269 /120709.

26 Ganji later published his findings in book form in *Alijenab-e Sorkhpoush va Alijenaban-e Khakestari: Asib-shenasi-ye Gozar be Dowlat-e Demokratic va Towse-e Gara* [Red eminence and gray eminences: The pathology of transition to the democratic and developmental government] (Tarh-e No, 2000).

27 Because of these similarities, many Iranians referred to Rafsanjani as "Akbar Shah."

28 In the Majles, too, conservative deputies attempted numerous times to impeach Khatami's minister of culture and Islamic guidance, Ata'ollah Mohajerani, for refusing to tighten restrictions on journalists and artists. But

while they failed to remove Mohajerani, they succeeded in impeaching another key reformist ally of Khatami's, the minister of interior, Abdollah Nuri. Public and legal harassment of other figures such as Tehran's mayor, Gholam-Hossein Karbaschi (on charges of corruption), the dissident cleric Mohsen Kadivar (on charges of spreading false information about the "sacred system of the Islamic Republic"), and Akbar Ganji (on charges of "spreading propaganda against the Islamic Republic"), among many others, rather swiftly halted the momentum of reforms.

29 As the *Economist*, with its famous print cover featuring an Iranian student holding up a bloodstained shirt at a protest, noted in its "Leader" at the time,

> All too often his progress is two steps back for each one forward. His is undoubtedly a government of good intentions. But he is trapped between the frustrated, impatient young—60% of today's Iranians were toddlers or not yet born at the time of the 1979 Islamic takeover—who urge him to race ahead, and conservative clerical overlords who wait watchfully to trip him up, and more often than not succeed in doing so. Now, with Iran's audacious students battling in the streets against the authorities in the most open act of political defiance since the earliest years of the Islamic republic, the future of Mr Khatami's gentle reforms are in doubt.

"Iran's Second Revolution?," *Economist*, July 19, 1999.

30 The message, in the respectful yet threatening and patronizing manner typical of conservative warnings, read as follows:

> We can see the footprints of the enemy in the aforementioned incidents and we can hear its drunken cackle. You should understand this today because tomorrow will be too late. If you regret this tomorrow, it will be impossible to retrieve the situation. O noble Seyyed: Look at the speeches made by your so-called friends and insiders at the gathering of students. Is what they said not tantamount to encouraging chaos and lawlessness? . . . Mr. Khatami: Look at foreign media and radios. Can you not hear their joyful music? Mr. President: If you do not make a revolutionary decision and if you do not fulfill your Islamic and national mission today, tomorrow will be far too late. It is unimaginable how irretrievable the situation will become. In the end, we would like to express our utmost respect for you excellency and to

declare that our patience has run out. We cannot tolerate this situation any longer if it is not dealt with.

See translated quote in Suzanne Maloney, "Remembering Iran's Student Protests, Fourteen Years Later," *Markaz*, Brookings Institution, July 9, 2013, https://www.brookings.edu/blog/markaz/2013/07/09/remembering-irans -student-protests-fourteen-years-later/.

31 See Azadeh Moaveni, "The Price of Reformist Victory?," *Al-Ahram Weekly*, no. 473, March 16–22, 2000, https://web.archive.org/web/20051227050708 /http://weekly.ahram.org.eg/2000/473/re3.htm.

32 As the arch-conservative *Wall Street Journal* editorial page proclaimed after the 18 Tir protests, "It is looking more and more as if he [Khatami] will come to resemble Mr. Gorbachev in an even more significant way, unintentionally presiding over the total collapse of his country's regime." "An Iranian Gorbachev?," editorial, *Wall Street Journal*, June 4, 1999, https:// www.wsj.com/articles/SB928445972894862564. For a comprehensive comparison of Gorbachev's and Khatami's reform efforts, see Zhand Shakibi, *Khatami and Gorbachev: Politics of Change in the Islamic Republic and the USSR* (Bloomsbury, 2010).

33 Ali Khamenei, "Reforms: Strategies, Challenges—Speech Delivered to Government Executives," July 10, 2000, https://english.khamenei.ir/news /170/Reforms-Strategies-Challenges.

34 Mohsen Sazegara, a one-time ally of Khatami, captured the commonly shared frustration with Khatami and the pace of reforms thus: "The basic problem is that the people around Khatami who call themselves reformers don't believe in freedom. Many of them are no different from the hardliners. . . . We didn't expect miracles. But we expected some progress. Instead, Khatami has thrown away many opportunities." Geneive Abdo, "Khatami Was 'Never a Rebel' and Has No 'Cause,' Critic Charges: Iran's Weary Would-Be Reformer," *International Herald Tribune*, December 1, 2000, https://www.nytimes.com/2000/12/01/news/khatami-was-never -a-rebel-and-has-no-cause-critic-charges-irans-weary.html.

35 In 1998, the UN General Assembly took up Khatami's proposal for such a dialogue, and the year 2001 was declared the "United Nations Year of Dialogue among Civilizations." See https://www.un.org/press/en/2001 /ga9952.doc.htm.

1 Kenneth M. Pollack, *The Persian Puzzle: The Conflict between Iran and America* (Random House, 2004), 303; Anwar Faruqi, "Velayati: New President Won't Change Foreign Policy," Associated Press International, May 18, 1997.

2 White House, Memorandum of Conversation, "Meeting with Russian President Yeltsin: NATO-Russia, Arms Control, Economics, Denver Summit of the Eight, Afghanistan, Iran," May 27, 1997.

3 AFP, "Israel Welcomes Khatami's Election in Iran," May 28, 1997; Laura Myers, "Qatar Leader Presses Clinton on Iraq, Iran," Associated Press, June 11, 1997; Amembassy Riyadh cable to Secretary of State, "Saudis View Iranian Election Outcome as Positive but Remain Skeptical about Likely Change in Policy," May 28, 1997.

4 White House, Memorandum of Conversation, "Meeting with Russian President Yeltsin."

5 Bruce Riedel, oral history conference, "Missed Opportunities? U.S.-Iran Relations, 1993–2001," Sess. 1, Musgrove Conference Center, St. Simons Island, GA, April 8–10, 2011.

6 Associated Press, December 6, 1996; Deutsche Presse Agentur, December 7, 1996; Madeleine Albright, *Madam Secretary: A Memoir* (Random House, 2003), 320.

7 State Department, "1996 Secretarial Transition Background Materials; Looking Ahead Memoranda," November 1996.

8 Deutsche Presse-Agentur, "U.S. Lawmakers Back Non-binding Call for Tougher Sanctions on Iran," July 23, 1997; The White House, "Letter from President to Speaker of House of Representatives & President of the Senate," August 21, 1997.

9 Richard A. Clarke, *Against All Enemies: Inside America's War on Terror* (Free Press, 2004), 120–21.

10 Dilip Hiro, *Neighbours, Not Friends: Iraq and Iran after the Gulf Wars* (Routledge, 2001), 229; Xinhua, "Iran Welcomes US Stance on Iranian Outlawed Group," October 11, 1997; Martin Indyk, *Innocent Abroad: An Intimate Account of American Peace Diplomacy in the Middle East* (New York: Simon & Schuster, 2009), 220.

11 CNN Special Event, "Iran: A New Opening," January 7, 1998.

12 AFP, "US, Iran Should Talk Directly: White House," January 8, 1998; Indyk, *Innocent Abroad*, 220–21; Martin Indyk, oral history conference, Musgrove, Sess. 4; "Khamenei Takes Hard Line on US," *White House Bulletin*, January 16, 1998.

13 Robin Wright, "Clinton Encourages More Exchanges, Better Ties with Iran," *Los Angeles Times*, January 30, 1998; Albright, *Madam Secretary*, 320; Indyk, *Innocent Abroad*, 218–21.

14 Albright, *Madam Secretary*, 322–23.

15 Transcript of Pentagon press briefing, "U.S.-Iran Relations," January 8, 1998.

16 Gen. J. H. Binford Peay III, oral history conference, Musgrove, Sess. 4.

17 President Bill Clinton, "Remarks at the Seventh Millennium Evening at the White House," April 12, 1999, *Public Papers of the Presidents of the United States: William J. Clinton*, bk. 1 (US Government Printing Office, 1999), 637.

18 Kamal Kharrazi, interview with *Kayhan International*, Tehran, May 8, 1999.

19 Louis Freeh, *My FBI: Bringing Down the Mafia, Investigating Bill Clinton, and Fighting the War on Terror* (St. Martin's Griffin, 2006), 4, 18.

20 Freeh, *My FBI*, 29 (emphasis added).

21 Released by the Clinton Library to the National Security Archive in 2010.

22 White House, "Message to President Khatami from President Clinton," June 1999.

23 "Clinton Urges Iran to Detain Hamas Leaders," *Al-Watan* (Kuwait), September 10, 1999; Riedel, oral history conference, Musgrove, Sess. 5.

24 The *Al-Watan* article went on to report at some length on the "stormy" interactions among Iranian leaders over how to respond to the Clinton letter, specifically pitting Khatami not against Khamenei but against Rafsanjani. Allegedly, Khatami and Khamenei agreed to have a joint committee respond to the White House.

25 Oral history conference, Musgrove, Sess. 5.

26 State Department, Madeleine Albright, "Remarks before the American-Iranian Council," March 17, 2000.

27 Hossein Mousavian, oral history conference, Musgrove, Sess. 5.

28 Martin Indyk, "The Clinton Administration's Approach to the Middle East," May 18, 1993.

29 Hiro, *Neighbours, Not Friends*, 306.

30 Agence France Presse, "Powell Hints at New Overtures to Iran," January 18, 2001.

31 Mousavian mentioned the experience with Lebanese hostages in the early 1990s as an example; see Mousavian, oral history conference, Musgrove, Sess. 5.

32 Riedel, oral history conference, Musgrove, Sess. 5.

7 Bush in the Khatami Era

1 Agence France Presse, January 17, 2001.

2 Rumsfeld's aides decided later that he also had an ulterior motive—to signal to a sluggish Pentagon bureaucracy that he planned to shake things up. David Crist, *The Twilight War: The Secret History of America's Thirty-Year Conflict with Iran* (Penguin, 2012), 418–20.

3 Zalmay Khalilzad, *The Envoy: From Kabul to the White House, My Journey through a Turbulent World* (St. Martin's Press, 2016), 110. For comparison, US officials attached high importance to the opening of diplomatic ties with the People's Republic of China in the 1970s purely from the standpoint of getting to know the country better.

4 Associated Press, "Cheney Pushed for More Trade with Iran," *Fox News*, October 9, 2004, https://www.foxnews.com/story/cheney-pushed-for -more-trade-with-iran.

5 Hugh Pope and Neil King, Jr., "Halliburton Connected to Iran Office: Firm Says It Doesn't Breach U.S. Law," *Wall Street Journal*, February 1, 2001.

6 White House statement, March 13, 2001, https://georgewbush-whitehouse .archives.gov/news/releases/2001/03/text/20010313-6.html.

7 Kenneth Katzman, "The Iran-Libya Sanctions Act (ILSA)," Congressional Research Service, updated April 19, 2005, https://apps.dtic.mil/dtic/tr/full text/u2/a475663.pdf.

8 Mousavian, MIT Conference, June 14, 2012; *Washington Post*, September 19, 2001.

9 Agence France Presse, September 16, 2001; Trita Parsi, *Treacherous Alliance: The Secret Dealings of Israel, Iran, and the U.S.* (Yale University Press, 2007), 225–26.

10 *Washington Post*, September 27, 2001; *New York Times*, October 6, 2001.

11 Mousavian, MIT Conference, June 14, 2012; Crocker interview with *Dallas News*, November 9, 2013.

12 George Tenet, *At the Center of the Storm: My Years at the CIA* (HarperCollins, 2007), 128–29.

13 *Washington Post*, October 25, 2001; *Washington Post*, February 4, 2002; Crist, *Twilight War*, 429–30.

14 Barbara Slavin, *Bitter Friends, Bosom Enemies: Iran, the U.S., and the Twisted Path to Confrontation* (St. Martin's, 2009),199; Barbara Slavin, "34 Years of Getting to No with Iran," *Politico*, November 19, 2013; Flynt Leverett, *Dealing with Tehran: Assessing U.S. Diplomatic Options toward Iran* (Century Foundation, 2006), 12, 23.

15 Had these meetings not been secret, these interactions probably would have had an impact on public opinion about Iran's intentions. When the State Department announced a willingness to reach out to Tehran, a policy analyst at the Heritage Foundation who said he was "extremely suspicious" told a reporter he might change his mind "if they would be willing to offer bases. That would be proof they would be serious." George Gedda, "State Dept. Says It'll Explore Iranian Role in Anti-terrorism Fight," Associated Press, September 16, 2001.

16 Crist, *Twilight War*, 431–32; Slavin, *Bitter Friends, Bosom Enemies*, 199; Hillary Mann communication excerpted in Jeffrey Goldberg, "Bad News for Hillary Mann Leverett," *Atlantic*, January 12, 2010.

17 *Independent* (London), October 16, 2001; *Washington Post*, October 6, 2001; *Washington Post*, October 29, 2001; *Washington Post*, February 4, 2002; *New York Times*, October 6, 2001.

18 *New York Times*, November 10, 2001; *New York Daily News*, November 14, 2001; James Dobbins, *After the Taliban: Nation-Building in Afghanistan* (Potomac Books, 2008), 49.

19 Crist, *Twilight War*, 433; Khalilzad, *Envoy*, 117.

20 James Dobbins, "Negotiating with Iran: Reflections from Personal Experience," *Washington Quarterly*, 33, no. 1 (January 2010): 150–51.

21 Dobbins, *After the Taliban*, 74–75; Dobbins, "Negotiating with Iran," 151; Khalilzad, *Envoy*, 119; Crist, *Twilight War*, 434.

22 Dobbins, MIT Conference, June 14, 2012.

23 Khalilzad, *Envoy*, 125–26; Dobbins, MIT Conference, June 14, 2012.

24 *New York Times*, January 22, 2002; James Dobbins, op-ed, *Washington Post*, May 6, 2004; CRS, "Afghanistan's Path to Reconstruction: Obstacles, Challenges, and Issues for Congress," September 20, 2002, 5; Crist, *Twilight War*, 436.

25 The CIA ultimately issued at least three internal "burn notices" against Ghorbanifar. During one polygraph exam, all but two of his answers were rated deceptive; responses regarding his name and birthplace were merely "inconclusive." CIA memorandum to chief of Near East Division, January 13, 1986, cited in Malcolm Byrne, *Iran-Contra: Reagan's Scandal and the Unchecked Abuse of Presidential Power* (University Press of Kansas, 2014), 160.

26 Byrne, *Iran-Contra*, 29; Tenet, *At the Center of the Storm*, 311–14.

27 Crist, *Twilight War*, 449–51; Tenet, *At the Center of the Storm*, 311–14.

28 Dobbins, MIT Conference, June 14, 2012.

29 *Washington Post*, January 7, 2002; Kenneth M. Pollack, *The Persian Puzzle: The Conflict between Iran and America* (Random House, 2004), 350–51; MIT Conference, June 14, 2012; Crist, *Twilight War*, 436.

30 Crist, *Twilight War*, 443–45; Pollack, *Persian Puzzle*, 345; *San Francisco Chronicle*, January 11, 2002.

31 George W. Bush, "The President's State of the Union Address," January 29, 2002, https://georgewbush-whitehouse.archives.gov/news/releases/2002 /01/20020129-11.html. One of the speechwriters devotes a chapter in his book on Bush's presidency to how the phrase wound up in the speech; David Frum, *The Right Man: An Inside Account of the Bush White House* (Random House, 2005); Condoleezza Rice, *No Higher Honor: A Memoir of My Years in Washington* (Crown, 2011), 148–51; Bob Woodward, *Plan of Attack* (Simon & Schuster, 2004), 88; Douglas J. Feith, *War and Decision: Inside the Pentagon at the Dawn of the War on Terrorism* (HarperCollins, 2008), 230–33.

32 Ebtekar interview with PBS *Frontline* correspondent Linden MacIntyre, February 2002; Hadi Semati, MIT Conference, June 14, 2012.

33 MIT Conference, June 14, 2012; Barbara Slavin, *Politico*, November 19, 2013; Dexter Filkins, "The Shadow Commander," *New Yorker*, September 30, 2013, https://www.newyorker.com/magazine/2013/09/30/the-shadow -commander.

34 Wilkerson, MIT Conference, June 14, 2012; Stephen J. Hadley oral history, The Miller Center, https://millercenter.org/the-presidency/presidential -oral-histories/stephen-j-hadley-oral-history; interviews with Feith, Chairman of the Joint Chiefs Gen. Richard Myers, and Vice Chairman Gen. Peter Pace, cited in Crist, *Twilight War*, 452–53; see also generally Suzanne Maloney, "U.S. Policy toward Iran: Missed Opportunities and Paths Forward," *Fletcher Forum* 32, no. 2 (Summer 2008).

35 Statement by the President, July 12, 2002, https://georgewbush-white house.archives.gov/news/releases/2002/07/20020712-9.html; *Washington Post*, July 23, 2002.

36 Rice, *No Higher Honor*, 150; "The National Security Strategy," September 2002, https://georgewbush-whitehouse.archives.gov/nsc/nss/2002/.

37 After a hiatus, Track 2 talks picked up again in the second half of 2005. On the initial round, see Hooshang Amirahmadi, Memo to Myself, "Meetings with Dr. Zarif and Dr. Kharrazi and in NSC and State Department," November 2002; Wilkerson, MIT Conference, June 14, 2012; William Luers, interview by Malcom Byrne, June 7, 2017; Laura Rozen, "Former US Diplomat Fosters US-Iran Ties behind the Scenes," *Al-Monitor*, October 7, 2014.

38 Wilkerson, MIT Conference, June 14, 2012.

39 *Gazette* (Montreal), February 25, 2002; *Daily Telegraph* (London), August 12, 2002; Slavin, *Bitter Friends, Bosom Enemies*, 199; Crist, *Twilight War*, 437–38.

40 Khalilzad, *Envoy*, 165; *New York Times*, May 26, 2003.

8 The Iraq War and Its Consequences

1 Alberto Bin, Richard Hill, and Archer Jones, *Desert Storm: A Forgotten War* (Greenwood, 1998), chap. 1.

2 Address before a Joint Session of the Congress on the State of the Union, January 29, 1991.

3 Shahram Chubin, "Iran and Regional Security in the Persian Gulf," *Survival* 34, no. 3 (1992): 62–80.

4 Javad Zarif, interview with authors Byrne and Tirman. On the airplanes, Kharrazi is quoted in Barton Gellman and David Hoffman, "Iran Assures U.S. It Will Hold Iraqi Planes," *Washington Post*, January 30, 1991, A1. On confiscation, see Youssef Ibrahim, "Tehran to Seize the Planes Iraq Sent to Iran for Safety," *New York Times*, July 31, 1992.

5 Chas Freeman, interview with Charles Stuart Kennedy, "Moments in U.S. Diplomatic History: An Opportunity Lost—the 1991 Iraqi Uprising," Association for Diplomatic Studies and Training, http://adst.org/about-adst/board-of-directors-2/. Thomas Pickering, America's UN ambassador at the time, recalls in the same set of interviews that he had formulated a plan that would help protect the Shi'a but he believed the military, possibly Schwarzkopf, vetoed it.

6 See the Nuclear Threat Initiative website on Iraq's program, http://www
   .nti.org/learn/countries/iraq.

7 Barton Gellman, "Allied Air War Struck Broadly in Iraq," *Washington Post*,
   June 23, 1991, https://www.washingtonpost.com/archive/politics/1991/06
   /23/allied-air-war-struck-broadly-in-iraq/e469877b-b1c1–44a9-bfe7–084
   da4e38e41/.

8 A. Ascherio et al., "Effect of the Gulf War on Infant and Child Mortality
   in Iraq," *New England Journal of Medicine* 327 (1992): 931–36. See also Joy
   Gordon, *Invisible War: The United States and Iraq Sanctions* (Harvard University Press, 2010); H. C. von Sponeck, *A Different Kind of War: The U.N.
   Sanctions Regime in Iraq* (Berghahn Books, 2006); Richard Garfield, *Mor-
   bidity and Mortality among Iraqi Children from 1990 through 1998: Assessing the Impact of the Gulf War and Economic Sanctions* (1999), http://
   www.casi.org.uk/info/garfield/dr-garfield.html. Von Sponeck was a UN
   official in Iraq responsible for implementing the sanctions, and he resigned
   in protest (as did others) owing to their harshness and capriciousness.
   Albright made her infamous statement to Leslie Stahl on "60 Minutes,"
   May 1996.

9 On mortality in the Iraq War, see John Tirman, *The Deaths of Others: The
   Fate of Civilians in America's Wars* (Oxford University Press, 2011); for a peer
   review of mortality studies, see Christine Tapp et al., "Iraq War Mortality
   Estimates: A Systematic Review," *Conflict and Health* 2, no. 1 (2008). The UN
   High Commissioner for Refugees keeps estimates of refugees and internally
   displaced. One summary by Roberta Cohen of the Brookings Institution at a
   lull in hostilities estimated the total at 4.7 million; Roberta Cohen, "Iraq's
   Displaced: Where to Turn?," Brookings Institution, December 31, 2008,
   https://www.brookings.edu/articles/iraqs-displaced-where-to-turn/.

10 Quoted in David Remnick, "War without End?," *New Yorker*, April 21, 2003.
   Remnick, editor of the magazine, supported the invasion. Years later, Gen.
   Wesley Clark (USA, Ret.) described a Defense Department memo he saw
   in 2002 that targeted seven countries in the region for regime change, including Iran. "Is General Wesley Clark's Prediction of a US Invasion of Iran
   at Hand?," *Democracy Now!*, September 28, 2018, https://www.presstv.com
   /Detail/2018/09/27/575411/General-Wesley-Clarks-warning-that-Iran-is
   -a-target-of-US-intentions-moving-closer.

11 "The National Security Strategy," chap. 3 (September 2002), Archive of the George W. Bush White House, https://georgewbush-whitehouse.archives .gov/nsc/nss/2002/nss3.html.

12 See the extensive material on this in the National Security Archive, such as "The Iraq War, Part I: The U.S. Prepares for Conflict," which has a number of internal, high-level memos outlining their intention to remove Saddam; http://nsarchive.gwu.edu/NSAEBB/NSAEBB326/.

13 "Remarks by the President at the 20th Anniversary of the National Endowment for Democracy," November 6, 2003, http://georgewbush-whitehouse .archives.gov/news/releases/2003/11/20031106-2.html.

14 Condoleezza Rice, interview with Nathan Gardels, *New Perspectives Quarterly*, Fall 2002, 8.

15 Mohammad Ali Abtahi, interview with *Frontline*, PBS, July 29, 2007.

16 Crocker recounts this in the BBC documentary "Shadow Commander: Iran's Military Mastermind," March 2019.

17 A British diplomat with nuclear nonproliferation duties speculated that the neocon Assistant Secretary of State John Bolton gave the information to the MEK; interviews of British policy makers with authors, October 2016. Mohamed ElBaradei, head of the IAEA at the time, hinted something similar in his memoir: "Whether the NCRI was used by Western intelligence to disseminate information about Iran's nuclear activities was a question I often pondered." Mohamed ElBaradei, *The Age of Deception: Nuclear Diplomacy in Treacherous Times* (Metropolitan Books, 2011), 112n.

18 Abbas Maleki, "Challenges in the U.S.-Iran Relationship 2001–2009" (unpublished conference proceedings), MIT, June 14, 2012. Maleki was deputy foreign minister during Rafsanjani's presidency.

19 Kemal Kharrazi, cable, US embassy Yerevan, from US Ambassador John Ordway to State Dept., relating conversation with Armenian foreign minister Vartan Oskanian, April 20, 2004.

20 Hossein Mousavian, "Challenges in the U.S.-Iran Relationship 2001–2009" (unpublished conference proceedings), MIT, June 13, 2012.

21 Stephen J. Hadley, "The George W. Bush Administration," Iran Primer (US Institute of Peace, 2010), http://iranprimer.usip.org/resource/george-w -bush-administration. Hadley was deputy national security adviser from 2001 to 2005 and national security adviser from 2005 to 2009.

22 Donald Rumsfeld, memorandum to President George W. Bush, December 8, 2006.

23 "Report to Congress on the Situation in Iraq," September 10–11, 2007, 4; available at https://tinyurl.com/24myxta3.

24 A State Department survey, which was not made public, was described in Amit R. Paley, "Most Iraqis Favor Immediate U.S. Pullout, Polls Show," *Washington Post*, September 27, 2006, http://www.washingtonpost.com/wp-dyn/content/article/2006/09/26/AR2006092601721.html. A 2009 poll for ABC, BBC, and other news organizations is found at http://abcnews.go.com/images/PollingUnit/1087a1IraqWhereThingsStand.pdf, which shows continuing opposition to US occupation and blames occupation forces for insecurity. Iran's role in Iraq was criticized by Iraqis in the poll, but not by such high numbers.

25 Lawrence Wilkerson, "Challenges in the U.S.-Iran Relationship 2001–2009" (unpublished conference proceedings), MIT, June 13, 2012.

26 James Dobbins, "Challenges in the U.S.-Iran Relationship 2001–2009" (unpublished conference proceedings), MIT, June 14, 2012.

27 Notably, the letter tracks with British envoy Jeremy Greenstock's assessment of Iran's goals in Iraq. "Iran's long-term aim was a stable, Shia-led neighbor, free of foreign interference, rich enough to offer good business and friendly enough not to present a threat," he recalled from his work with the Coalition Provisional Authority. "We judged that they wanted to influence but not dominate, and would take care not to provide the United States with a pretext to attack them. Iran wished to see a weak but not a turbulent Iraq." They also wanted the MEK sidelined. Jeremy Greenstock, *Iraq: The Cost of War* (William Heinemann, 2016), 313.

28 Zarif, interview; Sadeq Kharrazi, interview with authors Byrne and Tirman, December 13, 2014.

29 Richard Armitage, interview with *Frontline*, PBS, July 12, 2007.

30 Glenn Kessler, "Kerry's Claim That Iran Offered Bush a Nuclear Deal in 2003," *Washington Post*, December 9, 2013, https://www.washingtonpost.com/news/fact-checker/wp/2013/12/09/kerrys-claim-that-iran-offered-bush-a-nuclear-deal-in-2003/?utm_term=.2086061686ab. The text of the faxed "roadmap" and Guldimann's preamble are included in this article online.

31 Hadi Semati, "Challenges in the U.S.-Iran Relationship 2001–2009" (unpublished conference proceedings), MIT, June 13, 2012.

32 ElBaradei revealed in his memoir that he carried a note from Hassan Rouhani, then head of the Supreme National Security Council and Iran's chief nuclear negotiator, to President Bush in a meeting in the Oval Office in 2004. The note covered ground similar to the 2003 fax. Bush said he did not think Khamenei was open to dialogue and did not follow up. Rice and Armitage were both in the meeting. ElBaradei, *Age of Deception*, 132.

33 Paul Bremer, cable, "Message for SecDef," June 30, 2003.

34 Meghan O'Sullivan, "Challenges in the U.S.-Iran Relationship 2001–2009" (unpublished conference proceedings), MIT, June 14, 2012.

35 Michael R. Gordon and Andrew W. Lehren, "Leaked Reports Detail Iran's Aid for Iraqi Militias," *New York Times*, October 22, 2010, http://www.nytimes.com/2010/10/23/world/middleeast/23iran.html?pagewanted=all.

36 Mousavian, "Challenges."

37 Col. Joel D. Rayburn and Col. Frank K. Sobchak, eds., *The U.S. Army in the Iraq War* (Strategic Studies Institute and the Army War College Press, 2019), 1:499.

38 The device first appeared in 2003 but became much more commonplace from 2005 on. Brain injuries and post-traumatic stress disorder cases added to the toll. The Pentagon spent $75 billion to harden vehicles against IEDs and explosively formed projectiles, a more sophisticated device directly blamed on the Quds Force; see Marcus Weisgerber, "How Many US Troops Were Killed by Iranian IEDs in Iraq?," *Defense One*, September 8, 2015. Hence, the focus of concern about Iran's Revolutionary Guard killing US soldiers was at the center of interactions on Iraq in that period. The roadside bombs had another deleterious effect: US convoys, if seeing any Iraqi nearby who was using a cell phone or similar device, were authorized to attack that person, sometimes in cars on the road. Lethal "car accidents" increased fivefold during the war.

39 O'Sullivan, "Challenges."

40 Zalmay Khalilzad, interview with Malcolm Byrne, May 25, 2016. John Negroponte, a career diplomat, was briefly US ambassador in Iraq from 2004 to 2005.

41 Khalilzad, interview.

42 Hossein Shariatmadari, interview with *Frontline*, PBS, August 1, 2007. News reports had the figure to Saudi Arabia at $20 billion, with $30 billion in arms going to Israel. The arms for the Saudi monarchy were clearly about Iran. David Cloud, "U.S. Set to Offer Huge Arms Deal to Saudi Arabia," *New York Times*, July 25, 2007, http://www.nytimes.com/2007/07/28/washington/28weapons.html.

43 Donald Rumsfeld, *Known and Unknown: A Memoir* (Sentinel, 2011), 638.

44 Negar Azimi, "Hard Realities of Soft Power," *New York Times Magazine*, June 24, 2007, http://www.nytimes.com/2007/06/24/magazine/24ngo-t.html.

45 Armitage, interview.

46 Semati, "Challenges."

47 Mousavian, "Challenges."

48 Shariatmadari, interview.

49 Jack Straw, interview with the authors, October 25, 2016.

50 Kyle Rempfer, "Iran Killed More US Troops in Iraq Than Previously Known, Pentagon Says," *Military Times*, April 4, 2019, https://www.militarytimes.com/news/your-military/2019/04/04/iran-killed-more-us-troops-in-iraq-than-previously-known-pentagon-says/.

51 Sean Aday, "Chasing the Bad News: An Analysis of 2005 Iraq and Afghanistan War Coverage on NBC and Fox News Channel," *Journal of Communication* 60, no. 1 (March 2010): 144–64, https://doi.org/10.1111/j.1460-2466.2009.01472.x.

52 This was made clear by the official US army's comprehensive history *The U.S. Army in the Iraq War* (US Army War College Press, 2019). A good summary of their focus on Iran is provided by a reviewer:

> The first claim, which runs through the study like a subplot, is that the war's "only victor" was "an emboldened and expansionist Iran," which gained vast influence over its main regional adversary when Iraq's dictator was toppled and replaced by leaders with close ties to Iran. Washington "never formulated an effective strategy" for addressing this challenge, the study concludes, in part because it imposed "artificial geographic boundaries on the conflict" that "limited the war in a way that made it difficult to reach its desired end states." Put more succinctly: the United States erred not by waging a war far more expansive than its national interests warranted but by failing to take the fight far enough, including into neighboring Iran.

Jon Finer, "The Last War—and the Next? Learning the Wrong Lessons from Iraq," *Foreign Affairs*, July/August 2019, https://www.foreignaffairs.com/reviews/review-essay/2019-05-28/last-war-and-next.

53 Sarah Palin, "Palin on Ahmadinejad: 'He Must Be Stopped,'" *New York Sun*, September 22, 2008, https://www.nysun.com/opinion/palin-on-ahmadinejad-he-must-be-stopped/86311/. The remarks were meant for a rally against Ahmadinejad, but the protest organizers withdrew the invitation to Palin.

54 "Ahmadinejad: 'American Empire' Nearing Its End," CNN, September 23, 2008, https://www.cnn.com/2008/WORLD/meast/09/23/ahmadinejad.us/index.html.

9 The Nuclear File under Bush 43

1 As recently as 2015, Iran had 12,000 students at American universities. It peaked at 51,000 in 1980. See Stefan Trines, "Déjà Vu? The Rise and Fall of Iranian Student Enrollments in the U.S.," *World Education News and Review*, February 6, 2017, http://wenr.wes.org/2017/02/educating-iran-demographics-massification-and-missed-opportunities.

2 Gregory F. Treverton, *CIA Support to Policymakers: The 2007 National Intelligence Estimate on Iran's Nuclear Intentions and Capabilities* (RAND Corporation, 2013), https://documentcloud.adobe.com/link/review?uri=urn:aaid:scds:US:4698c22f-1131-4eb5-8f34-5114c080acof.

3 The Strategic Arms Limitation Talks (SALT) resulted in two treaties, SALT I (1972), which included the Anti-Ballistic Missile (ABM) Treaty limiting defensive weapons, and SALT II (1979). They limited the growth in nuclear arsenals of the United States and USSR. (The United States withdrew from the ABM Treaty in 2002.) The Strategic Arms Reduction Treaty, or START (1991), reduced strategic nuclear weapons; START II (1993) elaborated on the limits imposed by START I. A treaty banning intermediate nuclear forces, which were deployed in and against Europe, was signed in 1987.

4 See Matthew Evangelista, *Unarmed Forces: The Transnational Movement to End the Cold War* (Cornell University Press, 2002).

5 Joseph Cirincione, Jon Wolfsthal, and Miriam Rajkumar, *Deadly Arsenals: Nuclear, Biological, and Chemical Threats* (Carnegie Endowment for International Peace, 2005), chap. 15.

6 The release of the CIA report, or National Intelligence Estimate (NIE), in 2007 was itself a story indicative of the split in both the policy and political worlds of Washington. Those seeking regime change or heavy sanctions were incredulous, particularly since it was the Bush White House that declassified much of the NIE. It quashed much of the conservatives' case against Iran. Pro-arms control types had the opposite reaction. An excellent summary of the dispute is found in Gregory F. Treverton, *The 2007 National Intelligence Estimate on Iran's Nuclear Intentions and Capabilities* (Center for the Study of Intelligence, Central Intelligence Agency, May 2013). A 2010 NIE reaffirmed the 2007 key judgment.

7 Quoted in "The Iran Nuclear NIE of 2007: Revise, Reject, or Reiterate?," Arms Control Association Issue Briefs, vol. 1, no. 18 (August 12, 2010), https://www.armscontrol.org/issuebriefs/irannie2007#4.

8 A. Q. Khan was a Pakistani metallurgist who was trained in the Netherlands and gained knowledge of advanced enrichment techniques there. He was a key figure in Pakistan's development of nuclear weapons. He subsequently created a network of companies in Dubai and Malaysia to buy and sell centrifuges and other nuclear weapons technologies, notably to Iran, North Korea, and Libya. He was arrested in 2004 but pardoned the following day by President Musharraf of Pakistan.

9 Peter Jenkins, joint interview of British policy makers with the authors, London, October 18, 2016.

10 Jack Straw, joint interview of British policy makers with the authors, London, October 18, 2016.

11 *Implementation of the NPT Safeguards Agreement in the Islamic Republic of Iran, Report by the Director General* (IAEA Board of Governors, June 6, 2003), https://www.iaea.org/sites/default/files/gov2003-40.pdf. See Mohamed ElBaradei, *The Age of Deception: Nuclear Diplomacy in Treacherous Times* (Metropolitan Books, 2011), 116–22. The specific violations reported by IAEA were (1) failure to declare the import of natural uranium in 1991 and its subsequent transfer for further processing; (2) failure to declare the activities involving the subsequent processing and use of the imported natural uranium; (3) failure to declare the facilities where such material (including the waste) was received, stored, and processed; (4) failure to provide in a timely manner updated design information for the MIX Facility and for Tehran Research Reactor; and (5) failure to provide in a timely

manner information on the waste storage at Esfahan and at Anarak. There were also outstanding questions about other facilities and activities; see cited works for details.

12 Seyed Hossein Mousavian, *The Iranian Nuclear Crisis: A Memoir* (Carnegie Endowment for International Peace, 2012), 69.

13 Richard Dalton, British ambassador to Iran from 2003 to 2006, joint interview of British policy makers with the authors, London, October 18, 2016.

14 Stanislas de LaBoulaye, "Challenges in the U.S.-Iran Relationship 2001–2009" (unpublished conference proceedings), MIT, June 13, 2012.

15 Mousavian, *Iranian Nuclear Crisis*, 149–50.

16 "Communication dated 26 November 2004 received from the Permanent Representatives of France, Germany, the Islamic Republic of Iran and the United Kingdom concerning the agreement signed in Paris on 15 November 2004," International Atomic Energy Agency, November 26, 2004, https://www.iaea.org/sites/default/files/publications/documents/inf circs/2004/infcirc637.pdf.

17 ElBaradei, *Age of Deception*, 140.

18 Lawrence Wilkerson, "Challenges in the U.S.-Iran Relationship 2001–2009" (unpublished conference proceedings), MIT, June 13, 2012.

19 Peter Jenkins, "Challenges in the U.S.-Iran Relationship 2001–2009" (unpublished conference proceedings), MIT, June 13, 2012.

20 Condoleezza Rice, *No Higher Honor: A Memoir of My Years in Washington* (Crown, 2011), 158–59.

21 ElBaradei, *Age of Deception*, 137.

22 Thomas Pickering, "Challenges in the U.S.-Iran Relationship 2001–2009" (unpublished conference proceedings), MIT, June 14, 2012. Pickering had also been US ambassador to six countries and the United Nations, and he was active in Track 2 efforts on Iran for several years after leaving government.

23 In 2003, a *Los Angeles Times* poll had the public in favor of military strikes on Iran's nuclear assets by 50%–36%, and an ABC / *Washington Post* poll in 2003 had bombing favored by 56%–38%. A Fox News poll in January 2005 had the public against bombing Iran's nuclear assets, 46%–41%. An ABC / *Washington Post* poll in January 2006 opposed bombing by 54%–42%. (These polls are online at PollingReport.com.) In 2007, 18% told Gallup that military action should be taken to prevent Iran from developing nuclear weapons, with 28% backing military action should diplomacy fail,

and 45% opposed outright to military action. Gallup surveys show the consistency of deep disapproval of Iran by the public throughout that period (http://www.gallup.com/poll/116236/iran.aspx). As usual, polling results differed depending on the wording of questions asked, as well as recent events, and the trend described here has exceptions and outliers.

24 Nick Burns, "Challenges in the U.S.-Iran Relationship 2001–2009" (unpublished conference proceedings), MIT, June 13, 2012.

25 ElBaradei, *Age of Deception*, 196.

26 Hossein Mousavian, "Challenges in the U.S.-Iran Relationship 2001–2009" (unpublished conference proceedings), MIT, June 13, 2012.

27 Donald Rumsfeld, "Declaratory Policy and the Nuclear Programs of North Korea and Iran," memorandum to President Bush, October 5, 2006. Rumsfeld was suggesting that states who transfer WMD (technology, expertise, etc.) to terrorists would be targeted by the United States. The earlier memo (May 30, 2006) was unaddressed and likely circulated to senior staff.

28 On the "red line," see Abbas William Samii, "The Iranian Nuclear Issue and Informal Networks," *Naval War College Review* 59, no. 1 (Winter 2006): 78–79. Rouhani's comment about consensus on starting the gas diffusion plant in Esfahan is from an interview with Tehran Bureau, "Former Iran Nuclear Negotiator: Bush Negotiation Bid Was Rebuffed," May 12, 2012, trans. Muhammad Sahimi.

29 Quoted in Samii, "Iranian Nuclear Issue," 84. The original article appeared in *Kayhan*, November 17, 2004.

30 Hassan Rouhani, text of speech to the Supreme Cultural Revolution Council, published in *Rahbord*, September 30, 2005. The magazine is the publication of the Centre for Strategic Research, Tehran, considered a moderate think tank. Rouhani was later its director. The speech was from early 2005, translated from Persian and published by the Foreign Broadcast Information Service.

31 David Satterfield, "Insight from Iran's Worldview: Permrep Zarif's 1/14 Speech," memorandum to Secretary of State, January 27, 2005. Notably, two of the authors (Byrne and Tirman) heard Zarif give a similar speech in Tehran almost ten years later.

32 UN Security Council, Resolution 1737, December 27, 2006, https://www.iaea.org/sites/default/files/unsc_res1737-2006.pdf.

33 ElBaradei recalled an editorial in the *Washington Post*, likely penned by

editor Fred Hiatt, denouncing him for his diplomatic efforts to engage Iran "and to use his agency to thwart . . . the United States" (September 5, 2007). He got many reproaches like this, including from some of the key officials, but considered the nonproliferation function of the IAEA to warrant such activism. The *Washington Post* editorial page, in contrast, was a vociferous advocate of the war and occupation in Iraq and published numerous articles advocating war against Iran.

34 ElBaradei, *Age of Deception*, 274.

35 Gregor Peter Schmitz and Cordula Meyer, "U.S. War on Iran 'Closer to Reality,'" *Der Spiegel*, October 25, 2007, http://www.spiegel.de/internation al/world/us-war-on-iran-closer-to-reality-a-513572.html; Seymour Hersh, "Preparing the Battlefield," *New Yorker*, July 8, 2008.

36 Daniel H. Joyner, "Iran's Nuclear Program and International Law," *Penn State Journal of Law and International Affairs* 2, no. 2 (November 2013): 282–92, http://elibrary.law.psu.edu/cgi/viewcontent.cgi?article=1054& context=jlia.

37 Richard Dalton, "Iran Is Not in Breach of International Law," *Guardian*, June 9, 2011. The other coauthors were ambassadors from France, Belgium, Italy, Sweden, and Germany.

38 William O. Beeman, "Does Iran Have the Right to Enrich Uranium? The Answer Is Yes," *Huffington Post*, October 31, 2013, http://www.huffington post.com/william-o-beeman/does-iran-have-the-right-_b_4181347.html.

39 Stephen J. Hadley, "The George W. Bush Administration," *The Iran Primer* (US Institute of Peace, n.d.), https://iranprimer.usip.org/resource/george -w-bush-administration.

10 Obama Enters

1 Hendrik Hertzberg, "Obama Wins," *New Yorker*, November 9, 2008.

2 An early indicator of the global appeal of Obama's momentous rise was his historic campaign stop—before his official nomination as the Democratic candidate for president—in Berlin, Germany, where more than two hundred thousand spectators jammed the thoroughfares around the Siegessäule to hear his message of "improbable hope" and revel in the promise of restoring transatlantic ties to their previous glory. See Barack Obama, "Speech in

Berlin," Berlin, Germany, July 24, 2008, https://www.nytimes.com/2008/07/24/us/politics/24text-obama.html.

3 Michael R. Gordon and Jeff Zeleny, "Obama Envisions New Iran Approach," *New York Times*, November 2, 2007, https://www.nytimes.com/2007/11/02/us/politics/02obama.html.

4 Barack Obama, *Change We Can Believe In: Barack Obama's Plan to Renew America's Promise* (Three Rivers, 2008), 128.

5 William J. Burns, memorandum to Secretary of State Condoleezza Rice, "SUBJECT: Regaining the Strategic Initiative on Iran," May 27, 2008, 2.

6 Burns, memorandum to Rice.

7 Barack Obama, "Inaugural Address," Washington, DC, January 21, 2009, https://obamawhitehouse.archives.gov/blog/2009/01/21/president-barack-obamas-inaugural-address.

8 Obama's "ethical realism" was significantly influenced by the writings of the ethicist and Reformed theologian Reinhold Niebuhr. In a much-cited 2007 interview with the columnist David Brooks, Obama referred to Niebuhr as "one of my favorite philosophers," whose wisdom he boiled down to "the compelling idea that there's serious evil in the world, and hardship and pain. And we should be humble and modest in our belief we can eliminate those things. But we shouldn't use that as an excuse for cynicism and inaction. I take away ... the sense we have to make these efforts knowing they are hard, and not swinging from naïve idealism to bitter realism." David Brooks, "Obama, Gospel and Verse," *New York Times*, April 26, 2007, https://www.nytimes.com/2007/04/26/opinion/26brooks.html.

9 Office of the Press Secretary, "Videotaped Remarks by the President in Celebration of Nowruz," The White House, Washington, DC, March 20, 2009, https://obamawhitehouse.archives.gov/the-press-office/videotaped-remarks-president-celebration-nowruz.

10 As the then president of the National Iranian American Council, Trita Parsi, a persistent advocate of engaging Iran, later noted, "Everything about Obama's message was extraordinary: The respectful tone, the thoughtful message, the modern medium (the White House posted it on YouTube with Persian subtitles), as well as the very idea of speaking directly to the Iranian people and government." Trita Parsi, *Losing an Enemy: Obama, Iran, and the Triumph of Diplomacy* (Yale University Press, 2017), 70.

11 Republican presidents' messages on Nowruz, in contrast, were more ge-

neric and aimed mostly at the Iranian-American community inside the United States. The sole exception here was President George W. Bush's final Nowruz message, which included an extended interview with Voice of America Persian Service that included words of encouragement for reformers and pledged that "I would do nothing to undermine their efforts." Setareh Derakhshesh, "Bush Interview with VOA Persian Service," *Voice of America*, March 19, 2008, https://www.voanews.com/archive/bush-interview-voa-persian-service.

12 "Speech by Iranian Supreme Leader Ali Khamenei to a gathering at the Imam Reza shrine in Mashhad, on the occasion of Nowruz, the Iranian New Year," translated by the USG Open Source Center, March 22, 2009.

13 As Burns notes in his memoir, "The letter tried to thread a needle—the message needed to be clear but written in a way that would not cause too much controversy if it was leaked." William J. Burns, *The Back Channel: A Memoir of American Diplomacy and the Case for Its Renewal* (Random House, 2019), 348.

14 Burns, memorandum to Secretary of State Hillary Clinton, "A New Strategy toward Iran," January 24, 2009.

15 Burns, memorandum to Clinton. The substance of Burns's memo is further contextualized in his memoir; see Burns, *Back Channel*, 346–47.

16 "Text: New Conference with Obama and Lee," The White House, Washington, DC, June 16, 2009.

17 Charles Krauthammer, "Obama Misses the Point with Iran Response," *Washington Post*, June 19, 2009, https://www.washingtonpost.com/wp-dyn/content/article/2009/06/18/AR2009061803495.html. Neoconservative ideologues Bill Kristol and Stephen Hayes were even more damning, calling Obama "a de facto ally of President Mahmoud Ahmadinejad and Supreme Leader Ali Khamenei." Stephen F. Hayes and William Kristol, "Resolutely Irresolute," *Washington Examiner*, June 26, 2009, https://www.washingtonexaminer.com/weekly-standard/resolutely-irresolute.

18 A widely cited passage from Obama's Cairo speech reads,

America does not presume to know what is best for everyone, just as we would not presume to pick the outcome of a peaceful election. But I do have an unyielding belief that all people yearn for certain things: the ability to speak your mind and have a say in how you are governed; confidence in the rule of law and the equal administration of justice; government that is transparent and doesn't steal from the people; the freedom to live as you choose. Those are not just American ideas, they are human rights, and that is why we will support them everywhere.

See Barack Obama, "The President's Speech in Cairo: A New Beginning," Cairo University, Cairo, Egypt, June 4, 2009, https://obamawhitehouse.ar chives.gov/issues/foreign-policy/presidents-speech-cairo-a-new-beginning.

19 As one commentator asked, "If Obama is unwilling to state that Iran's treatment of its people during this incident will have a bearing on his desire to engage with Iran's government, then why not say that one of the issues he now plans to raise when they do finally talk is the fate of the many, many peaceful Iranian protestors who the world has watched savagely clubbed in the streets and then hauled away to God knows where?" Christian Brose, *Foreign Policy*, June 16, 2009, https://foreignpolicy.com /2009/06/16/more-things-obama-should-be-saying-and-doing-about -iran/.

20 "President's Speech in Cairo."

21 Abbas Milani and Larry Diamond, "Let's Hear the Democracies," *New York Times*, July 6, 2009.

22 Barack H. Obama, "A Just and Lasting Peace," Nobel Lecture, Oslo, Norway, October, 10, 2009, https://www.nobelprize.org/prizes/peace/2009/obama /lecture/.

23 Montazeri, who lived under house arrest owing largely to his renunciation of concept of the *velayat-e faqih* and sharp criticisms of Khamenei, issued perhaps the harshest indictments of Khamenei's rule. In a statement attributed to his office, he inveighed that the Islamic Republic was no longer Islamic nor republican, but "a military regime." See Michael Theodoulou, "The Grand Ayatollah Unleashes His Wrath," *National*, September 21, 2009, https://www.thenational.ae/world/mena/the-grand-ayatollah -unleashes-his-wrath-1.540914.

24 See, e.g., collected essays in Nader Hashemi and Danny Postel, eds., *The People Reloaded: The Green Movement and the Struggle for Iran's Future* (Melville House, 2011); Negin Nabavi, ed., *Iran: From Theocracy to the Green Movement* (Springer, 2012); Abbas Milani, "The New Democrats," *New Republic*, July 15, 2009; and Abbas Milani, "Beating Bad Karma," *Boston Review*, July 1, 2009. Hamid Dabashi's almost daily writings during the

protests best captured the granularity of events and shifting circumstances and are collected in *The Green Movement in Iran* (Transaction, 2011); for his critical commentary on US-Iran dynamics surrounding the Green Movement, see Hamid Dabashi, *Iran, The Green Movement and the USA: The Fox and the Paradox* (Zed Books, 2010).

25 Mousavi's key public statements and interviews in this period are compiled at https://irandataportal.syr.edu/mir-hossein-mousavi. For his evocation of Islamic Revolution ideals in defending the post-election protests, see his statement "To the Green Path of Hope," September 5, 2009, https://irandataportal.syr.edu/to-the-green-path-of-hope-5-september-2009.

26 As Burns reflected later, "In hindsight, we should have politely ignored those entreaties and been sharper in our public criticism from the start. Such criticism, which we eventually made quite strongly, was not only the right thing to do, it was also a useful reminder to the Iranian regime that we weren't so desperate to get nuclear talks started that we'd turn a blind eye to threatening behavior, whether against Iran's own citizens or our friends in the region." Burns, *Back Channel*, 349.

27 Burns, *Back Channel*, 352.

28 For their part, American officials reasoned that the rejection was essentially an act of sabotage by Ahmadinejad's political rivals inside Iran—i.e., national security officials close to the former pragmatist president Rafsanjani—who wished to deny him any victories on the diplomatic front. As Burns later reflected, "The Iranian president's political rivals, some of whom had been involved in the nuclear negotiations before and might otherwise have taken more supportive positions, didn't want Ahmadinejad to get the credit for any breakthroughs, however modest. Iranian politics are a brutal contact sport, and the TRR deal was one of its many casualties." Burns, *Back Channel*, 353.

29 "Israel Urges Crippling Sanctions Now," *Reuters*, February 9, 2010.

30 For a good summary of the uncertainties around Iran's intentions, as well as the diplomatic process at the time, see Thomas R. Pickering, "The Iranian Quagmire: How to Move Forward," *Bulletin of the Atomic Scientists* 66, no. 6 (2010): 88–94.

31 "Joint Declaration by Iran, Turkey and Brazil," May 17, 2010, https://fas.org/nuke/guide/iran/joint-decl.pdf.

32 Peter Baker and David E. Sanger, "U.S. Makes Concessions to Russia for

Iran Sanctions," *New York Times*, May 21, 2010, https://www.nytimes.com/2010/05/22/world/22sanctions.html.

33 For a detail explanation and assessment of the diplomatic jockeying for concessions by China and Russia, see Parsi, *Losing an Enemy*, 98–115.

34 S/RES/1929 (2010), United National Security Council, June 9, 2010, https://www.undocs.org/S/RES/1929%20(2010).

35 "Ahmadinejad: New Sanctions 'Fit for Dustbin,'" *BBC News*, June 9, 2010.

36 Office of the Press Secretary, "Remarks by President on United Nations Security Council Resolution on Iran Sanctions," The White House, June 9, 2010.

37 Office of the Press Secretary, "Remarks by President at the Signing of the Iran Sanctions Act," The White House, July 1, 2010.

38 For a detailed account of the initial back-channel meeting, see Mark Landler, *Alter Egos: Hillary Clinton, Barack Obama, and the Twilight Struggle over American Power* (Random House, 2016), chap. 10. As Sullivan later explained, "Without that channel we likely would have spent the fall of 2013 trying to figure out who to talk to and how." See David Ignatius, "The Omani Back Channel to Iran and the Secrecy Surrounding the Nuclear Deal," *Washington Post*, June 7, 2016.

39 Barack Obama, "Inaugural Address," Washington, DC, January 21, 2013, https://obamawhitehouse.archives.gov/the-press-office/2013/01/21/inaugural-address-president-barack-obama.

11 Rouhani, Zarif, and the Nuclear Deal

1 In 2007, Kerry participated in a panel discussion alongside former Iranian reformist president Mohammad Khatami in Davos, Switzerland, and had become acquainted with Iranian expatriates, lobby organizations, and think tank experts in Washington.

2 The Guardian Council also disqualified Ahmadinejad's chief of staff, Esfandiyar Rahim Mashaie, as well as his foreign minister Manouchehr Mottaki. Jason Rezaian, "Iranian Presidential Candidates Announced; Rafsanjani Disqualified," *Washington Post*, May 22, 2013.

3 See Mohsen Milani, "Why the Islamic Republic Disqualified One of Its Founding Fathers from Running for President," *Atlantic*, June 7, 2013,

https://www.theatlantic.com/international/archive/2013/06/why-the
-islamic-republic-disqualified-one-of-its-founding-fathers-from-running
-for-president/276671/.

4 The two men had been erstwhile comrades during the first decade following the 1979 revolution, but they gradually grew apart as their visions for a
post-Khomeini Islamic Republic pitted their respective interests against
each other. In this ill-fated rivalry, however, Khamenei always had the upper hand owing to his position in the hierarchy of power (a post that, in an
especially cruel irony of history, he owed almost entirely to Rafsanjani's
public support and private maneuverings shortly after Khomeini's death).

5 Rouhani's actual surname is Fereydoun, which he changed early in his clerical training to reflect his spiritual transformation into a clergyman.

6 For a summary of the backgrounds and political histories of Aref and Rouhani, see Mehrzad Boroujerdi and Kourosh Rahimkhani, *Postrevolutionary
Iran: A Political Handbook* (Syracuse University Press, 2018), 394–95, 702–3.

7 For an overview of Ahmadinejad's economic legacy, see Nader Habibi,
"The Economic Legacy of Mahmoud Ahmadinejad" (Working Paper 5,
Crown Center for Middle East Studies, Brandeis University, April 2014),
https://www.brandeis.edu/economics/RePEc/brd/doc/Brandeis_WP69
.pdf. Djavad Salehi-Isfahani provides an insightful picture of fiscal policy
dilemmas and decision-making in the Ahmadinajed years through a critical assessment of his controversial subsidy reform policy in "Iran's Subsidy
Reform: From Promise to Disappointment," *Policy Perspective*, no. 13, Economic Research Forum, June 2014, https://erf.org.eg/wp-content/uploads
/2015/12/PP13_2014.pdf.

8 International Monetary Fund, *World Economic Outlook Database*, October
2012. However, it must be noted that by 2011 the standard measure of economic inequality, the Gini coefficient, fell to its lowest rate since 1990, indicating a decline in the rate of inequality. See data from the Statistical Center of Iran, 2006–11; and Ali Enami, Nora Lustig, and Alireza Taqdiri, "Fiscal
Policy, Inequality, and Poverty in Iran: Assessing the Impact and Effectiveness of Taxes and Transfers," *Middle East Development Journal* 11, no. 1
(2019): 49–74.

9 Saeed Kamali Dehghan, "Iran Presidential Candidates' Debate—as It Happened," *Guardian*, June 5, 2013, https://www.theguardian.com/world/blog
/2013/jun/05/iran-presidential-candidates-debate-live-coverage.

10 Jason Rezaian, "Iran's Presidential Election Gets Personal," *Washington Post*, June 7, 2013. Notably, Rouhani was not alone in advocating for a more flexible and thoughtful diplomatic approach toward Western powers. Moments into the debates, Ali Akbar Velayati, one of Khamenei's most trusted advisors, also criticized Jalili's hard-line approach: "You were in charge of the nuclear case for several years, and we haven't taken a single step forward. . . . Diplomacy isn't about toughness or stubbornness."

11 See Suzanne Maloney, "Rouhani Goes to Isfahan: Why Iran's Elections May Yet Get Interesting," *Markaz*, Brookings Institution, June 4, 2013, https://www.brookings.edu/blog/markaz/2013/06/04/rouhani-goes-to-isfahan-why-irans-elections-may-yet-get-interesting/.

12 Behind the scenes, the political jockeying and lobbying efforts of former presidents Rafsanjani and Khatami were crucially important in coordinating the support of these groups on Rouhani's behalf.

13 Ali M. Pedram, "In Conversation with Hassan Rouhani," *Asharq Al-Awsat*, June 13, 2013, https://web.archive.org/web/20131209055728/http://en-maktoob.news.yahoo.com/conversation-hassan-rouhani-182743986.html.

14 For detailed results of the 2013 presidential election, see Boroujerdi and Rahimkhani, *Postrevolutionary Iran*, pp. 100–101. The same information can also be found at https://irandataportal.syr.edu/2013-presidential-election. Qalibaf and Jalili finished a distant second (16.5%) and third (11.3%) behind Rouhani, respectively.

15 See Hussein Banai, "A Test of Wills in Iran," *Los Angeles Times*, June 18, 2013, https://www.latimes.com/opinion/la-xpm-2013-jun-18-la-oe-banai-iran-hassan-rowhani-20130618-story.html.

16 As some of Rouhani's advisors relayed to Trita Parsi, "while Khamenei might not have wanted Rouhani to win, his very narrow margin of victory rendered a conservative challenge to the election results and demand for recount very likely. The most probable reason why such challenge never was mounted, they argue, 'must have been because of direct orders from Khamenei.'" Trita Parsi, *Losing an Enemy: Obama, Iran, and the Triumph of Diplomacy* (Yale University Press, 2017), 205.

17 For a summary of his proposals and accomplishments, see Amir Paivar, "Iran: Rouhani's First 100 Days," *BBC Persian*, November 12, 2013, https://www.bbc.com/news/world-middle-east-24908733.

18 See Andrew Detsch, "The 'Brain Trust' behind Iran's New President," *Diplomat*, August 3, 2013, https://thediplomat.com/2013/08/the-brain-trust-behind-irans-new-president/.

19 See chap. 5.

20 Boroujerdi and Rahimkhani, *Postrevolutionary Iran*, 792.

21 For an in-depth profile of Zarif, see Robin Wright, "The Adversary," *New Yorker*, May 19, 2014.

22 Wright, "Adversary." Feinstein told Wright, "He doesn't produce incendiary sentences. He is thoughtful. He is real. He wants to help his people and lead them in a different direction. That's important to me in my measurement of a person."

23 "Iran Election: Israel Issues Warning after Rouhani Win," *BBC News*, June 16, 2013, https://www.bbc.com/news/world-middle-east-22927408.

24 Robert Tate, "Holocaust Deniers Gather in Iran for 'Scientific' Conference," *Guardian*, December 12, 2006, https://www.theguardian.com/world/2006/dec/12/iran.israel. Ahmadinejd's anti-Semitism was complemented by a host of other discriminatory remarks targeting the Baha'i community and denying the existence of gay and transgender people in Iran.

25 The message, which quickly went viral, also included a picture of a Jewish person in prayer pose; https://twitter.com/HassanRouhani/status/375278962718412800.

26 See Wright, "Adversary."

27 Hassan Rouhani, "Time to Engage," *Washington Post*, September 19, 2013, https://www.washingtonpost.com/opinions/president-of-iran-hassan-rouhani-time-to-engage/2013/09/19/4d2da564-213e-11e3-966c-9c4293c47ebe_story.html.

28 Ben Rhodes, *The World as It Is: A Memoir of the Obama White House* (Random House, 2018), 248.

29 Interestingly, the existence of a back channel was not known to either Rouhani or Zarif until after the election.

30 He added, "It also cost Rouhani far less political capital to push for direct talks with the Americans when the more hawkish Ahmadinejad government had already crossed that Rubicon." William J. Burns, *The Back Channel: A Memoir of American Diplomacy and the Case for Its Renewal* (Random House, 2019), 368.

31 Burns, *Back Channel*, 371.

32 "Leader's Speech in Meeting with the Commanders of the Islamic Revolutionary Guards Corps," *Khamenei.ir*, Tehran, Iran, September 17, 2013,
https://english.khamenei.ir/news/1827/Leader-s-Speech-in-Meeting
-with-Commanders-of-Islamic-Revolutionary.

33 Rhodes, *World as It Is*, 249.

34 The intricacies of narrative were not lost on American officials, but they
still very much looked at opportunities like these in purely instrumental
terms. As Rhodes, who leaked the news of the failed meeting to the press
pool afterward (with Obama's approval), reflects in his memoir, "Rouhani
had been trying to portray himself, at home and around the world, as a reasonable man, committed to dialogue. We were undercutting that narrative,
which was its own form of pressure." Rhodes, *World as It Is*, 250. It must be
noted that there are slight differences of interpretation in accounts of
American officials as to why the meeting did not take place. In his memoir,
Burns gives the impression that the effort fell through after the Iranians
floated some preconditions: "Once the Iranians began to press us to agree
to preconditions for even a brief pull-aside encounter, invoking the familiar
plea for some recognition of a 'right' to enrich, it was apparent that the effort to engineer a meeting was not worth it." Burns, *Back Channel*, 374.

35 "U.S. Senators Urge Obama to Take Tough Line on Iran," *Reuters*, September 23, 2013, https://www.reuters.com/article/us-un-assembly-iran-con
gress/u-s-senators-urge-obama-to-take-tough-line-on-iran-idUSBRE98
MoU020130923.

36 Laura Rozen, "Obama Calls Iran's Rouhani," *Al-Monitor*, September 27,
2013, https://www.al-monitor.com/pulse/originals/2013/09/zarif-kerry
-israel-netanyahu-nuclear-1979-miryusefi-un-p51.html.

37 As a report by the Arms Control Association pointed out, "Prior to the
November 2013 interim agreement, Iran had produced about 11,100 kilograms of 3.5 percent-enriched uranium, an amount sufficient for several
nuclear weapons if enriched further to weapons grade and then fabricated
into the weapons' metallic cores." Kelsey Davenport, Daryl G. Kimball, and
Greg Thielmann, *Solving the Iranian Nuclear Puzzle: Toward an Effective
and Comprehensive Nuclear Agreement*, 3rd ed. (The Arms Control Association, June 2014), 12.

38 Burns, *Back Channel*, 377.

39 Managing Netanyahu's gripes and interventions would indeed become the White House's single biggest challenge in selling a nuclear deal with Iran to the American public, but with a united P5+1 behind him and a cooperative Iranian government, Obama's narrative of engagement resonated more than Netanyahu's hyperbolic predictions of doom and gloom.

40 For how Iranian leaders'—especially Zarif's—use of social media transformed Iran's diplomatic approach, see Constance Duncombe, "Twitter and Transformative Diplomacy: Social Media and Iran-US Relations," *International Affairs* 93, no. 3 (May 2017): 545–62.

41 Mohammad-Javad Zarif, "Iran's Message: There Is a Way Forward," Javad Zarif YouTube Channel, https://youtu.be/Ao2WH6GDWz4.

42 "Joint Plan of Action," Geneva, Switzerland, November 24, 2013, https://assets.documentcloud.org/documents/839276/joint-plan-of-action-24-november-2013-the-final-1.pdf.

43 Associated Press, "Netanyahu: Deal 'Historic Mistake,'" *Politico*, November 24, 2013, https://www.politico.com/story/2013/11/iran-israel-netanyahu-deal-historic-mistake-100298.

44 He added, "ISIS is a group of adventurers with a very aggressive ideology. But they have to conquer more and more territory before they can became [*sic*] a geo-strategic, permanent reality. I think a conflict with ISIS—important as it is—is more manageable than a confrontation with Iran." "Henry Kissinger's Thoughts on the Islamic State, Ukraine and 'World Order,'" *Weekend Edition Saturday*, September 6, 2014, https://www.npr.org/2014/09/06/346114326/henry-kissingers-thoughts-on-the-islamic-state-ukraine-and-world-order. For a counterperspective, see Hussein Banai, "The Myth of Iranian Hegemony," *Policy Options*, November 2, 2014, https://policyoptions.irpp.org/magazines/policyflix/banai/.

45 "Benjamin Netanyahu's Address to a Joint Meeting of Congress," *Washington Post*, March 3, 2015, https://www.washingtonpost.com/news/post-politics/wp/2015/03/03/full-text-netanyahus-address-to-congress/.

46 For a representative sample of criticisms of the deal, see Robert Satloff, "What's Really Wrong with the Iran Nuclear Deal," *New York Daily News*, July 14, 2015; for a rebuttal to these criticisms, see Graham Allison, "A Point-by-Point Response to the Iran Deal Critics," *Atlantic*, July 8, 2015, https://www.theatlantic.com/international/archive/2015/07/iran-nuclear-nietzsche/397970/.

47 "U.S, Israel Sign $38 Billion Military Aid Package," *Reuters*, September 14, 2016; and "Obama Administration Arms Sales Offers to Saudi Top $115 Billion," *Reuters*, September 6, 2016.

48 "Transcript: President Obama's Full NPR Interview on Iran Nuclear Deal," *National Public Radio*, April 7, 2015, https://www.npr.org/2015/04/07/3979 33577/transcript-president-obamas-full-npr-interview-on-iran-nuclear-deal.

49 The Iran deal, and Obama's deft handling of the public justifications behind it, represented a classic case study in how principles and consequences could be balanced to produce an optimal result. For an elaboration of Obama's balancing act in this case, see Hussein Banai, "How Obama Solved U.S.-Iran Relations' 'Trolley Problem,'" *Ethics and International Affairs*, July 2015, https://www.ethicsandinternationalaffairs.org /2015/how-obama-solved-u-s-iran-relations-trolley-problem/.

50 Thomas L. Friedman, "Iran and the Obama Doctrine," *New York Times*, April 5, 2015. For a longer exposition of the "Obama doctrine" and Iran, see Jeffrey Goldberg, "The Obama Doctrine," *Atlantic*, April 2016, https://www .theatlantic.com/magazine/archive/2016/04/the-obama-doctrine/471525/.

12 Trump and Regeneration through Violence

1 See John Mearsheimer and Stephen Walt, *The Israel Lobby and U.S. Foreign Policy* (Farrar, Straus & Giroux, 2007). While published long before the Trump administration, it makes a convincing, if controversial, case for the pro-Israel lobby's influence.

2 See, e.g., Susan Lope, "Indian Giver: The Illusion of Effective Legal Redress for Native American Land Claims," *Southwestern University Law Review* 23 (1991–92): 331–60; and Matthew Atkinson, "Red Tape: How American Laws Ensnare Native American Lands, Resources, and People," *Oklahoma City University Law Review* 23, nos. 1 and 2 (Summer 1998): 379–432.

3 "Transcript: Trump's Remarks on Iran Nuclear Deal," *National Public Radio*, October 13, 2017, https://www.npr.org/2017/10/13/557622096/tran script-trump-s-remarks-on-iran-nuclear-deal.

4 "Full Transcript of Trump's Speech on the Iran Nuclear Deal," *New York Times*, May 8, 2018, https://www.nytimes.com/2018/05/08/us/politics /trump-speech-iran-deal.html.

5 Bolton was a key participant in the decision by President George W. Bush in 2001–2 to withdraw from the Anti-Ballistic Missile Treaty, which prohibited systems that could shoot down ballistic missiles and thereby stabilize deterrence. Vladimir Putin later described this as the beginning of a new arms race. The ostensible reason for quitting the ABM Treaty was to develop antimissile capabilities against "terrorist" states like Iran. As of 2019, very little ABM capability was in place.

6 The twelve demands were (1) declare to the IAEA a full account of the prior military dimensions of its nuclear program and permanently and verifiably abandon such work in perpetuity; (2) stop enrichment and never pursue plutonium reprocessing; (3) provide the IAEA with unqualified access to all sites throughout the entire country; (4) end ballistic missile and nuclear-capable missile systems; (5) release all US citizens and citizens of our partners and allies; (6) end support to Middle East terrorist groups, including Lebanese Hezbollah, Hamas, and the Palestinian Islamic Jihad; (7) respect the sovereignty of the Iraqi government and permit the disarming, demobilization, and reintegration of Shi'a militias; (8) end military support for the Houthi militia and work toward a peaceful political settlement in Yemen; (9) withdraw all forces under Iranian command from Syria; (10) end support for the Taliban and other terrorists in Afghanistan and the region, and cease harboring senior Al-Qaeda leaders; (11) end the IRG Qods Force's support for terrorists and militant partners around the world; and (12) end its threatening behavior against its neighbors, threats to international shipping, and destructive cyberattacks. See https://www.heritage.org/defense/event/after-the-deal-new-iran-strategy.

7 Memorandum to Trump, published in the *National Review*, August 28, 2017, https://www.nationalreview.com/2017/08/iran-nuclear-deal-exit-strategy-john-bolton-memo-trump; op-ed, "Beyond the Iran Nuclear Deal," *Wall Street Journal*, January 15, 2018; "Bolton Warns Iran of 'Hell to Pay' in Impassioned NY Speech," *Times of Israel*, September 25, 2018, https://www.timesofisrael.com/bolton-to-warn-iran-of-hell-to-pay-in-impassioned-ny-speech/.

8 Salvador Rizzo, "A Guide to Understanding the Administration's Spin on Terrorists at the Border," *Washington Post*, January 14, 2019, https://www.washingtonpost.com/politics/2019/01/14/guide-understanding-administrations-spin-terrorists-border/?utm_term=.e4affd1f9883.

9   See Alex Nowrasteh, "Terrorists Are Not Crossing the Mexican Border," CATO Institute blog, March 18, 2021, https://www.cato.org/blog/terrorists-are-not-crossing-mexican-border.

10 See the polling data from various organizations (Gallup, CNN, etc.) at http://www.pollingreport.com/iran.htm. One striking finding is that, when asked, about 15%–30% said they did not know enough to have an opinion.

11 The statement was made on April 30, 2018, but later retracted. See Brandon Conradis, "White House Revises Statement Saying Iran 'Has' Secret Nuclear Weapons Program," *Hill*, April 30, 2018, https://thehill.com/business-a-lobbying/385595-white-house-adjusts-statement-that-said-iran-has-secret-nuclear-weapons.

12 Noa Landau, "Pompeo to Netanyahu: Confronting Iran Key to Mideast Stability, Peace," *Haaretz*, February 14, 2019, https://www.haaretz.com/middle-east-news/pompeo-impossible-to-achieve-mideast-stability-peace-without-confronting-iran-1.6936439.

13 All IAEA reports on Iran are available on the agency's website, https://www.iaea.org/newscenter/focus/iran/iaea-and-iran-iaea-reports.

14 Kelsey Davenport, "The IAEA Reports—Yet Again—Iran's Compliance with the JCPOA," Arms Control Association, November 30, 2018, https://www.armscontrol.org/blog/2018-11-30/iaea-reports-yet-again-irans-compliance-jcpoa.

15 James W. Carey, "A Cultural Approach to Communication," in *Communication as Culture: Essays on Media and Society*, 2nd ed. (Routledge, 2008), 5, https://documentcloud.adobe.com/link/review?uri=urn:aaid:scds:US:519fd96a-1f72-4d85-ab5e-5862b6cfd0eb. Carey also wrote in this essay, apropos of Trump, "Under a ritual view, then, news is not information but drama. It does not describe the world but portrays an arena of dramatic forces and action; it exists solely in historical time; and it invites our participation on the basis of our assuming, often vicariously, social roles within it" (7).

16 Albert O. Hirschman, "Two Hundred Years of Reactionary Rhetoric: The Case of the Perverse Effect," The Tanner Lectures on Human Values, University of Michigan, April 8, 1988, 9–11, https://tannerlectures.utah.edu/_documents/a-to-z/h/hirschman89.pdf.

17 Mark Dubowitz, "With John Bolton, the Iran Deal 'Nixers' Have an Upper Hand over the 'Fixers,'" *New York Daily News*, March 23, 2018, https://www

.fdd.org/analysis/2018/03/23/with-john-bolton-the-iran-deal-nixers-have
-an-upper-hand-over-the-fixers/. On Pletka's view, see Danielle Pletka,
"How to Think about the End of the JCPOA," *AEIdeas*, May 8, 2018, http://
www.aei.org/publication/how-to-think-about-the-end-of-the-jcpoa/.

18 "Outlaw Regime: A Chronicle of Iran's Destructive Activities," Department
of State (May 2018), 4, https://documentcloud.adobe.com/link/review?uri
=urn:aaid:scds:US:37fed350–5b6a-4036–81d2–238133309b6f.

19 Not all pro-Israel groups opposed the JCPOA. J Street and similar organizations supported the deal. In polling of Jewish Americans, a majority supported the agreement. The split in the community reflected to some extent
the split in Israel, where the Netanyahu government went to great lengths
to undermine the negotiations, but several former military and intelligence
community leaders saw the JCPOA as a net plus for Israeli security.

20 An example of a strategy for radical change prompted by the United States
that contains these elements is Frederick Kagan, "Can We Pursue a Victory
Strategy against Iran?," *Commentary*, September 2018, 22–30.

21 Michael Rubin, "Ending the Iran Nuclear Deal Isn't Enough: Trump Must
Wage Economic Warfare," *Washington Examiner*, May 8, 2018, http://www
.aei.org/publication/ending-the-iran-nuclear-deal-isnt-enough-trump-must
-wage-economic-warfare/.

22 Mearsheimer and Walt, *Israel Lobby*. See also Robert Dreyfuss, "AIPAC
from the Inside, Part 1: Isolating Iran," *Tehran Bureau*, June 11, 2011, https://
www.pbs.org/wgbh/pages/frontline/tehranbureau/2011/06/aipac-from
-the-inside-1-isolating-iran.html.

23 "Iran's Leader Ordered Crackdown on Unrest—'Do Whatever It Takes to
End It,'" *Reuters*, December 23, 2019, https://www.reuters.com/article/us
-iran-protests-specialreport/special-report-irans-leader-ordered-crack
down-on-unrest-do-whatever-it-takes-to-end-it-idUSKBN1YR0QR.

24 Dina Esfandiari and Ali Vaez, "The Hard-Liners Won in Iran. That's Not All
Bad News," *New York Times*, June 22, 2021, https://www.nytimes.com/2021
/06/22/opinion/iran-election-raisi-nuclear-deal.html?smid=tw-share.

25 Patrick Wintour and Julian Border, "Trump Says He Stopped Airstrike on
Iran Because 150 Would Have Died," *Guardian*, June 21, 2019, https://www
.theguardian.com/world/2019/jun/21/donald-trump-retaliatory-iran-air
strike-cancelled-10-minutes-before.

26 Emily Meierding, "The Real Reason Trump Won't Attack Iran," *Foreign Policy*, September 18, 2019, https://foreignpolicy.com/2019/09/18/the-real -reason-trump-wont-attack-iran-saudi/.

27 The violence of sanctions has yet to be adequately measured. The Harvard team that calculated infant mortality as a consequence of US sanctions on Iraq from 1990 to 2003 remains the gold standard. They found through a large (>23,000) household survey conducted in 1999 that five hundred thousand children died in excess of normal mortality. "Infant mortality rose from 47 per 1000 live births during 1984–89 to 108 per 1000 in 1994–99, and under-5 mortality rose from 56 to 131 per 1000 live births." Mohamed M. Ali and Iqbal H. Shah, "Sanctions and Childhood Mortality in Iraq," *Lancet* 355, no. 9218 (May 27, 2000): 1851–57. Other studies have established a correlation between poor economic conditions and mortality, particularly in childhood. See, e.g., Oliver Ezechi and Karen Odberg-Petterson, *Perinatal Mortality* (Books on Demand, 2012); M. S. Kulkarni, N. R. Pinto, and A. M. Ferreira, "Socioeconomic Correlates and Trends of Infant Mortality Rate in Goa and Kerala," *Indian Journal of Maternal Child Health* 6, no. 3 (July– September 1995): 84–86, https://pubmed.ncbi.nlm.nih.gov/12346504/; Olle Lundberg, "The Impact of Childhood Living Conditions on Illness and Mortality in Adulthood," *Social Science and Medicine* 36, no. 8 (April 1993): 1047–52.

28 Samira Saramo, "The Meta-violence of Trumpism," *European Journal of American Studies*, Summer 2017, abstract.

29 Ali Harb, "Blinken Defends Iran Deal but Says No Concessions to Renew Talks," *Middle East Eye*, March 10, 2021, https://www.middleeasteye.net /news/secretary-state-tony-blinken-defends-iran-deal-no-concessions.

About the Authors

Hussein Banai is assistant professor of international studies at the Hamilton Lugar School of Global and International Studies, Indiana University, Bloomington, and a Research Affiliate at the Center for International Studies, Massachusetts Institute of Technology. He is the author of *Hidden Liberalism: Burdened Visions of Progress in Modern Iran* and coauthor of *Becoming Enemies: U.S.-Iran Relations and the Iran-Iraq War, 1979–1988*. His articles on Iran's political development, US-Iran relations, diplomatic theory and practice, and democratic thought have appeared in academic, policy, and popular periodicals.

Malcolm Byrne is deputy director and research director of the nongovernmental National Security Archive, where since 1997 he has also run the Iran-U.S. Relations Project, a multinational archival exploration. He is the author, coauthor, or editor of several books on US policy toward Iran, including the award-winning *Mohammad Mosaddeq* *and the 1953 Coup in Iran* and, most recently, *Worlds Apart: A Documentary History of US-Iranian Relations, 1978–2018.* He has traveled numerous times to the Islamic Republic for research and conferences.

John Tirman has been, since 2004, executive director of the Center for International Studies at the Massachusetts Institute of Technology, where he is also principal research scientist. Previously, he was program director at the Social Science Research Council and executive director of the Winston Foundation for World Peace. He is author or coauthor of fourteen books, including *Becoming Enemies: U.S.-Iran Relations and the Iran-Iraq War, 1979–1988,* and *U.S.-Iran Misperceptions.* He has conducted pioneering research on the human costs of war, including the book *The Deaths of Others: The Fate of Civilians in America's Wars.*

Index

Abdi, Abbas, 369n8
Abdoli, Fattah, 119
Abdullah (Saudi Arabia), 114
Abtahi, Mohammad Ali, 206
Achaemenid Empire, 27, 30
Adams, Brooks, 45
al-Afghani, Jamal al-Din, 27
Afghanistan: al-Qaeda in, 180; September 11, 2001 terrorist attacks and, 179; Soviet invasion of, 85
Afghanistan War, 6, 44, 181–88
Agnew, Spiro, 349n17
Ahmad, Jalal Al-e, 34, 368n1
Ahmadinejad, Mahmoud: economic growth under, 277, 281; election of, 7, 8, 149, 266, 350n21; Iran's nuclear program and, 236, 239–40, 244, 246, 268; Iraq War and, 215, 220; Obama and, 260
AIPAC (American Israel Public Affairs Committee), 11, 318–19

Airborne Warning and Control System (AWACS), 70
Akhundzadeh, Mirza Fatali, 26–27
Alavi-Tabar, Alireza, 369n8
Albright, Madeleine, 153, 155–58, 166–67, 179, 201
Algiers Agreement (1975), 113, 116
Ali (caliph), 32–33
Amanpour, Christiane, 5, 137
American Enterprise Institute, 318
American exceptionalism, 37–38, 43
American Israel Public Affairs Committee (AIPAC), 11, 318–19
American national narrative: clashing narratives and, 47–53; frontier myth in, 13–14, 38–42, 46–47, 219, 316, 352–53n40; narrative trap and, 37–47; Trump's revival of, 314–20, 328–29
Amuzegar, Jahangir, 363n10
Anderson, Benedict, 19

Anderson, Terry, 117
Anglo-Iranian Oil Company, 62
Anglo-Russian agreement (1907), 29
Ansar al-Allah (group), 125
Ansar-e Hezbollah, 145
Ansari, Ali, 51
Anti-Ballistic Missile Treaty (ABM),
    401n5
Arab-Israeli conflict, 66, 174
Arab Spring, 274, 277
Arafat, Yasser, 112, 157, 188
Araghchi, Abbas, 289–90, 291, 297–98
Arak heavy water plant, 230–31, 302
Aramco, 126
Ardalan, Homayoun, 119
Aref, Mohammad Reza, 280, 281
Argentina: Iran's nuclear program and,
    229; national narrative in, 53; terrorist
    attacks in, 118–19, 125
Argentine Israelite Mutual Association
    bombing (1994), 125
Arjomand, Said Amir, 363n9, 364n12
Armitage, Richard, 173, 180, 187, 210, 211, 217
arms control: industry of, 224–28; Trump
    and, 309. See also specific agreements
Arms Control Association, 11, 398n37
Arnold, Matthew, 75–76
Aryan narrative, 27–29, 31, 35–36, 332,
    349n12, 350n18, 352n33
al-Assad, Bashar, 319
assassinations: of Imam Hussein, 33; of
    Iranian dissidents, 106, 110, 119, 120, 124,
    136, 143–44, 170; of Kurdish activists, 14;
    of Masoud, 177; of Rabin, 153; of Solei-
    mani, 321, 323–24
Association of Combatant Clergy, 130–31,
    144
Atatürk (Mustapha Kemal), 28, 30
Atlantic Charter, 56–57
Atoms for Peace program, 229
AWACS (Airborne Warning and Control
    System), 70

Badr Brigade, 202, 212, 214
Baha'i, 19, 48, 159

Baker, James, 116
Bakhtiar, Shahpour, 72, 118, 119
Ball, George, 71, 72
Bancroft, George, 41
Baruch, Bernard, 224
Bazargan, Mehdi, 73, 74
Beeman, William, 249
Behbehani, Ayatollah, 62
Berger, Sandy, 163
Berlin, Isaiah, 348n6; "The Bent Twig,"
    23–24
Biden, Joe: JCPOA and, 16, 329–30; Zarif
    and, 286
bin Alawi, Yusuf, 163–64, 165
bin Laden, Osama, 45, 177, 179
bin Salman, Mohammed, 311, 323
Blair, Tony, 152, 232
Blinken, Anthony, 329
Bolton, John: Anti-Ballistic Missile Treaty
    and, 401n5; in Bush (G.W.) administra-
    tion, 179, 232, 234, 237, 381n17; in Trump
    administration, 309, 311, 314
Bonn Conference (2001), 181–88
Boroumand, Abdorrahman, 118
Brahimi, Lakhdar, 182, 183
Bremer, Paul, 212
Bretton Woods system, 46
Britain. See United Kingdom
Brooks, David, 390n8
Brown, Gordon, 267
Brzezinski, Zbigniew, 70–71, 72, 82, 84
Buckley, William, 90
Burns, Nicolas, 239
Burns, William: Iraq War and, 208, 211;
    JCPOA and, 289–90, 398n34; Obama
    and, 253, 257–59, 267; US-Iran relations
    and, 194, 391n13, 393n26
Bush, George H. W., 4, 52, 114–15, 198–99,
    361n34
Bush, George W.: advisors to, 172–73; "axis
    of evil" speech, 6, 189–90, 193–94, 206,
    218; Bonn Conference and, 181–88; first
    months of administration, 173–76; inau-
    gural address (2005), 205; Iran's nuclear
    program and, 222–50; Iraq War and,

197–221; national narratives and, 5–6; September 11, 2001 terrorist attacks and, 176–81; State of the Union address (2002), 6, 189–90, 193–94
Bush Doctrine, 203–4

Carey, James, 316, 402n15
Carter, Jimmy: Iran-Iraq War and, 4, 82–85; national narratives and, 49; Tehran embassy hostages and, 54, 75, 228; US-Iran relations and, 54–55, 69–75, 77
Casey, George W., 213
Cave, George, 83
Center for Strategic Research, 133, 285, 388n30
chemical weapons, 92–94, 100
Chemical Weapons Convention, 92
Cheney, Dick, 173, 175, 192, 194, 207, 215, 237–38, 242, 247
Cheney, Liz, 216
Chevron, 175
child soldiers, 80
China: Bush (G.W.) and, 174; Iran's nuclear program and, 229, 270; Iran's trade cooperation with, 323; JCPOA and, 1–2; North Korea's nuclear program and, 317; nuclear weapons development in, 225, 310
Christopher, Warren, 153
Churchill, Winston, 61
CIA (Central Intelligence Agency): Ghorbanifar and, 187, 378n25; Iran-Iraq War and, 83, 86–87, 96; Iran's nuclear program and, 223, 231, 248, 313; Khobar Towers bombing investigation, 126; Mossadeq and, 22, 35, 61, 62; National Intelligence Estimate (2007), 386n6; on shah's political longevity, 71
civil society, 11–12, 128, 135–36, 142
Clark, Wesley, 380n10
Clark, William P., 86
Clarke, Richard, 155
Clinton, William: Khatami and, 151–52; national narratives and, 4–5, 52; US-Iran relations and, 120–27, 153–61

Clinton, Hillary, 258
Cogan, Charles, 94
Cohen, Roberta, 380n9
Cohen, William, 153
Cold War politics, 59, 82, 85, 224–28
colonialism in national narratives, 19. *See also* imperialism
Comprehensive Iran Sanctions, Accountability, and Divestment Act of 2010 (US), 271
confirmation bias, 332
Conoco, 125–26, 175
Constitutional Revolution (Iran), 27
cosmopolitanism, 24
Crocker, Ryan, 178, 180, 191–92, 195, 206, 210, 215
Crowe, William, 98
Cuban Missile Crisis (1962), 224
Cyrus the Great, 21, 25, 27, 30, 31, 35
Cyrus Cylinder, 21, 350n18

Dabashi, Hamid, 392–93n24
Dalton, Richard, 249
D'Amato, Alfonse M., 126
Darius the Great, 30, 35
decolonization movement, 59
Defense Intelligence Agency (US), 187
Dehkordi, Nouri, 119
democracy promotion, 264–65, 266
Desert Shield Operation, 198–99
Desert Storm Operation, 4, 199–202
Dobbins, James, 6, 182–84, 187, 191, 208, 210, 215
Dole, Robert, 126
dual containment policy, 121–27, 155
dual-use technologies, 229–30
Dubowitz, Mark, 318

Eagle Claw Operation, 97
Earnest Will Operation, 96
Ebtekar, Massoumeh, 190
Egypt: Arab Spring in, 274; military rule in, 298
Einstein, Albert, 225
Eisenhower, Dwight, 60–61, 77, 229

ElBaradei, Mohamed, 232–41, 246–48, 381n17, 383n32
Emery, Christian, 357n42
Enduring Freedom Operation, 44–45, 180. *See also* Afghanistan War
Enlightenment, 29
Erdogan, Recep Tayyip, 269
Eshkevari, Hassan Yousefi, 133, 369n8
Esmǣil, 32
ethnicity and national narratives, 19–20, 350n18
Export-Import Bank of the United States, 87
ExxonMobil, 175

Fadlallah, Mohammad Hossein, 162
Faisal Al Saud, 113
Fallahian, Ali, 120, 143–44
Faludi, Susan, 352n38
Farsi language, 349n16
FBI (Federal Bureau of Investigation), 126, 162
Feinstein, Dianne, 286, 397n22
Feith, Douglas, 177, 190, 192, 207
Fernández de Kirchner, Cristina, 367n43
Fischer, Michael M. J., 33–34, 350n21
Fisher, Joschka, 232, 234
Ford, Gerald, 69
Fordow nuclear enrichment facility (Iran), 272
Foundation for the Defense of Democracy, 315, 318
Foundation for the Dispossessed and War Veterans, 107–8
France: Iran's nuclear program and, 7, 231–36; JCPOA and, 1–2, 9, 295, 318; nuclear weapons development in, 225
Franco, Francisco, 30
Freeh, Louis J., 126–27, 162–63
Freeman, Chas, 200
Friedman, Thomas, 162, 302
frontier myth in America's national narrative, 13–14, 38–42, 46–47, 219, 316, 352–53n40
futility thesis, 317, 319

Ganji, Akbar, 133, 143, 369n8, 369n10, 371n26, 372n28
Gates, Robert, 215
Gellner, Ernest: *Nations and Nationalism*, 23
Geranmayeh, Ellie, 322
Germany: Iran's nuclear program and, 7, 229, 231–36; JCPOA and, 1–2, 318
Ghalibaf, Mohammed Bagher, 322
Gharazi, Mohammad, 280
Ghassemlou, Abdul-Rahman, 120
Ghorbanifar, Manucher, 186–87, 378n25
Gingrich, Newt, 160
Golpayegani, Mohammad-Reza, 361n1
Gorbachev, Mikhail, 309
Gore, Al, 158
Graham, Lindsey, 292
Green Movement, 260–62, 266, 268, 350n21
Greenstock, Jeremy, 382n27
Guardian Council (Iran), 12, 131–32, 279–80, 284, 322
Guldimann, Tim, 209, 210
Gulf Cooperation Council, 112, 113

Haddad-Adel, Gholam-Ali, 280
Hadley, Stephen, 173, 186–87, 207, 250, 381n21
Hagel, Chuck, 286
Haig, Alexander, 358n4
Hajjarian, Saeed, 145–46, 168, 369n8, 371n24
Hajj pilgrimages, 113–14
al-Hakim, Abdul Aziz, 202, 212, 214
al-Hakim, Mohammad Baqir, 202
Haley, Nikki, 308
Halliburton, 175
Hamas, 154, 209
al-Hamdani, Majid Rashid, 360n26
Hannity, Sean, 312
Hayes, Stephen, 391n17
Henderson, Loy, 62
Herder, Johann Gottfried, 24
Heritage Foundation, 377n15
Hersh, Seymour, 247

Hertzberg, Hendrik, 251, 252
Hezbollah: Argentine Israelite Mutual
    Association bombing (1994) and, 125;
    hostages in Lebanon held by, 90, 113,
    114–15, 117, 199; Iran's support for, 90,
    125, 154, 209, 333; IRGC and, 86; Khobar
    Towers bombing and, 126–27, 164
Hiatt, Fred, 389n33
Higgins, William, 115, 365n26
Hirschman, Albert O., 317–18
Horthy, Miklós, 30
Hosseinian, Hadi Nejad, 181
Hull, Cordell, 56
Hurley, Patrick J., 57
Hussein, Imam, 25, 32–33, 34, 49, 332,
    350n20
Hussein, Saddam. See Saddam Hussein
Huyser, Robert, 72

IAEA. See International Atomic Energy
    Agency
idealism, 45–46, 205, 265
ideology in national narratives, 21–23
imagined communities, 19
imperialism: America's national narrative
    and, 45; decolonization movement and,
    59; Khamenei on, 146–48; national nar-
    ratives and, 13, 14, 19; protests against,
    348n10; Soviet perspectives on, 227;
    Truman Doctrine and, 59–60
India's nuclear program, 250, 310
individualism, 41
Indyk, Martin, 121–23, 154, 156–57, 163,
    165, 168, 367n39
Institute for Political and International
    Studies, 110, 234
Intermediate-Range Nuclear Forces (INF)
    Treaty (1987), 309
International Atomic Energy Agency
    (IAEA): Iran's nuclear program and,
    206, 209, 223, 230, 233, 235, 248, 267,
    386n11; Iraq's WMD program and, 201;
    JCPOA and, 7, 9–10, 16, 314–15
Iran and Libya Sanctions Act of 1996
    (US), 4, 126, 155, 175–76, 319

Iran-Contra affair, 91–92, 101, 186
Iran-e Farda (periodical), 142
Iranian national narrative: Aryan narra-
    tive in, 27–29, 31, 35–36, 332, 349n12,
    350n18, 352n33; clashing narratives
    and, 47–53; martyrdom in, 33–34, 49,
    80, 332, 353n43; narrative trap and,
    25–37
Iran-Iraq War (1980–88), 79–102; chem-
    ical weapons and, 92–94; final stages,
    95–98; initial invasion and counterin-
    vasion, 80–88; Iran-Contra affair and,
    90–92; Iran's national narrative and, 4,
    49, 332; stalemate, 88–90; War of the
    Cities, 88–89, 95
Iran Non-Proliferation Act of 2000 (US),
    168
Iraq: in "axis of evil," 189–90; dual con-
    tainment policy and, 121–27, 155;
    insurgency in, 211–16; Iranian support
    for insurgency in, 277, 307; Operation
    Desert Shield and, 198–99; Operation
    Desert Storm and, 199–202. See also
    Iran-Iraq War; Iraq War; Persian Gulf
    War; Saddam Hussein
Iraqi Freedom Operation, 45, 193, 202–21.
    See also Iraq War
Iraq War, 8, 15, 44–45, 193, 202–21
IRGC. See Islamic Revolutionary Guard
    Corps
ISIS. See Islamic State of Iraq and Syria
Islamic Azad University, 108
Islamic Jihad Organization, 90
Islamic narrative in Iran's national narra-
    tive, 32, 36, 37, 332. See also Shi'a Islam
Islamic Revolutionary Guard Corps
    (IRGC): Arab Spring and, 277; Iran-Iraq
    War and, 79; Khatami and, 145; Kho-
    bar Towers bombing and, 162–63, 164,
    170; Obama and, 260; post-Khomeini
    political order and, 105, 107; reformers
    and, 12
Islamic State of Iraq and Syria (ISIS), 35,
    298, 399n44
al-Ismaily, Salem Ben Nasser, 272–73

Israel: Ahmadinejad on, 8; Argentina
    embassy bombing (1992), 118–19;
    attacks on Iranian nuclear facilities,
    323; Hezbollah and, 90; JCPOA and,
    298, 300, 403n19; *Karine A* interception
    by, 188; Lebanon invasion (1982), 86;
    nuclear program in, 250
Israeli-Palestinian peace process, 114, 119,
    121

Jalili, Saeed, 267, 280, 282, 284, 396n10
Jame'eh (periodical), 142–43, 371n24
Javits, Jacob, 75
JCPOA. *See* Joint Comprehensive Plan of
    Action
JCS (Joint Chiefs of Staff), 173
Jefferson, Thomas, 40
Jenkins, Peter, 232, 237
jeopardy thesis, 318, 319
Jernegan, John, 56
Jews: in Iran, 32, 168, 287; JCPOA support
    from, 403n19
Johnson, Lyndon, 64–65, 66
Joint Chiefs of Staff (JCS), 173
Joint Comprehensive Plan of Action
    (JCPOA), 276–304; Biden and, 16, 329–
    30; IAEA and, 7, 9–10, 16; negotiation
    and signing of, 288–304; Obama and,
    1–2, 9–10, 11, 297–304, 333; Rouhani's
    diplomatic efforts and, 1–2, 9, 11, 279–
    95, 333; Trump and, 2, 10, 16, 307–14;
    Zarif and, 11, 295–97, 303
J Street (organization), 403n19

Kadivar, Mohsen, 369n8, 372n28
Karbala Paradigm, 25, 33–34, 334–35,
    350n21
Karbaschi, Gholam-Hossein, 109, 372n28
Karine A interception, 188
Karroubi, Mehdi, 261, 266
Karzai, Hamid, 182–83, 185
Kashani, Abol-Qasem, 62
Kashmir War (1965), 66
Katibeh, Kourosh, 118
Kennedy, John F., 63–64

Kenya embassy bombing (1998), 160, 162
Kermani, Mirza Aqa Khan, 26–27, 28, 30
Kerry, John, 11, 278, 286, 291, 294, 394n1
Khalilzad, Zalmay, 174–75, 179, 183–84,
    210, 214–15
Khamenei, Ali: on "axis of evil" speech,
    190; Clinton and, 168, 171; diplomatic
    efforts by, 290–91; election as supreme
    leader, 103–4; Iran-Iraq War and, 99;
    Iran's national narrative and, 36–37;
    Iran's nuclear program and, 233, 234,
    236, 243; JCPOA and, 302; Khatami
    and, 132, 141; national narratives and,
    7; Obama and, 256–57, 271; political
    longevity of, 363n8; post-Khomenei
    political order and, 104–27; Rafsanjani
    and, 395n4; Rouhani and, 279, 289; Sep-
    tember 11, 2001 terrorist attacks and,
    177; Trump and, 320, 321, 324; US-Iran
    relations and, 159
Khan, A. Q., 231–32, 386n8
Kharrazi, Kamal, 116, 157–59, 161, 165, 179,
    181, 194, 199, 206
Kharrazi, Sadeq, 175, 209–10
Khatami, Mohammad: Ahmadinejad and,
    261; "axis of evil" speech and, 218; Bonn
    Conference and, 181–88; Bush (G.W.)
    and, 172–96; conservative backlash
    against, 141–48; diplomacy by, 136–41,
    218; economic growth under, 281; elec-
    tion of, 4, 12, 129–36, 151; Iran's national
    narrative and, 6, 7, 36, 52; Iran's nuclear
    program and, 233, 234, 236, 244, 246;
    Obama and, 260; Rafsanjani and, 108;
    reform movement and, 128–29, 148–50;
    September 11, 2001 terrorist attacks
    and, 176, 181; US-Iran relations and, 4–5
Khobar Towers bombing (1996), 4, 15,
    126–27, 152–71
Khomeini, Ruhollah: death of, 103; Iran-
    Contra affair and, 92; Iran-Iraq War
    and, 81–82, 84–86, 95, 98–99; Iran's
    national narrative and, 3–4, 8, 34, 49;
    Iran's nuclear program and, 229; legacy
    of, 105–6, 132; MEK and, 223; revolution

of 1979 and, 72–73, 75; suppression of
dissent by, 362n3; US-Iran relations
and, 66, 72
Kim Jong-un, 309, 316
Kissinger, Henry, 67–69, 299
Kiyan (periodical), 142
Kiyan Circle, 369n9
Komer, Robert, 64
Korean War, 43–44, 58
Krauthammer, Charles, 263
Krebs, Ronald, 25, 332
Kristol, William, 391n17
Kuniholm, Bruce, 57
Kurds: assassination of Kurdish activists,
14; Iran-Iraq War and, 93, 112; Iraq
War and, 200; national narratives and,
31–32, 48, 57–58, 68
Kuwait invasion by Iraq (1990), 112–13,
119, 198
Kyoto Protocol, 174

LaBoulaye, Stanislas de, 234
Laingen, Bruce, 63, 73, 74–75, 77
language and national narratives, 20, 31,
349n16
Larijani, Ali, 240–41, 244, 247
Lavrov, Sergei, 239
Lebanon: Hezbollah in, 90, 110, 113, 114–15;
Iranian support for organizations in,
299, 307; Israel's invasion of (1982), 86
Ledeen, Michael, 186–87
Levy, David, 152
Libya: Arab Spring protests in, 274; failed
state in, 298
Lincoln, Abraham, 40
Lula da Silva, Luiz Inácio, 269
Luti, William, 179

MacArthur, Douglas, II, 67, 69
Maleki, Abbas, 381n18
Malley, Robert, 329
Mann, Hillary, 179
Marshall Plan, 59
martyrdom, 33–34, 49, 80, 332, 353n43
Mashaie, Esfandiyar Rahim, 394n2

Masoud, Ahmad Shah, 177
Mattis, James, 308–9
McCain, John, 292
McFarlane, Bud, 285
McKinley, William, 42
McMaster, H. R., 309
Medvedev, Dmitry, 270
MEK. *See* Mujahedin-e-Khalq
Menendez, Robert, 292
Miller, William G., 77
MI6 (UK), 61
Mohajerani, Ata'ollah, 371–72n28
Mohammad, succession struggle follow-
ing death of, 32–33
Mohammad Reza Shah Pahlavi. *See*
Pahlavi, Mohammad Reza Shah
Mojtahed-Shabestari, Mohammad, 369n8
Moniz, Ernest, 298
Montazeri, Hossein-Ali, 265, 285, 362n3,
392n23
Mosaddeq, Mohammad: Iranian national
narrative and, 3, 34–35; nationalization
of oil industry and, 58–59; overthrow
of, 22, 34, 54–55, 61–62, 139–40, 332, 336
Mottaki, Manouchehr, 215, 394n2
Mousavi, Mir-Hossein, 12–13, 130, 260–62,
266
Mousavian, Hossein: Iran's nuclear pro-
gram and, 236, 241; Iraq War and, 207,
213, 218; Khatami and, 176, 178, 188, 191;
post-Khomeini political order and, 114,
124; US-Iran relations and, 168, 171
Mughniyah, Imad, 90, 181
Mujahedin-e-Khalq (MEK, People's
Mojahedin of Iran), 156, 195, 206, 222,
229–30, 248
Murphy, Richard, 94
al-Mussawi, Abbas, 365n26
Mussolini, Benito, 30
Mutahhari, Ayatollah, 49

Nafisi, Said, 31
Naser al-Din Shah, 26
Nasrallah, Hassan, 162, 286
Nasser, Gamal Abdel, 30

Nasseri, Cyrus, 236
Natanz nuclear enrichment facility (Iran), 7, 195, 230–31, 236, 272
Nategh-Nouri, Ali Akbar, 133–34, 151
National Council of Resistance, 195, 206, 222
nationalism in national narratives, 19–22, 28, 29, 48
nationalization of oil industry in Iran, 58–59
national narratives: Aryan narrative, 27–29, 31, 35–36, 332, 349n12, 350n18, 352n33; clashing narratives, 47–53; confirmation bias and, 332; defined, 2–3; frontier myth in, 13–14, 38–42, 46–47, 219, 316, 352–53n40; narrative trap, 18–53; national interests and, 331–45; Trump's revival of America's narrative, 314–20, 328–29. *See also* American national narrative; Iranian national narrative
NATO (North Atlantic Treaty Organization), 270
Negroponte, John, 383n40
Netanyahu, Benjamin: election of, 153–54; Iran's nuclear program and, 268, 272; JCPOA and, 286–87, 293, 298–300, 314, 399n39, 403n19; US-Iran relations and, 157
Niebuhr, Reinhold, 390n8
Nielsen, Kirstjen, 312
Nisman, Alberto, 367n43
Nixon, Richard, 64, 67–69
Nixon Doctrine, 67
Noble, David W., 40–41
Non-Proliferation Treaty (NPT), 7, 16, 224, 229, 249, 294; Additional Protocol, 233, 234–35, 240, 243
Noori, Sheikh Fazlollah, 27
North, Oliver, 91
North Atlantic Treaty Organization (NATO), 270
Northern Alliance, 177, 181, 182, 184–85
North Korea: in "axis of evil," 189–90; Bush (G.W.) and, 174; Trump's diplomatic efforts with, 309–10, 316–17

NPT. *See* Non-Proliferation Treaty
nuclear program in Iran: ambitions of, 229–31; arms control industry and, 224–28; back channel diplomacy, 272–75; European diplomatic responses to, 231–36; Fordow nuclear enrichment facility, 272; Iran's policy responses, 243–47; Natanz nuclear enrichment facility, 7, 195, 230–31, 236, 272; Non-Proliferation Treaty and, 7, 16, 224, 229, 233–35, 240, 243, 249, 294; Obama's policies and, 267–75; Shahab-3 missile development, 159; US diplomatic responses, 237–42. *See also* Joint Comprehensive Plan of Action
Nuri, Abdollah, 372n28

Obama, Barack: diplomatic efforts by, 254–59; election of, 9, 251–53; Iran's nuclear program and, 267–75; JCPOA and, 1–2, 9–10, 11, 297–304, 333; reformist movements in Iran and, 259–66; Rouhani and, 289, 291, 292–93
Ogata, Sadako, 185
OIC (Organization of Islamic Cooperation), 136, 157
oil industry in Iran: Bush (G.W.) and, 175; diplomatic relations and, 168; nationalization of, 58–59; offshore development, 125–26
Oman's back channel diplomacy, 115, 163, 272–75, 289, 293
O'Neill, Paul, 185
OPEC (Organization of Petroleum Exporting Countries), 112, 198
Open Society Institute, 244
Operation Desert Shield, 198–99
Operation Desert Storm, 4, 199–202
Operation Eagle Claw, 97
Operation Earnest Will, 96
Operation Enduring Freedom, 44–45, 180. *See also* Afghanistan War
Operation Iraqi Freedom, 45, 193, 202–21. *See also* Iraq War
Operation Praying Mantis, 97

Operation Staunch, 87–88
Operation TPAJAX, 61
Organization of Islamic Cooperation (OIC), 136, 157
Organization of Petroleum Exporting Countries (OPEC), 112, 198
orientalism, 27, 42, 349n12, 350n18
Oslo Accords, 154
O'Sullivan, Meghan, 212, 214
Ottoman Empire, 28
Oveissi, Gholam Ali, 83

Pahlavi, Mohammad Reza Shah: evacuation from Iran, 72–73; Iraq and, 81; national narratives and, 31; Nixon and, 67–69; US-Iran relations and, 3–4, 65
Pahlavi, Reza Shah, 28, 29–30
Pakistan: Afghanistan War and, 182–83; Iran's nuclear program and, 229; nuclear program in, 250, 386n8; nuclear weapons program in, 310
Palestinian Islamic Jihad, 119, 125
Palin, Sarah, 220
Paris Agreement (2004), 235–36
Parsi, Trita, 390n10, 396n16
Partial Test Ban Treaty (1963), 224
Pelosi, Christine, 287
People's Mojahedin of Iran. See Mujahedin-e-Khalq
Peres, Shimon, 90, 153
Pérez de Cuéllar, Javier, 92, 116, 117, 365n21
Perle, Richard, 203
Peron, Juan, 30
Perry, William, 153
Persian Gulf War (1990–91), 113, 198–202
perversity thesis, 317, 318
Petraeus, David, 15, 206, 207–8
P5+1: Iran's nuclear program and, 239–40, 243–48, 250, 257, 267–69; JCPOA and, 9, 290–91, 293–97, 302
Philippines, American imperialism and, 42–43
Picco, Giandomenico, 116, 117, 118, 341
Pickering, Thomas, 156, 238, 379n5, 387n22

Pincus, Steven, 347n2
Pletka, Danielle, 318
pluralism, 142
political assassinations. See assassinations
Pompeo, Mike, 309, 310, 314, 318, 325, 326, 328
Powell, Colin, 173, 177, 181–83, 188, 195, 211, 217, 238
pragmatism, 109, 265, 277
Praying Mantis Operation, 97
Precht, Henry, 75–76, 77
preemption doctrine, 203–4
Pugwash (organization), 11, 342
Puritans, 38–39
Putin, Vladimir, 401n5

Qaboos bin Said, 115, 163, 272–73, 289
al-Qaeda, 5–6, 178–80, 195, 214
Qajar dynasty (1785-1925), 26–27, 28–29
Qalibaf, Mohsen, 280, 284
Qanooni, Younis, 184–85
Quds Force, 178, 191, 212–13, 219, 220, 321

Rabin, Yitzhak, 153, 154
Radio Free Europe, 160
Rafiqdoost, Mohsen, 108
Rafsanjani, Ali Akbar Hashemi: Ahmadinejad and, 261, 277–78; Bush (G.H.W.) and, 115, 117–18; Center for Strategic Research and, 285; disqualification from 2013 election, 279–80; dual containment policy and, 123–24; economic growth under, 281; on election legitimacy, 265; Iran-Iraq War and, 91, 97, 98–99; Iran's nuclear program and, 246; Iraq War and, 206; Khamenei and, 395n4; Khatami and, 130; Khobar Towers bombing and, 127; political assassinations and, 143–44; political longevity of, 363n8; post-Khomenei political order and, 104–27; Saudi Arabia and, 199; September 11, 2001 terrorist attacks and, 176–77, 178
Rafsanjani, Mehdi, 114

Rahnavard, Zahra, 260

Raisi, Ebrahim, 324

Ravanchi, Majid Takht, 289–90, 291, 297–98

Reagan, Ronald: arms control and, 227; Intermediate-Range Nuclear Forces (INF) Treaty (1987) and, 309; Iran-Contra affair and, 90, 92; Iran-Iraq War and, 4, 86, 93, 98

Reformist Front Coordination Council, 283

Reyshahri, Mohammad, 370n13

Rezaie, Mohsen, 98–99, 180, 261, 280

Reza Shah Pahlavi. See Pahlavi, Reza Shah

Rhodes, Ben, 398n34

Rice, Condoleezza: Bush (G.W.) administration and, 172–75, 185, 189–90, 193, 195; Iran's nuclear program and, 237–40; Iraq War and, 205, 211, 215–16; US-Iran relations and, 51, 253

Richardson, Bill, 157

Riedel, Bruce, 119, 153, 156, 163, 171, 366n36

Rogers, Will, 98

Rokhsefat, Mostafa, 369n11

Romanticism, 24

Romney, Mitt, 274

Roosevelt, Franklin, 46, 55–56

Roosevelt, Kermit, 61, 65

Roosevelt, Theodore, 40, 42, 46, 352n33

Rostow, Walt, 64

Rouhani, Hassan: Center for Strategic Research and, 388n30; diplomatic efforts by, 288–97; economic growth under, 322–23; election of, 279–84; foreign policy advisors to, 285–88; Iran's nuclear program and, 233, 234, 236, 243, 244, 245; JCPOA and, 1–2, 9, 11, 279–95, 333; national narratives and, 7, 13; Trump and, 320, 322, 324

Rubin, Michael, 319

Rumsfeld, Donald: Iran-Iraq War and, 88; Iran's nuclear program and, 237–38, 242; Iraq War and, 207, 215, 216; US-Iran relations, 173–74, 189, 192, 194–95

Rushdie, Salman, 110, 158, 364n17

Rusk, Dean, 65

Russell, Bertrand, 225

Russia: Bush (G.W.) and, 174; Iran's national narrative and, 28; Iran's nuclear program and, 229, 270; JCPOA and, 1–2, 9; nuclear weapons program in, 310; Trump and, 309–10. See also Soviet Union

Saanei, Yousef, 265

Saddam Hussein: Bush (G.W.) and, 192; Clinton and, 154; Iran-Iraq War and, 4, 80–81, 85, 86–89, 93, 95, 100, 223, 332; Kuwait invasion (1990), 112–13, 119; national narratives and, 6, 16; Persian Gulf security cooperation and, 112; Persian Gulf War and, 113, 198–202; WMDs and, 45, 201, 203–4

Sadjadpour, Karim, 363n8

al-Sadr, Muqtada, 8, 202–3, 206, 212

Safavi, Yahya Rahim, 179

Safavids, 32

Sahabi, Ezatollah, 369n8

Salaam (periodical), 144

Salami, Hossein, 321

Salehi, Ali Akbar, 245, 298

Salehi-Isfahani, Djavad, 395n7

sanctions: against Iran, 268–72, 318, 327, 332, 404n27; against Iraq, 201–2

Sanders, Sarah Huckabee, 313–14

Sarkozy, Nicholas, 267

Al Saud, Faisal, 113

Saudi Arabia: Iran's relations with, 110–11, 113; JCPOA and, 298, 300; Khobar Towers bombing (1996), 126–27; Operation Desert Shield and, 198–99; Persian Gulf War and, 113; truck bombings (2003), 195

Sawers, John, 237

Sazegara, Mohsen, 371n24, 373n34

Schelling, Thomas, 225

Schumer, Charles, 292

Schwarzkopf, Norman, 200

Scowcroft, Brent, 116, 117, 119
Second of Khordad network, 135–36, 148–49
Secor, Laura, 368n3, 369n11
Security Council (UN): Iran-Iraq War and, 84, 99, 365n20; Iran's nuclear program and, 8–9, 232, 235, 245–46; Iraq's invasion of Kuwait and, 112–13, 154; sanctions against Iran, 270, 278
Semati, Hadi, 190, 191, 211, 218
Sembler, Melvin, 187
September 11, 2001 terrorist attacks, 5–6, 176–81
Sharafkandi, Sadegh, 119
Shari'ati, Ali, 350n20
Shariatmadari, Hossein, 216, 244
Sharoudi, Mahmoud Hashemi, 144
Sherman, Wendy, 293, 297–98
Sheybani, Abbas, 362n6
Shi'a Islam: Iran-Iraq War and, 81; Iran's national narrative and, 25, 26, 32–34; in Iraq, 200, 202–3, 207; in Lebanon, 86; Sunni insurgency in Iraq and, 212
Shultz, George, 87–88
al-Sistani, Ali, 192, 202
Six plus Two group on Afghanistan, 179, 191
Slotkin, Richard, 39, 40, 42, 48, 353n40
Smith, Anthony D., 20
Sobh-e Emrooz (periodical), 143, 371n24
Solana, Javier, 240–41, 246
Soleimani, Qasem: assassination of, 321, 322, 324–25, 332; as Quds Force leader, 178, 191, 206, 220, 299
Soroush, Abdolkarim, 133, 369n8, 369n10
Soviet Union: arms control industry and, 224–28; arms sales to Iraq, 360n27; fall of, 109, 119, 133; Iran-Iraq War and, 82, 85, 95; nuclear weapons development in, 224; post-World War II policies on Iran, 57–58; US-Iran relations and, 66. See also Cold War politics; Russia
Specter, Arlen, 181
Stalin, Joseph, 57–58

Status of Forces Agreement (1964), 65–66
Staunch Operation, 87–88
Straw, Jack, 218, 232, 234
Sullivan, Jake, 273, 290, 291
Sullivan, William, 71, 72
Sunni Islam: Iran-Iraq War and, 81; Iran's national narrative and, 32, 33; Iraq War and, 202, 207
Supreme Cultural Revolution Council, 244
Supreme National Security Council (Iran), 171, 176, 234, 243, 280
Syria, Iranian support for organizations in, 277, 299, 307

Taheri, Jalaleddin, 193
Taherian, Mohammad, 179, 182
Tajzadeh, Mostafa, 369n8
Taliban, 6, 16, 35, 158, 177–78, 180, 182
Talwar, Puneet, 257, 273
Tanzania embassy bombing (1998), 160, 162
Tehran Agreement (2003), 234–35
Tehran Conference (1943), 57–58
Tehran Declaration (2010), 9, 269, 370n16
Tehran embassy takeover (1979), 54, 75, 228
Tenet, George, 178
terrorism: Argentina embassy bombing (1992), 118–19; Argentine Israelite Mutual Association bombing (1994), 125; Bush Doctrine and, 204; Khatami and, 156–57; Khobar Towers bombing (1996), 4, 15, 126–27, 152–71; Tanzania embassy bombing (1998), 160, 162; truck bombings in Saudi Arabia (2003), 195. See also specific terrorist groups
Teutonism, 352n33
Thatcher, Margaret, 198
Tillerson, Rex, 308–9
Tocqueville, Alexis de: Democracy in America, 38
TPAJAX Operation, 61
Truman, Harry, 57–58, 59–60, 355n9
Truman Doctrine, 46, 59–60

Trump, Donald, 305–30; American national narrative revived by, 314–20, 328–29; Iran's response to rhetoric of, 320–24; Iraq War and, 220; JCPOA terminated by, 2, 10, 16, 307–14; US-Iran relations and, 324–28
Tunisia, Arab Spring protests in, 274
Turner, Frederick Jackson, 41, 45
Turner, Stansfield, 356n34
Tutwiler, Margaret, 365n29
Twetten, Thomas, 86

Umayyad dynasty, 32–33
Union of Concerned Scientists, 11
United Against Nuclear Iran, 315
United Arab Emirates, 298
United Kingdom: imperialism and, 148; Iran's national narrative and, 28; Iran's nuclear program and, 7, 231–36; JCPOA and, 1–2, 318; nuclear weapons development in, 225; post–World War II policies on Iran, 57–58
United Nations, 56–57, 181–82. See also Security Council
universalism, 24

Vance, Cyrus, 70–71, 72
Velayati, Ali Akbar, 112, 116, 233, 273, 280, 365n20, 396n10
Veliotes, Nicholas, 87
Vienna Group, 9, 269
Vietnam War, 43–44
Villepin, Dominique de, 232, 234
Voice of America, 157, 160
Von Sponeck, H. C., 380n8

War of the Cities (1984), 88–89, 95
Washington Institute for Near East Policy, 11

weapons of mass destruction (WMDs), 45, 154, 193, 201, 202, 203–4, 208, 231, 388n27
Welch, David, 156
Wilkerson, Lawrence, 192, 194, 195, 208, 211, 237
Williams, William Appleman, 46
Wilson, Woodrow, 42, 43, 45–46
Winthrop, John, 37
WMDs. See weapons of mass destruction
Wolfowitz, Paul, 179, 186–87, 207
World Bank, 168, 322
World Trade Organization (WTO), 9

Xerxes, 30, 35

Yazdi, Ibrahim, 74
Yazdi, Mohammad, 144
Yazid (caliph), 33, 34
Yeltsin, Boris, 151, 152
Yemen: Arab Spring in, 274; civil war in, 298, 323; Iranian support for organizations in, 277, 307

Zarif, Mohammad Javad: diplomatic efforts by, 289, 291–92, 294; Iran's nuclear program and, 244; Iraq War and, 199, 210, 217; JCPOA and, 11, 295–97, 303; national narratives and, 6; Pompeo and, 310; post-Khomeini political order and, 118; Rouhani and, 285–88; Trump and, 320, 322, 323; US-Iran relations and, 158, 179, 183–85, 194
al-Zarqawi, Abu Musab, 195
Zavarehi, Seyyed Reza, 370n13
Zia-Ebrahimi, Reza, 28, 36
Zoroastrianism, 32

Index